598.07 PB

Devine, Arnold
Connecticut birding guide

19.95
3/00

DISCARD

Southbury Public Library
561 Main Street South
Southbury, Conn. 06488

GAYLORD MG

CONNECTICUT BIRDING GUIDE

Arnold Devine and Dwight G. Smith

Illustrations by Mark Szantyr

Foreword by Noble S. Proctor

Maps by Trevor Becker

General Editor: Marcia Schultz

**Computer Graphics by Lisa Galvin
and Danielle Joslin**

THOMSON-SHORE, INC.
Dexter, Michigan

Illustrations by Mark Szantyr

Maps by Trevor Becker

General Editor: Marcia Schultz
Computer Design by Lisa Galvin and Danielle Joslin

Library of Congress Cataloging Data

Devine, Arnold
Smith, Dwight G.
Connecticut Birding Guide
  Bibliography
  Index
I. Bird watching---Bird Finding---Connecticut --Guide Books
Library of Congress Catalog Card Number 97-60069
ISBN 0-9657185-0-6
Printed on Opague 60% Recycled Natural Paper (90% Post Consumer)

Connecticut Birding Sites

1 White Memorial Foundation
2 Mt. Riga Area
3 Under Mountain Road
4 American Legion/Peoples SF
5 Barkhamsted Reservoir .
6 Northeast Audubon Center
7 Northwestern Highlands Tour
8 Mohawk State Forest
9 Nepaug Reservoir
10 River Road in Kent
11 Steep Rock Reservoir
12 New Milford Tour
13A Skiff Mountain WMA
13B Macedonia Brook State Park
14 Flander's Nature Center
15. Sperry Park
16. River Road in Southbury
17 Naugatuck State Forest
18 Stevenson's Dam
19 C. P. Huntington State Park
20 Devil's Den Preserve
21 Valley Road
22 Osbornedale State Park
23A Southbury Training School Pond
23B Aspetuck Reservoir
24 Quarry Road
25 Connecticut River in Enfield
26 Bradley International Airport
27 Northwest Park
28 Station 43
29 Great Pond State Forest
30 Roaring Brook Nature Center
31 Talcott Mountain Reservoir Area
32 Farmington Meadows Area
33 Batterson Park Pond
34 Cromwell Meadows WMA
35 Black Pond and Bishops Pond
36 Durham Meadows
37A Sleeping Giant State Park
37B Quinnipiac River State Park
38 Bigelow Hollow State Park
39 Boston Hollow and Yale Forest
40 Natchaug State Forest Area
41 Storrs Area Tour
42 Mansfield Hollow State Park
43 Quinebaug River WMA
44 Pachaug State Forest
45 Devil's Hopyard State Park
46 Hartman Park
47 Nehantic State Forest
48A Trailwood
48B West Thompson Lake
49 Audubon Center of Greenwich
50 Greenwich Point Park
51 Southwest Shoreline Tour
52 Norwalk Harbor Tour
53 Sherwood Island State Park
54 Connecticut Audubon Sanctuary
55 Fairfield to Bridgeport Tour
56 Great Meadows Marsh Area
57 Milford Point
58 Gulf Pond
59 Laurel Reservoir
60 New Haven Harbor Tour
61 West Rock Ridge State Park
62 Lighthouse Point Park
63 East Rock Park
64 Branford Supply Ponds
65 Guilford Sluice
66 Falkner Island
67 Middle Beach
68 Hammonasset Beach State Park
69 Lower Connecticut River Tour
70 Furnace Pond
71 Great Island WMA
72 Griswold Point Preserve
73 Rocky Neck State Park
74 Harkness Memorial State Park
75 Connecticut College Arboretum
76 Smith Cove, Thames River
77 Eastern Point
78 Bluff Point Coastal Reserve
79 Haley Farm State Park
80 Mystic River
81 Denison-Pequotsepos NC
82 Stonington Point
83 Barn Island WMA
84 Assekonk Swamp WMA

TABLE OF CONTENTS

Acknowledgements

Innumerable people have helped in many ways during the preparation of the Connecticut Birding Guide. When we initially started the project information on regional birding sites was gleaned from several friends located throughout the state. These individuals included Louis Bevier, Paul Desjardins, Betty Kleiner, Bill Gaunya, Debbie Martin, and Dave Provencher. John Gaskell was particularly helpful with providing information on dozens of sites in the southcentral and eastern portions of the state. Many friends and associates including Andy Brand, Tom Baptist, Milan Bull, Jerry Connolly, Paul Desjardins, Fran D'Amico, John Gaskell, Ted Gilman, Bill Gaunya, Jay Kaplan, Gordon Loery, Will Stoddard, Robert Winkler, Chris Wood, and Joe Zeranski also reviewed our earlier versions of one or more site accounts and provided helpful advice and corrections.

Louis Bevier and Noble Proctor critiqued an earlier version of this book and offered many valuable suggestions regarding its final form and content. George Clark, Robert Askin, Wendy Howes, Greg Hanisek, Frank Mantlik, and Mark Szantyr also reviewed significant portions of this book and provided helpful and constructive criticism.

We owe Noble Proctor a debt of gratitude for his earlier book, *25 Birding Sites in Connecticut*, which represents the first field guide to several of Connecticut's birding sites. Noble graciously wrote the foreword for the *Connecticut Birding Guide*. Noble has been a friend, instructor (BD), and coworker (DGS) through many years at Southern Connecticut State University.

Danielle Joslin, Tara Casanova, and Lisa Galvin worked on the initial site guide maps for the book. Trevor Becker used his extensive knowledge of computer graghics including Adobe Illustrator and Adobe Photoshop to prepare the final maps. Gerald Schultz and Alex Turko, professors of biology at Southern Connecticut State University, provided their considerable computer expertise.

Marcia Schultz and Joyce Wall helped edit and format the project, reviewing the entire manuscript for typos, grammer, and consistency.

We extend our thanks to all involved in this project. Their efforts and assistance have constantly and consistently improved the final book.

Arnold Devine
Dwight G. Smith

About the Authors and Artist

Arnold "Buzz" Devine has studied the birds of Connecticut for the past 20 years. He is a member of the Connecticut Ornithological Association's (COA) Board of Directors, the Avian Records Committee of Connecticut, and Connecticut's Endangered Species Advisory Committee for Birds. Buzz has published numerous scientific articles related to bird behavior and ecology. He works for the Connecticut Department of Environmental Protection in the Hazardous Waste Enforcement Section.

Dwight Glenn Smith is a professor at Southern Connecticut State University where he has taught zoology and ecology since 1970. He has conducted research on birds in Siberia, South Africa, Venezuela, Alaska and much of the western United States. Dwight has published 10 books and about 300 scientific papers, and is currently editor of the *COA Bulletin*.

Mark Szantyr is an artist and illustrator living in Storrs, Connecticut, with his wife Gail, and his son, Bobby. A long-time Connecticut birder, he is a licensed bird-bander, a founding member of the Connecticut Ornithological Association, and was the first and is current secretary of the Avian Records Committee of Connecticut. Mark serves on the Board of Directors of the COA and is one of the "voices" of the Connecticut Rare Bird Alert. Mark received his Master of Fine Arts degree in painting from the University of Connecticut in 1992. He has illustrated a number of texts and ornithological journals, including numerous covers for *The Connecticut Warbler*, the journal of the Connecticut Ornithological Association. He also co-illustrated the revised *Birds of Storrs, Connecticut, and Vicinity*.

FOREWORD

One of the most asked questions of me is "When are you going to update your bird finding guide". My patent answer of the past five years has been "Just wait--there is an excellent guide being written". That guide is now at hand!

Devine, a tireless field birder over the years and Smith a nationally recognized authority on birds of prey have combined to produce an outstanding guide that has long been needed for Connecticut. Over the past few years we have had glimpses of what to expect from this book with location and site guides appearing in a variety of publications. However, not even these glimpses of what was coming has the impact of this completed work. Nearly 100 sites are detailed in this complete work for the state. The book covers not just the well known parks but sites that are more obscure but have proven to be excellent birding through the years. Devine and Smith have painstakingly researched each site not by simply going through past information on the areas but going afield and birding at the sites themselves. In addition, they have talked with other birders familiar with the sites and have gone over the past records for each location to get as detailed and accurate a picture of what species can be found for every season. Unlike some finding guides that rely on local maps that may be inaccurate, for this book, each trail has been walked to assure exacting information and no-fail instructions for finding the best birding. Add to this, newly drawn and accurate maps detail the trails and highlight the best birding sites to make this the best possible reference for the birder. Complete details are listed on reaching the site with accurately measured distances from the principle road nearest the location.

Scattered throughout the book is the artwork of Mark Szantyr, another long time birder in the state. Mark knows not only the bird life, but has the ability to capture these birds with striking sketches, both beautiful and accurate in their scope.

Devine, Smith and Szantyr are to be congratulated on this long awaited and outstanding book. It will remain the standard for Connecticut birders for many years to come.

Now you have it in hand, get out and get birding and have the fun of investigating many new sites that will open up wonderful birding adventures in the state.

Noble S. Proctor

I BIRDING CONNECTICUT

Despite its small size and high population density, Connecticut provides an excellent array of birding opportunities, both for the novice and advanced birder. Nearly 400 species have been confirmed for the state, including 182 nesting species that were recorded during the Connecticut Breeding Bird Atlas survey conducted from 1982-1986. Furthermore, each year birders scours the state for new and unusual species and manage to turn up a new state species quite often, so the list of species that may occur in the state just keeps growing.

Habitat, geography, and happenstance all contribute to Connecticut's bird diversity. The wealth of habitats within the state range from seashores to highlands. Connecticut's southern border fronts on Long Island Sound, resulting in a convoluted coastline of 618 miles. This shoreline includes a variety of coastal habitats---islands, bays, inlets, estuaries, rocky coves, and salt marsh---which attract waterfowl, shorebirds, rails, and herons. Several major river systems, hundreds of lakes and ponds, and innumerable wetlands all provide inland habitats for nesting and migrating aquatic birds.

Topographically, the state is also diverse. A wedge-shaped central valley is bordered by eastern hills and even higher western hills. Elevations range from sea level along the coast to the highest point in the Northwest Highlands at 2380 feet, located on the southern slope of Mt. Frissel. This varied topography produces equally varied ecological habitats. About 65 percent of Connecticut is woodland, much of which is interspersed with fields, meadows, and farmlands. Although residences and residential areas dot most of the state, most of the large urban, industrial and commercial complexes are limited to the southern coastline with the notable exceptions of the cities of Hartford, Danbury, and Waterbury. The state's woodlands are of three main types, deciduous, coniferous, and mixed, each of which provide distinctive habitats for a variety of woodpeckers, warblers, thrushes, vireos, and other woodland birds. Most of Connecticut's woodland is deciduous, but in the northern half of the state mixed stands of hardwoods and conifers occur more frequently. Stands of hemlock are found in cool ravines, while plantations of white and red pine have been planted around reservoirs and along some waterways. A few black spruce bogs occur at widely scattered locations in the central and northwestern parts of the state.

Geographically, Connecticut is advantageously placed for birding opportunities. The Atlantic Coast Flyway, one of the five major migratory routes in North America, traverses the state and birders are treated each fall and spring to the movement of warblers, vireos, thrushes, flycatchers, sparrows and raptors. The spring push of warblers and vireos is usually spectacular and concentrated in several sites described in this guide, especially East Rock Park in New Haven and River Road in Kent. The fall songbird migration is more dispersed, although several shoreline sites such as Hammonasset Beach State Park and Bluff Point Coastal Reserve are noted for their songbird movements. Fall is also the time for spectacular concentrations of migrating shorebirds that pile up at Milford Point and Griswold Point Preserve while the hawk movement at Lighthouse Point Park and Quaker Ridge can draw hordes of skywatchers.

Connecticut is located at a geographical and ecological transition zone for many birds. For example, the northern range of a number of more southerly species such as the Orchard Oriole, Summer Tanager, Yellow-throated Warbler, Prothonotary Warbler, and Blue Grosbeak extends into Connecticut. Conversely, several species such as the Alder Flycatcher and Golden-winged Warbler, which are normally associated with more northern habitats, breed in the higher, cooler Northwest Highlands.

Special circumstances have also played a role in adding to Connecticut's array of birds, for the state lies along the northward weather track of autumn hurricanes. For days after the passage of a September hurricane through the state, birders scour Stonington Point, Sandy Point, Milford Point, Griswold Point Preserve, and other coastal areas for tropical and pelagic oddities such as the Brown Pelican, Sooty Tern, Sandwich Tern, shearwaters, and Wilson's Storm-Petrel which may be blown in by the storm track.

Connecticut birders are also occasionally treated to a few exotic species that represent vagrants or possibly captive birds that have escaped, such as the Ruddy Shelduck, Chough, and Eurasian Jackdaw. Usually, such species never become part of the official state bird record, but still offer interesting discussion and speculation among birders.

Seasonal Birding Opportunities

Avid birders may keep daily, monthly, seasonal and yearly lists and compete with themselves and their friends to record the highest totals or spot the rarest species. The state's diversity of habitats offers birders the chance to see a wide variety of birds in every month of the year, and Connecticut is small enough that many, perhaps most, of its basic habitats can be birded in a single day. By birding specific sites at certain times through the year, a good birder, with diligence, can easily list over 200 species in a year. Connecticut's advanced birders, who routinely bird several times a week, usually record 240-260 species annually. To guide birders through the Connecticut year we suggest the following seasonal list of sites to visit during each month of the year.

Winter Months. Despite the normally cold and dreary winter weather, January and February offer a surprising number of birding opportunities. Mixed foraging flocks of nuthatches, chickadees, woodpeckers, and other wintering songbirds can be found along the trails of most inland birding sites such as White Memorial Foundation, Mohawk State Forest, Mansfield Hollow State Park, Devil's Hopyard State Park, and Nehantic State Forest. Winter finches (grosbeaks, redpolls, crossbills, Pine Siskin, and Purple Finch) frequently can be turned up in the pine, spruce, and hemlock woodlands at Mohawk State Forest, Bigelow Hollow State Park, Barkhamsted Reservoir, and Pachaug State Forest. Connecticut's major rivers, ice free lakes, and reservoirs are generally good for wintering waterfowl and raptors. Bald Eagle, Golden Eagle (rare), flocks of Common Goldeneye, Common Merganser, and other waterfowl that the eagles may prey on can usually be spotted at Barkhamsted Reservoir, along the Connecticut River at Enfield, and also along the Housatonic River near the Shepaug and Stevenson's Dams.

The best winter birding is usually found along the coast. Norwalk Harbor, Sherwood Island State Park, New Haven Harbor, the mouth of the Connecticut River, and the Thames River can be good for a variety of wintering waterfowl. Here you may find Snowy Owls at Milford Point or Great Meadows Marsh, Purple Sandpipers at Merwin Point or

Eastern Point, and the chance to pick up white-winged gulls (Glaucous, Iceland) or the Lesser Black-backed Gull at Oyster River, Bradley Point, or Sandy Point. Offshore waters at these sites can also produce a wide variety of sea ducks, loons, grebes, and mergansers. Eastern Point in Groton is usually good for Brant and sometimes Common Eider. Smith Cove in Waterford and the Mamacoke Island Natural Area part of the Connecticut College Arboretum are consistently good for a variety of bay and diving ducks, as well as cormorants and loons. This is also a good time to check shoreline sites such as Hammonasset Beach State Park, Great Meadows Marsh, and Bluff Point Coastal Reserve for winter visitors such as Rough-legged Hawk, Snow Bunting, Lapland Longspur, and Short-eared Owl.

Winter months can be excellent for calling owls. Eastern Screech-owl, Great Horned and Barred Owls often respond to tape or vocal imitation of their songs during the early evening hours of darkness or just before dawn. A search of the conifer stands at Greenwich Point Park, Hammonasset Beach State Park, or inland at Quinnipiac River State Park, and Sperry Park frequently yields Northern Saw-whet Owl or Great Horned Owl, and sometimes Long-eared Owl. Durham Meadows is also good for wintering raptors and is fairly consistent for Northern Shrike (every other year or so).

The Spring Migration. March is a time of transition for both weather and birds. Bright and sunny days increasingly mix with and alleviate the worst of winter's cold and snow. Winter birds start moving northward, especially toward the end of the month. Meanwhile, spring migrants begin to build in numbers and variety in the state. The Connecticut and Housatonic Rivers are important migration corridors for Osprey, Tree Swallow, inland shorebirds (Killdeer and American Woodcock), and waterfowl. Other early migrants such as Eastern Phoebe, American Robin, Eastern Meadowlark, Red-winged Blackbird, Common Grackle, Rusty Blackbird, and Brown-headed Cowbird begin to appear throughout the state. Blackbirds usually start appearing in late February. In late March and early April, large flocks of Bonaparte's Gull mass at the mouth of Oyster River, South Cove in Old Saybrook, and Long Wharf in New Haven. These sites usually yield Black-headed Gull and frequently Little Gull among the migrants.

The migration scene continues in April. Waterfowl concentrations can be found at Greenwich Point Park, Great Island WMA, Milford Point, Gulf Pond, and Rocky Neck State Park. The spring hawk migration is less concentrated than in fall, but returning accipiters and Red-tailed, Red-shouldered and Broad-winged Hawks can be spotted at River Road in Kent, Naugatuck State Forest, Osbornedale State Park, and elsewhere. From mid-April into early May the herons, egrets, and shorebirds return to the coastal marshes and can be spotted at Manresa, Great Meadows Marsh, Milford Point, Griswold Point, Barn Island, and elsewhere along the shoreline.

The spring migration of warblers, songbirds, and vireos peaks during the first three weeks of May and Connecticut birders are galvanized by an urgent necessity to visit River Road in Kent, Boston Hollow in Ashford, and East Rock Park in New Haven, to catch concentrations of spring warblers. A good day's birding at these and other sites can frequently tally two dozen warbler species. Scanning the flocks of swallows that build at Konold's Pond or Nepaug Reservoir should produce Tree, Northern Rough-winged, Barn, Bank, and occasionally Cliff Swallows. By late May, Bluff Point Coastal Reserve, Lighthouse Point Park, Boston Hollow, and Devil's Hopyard State Park can host good songbird concentrations.

The Nesting Season. By late spring, many species such as Great Horned Owls, Killdeer, and European Starlings have already fledged young. In May and June, the nesting season of passerines is in full swing throughout the state. Breeding birds can be tallied at every birding site in the state, so pick sites which offer a variety of habitats and plan to bird them either early in the morning, just after first light, or in late evening hours to enjoy the song serenades. Good sites for woodland nesting birds include White Memorial Foundation, Mohawk State Forest, Northwest Highlands Tour, Pachaug State Forest, Nehantic State Forest, Naugatuck State Forest, Natchaug State Forest, and Connecticut College Arboretum.

The wetlands at Station 43, Mohawk State Forest, and White Memorial Foundation all provide good summer birding for rails, ducks, flycatchers, and possibly bitterns. Visit shoreline sites to see the long-legged waders in action as they forage for food for themselves and their young. Herons and egrets stand out against the marsh background at Barn Island Wildlife Management Area, Great Island Wildlife

Management Area, Hammonasset Beach State Park, Milford Point, and other shoreline sites. This is also a good time to watch the behavioral antics of the nesting Least Terns and Piping Plovers from the elevated boardwalk at Milford Point. Protected areas for these species are also found at Long Beach, Sandy Point, and Griswold Point Preserve.

By midsummer, most nesting species have already fledged their young although a few of the late nesters, renesters, and double-nesting species such as the American Robin, American Goldfinch, Cedar Waxwing, and House Sparrow may still be attending nestlings. Most of the shoreline sites are now crowded with bathers and recreational boaters and even inland sites tend to be hot, humid, and too buggy to bird. Best bets for inland birders in July and early August are to take cool evening or early morning hikes in hemlock woodlands at People's State Forest, White Memorial Foundation, Devil's Hopyard State Park, or Boston Hollow, all of which will produce some warblers, thrushes, and flycatchers. By mid-July, adults and newly fledged young of Barn, Tree, Bank, and Northern Rough-winged Swallows are flocking in those long lines on telephone wires while the late afternoon aerial displays of starling flights grow larger each day.

The Fall Migration. From mid-July onward, shorebirds migrating from their nesting grounds on the Canadian Arctic begin to appear all along the coast. Bluff Point Coastal Reserve, Milford Point, Griswold Point, Sandy Point, and Hammonasset Beach State Park become the hottest birding sites in Connecticut.

In August, the shorebird movement is in full swing. Barn Island Wildlife Management Area, Bluff Point Coastal Reserve, Great Island Wildlife Management Area, Hammonasset Beach State Park, Long Wharf, Sandy Point, Greenwich Point Park, and especially Milford Point can feature spectacular concentrations of shorebird flocks. Less common shorebirds such as American Golden-Plover and Pectoral and Upland Sandpipers are frequently tallied during this time as well. Concentrations of Common Tern begin to swell towards the end of the month and should be checked for stragglers such as Forster's, Royal, Caspian and Roseate Terns, all of which occur annually. During July and August, migrating songbird begin to appear in the woods and thickets at Hammonasset Beach State Park, Bluff Point Coastal Reserve, Lighthouse Point Park, and various inland locations such as Osbornedale

State Park, and Station 43. Late August also heralds the start of the evening migration of Common Nighthawks which can often be seen during late evening hours at Naugatuck State Forest, West Rock Ridge State Park, Sherwood Island State Park, and many other locations. The fall migration of shorebirds and swallows peaks just as the hawk migration begins. In September, hawk watchers are active at Quaker Ridge, Lighthouse Point Park and other hawk watching stations in the state. Streams of accipiters, especially Sharp-shinned and Cooper's Hawks, and buteos including the Red-tailed, Broad-winged and Red-shouldered Hawks are seen along with Osprey and American Kestrel. Less common but consistent migrant raptors include Northern Harrier, Turkey Vulture, Peregrine Falcon, and Merlin. The overlook at East Rock Park and the ridgetop at Bald Peak are used for watching hawks at eye level. In late September and early October, the migrating songbirds continue to stack up in number and variety at the major shoreline birding sites---best bets are Lighthouse Point Park, Hammonasset Beach State Park, and Bluff Point Coastal Reserve.

For many birders, October is a favorite month. Cool temperatures cause a sharp drop in the number of visitors to state parks and other lands just at the time when lots of birds are moving about. Inland, birders should schedule a visit to Bantam Lake in Litchfield for Ruddy Duck, American Coot, Pied-billed Grebe, and other waterbirds. October is also a good month for fall sparrows. Savannah, Lincoln's, White-throated, White-crowned, and the rarer Lark, Clay-colored, and Henslow's Sparrows may occur at coastal birding sites such as Lighthouse Point Park and Hammonasset Beach State Park. White Memorial Foundation and the pastures at Station 43 also get good sparrow concentrations at this time. American Pipit arrive in October, and may be found in the field furrows at Farmington Meadows, Station 43, Horse Barn Hill, and other inland and coastal sites.

Late Autumn and Early Winter. Late autumn is a relatively quiet period for birders following the excitement of the fall migration, but this is the time when some of Connecticut's best rarities have occurred, such as Tropical Kingbird, Gray Kingbird, and Black-throated Gray Warbler. Waterfowl concentrations can still be found at many lakes, rivers, and coastal sites. Most of the migrating raptors, shorebirds, and songbirds have passed through the state although a few procrastinators may appear at shoreline birding sites. This is also the season to keep tabs on the Rare Bird Alert, as errant migrants or storm blown species can turn up almost anywhere. Sea ducks, Red-throated and Common Loons, and Horned Grebes can appear along the coast, especially at Greenwich Point Park, Hammonasset Beach State Park, Griswold Point Preserve, Harkness Memorial State Park and Bluff Point Coastal Reserve. The Northern Gannet has also been regularly appearing in November along the coast.

Winter birds start arriving during this period. Early snowfalls and sharp cold spells may send crossbills, siskins, Northern Saw-whet Owls, and Snowy Owls into the state. Snowy Owls can turn up anywhere in the state, but Milford Point and Great Meadows Marsh are always good possibilities.

December birding is limited by the short winter days and is always weather dependent. Warm clothing, good gloves and a spare pair of dry socks and shoes can be helpful if you plan to spend the day in the field. Inland, hikes along any of the passable trails at Mohawk Mountain, Osbornedale State Park, Natchaug State Forest, Bigelow Hollow State Park, and most of the other interior birding sites listed in this guide will turn up many residents and winter visitors. The North American Christmas Bird Count in Connecticut is conducted in the last weeks of December and the first days of January. To participate in one or more counts, contact local birding clubs, Audubon chapters, or nature centers.

Birding Equipment

Your primary pair of binoculars is a matter of choice and there are as many opinions about these as there are birders. Because Connecticut birding opportunities often involves trips to the shoreline combined with inland trips we recommend using 10 x 42 binoculars. Other traditional favorites are the 8 x 40's or 7 x 35's. A good spotting scope mounted on a sturdy tripod is essential for most trips to shoreline sites and inland lakes and reservoirs, especially when you want to identify those occasional rarities such as the European gulls, offshore waterfowl, and other water birds.

Birding equipment should include a small, comfortable backpack with a packet of maps, pocket knife, and a compass. From spring through fall, a rain poncho, extra cap, sunglasses, insect repellent, sun screen, and drinking water should also be carried. In winter, keep an extra pair of heavy socks and possibly an extra pair of gloves in the backpack. Additional items to carry include favorite field guides, a spare pair of binoculars, camera, pen or pencil, and notebook. Lens cleaning paper, and an extra binocular strap can also be useful.

Weather and Clothing

Connecticut's weather is New England's weather so it helps to pay heed to the old proverb "there is nothing so changeable as New England weather" and be prepared with proper seasonal clothing. A sampling of the average monthly temperatures across regions of the state is presented in the table below.

Representative Average Monthly Temperatures for Connecticut Regions
Temperatures in degrees Fahrenheit

Month	Northwest Hills	Interior Valley	Coastal Slope	Eastern Hills
Jan	27.7	27.5	29.1	26.0
Feb	25.5	30.0	30.0	27.5
Mar	33.6	38.7	37.3	35.0
Apr	45.4	49.9	47.5	46.0
May	56.9	60.1	58.1	56.3
June	65.6	68.5	65.2	65.2
July	70.3	74.6	73.2	70.0
Aug	68.5	71.5	72.4	68.4
Sept	61.4	64.0	64.0	61.6
Oct	51.5	53.8	53.7	51.5
Nov	39.6	43.0	42.8	41.0
Dec	27.7	30.5	31.5	29.3

* Data from *The Climate of Connecticut.*

In winter, much of your birding activity will probably concentrate along the coast; here the danger lies in the frequently strong and bitter sea winds which increase the wind chill factor, even on bright and sunny days. Inland winter birding can be just as climatically strenuous when hiking in frost hollows and colder ravines where snow accumulation and wind drifts can be difficult to traverse. Winds are usually, but not always, less of a problem for the inland birder but snows can be deeper than anticipated along woodland trails. A parka, wool scarf, hat, appropriate shoes, and a good pair of gloves should be the minimum clothing necessities for winter birding.

A layered approach works best for all kinds of birding weather. The first, or outer layer, should function as a protective barrier between you and the weather. A waterproof jacket and pants of shell fabric such as Gore-Tex helps keep out wind and water but still allows water vapor from your body to escape. The middle layer of clothing functions as the warm, insulating layer. Wool, down, or polyester sweaters, and vests, and jackets of materials such as Thinsulate and Polarguard HV retain body heat. The inner layer of winter clothing is the most important and usually the most neglected layer. For your comfort and safety, it should consist of a fabric such as polyester or nylon such as Environtherm, Thermex, or Fieldsensor which transports body moisture away from your skin. A good pair of gloves provides much better protection than merely placing your hands in your pockets from time to time. Socks are just as important as upper body clothing; use acrylic-based blends of wool, nylon, or spandex along with a pair of no-bulk high-tech fiber liner socks for added warmth. A woolen cap is also recommended, first because it prevents excess heat loss from the most exposed part of the body, the head, and also because you can use it to regulate body heat; as you warm up, remove the cap until you feel comfortable.

Spring and fall generally offer the best birding weather. Cool, bright and sunny days make for enjoyable hikes throughout the day and evening. Temperatures can be brisk in early morning and evening so a medium weight jacket is a good clothing item to take along.

July and August can be hot and humid with prolonged heat waves invariably accompanied by high humidity. Restrict hiking to the cooler early morning and late evening hours.

Tides and Tide Tables

Birding at the right turn of the tide can play a big part when visiting coastal areas. Generally, two hours before and after high tide is the best time to spot shorebirds and ducks. However, some low mudflats and sandbars may only be exposed during mean low tide.

Long Island Sound experiences two tidal cycles (periods of high and low tides) daily. Actually, a complete tidal cycle (high-low-high) takes 12 hours and 25 minutes. Most state and local newspapers include tide tables that can be clipped and periodically consulted. Keep in mind that the exact time of high and low tides is earlier to the east and later along the western part of the Connecticut coast. For example, high tide at Stonington Point is about 2:25 hours earlier than at Greenwich, while low tide is about 2:40 minutes earlier. Because of the narrowing waters of western Long Island Sound, tides are considerably more pronounced from Fairfield westward along the shore. For example, at Stamford the average tidal range is about 7.2 feet (2.2 meters) while at New London the range is only 3.0 feet (0.9 meters).

General Precautions

Birding in the field often means that you will be exposed to common and sometimes not so common plant and animal pests.

Undoubtedly, the most troublesome plant pest in Connecticut is poison ivy. This plant, with its glossy green leaves in clusters of three, is especially widespread in disturbed areas such as roadsides, fields, along stone walls, and around outbuildings and old foundations. In some places poison ivy forms a ground cover, in others it becomes a vine growing up the sides of trees, fence posts, and telephone poles. When the twigs or leaves of poison ivy are broken or crushed they release an oil which can penetrate the skin, causing irritation.

If you have been exposed to poison ivy, wash the exposed skin with soap and water as soon as possible. If you are hiking in wetlands or seep areas find some jewelweed (the pale green herb with bright orange fall flowers). Some naturalists maintain that rubbing the juices of jewelweed on the affected skin will alleviate poison ivy symptoms. Serious cases of poison ivy should be treated by a physician. Birders hiking in swamps, bogs, and along the edges of wetlands may encounter a tall shrub or small tree that looks like sumac. This is poison sumac, which can be identified by its white berries and sumac-like leaves that lack teeth. Poison sumac is closely related to poison ivy. Like its better known relative, the oils of poison sumac can cause itching, irritation, and a painful and aggravating rash.

Ticks, mosquitos, deer flies, black flies, spiders, wasps, and bees should pose no problem if you take some very general precautions before and after the day's birding trip. Ticks are potentially dangerous because some of them may carry Lyme Disease, a multisystem affliction that affects the skin, joints, and nervous system, and sometimes the heart and eyes. Named for the town of Lyme, Connecticut, in which the disease was first identified in 1975, Lyme Disease is one of several tick-transmitted diseases; others include Ehrlichiosis, Babesiosis, and Tick Paralysis, but these are rare in Connecticut.

Ticks can be abundant in grassy and shrubby fields, thickets, and shrubby woodland edges from March through October, and are most prevalent in May, June and July. During warm spells ticks may be out in every month of the year. To avoid ticks, try to limit off-trail hiking, especially through overgrown fields and thickets. Wear light clothing, with the trouser legs tucked into the socks or hightops and sprayed with insect repellant. Permethrin Tick Repellent and Duranon Tick Repellent are effective against ticks, mosquitos, and chiggers. Permethrin and Duranon (and other insect sprays containing Permethrin) are applied directly on the clothing prior to wearing. Let the clothing dry first before you put it on. **Don't apply insecticides directly on your skin.** Using a combination of insecticides with an insect repellant (active ingredient DEET, as found in Cutter's and other brands) will protect you from most insect bites. Insect repellents can be applied directly to the skin. The use of insect repellents and insecticides doesn't entirely eliminate the chance of getting ticks so check yourself thoroughly after every birding trip. A good shower after spending some time in the field is always advisable as well---for a variety of good reasons!

From April through mid-October, mosquitos can be a problem when birding inland and coastal marshes, around the shores of ponds and lakes, and even in wet woodlands. A hat, long-sleeved shirt and periodic spraying with insect repellent usually discourages them, although during a long hike repellent should be applied several times.

Deer flies can be an abominable nuisance and seem to be especially numerous on hot, muggy days in woodlands. For some reason, deer flies like to get into your hair, so a hat helps to keep them away. They and black flies can be dissuaded by the judicious use of insect repellent.

Spiders are another common arthropod that seem to have become more troublesome--- in recent years several people have been bitten by

wintering species which are normally seen only between late October and March, another 70 are usually observed only during spring or fall migration, and another 170 or so birds are nesting species. While memorizing even a hundred species can be initially daunting for the novice birder, the numbers can be made more manageable by using this guide. Each of the birding site guides provides a detailed list of the birds that are likely to be seen and the specific areas where they can be found.

Before your next birding trip to one of the birding sites we describe in this guide, read the description of the site and make a list of the birds likely to be found there which you might have difficulty with. Review the field marks and when possible, listen to their typical songs. With these preparations you may be pleasantly surprised to find an immediate improvement in your birding skills which in turn will stimulate you to undertake more field trips.

Connecticut Birding Hotline

Any rare and unusual birds that turn up in Connecticut are listed on a statewide birding hotline. The Birding Hotline, also known as the Rare Bird Alert, is a tape recorded message sponsored by the Connecticut Ornithological Association and the Audubon Council of Connecticut. The hotline is updated weekly with new sightings and information, including directions about where to find rare birds. Connecticut birders should get into the habit of periodically checking the birding hotline for the latest information on rarities spotted in the state. The Rare Bird Alert number for Connecticut is:

RARE BIRD ALERT 203-254-3665

For computer users, the Connecticut Rare Bird alert is also available on Internet. If you want to receive rare bird alerts for the eastern states (including Connecticut), send the two-word message: SUBSCRIBE BIRDEAST.

General Information

For further information about the ecology of Connecticut birds and birding habitats, contact the following agencies:

DEP Bureau of Natural Resources
Wildlife Division
79 Elm Street
Hartford, Connecticut   06106-1632   phone (860)-424-3011

To obtain topographic maps, county maps, and publications including a copy of *The Atlas of Breeding Birds of Connecticut* contact:

DEP Maps and Publications Sales
79 Elm Street
Hartford, CT 06106-1632   phone (860)-424-3555

For further tourist information including a state map, vacation guide packets, information and reservations for motels and more contact:

Connecticut Tourism Division
865 Brook Street
Rocky Hill, CT 06067-3405   phone (800)-282-6863

Connecticut Birding Organizations

We also recommend that you join a local, regional or statewide bird club. Connecticut's leading birding organization is the Connecticut Ornithological Association (COA). The COA produces two informative periodicals; a quarterly journal, *The Connecticut Warbler,* and, a quarterly newsletter, the *COA Bulletin* which provides the latest information about birds, birders, and birding activity in the state. The COA also publishes a *Field Checklist, Birds of Connecticut* which is available for a nominal fee. For further information about any of these publications as well as membership in COA write:

The Connecticut Ornithological Association
314 Unquowa Road
Fairfield, CT   06430

In addition to the COA, Connecticut has a number of important bird clubs and environmental organizations that emphasize birding. Many of these, such as the Connecticut Audubon Society, Hartford Audubon Society, New Haven Bird Club, and Natchaug Ornithological Society have a long history of operation in the state. The Connecticut Audubon Society owns and manages more than a dozen nature sanctuaries, several of which (Larsen, Trailwood, Milford Point) are featured in this birding guide. The National Audubon Society (NAS) also has several Audubon centers in Connecticut, which offer birding opportunities. In addition, the NAS has numerous state chapters that sponsor birding trips and events (e.g., Christmas bird counts). A list of organizations in Connecticut that manage sanctuaries and nature centers or promote birding activities is included in Chapter VI.

How to use this Guide

This book is written as a guide to the best birding sites in Connecticut. We have tried to write this guide in such a way that it will prove useful to novices, seasoned birders, and visitors, as well as state residents. Throughout the individual site guides, we describe interesting natural features, where appropriate, to enliven and inform your birding adventures.

This guide is divided into four sections. A chapter on the major ecological habitats in the state follows this introductory chapter. Each habitat is described, and some birds characteristic of the habitat are listed. Section three, comprising the bulk of the text, consists of the birding site guides. The birding sites are grouped into seven regional areas of the state, the Northwest Highlands, Western Hills, Central Valley, Eastern Hills, Southwestern Coastal, Central Coastal, and Southeastern Coastal.

For each area we have provided guides for ten or more good birding sites. Birding sites were selected for the range of habitats and birds that may be found, plus their accessibility to birders. Directions to each birding site begin from one of the following major highways; Interstate 95, Interstate 91, Interstate 395, Interstate 84, the Wilbur-Cross and Merritt Parkway (Route 15), Route 8, Route 9, or other state routes. For each exit we have also included the information printed on the exit signs. For example, the directions to Bluff Point Coastal Reserve begin with "From Interstate 95 take Exit 88 (Route 117)...." In this case, Route 117 is the information placed on the exit sign. Most directions include distances between major points, but keep in mind that vehicle odometers may vary slightly so mileages over longer distances should be taken as reasonable approximations.

Each birding site guide includes a brief list of the birding highlights offered at that site, the best times to bird the site, and, as applicable, specific information on birding trails to hike. For each site, we have provided a list of birds that can be expected during certain seasons, as well as uncommon or rare species that might be possible. The listings consist of birds we observed or that have been observed by knowledgeable birders. A map is provided for each of the major birding sites. For clarity, most maps include only the major access roads to, from, and around a birding site. Map scales are approximate. The most frequently used map symbols are illustrated on page 23.

Chapter IV is an annotated species list of the birds accepted by the Connecticut Rare Record Committee. The species list includes a brief description of the habitat and season in which a species is most likely to occur in the state, along with a short list of birding sites where they may be found, in season. The birding guide concludes with a bibliography including a list of books useful for Connecticut birders and a list of Connecticut's birding and other nature organizations.

Regional Birding Areas of Connecticut

LEGEND

ⓟ	Parking
⚠	Camping Area
🜊	Picnic Area
◈Ⓑ	Boat Launch
◇Ⓒ	Canoe Launch
╈	Power Lines
♧	Conifers
🜉	Wet Lands
+++	Railroad Lines

Major symbols used in maps for the birding site guides.

into a variety of upland terrestrial habitats such as meadows, old fields, and shrubby thickets. Natural factors such as local soil, wildfire, and climate may also dictate different habitats such as sand plains and grasslands that exist within an otherwise wooded landscape. Where fields, plains, and thickets border woodlands an important habitat called woodland edge occurs. The fields, thickets and edge habitat created by human and natural circumstances enhance local and regional habitat diversity, which in turn provides birders with the chance to find many more species than would occur if Connecticut was entirely covered by deciduous woodlands.

Fields
Abandoned fields, pastures, and former croplands will naturally revert by ecological succession to woodlands on a time scale of 80 to about 150 years. The process begins when abandoned fields are invaded by forbs, grasses, and shrubs that transform the abandoned area into a field of asters, goldenrod, milkweed, mullein, and other wildflowers. Within a few years grasses such as little bluestem, ticklegrass, and orchard grass invade the pioneer weed field and transform it into a grassy field.

Two other distinctive types of field habitats that occur in Connecticut are mowed fields and lawns around commercial establishments, airports, and cemeteries and the patches of edaphic prairie found on well drained soils in the central lowlands and the crests of trap rock ridges. Some of the birds of pastures, hayfields, croplands, large airports, and open fields include:

American Kestrel, Northern Bobwhite, Ring-necked Pheasant, Mourning Dove, Horned Lark, Purple Martin, Eastern Meadowlark, Common Grackle, American Goldfinch, and Savannah, Grasshopper, Chipping, and Field Sparrows

Some birding sites with representative field habitats are: Bradley International Airport, Haley Farm State Park, Harkness Memorial State Park, Osbornedale State Park, and Mansfield Hollow State Park.

Thickets
Like fields, thickets are temporary habitats in Connecticut, giving way,

in time, to woodlands. Thickets are formed when shrubby vegetation such as red cedar, multiflora rose, raspberry, sumac, greenbrier, Oriental bittersweet, cherry and other shrubs and vines take root in the grassy fields, often producing dense, almost impenetrable bramble thickets.

The shrubby growth found along utility rights-of-way is also thicket habitat. To install power lines, utility companies cut long swaths across the landscape, then placed the power line or gas line in the middle of the swath. Initially, the vegetation along many of these power line cuts were managed by periodic spraying of herbicides, or cutting, or both cutting and spraying to reduce the growth of woody vegetation. In recent years, most utilities have abandoned these practices and have maintained corridors primarily by selective removal of tree saplings. The result is powerline habitats that consist of long tracts of shrubby growth with an understory of grasses and herbs such as goldenrod and mugwort. In essence, powerlines have become relatively stable thickets, consisting of rose and other bramble amidst which grow small white pine, black cherry, and other early woodland pioneering species.

Whatever their origin, thickets are exceptionally valuable bird habitats, providing not only high quality foods but also good cover, and many birds of field and forest roost and forage in thickets and woodland edge. Some typical birds of thickets include:

Gray Catbird, Brown Thrasher, White-eyed Vireo, Blue-winged and Prairie Warblers, Common Yellowthroat, Northern Cardinal, Field Sparrow, and Indigo Bunting

Birding sites with good thickets include Audubon Center of Greenwich, Barn Island Wildlife Management Area, Connecticut College Arboretum, Haley Farm State Park, Mansfield Hollow State Park, Northwest Highlands, and Quinibaug Wildlife Management Area.

Edge

In Connecticut, edge habitat most often is represented by the transitional boundary between woodlands and adjacent fields, wetlands, or developed habitats. Edge usually includes a mix of smaller woodland trees, herbs, and shrubs. Some of the birds that nest, roost, or forage in woodland edge include:

Eastern Screech-Owl, Mourning Dove, House and Carolina Wrens, Northern Mockingbird, Gray Catbird, White-eyed Vireo, Yellow Warbler, Common Yellowthroat, Indigo Bunting, Northern Cardinal, Song Sparrow, and Brown-headed Cowbird

Most interior birding sites have some edge habitat.

DEVELOPED HABITATS

While much of the Connecticut landscape is comprised of natural habitats, some have been transformed by suburban, urban, commercial, and industrial development. Greenbelts, lawns, and ornamentals all contribute to birdscaping habitats that entice certain species tolerant of these modified landscapes. Some of the birds of suburbs, urban open space, and landscaped commercial or industrial habitats include:

American Kestrel, Rock Dove, Barn and Eastern Screech Owls, European Starling, American Crow, House Wren, Carolina Wren, Northern Mockingbird, Brown-headed Cowbird, Northern Cardinal, House Finch, and House Sparrow.

FRESHWATER LANDSCAPES

Innumerable wetlands, ponds and lakes dot the Connecticut countryside while rivulets, rills, brooks, creeks, and rivers wind and curve through the landscape. Together, these freshwater habitats add diversity to Connecticut and attract a varied assortment of birds that require these specialized habitats for nesting, resting, and foraging.

Wetlands

Wetlands are interface habitats between land and water. Connecticut's freshwater wetlands range from ponds to marshes to shrub swamps to wooded red maple swamps. In addition to being habitats for wildlife, wetlands have a number of significant functions. They serve as water storage reservoirs, holding excess waters during high water periods following spring rains, for example, and releasing it slowly as water levels decline, preventing floods. Wetlands also purify water; wetland plants entrap sediment and other debris, thereby reducing erosion and water turbidity downstream. Some wetland plants also extract heavy metals and other pollutants from the water. Wetlands are important nurseries for fish and serve as habitat for a variety of amphibians, reptiles and mammals. Some of the many species of birds that nest and forage in freshwater wetlands of Connecticut include:

Great Blue and Green Herons, Canada Goose, Mallard, American Black and Wood Ducks, Red-shouldered Hawk, Virginia Rail, Sora, American Woodcock, Barred Owl, Marsh Wren, Red-winged Blackbird, and Swamp Sparrow.

Birding sites that have representative examples of wetlands include Audubon Center of Greenwich (shrub swamp, red maple swamp), Devil's Den Preserve (red maple swamp), Natchaug State Forest (red maple swamp, cattail marsh, shrub swamp), Quinnipiac River State Park (red maple swamp), Station 43 (extensive marshes of cattail, pickerelweed, purple loosestrife), and White Memorial Foundation (cattail marsh, shrub swamp).

Bogs
Bogs are scarce and unusual habitats in Connecticut. Bogs occur in natural depressions, often glacial kettles with poor drainage and cold microclimates. The cold, acidic bog water slows normal decomposition and dead plants accumulate in a mass of organic debris that floats on the water. Most bogs include a number of unique and interesting plant species such as black spruce, pitcher plant, bog cranberry, and sundew. Some typical birds of bogs include:

Yellow-bellied Flycatcher, Northern Waterthrush, Nashville Warbler, and Lincoln's Sparrow.

Birding sites that have good examples of bogs include Flanders Nature Center (pitcher plant, leatherleaf, cranberry bog) and Mohawk State Forest (black spruce bog).

Ponds and Lakes
Connecticut has hundreds of ponds, lakes, impoundments, and

reservoirs, many of which have been enlarged through the construction of earth or concrete dams. Lakes and ponds serve as recreational sites for seasonal boating, swimming, fishing, and other water activities and many feature extensive shoreline development. Despite their often heavy seasonal use, most lakes and ponds are nesting and resting areas for a variety of waterfowl and other waterbirds and as roosting and refueling areas for many migrant species. Some characteristic birds of ponds and lakes include:

Great Blue and Green Herons, Mute Swan, Canada Goose, Mallard, Ring-necked Duck, Bufflehead, Hooded Merganser, American Coot, Osprey, Belted Kingfisher, Tree Swallow, and Red-winged Blackbird

Birding sites that include good examples of ponds and lakes are Barkhamsted Reservoir, Bigelow Hollow State Park (Bigelow Pond and Mashapaug Pond), Great Pond State Forest, Mansfield Hollow State Park, Nepaug Reservoir, and White Memorial Foundation (Bantam Lake, Cemetery Pond, Little Pond).

Riverine Systems
Connecticut rivers carve and shape the landscape. The largest river complexes---the Connecticut, Naugatuck, Housatonic, and Thames---run from north to south through the state, discharging into Long Island Sound. These rivers serve as migration corridors for a wide variety of species that traverse the state during their spring and fall migrations along the Atlantic Flyway. The riparian woodlands that occur along these rivers comprise an important habitat for birds and other wildlife. Some birds that may be found along Connecticut rivers include:

Common Goldeneye, Common Merganser, Bald Eagle, Osprey, Spotted Sandpiper, Belted Kingfisher, Barn, Tree, Bank, and Northern Rough-winged Swallows, Warbling Vireo, and Baltimore Oriole.

Birding sites that include riverine systems are: Connecticut River in Enfield and Suffield, Lower Connecticut River Tour, Mystic River, River Road in Kent, and River Road in Southbury.

COASTAL HABITATS

The Connecticut shoreline consists of several hundred miles of bays, estuaries, rocky shores, beaches, tidal flats, sand beaches, and salt marshes. Collectively, these shoreline habitats support a rich diversity of waterfowl, shorebirds, gulls, and waterbirds. During spring and fall, coastal marshes provide resources for the thousands of birds that migrate along the Atlantic Coast Flyway, both for stopover and staging areas where they rest and feed before resuming migration.

A typical sequence of shoreline habitats exhibits distinct zones that occur in a specific sequence from shore to upland. From water to upland these zones may include mud flats, sand beach, low salt marsh, high salt marsh, and marsh-upland edge. Most of Connecticut's salt marshes are cut with mosquito ditches which were dredged to drain the natural pools that provided habitat for marsh birds. Pools are being restored in some marshes which, in combination with hummocks and wooded islands, add important birding habitat diversity to the otherwise fairly uniform salt marshes.

Mudflats and Sand Beaches

Extensive areas of mud flats and/or sand beaches are a characteristic and common feature of Connecticut shorelines. In many areas along the coast, long, low stretches of mud flats and sand beaches or sand bars often occur just offshore as well. The mud flats, and, to a lesser extent, the sandy beaches are used by a wide variety of shorebirds and gulls for feeding and resting. Some characteristic birds that may be found on sand beaches and mud flats include:

Piping and Semipalmated Plovers, Semipalmated Sandpiper, Greater and Lesser Yellowlegs, Willet, Great Black-backed, Herring and Ring-billed Gulls, and Least Tern.

Birding sites with great areas of mud flats and sandy beaches include Bluff Point Coastal Reserve, Great Meadows Marsh, Griswold Point, Hammonasset Beach State Park, and Milford Point.

Rocky Shore

Naturally occurring and human versions of rocky shores (jetties, pilings, sea walls) provide important habitat for foraging and resting waterbirds. Some birds that occur along rocky shores include:

Ruddy Turnstone, Spotted and Purple Sandpipers, Double-crested and Great Cormorants, Herring and Great Black-backed Gulls, and Common Tern.

Salt Marsh

Two salt marsh zones can be identified, low and high salt marsh. The low salt marsh lies in the intertidal zone and is inundated at high tide. It is most easily identified by the vegetative belt of salt water cordgrass that grows from 3-7 feet tall. The tall, dense growth of plants form a protective cover for salt marsh birds and other wildlife while the rootstalks are an important food source for wintering ducks and geese. Because the low salt marsh is periodically flooded, most birds nest in the high salt marsh or adjacent uplands, but a number of waterfowl and shorebirds use the low salt marsh for feeding and finding cover.

The high salt marsh is the most common salt marsh in Connecticut, often covering large expanses along the shoreline. The high salt marsh extends from the low salt marsh to the marsh-upland interface. In summer, the high salt marsh is a sea of grassy-green salt meadow cordgrass, intermixed with spikegrass, blackgrass, and showy forbes such as sea lavender and seaside goldenrod. In fall and winter, the high salt marsh is marked by the dry brown stems of cordgrass. The high salt marsh usually has a distinctive upland interface belt of scrubby vegetation of marsh elder, switchgrass, and groundsel-tree. In some areas the marsh-upland interface may consist of a dense, but narrow belt of reedgrass. The high salt marsh is an important habitat for birds. Because tidal flooding is reduced or absent, many species nest, forage or raise their young in the high salt marsh. Others take refuge in the tall cover provided by the grasses, sedges, and forbes. Furthermore, the marsh-upland ecotone creates an edge effect which, in this case, is beneficial for many species that nest and roost in the shrubby or wooded vegetation of adjacent uplands and feed in the high salt marsh. Some of the birds that nest or forage in salt marshes include:

Great Blue and Green Herons, Black-crowned and Yellow-crowned Night-Herons, Great and Snowy Egrets, Glossy Ibis, Green-winged

Teal, Clapper Rail, Willet, Least Sandpiper, Least and Common Terns, Rough-legged Hawk, Northern Harrier, Osprey, Short-eared Owl, Tree Swallow, Purple Martin, Marsh Wren, and Saltmarsh Sharp-tailed and Seaside Sparrows.

Birding sites with extensive areas of salt marsh include: Barn Island Wildlife Management Area, Great Island Wildlife Management Area, Great Meadows Marsh, Hammonasset Beach State Park, Rocky Neck State Park, and Sherwood Island State Park.

CHANGES IN THE LANDSCAPE

The natural habitats of Connecticut are constantly in flux. Forests are cleared by hurricanes, tornadoes, or humans. As farms are abandoned, the land is either sold for development or ecologically reverts to woodland. Conversion of forest and farmlands for commercial, industrial, and residential development is constantly displacing natural habitats. Humans and animals (e.g., beaver) divert, dam, or pollute streams and wetlands both inland and along the coast. Some of these transgressions are avoidable, but others are the price that we pay for civilization. On the positive side of the ledger, Connecticut has many good examples of natural habitat still available and much of that has been protected from further human encroachment.

The birding sites that we describe are a selection of Connecticut's best natural and modified landscapes, but even they may be subject to further alteration. These changes threaten the complexion and composition of Connecticut's aquatic and terrestrial habitats. For example, the eastern hemlock, *Tsuga canadensis*, normally a tall, long-lived native tree, is in trouble. This valuable and attractive tree comprises about 6% of Connecticut's woodlands but also occurs in relatively pure stands in hemlock ravines and on north-facing slopes of hills and mountains. The hemlock is seriously threatened by an infestation of the woolly adelgid, *Adelgid tsugae*, a small, sap-sucking insect that causes defoliation and eventually the death of the infected tree. First noticed in Connecticut following Hurricane Gloria in 1985, the woolly adelgid has spread rapidly and now threatens to destroy Connecticut's hemlocks.

The cool, hemlock-clad ravines offer important breeding habitat for a number of birds such as the Solitary Vireo, Acadian Flycatcher, and

Black-throated Green and Blackburnian Warblers, as well as red squirrel, fisher, and white-tailed deer. The demise of hemlock stands has already figured in the decline of the nesting colony of Fish Crows at East Rock Park and the ultimate effects on other species throughout the state is problematical.

American elm and red pine have also been devastated by disease in Connecticut. By the 1950's, American elm had been mostly eliminated from Connecticut woodlands by the Dutch Elm Disease. Other native hardwoods replaced the elm, leaving the basic nature of the deciduous forest intact. The loss of red pine is a more serious concern, however.

Red pine grows naturally only in the northwestern corner of the state but thousands of seedlings were planted for reforestation of old fields in many state parks and forests at the turn of the century and also during the Civilian Conservation Corp era in the 1930's. The tall pines with a dark, symmetrical crown lend a pleasing alpine aspect to landscapes as well as provide shade for trails and picnic areas in state parks and state forests. Unfortunately, Connecticut red pine stands are plagued by two destructive pests; the red pine scale, which was discovered in Connecticut in 1946, and the red pine adelgid, which was first found in 1979. To stop further destruction by the red pine scale, conservation agencies have clear-cut red pine stands in many areas of the state such as at Mohawk State Forest. Some of the harvested pine stands have been planted with white pine seedlings, but other areas will eventually regenerate as hardwood forests.

Hemlock and red pine losses will reduce the abundance and local distribution of conifer stands throughout the state and result in their replacement by hardwoods. Again, the loss of conifer stands will undoubtedly lead to a loss of birds and other wildlife that require evergreen habitat.

III BIRDING SITES

Northwest Highlands

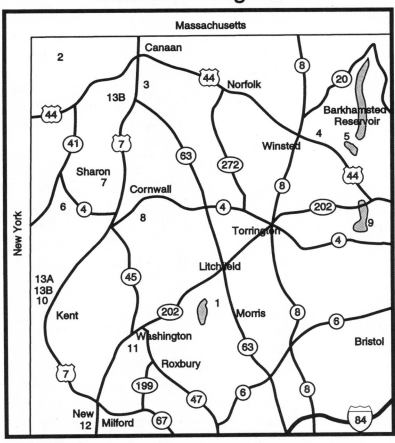

1. White Memorial Foundation
2. Mt. Riga Area
3. Under Mountain Road
4. American Legion and Peoples State Forest
5. Barkhamsted Reservoir
6. Northeast Audubon Center
7. Northwestern Highlands Tour
8. Mohawk State Forest
9. Nepaug Reservoir
10. River Road in Kent
11. Steep Rock Reservation
12. New Milford Tour
13A. Skiff Mountain Wildlife Management Area
13B. Macedonia Brook State Park

1 WHITE MEMORIAL FOUNDATION

Litchfield and Morris

The 4000-acre White Memorial Foundation (WMF) is one of Connecticut's most beautiful and exciting interior birding locales. Habitats at WMF include 1,500 acres of hardwoods, mixed woodlands, and conifer plantations intermixed with fields, pastures, clear-cuts, and thickets. Aquatic habitats at the foundation feature wetlands, streams, ponds, and property bordering Bantam Lake.

Over 35 miles of woodland roads, trails, and boardwalks provide access to birding habitats at WMF. Most trailheads are clearly marked with signs and trail map displays. Bantam River and Bantam Lake can also be birded by canoe during most of the year.

Some 246 species of birds have been observed within the varied wetland and upland habitats of White Memorial Foundation including 115 breeding species. At least 18 species of warblers, 8 species of raptors, and 7 species of flycatchers nest on foundation property.

Some of the notable birds observed at WMF are Eared Grebe, Northern Shoveler, Ruddy Duck, Black Vulture, Olive-sided and Yellow-bellied Flycatchers, Northern Shrike, Mourning Warbler, Rusty Blackbird, Pine Grosbeak, and Red and White-winged Crossbills.

Interesting nesting species are Pied-billed Grebe (rare), American Bittern (rare), Least Bittern (rare), Hooded Merganser, Sharp-shinned Hawk, Northern Goshawk, Yellow-bellied Sapsucker, Virginia Rail, Sora, Marsh and Winter Wrens, Solitary Vireo, Nashville and Blackburnian Warblers, and Golden-crowned Kinglet.

The White Memorial Foundation has a Conservation Center with a Visitor Information Booth, a Nature Museum, library (the natural history library of 30,000 volumes is considered one of the best in the state), wildlife dioramas, a book store, dormitories, and classrooms.

The Holbrook Bird Observatory at WMF overlooks a uniquely landscaped birding area with bird blinds provided for viewing and photographing birds at close range. Other facilities at the Foundation include picnic areas, family campgrounds, and a boat launch. Observation platforms are placed at several rewarding birding sites.

WMF functions as a nature preserve and also as a center for research on birds and other wildlife. In the 1960's Leon Gorski studied the

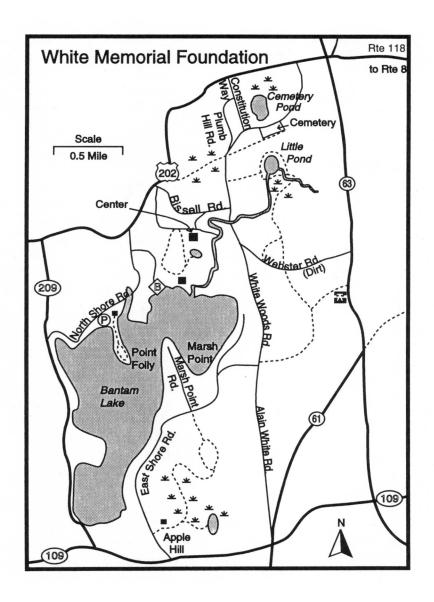

White Memorial Foundation

ecology and behavior of flycatchers that nested in wetland habitats on the White Memorial Foundation. His research helped determine that Trail's Flycatcher consisted of two distinct species, the Alder Flycatcher and Willow Flycatcher. Today, both of these flycatchers nest at WMF. Since 1978, Gordon Loery has conducted studies on the population dynamics of Black-capped Chickadee and Tufted Titmouse wintering populations at WMF.

DIRECTIONS

Take Route 8 to Exit 42 (Route 118, Litchfield and Harwinton) and follow Route 118 west for 4.8 miles to Route 202 in Litchfield. Follow Route 202 west for about 2.0 miles to Bissell Road on the left. Turn left onto Bissell Road and immediately turn right onto a dirt road (road is well marked) which leads to the Visitor Center. Directions to most of the WMF sites will be given from the Route 202 and Bissell Road junction.

BIRDING

You can obtain a copy of *White Memorial Foundation Guide to Birding* at the bookstore along with a bird list detailing information on nesting species, and the arrival and departure dates for summer residents and fall migrants The birding guide published by White Memorial Foundation lists 30 birding sites on the property, and the seasons that they can best be birded. You can also purchase a detailed map of the White Memorial Foundation which shows the roadways, topographic features, trails, and other pertinent information. Because of the size of the White Memorial Foundation and the large number of trails, we recommend purchasing this map.

From late April through May, members of the Litchfield Hills Audubon Society lead free bird walks starting at the museum every Sunday, beginning at 7:30 am. Non-members are welcome on these bird walks. Free guided tours of WMF are given every Saturday (except in winter), usually starting at 2:00 pm, from the museum. The afternoon tours often feature bird walks.

Visitor Center. During all seasons there is ample bird activity in the fields, bird feeders, and gardens around the Visitor Center. Bird feeders, some with blinds, are placed throughout the area. Permanent residents typically observed at the feeders include Hairy and Downy Woodpeckers, Black-capped Chickadee, Tufted Titmouse, White-breasted Nuthatch, Northern Cardinal, House Finch, and American Goldfinch. In colder months (October-April), these may be joined by winter finches, especially Purple Finch, Pine Siskin, and Evening Grosbeak; both the siskin and grosbeak are irregular from year to year.

In summer, American Kestrel has nested in the trees bordering the open field. Other birds nesting in the thickets and trees around the Visitor Center include Northern Mockingbird, Chipping Sparrow, Rose-breasted Grosbeak, and Baltimore Oriole.

Behind the Visitor Center is Ongley Pond, an area often bustling with wildlife. From the pond, a 0.3 mile long trail leads to an observation platform overlooking Bantam Lake. The trail passes through wet woodland, then a shrubby swamp with a cattail fringe. From April through September, these wetlands may harbor Black-billed and Yellow-billed Cuckoos, Northern Flicker, Eastern Wood-Pewee, House Wren, Wood Thrush, Veery, Gray Catbird, Red-eyed Vireo, and Cedar Waxwing. Common trailside birds may also include Blue-winged, and Black-and-white Warblers, Common Yellowthroat, Ovenbird, Northern Waterthrush, and American Redstart.

Typical birds nesting along the river are Willow Flycatcher, Marsh Wren (in the cattails) and Yellow-throated and Warbling Vireos. In spring and fall, the shrubs may harbor a variety of migrant warblers, vireos, and sparrows.

Built on the foundation of an ice house, the observation platform provides a good view of the lake. It also offers roosting sites for gulls and occasionally, waterfowl during fall and winter.

Catlin Woods. To get to Catlin Woods from the junction of Route 202 and Bissell Road, follow Bissell Road east to White Woods Road (0.8 miles). Turn right and head south on White Woods Road for 0.3 miles and turn left onto Webster Road (dirt). Follow Webster Road east (0.3 miles) until a dirt road/trail (with barrier gates on both sides of Webster Road) intersects the roadway. Catlin Woods is located to the left (north) of the road.

The towering hemlocks of this beautiful woodland stand are majestic reminders of what the mature forests of the Northeast must have looked like to the American natives and early European settlers. The dense canopy shadows the gloomy forest interior which is illuminated by light shafts and sun flecks. The deep forest remains cool and damp, even on hot summer days. Hopefully, this magnificent hemlock stand won't fall victim to the fungal and insect pests that now plague many hemlock woodlands in parts of the Northeast.

In summer, the cold, damp microclimate of Catlin Woods hosts a variety of noteworthy nesting species including Northern Goshawk (rare), Winter Wren, Black-throated Green, Blackburnian and Yellow-rumped Warblers, Northern Waterthrush (near the wooded wetland edge), Solitary Vireo, Red-breasted Nuthatch, and White-throated Sparrow (occasionally). Other breeding regulars may include Ruffed Grouse, Barred and Great Horned Owls, Pileated Woodpecker, Black-capped Chickadee, Veery, Wood Thrush, Red-eyed Vireo, and Ovenbird.

During spring and fall migration, check the evergreens for Yellow-bellied Flycatcher, a number of northern warblers (Tennessee, Bay-breasted, Cape May, and Blackpoll), and the wooded understory for Swainson's and Gray-cheeked Thrushes.

Catlin Woods can be good for winter finches during incursion years; Pine and Evening Grosbeaks, Red and White-winged Crossbills, and Pine Siskin have been found in past winters. Of these, Pine Siskin is generally an annual winter visitor. From late October into February, Great Horned Owls can sometimes be heard calling in the late evening and early morning hours. Although less vocal, Barred Owls can usually be tempted to respond to vocal imitations or tape recorded playback.

Little Pond. From the junction of Bissell Road and Route 202, follow Bissell Road for 0.8 miles east and turn left onto White Woods Road. The trail to Little Pond is located on White Woods Road, just north of its junction with Bissel Road. Park along White Woods Road about 100 yards north of the junction. A barrier gate on the right (east) with a trail map identifies the start of the trail to Little Pond.

Little Pond features an outstanding elevated boardwalk trail over a mile in length which winds through cattail and shrub marsh edging the perimeter of the pond. Wetland communities along the boardwalk offer wonderful opportunities for birding and wildlife observation. The boardwalk has only recently been renovated, at a cost of $70,000 (for wildlife enthusiasts, the cost is well worthwhile).

The trail to Little Pond first goes through a Scotch pine-hemlock woodland with an edge understory of knotweed and berry bramble thickets. Along the trail, watch and listen for Pileated Woodpecker, White-breasted Nuthatch, Red-breasted Nuthatch, and Brown Creeper. The Brown Creeper nests beneath the loose bark of the dead and diseased trees to the left. In spring and summer, Pine, Black-throated Green, and Blackburnian Warblers also nest in the tall conifers. From May into July, the organ-like musical song of the Veery can be heard as they proclaim their breeding territories along the trail.

After 200 yards along, the trail emerges along the left edge of an overgrown field of goldenrod, bramble, knotweed and pine saplings. Check the thickets and goldenrod fields on the right for Brown Thrasher (uncommon from April through September), American Goldfinch, and Field and Song (permanent resident) Sparrows. Nest boxes in the field may have broods of Eastern Bluebirds or Tree Swallows. In past years a red fox denned in the sandy soils beneath the grassy and scrubby undergrowth. Fall sparrow migration (October and November) can yield an impressive variety in the fields and thickets---Chipping, White-throated, Swamp, and Savannah Sparrows, and Dark-eyed Junco, as well as the uncommon Lincoln's, White-crowned, and Fox Sparrows.

The trail ends in a "T" at the loop trail around the pond. Take the right trail through the cattails to an iron footbridge over the Bantam River. From the footbridge you can view the marsh (south) of the bridge and the open waters of Little Pond in the distance to the north. Scan the vegetation along the river's edge for waterfowl including Canada Goose, Mallard, American Black Duck, Blue-winged Teal, and Wood Duck, and for waders such as the American Bittern (rare), Least Bittern (rare), and Green Heron. Shorebirds are regular from April to June, and from August into September. Possible shorebirds include Least, Semipalmated, Solitary, and Spotted Sandpipers, and Greater and Lesser Yellowlegs. American Woodcock are seen or heard at dusk. Common Snipe are regular but elusive migrants.

Early spring migrants to the marsh (March and April) include Red-winged Blackbird, Common Grackle and Eastern Phoebe, all of which nest nearby. Rusty Blackbird is a regular spring (March and April) and fall (October through November) migrant. Migrating Barn, Bank, Northern Rough-winged, Tree, and Cliff Swallows are often spotted just over the vegetation or along the river. All but the Cliff Swallow nest on or near WMF property.

In spring and summer, Swamp Sparrow is a common breeding species that places its nest in the cattails or bushes, directly over the water. The Eastern Bluebird nests intermittently in the swamp, seeking out cavities in dead standing timber. Several flycatchers including the Eastern Kingbird, and Willow and Alder Flycatchers nest in the marsh and swamp.

After scanning Little Pond from the bridge, retrace your steps to the "T" junction and walk the trail around the pond clockwise. This trail soon puts you on the boardwalk around Little Pond and the adjacent marsh where most of the birding action will be. The elevated boardwalk threads through marsh and low shrub swamps of silky dogwood, alder, willow, and arrowwood as it makes its way around Little Pond.

Birding along this extensive stretch of boardwalk can be a fascinating dawn adventure, especially in May or June, when the breeding season is in full swing. The marsh and shrub swamp come alive with the calls of avian, amphibian, and insect inhabitants. The ruckus raised by this myriad of vocalists leaves the visitor with a long lasting impression of wildlife at WMF.

Lodges and tree stumps testify the presence of American beaver. With patience, the quiet birder may observe these industrious mammals at work. Many of the bird species seen by the footbridge will also be seen along the boardwalk, where they can often be studied at closer quarters. Scan the area for Virginia Rail and other elusive swamp species. Yellow-billed and Black-billed Cuckoos (the cuckoo populations are irregular) are occasionally seen. Songbirds found among the wetland shrubs may include Common Yellowthroat, and Yellow, Chestnut-sided, and Blue-winged Warblers. Both Alder and Willow Flycatchers were common summer breeders along the boardwalk, nesting in upright forks of shrubs and small trees. Alder Flycatcher has declined in abundance, but can still be found along the north part of the loop. In fall, this stretch of boardwalk can frequently yield Rusty Blackbird and American Tree Sparrow (October to April).

Waterbirds often spotted on Little Pond include Pied-billed Grebe,

Canada Goose, Mute Swan, Mallard, and Blue-winged Teal. Great Blue and Green Herons hunt and hide in the edge vegetation. Migrants can include Ring-necked Duck, Common Merganser, and occasionally American Coot. The boardwalk ends for a short distance. The trail continues through a scrubby red maple swamp, crosses a small footbridge, and eventually winds around back to the first footbridge overlooking the Bantam River. From here it is a short distance to the "T" and back to the car.

Cemetery Pond. Located just east of the junction of White Woods Road and Constitution Way, the pond takes its name from the small cemetery nearby. To reach Cemetery Pond from the junction of Bissell Road and Route 202, follow Bissell Road east to White Woods Road (0.8 miles). Turn left and continue 0.7 miles to Constitution Way on the left. Park along Constitution Way.

Cemetery Pond is a good example of how animals other than humans can transform a landscape. The pond was created about 25 years ago when beavers constructed a dam across the natural outlet of a small stream. Note how the beaver dam arches toward the pond, an architectural feature common to many dams constructed by both humans and beavers. The dam actually maintains an elevated water level in the pond.

Cemetery Pond includes cattail and reedgrass marshes, and willow, alder, and maple shrubs, the whole forming a diverse and thriving wildlife community that supports many nesting species, avian migrants, and winter visitors.

Scope the wetland edge for waterbirds. Waders and waterfowl often forage and take shelter among the cattail and periodically come into view. Some species encountered from early spring through fall include the Pied-billed Grebe, Least Bittern (rare), Great Blue and Green Herons, Wood Duck, and Blue-winged Teal. Great Egret occurs regularly during post breeding dispersal (late July into August). A local birding highlight was the occurrence of an Eared Grebe (rare) that spent a couple of days on the pond in September, 1994. Migrant waterfowl seen on the pond may include Green-winged Teal, Northern Shoveler (occasional), Gadwall, American Black Duck, and Ring-necked Duck.

Mute Swan, Virginia Rail, and the rarer Common Moorhen may nest at the pond, while American Woodcock nest nearby. Several passerines including Least Flycatcher, Eastern Phoebe, Eastern Kingbird, Tree Swallow, House Wren, Eastern Bluebird, Gray Catbird, Cedar Waxwing, Common Yellowthroat, Yellow Warbler, Swamp Sparrow, Common Grackle, Baltimore Oriole, House Finch, and Purple Finch (uncommon), nest in the cattail marsh or among the scattered shrubs and trees surrounding the pond. A small Marsh Wren population nests in the cattails along the northern shore.

Most excursions to Cemetery Pond will produce raptors, especially the Red-tailed Hawk and Turkey Vulture. Less common species to look for along the wooded edge or foraging over the pond include the Northern Goshawk, and Cooper's and Sharp-shinned Hawks; all of which nest on WMF property. Between April/May and again from September/October, Osprey migrate through this area and fish the pond.

Railroad Bed Trail. This stop takes only a few minutes, but provides access to extensive wetland habitats. From Cemetery Pond, follow White Woods Road south to its junction with Plumb Hill Road (0.2 miles). The Railroad Bed Trail is located about 250 feet south of the junction. Park near the trail, which is visible on either side of the road.

The black-topped cinder trail is actually an old railroad bed. On the right (west of the road), the trail opens on Mallard Marsh which supports a large nesting population of Red-winged Blackbirds. Virginia Rail also nests in the marsh and possibly Common Moorhen and American Bittern (both species are sometimes seen or heard in May and June).

After birding Mallard Marsh, cross the road and walk along the roadbed which cuts through shrubby wetlands. During the breeding season, the water level to the left is artificially maintained for the propagation of Northern Pike. Following hatching and a period of growth, the sluice gates are opened and the young pike follow the waterways to Bantam River. April is a good month to observe the spawning behavior of the pike within this shallow, weed filled impoundment.

In spring, Blue-winged Teal is uncommon, but regular in the marsh. Other wetland associated species noted at Little Pond and Cemetery Pond may be observed along the trail.

Laurel Hill and Apple Hill. This site is most productive during the nesting season from May into August. A number of bird species difficult to locate elsewhere at WMF can usually be found here. To get to Laurel Hill from the junction of Route 202 and Bissell Road, follow Bissell Road east for 0.8 miles to White Woods Road, turn right and continue 1.5 miles to East Shore Drive (White Woods Road becomes Alain White Road in the town of Morris). Turn right and continue on East Shore Drive about 0.5 miles until the woodland road to Laurel Hill is seen on the left (immediately opposite Marsh Point Drive).

Park and survey the deciduous woodland before hiking up the trail. Laurel Hill consists primarily of old field habitat reverting to shrub fields and second growth woodlands that include an extensive mountain laurel understory.

Scout the area for warblers, especially Black-throated Blue, Canada, Hooded (irregular), Blue-winged, Chestnut-sided, American Redstart, Louisiana Waterthrush, and Ovenbird. Sharp-shinned and Cooper's Hawks have nested nearby, and (with luck and diligent watching) may be spotted foraging over the hillside. The hardwoods support the usual variety of woodland nesting species including Eastern Wood-Pewee, Scarlet Tanager, Wood Thrush, Red-eyed Vireo, Rose-breasted Grosbeak, and Eastern Towhee.

To bird Laurel Hill, follow the trail up to the hilltop and to the bottomland beyond (about 0.6 miles from the trailhead). A short boardwalk bisects a wooded wetland reminiscent of a southern bald cypress swamp. In spring and summer, the swamp and adjacent woodland are usually bustling with birds. Watch and listen for Red-shouldered Hawk, Ruffed Grouse, Barred Owl, Pileated Woodpecker, Yellow-bellied Sapsucker, Great Crested Flycatcher, Winter Wren, Hermit Thrush, Blue-gray Gnatcatcher, Yellow-throated and Solitary Vireos, Northern Waterthrush, and numerous other species.

Once you cross the boardwalk, the trail continues through deciduous woodland and breaks out into old field habitat at Apple Hill (about 0.7 miles) before terminating on East Shore Drive near a lumber mill. The fields and thickets support Wild Turkey (vocal early morning in April and May), Black-billed Cuckoo, Eastern Bluebird, White-eyed Vireo (uncommon), Prairie Warbler, Eastern Meadowlark, Bobolink, Field Sparrow, and Indigo Bunting. In fall, the viewing platform on top of Apple Hill provides a panoramic view of the northwestern highlands and Bantam Lake, and offers good fall hawk watching. If you want to explore Apple Hill, but do not want to take the entire hike, return to your car and drive 1.0 miles farther along East Shore Drive. Turn left just past the lumber mill and follow the driveway to the small parking area on the right. Follow the trail uphill and behind the house to Apple Hill.

Point Folly. To get to Point Folly from the junction of Route 202 and Bissell Road, follow Route 202 west 0.5 miles to North Shore Road. Turn left and go south on North Shore Road for 1.0 miles. Park on the left near the lake.

Point Folly is a narrow peninsula projecting about 0.4 miles southward into Bantam Lake. East of the peninsula is the outlet to Bantam River. Keeler Cove forms the inlet along Point Folly's western shoreline. During summer, camping is allowed at Point Folly for a fee.

In autumn (mid-October to December) and again in spring, Point Folly can be exceptionally productive for waterfowl and waterbirds; loons, mergansers, dabbling ducks, geese, swans, grebes, and gulls.

During winter, the lake normally freezes and birding is limited to scouting out the occasional gull or watching the mixed foraging flocks of passerines in the adjacent woods and thickets. In summer, Bantam Lake is a high use recreational area for boating, swimming, and water skiing and opportunities for birding are drastically curtailed.

The small inlet directly in front of the parking area is Keeler Cove. In fall, this is one of the best spots in Connecticut to find flocks (sometimes numbering up to a hundred individuals or more) of Ruddy Duck and American Coot, which feed on invertebrates and aquatic vegetation in the quiet waters of the cove.

After birding Keeler Cove, walk to the point, and stop at the observation platform to check out North Bay and the Bantam River outlet on the east side of Point Folly. Scan the vegetation edge carefully all along the outlet as many waterbirds mainly work the interior of the emergent vegetation and only occasionally come into view. Great Blue and Green Herons can be found here from spring through fall. Waterbirds usually encountered include Common Loon,

Pied-billed Grebe, Canada Goose, Wood Duck, Green-winged and Blue-winged Teals, Gadwall, Northern Pintail, Canvasback, Ring-necked Duck, Bufflehead, Common Goldeneye, and Hooded and Common Mergansers. Less common species that can turn up include Red-throated Loon, Red-necked Grebe, Double-crested Cormorant, Snow Goose, Greater and Lesser Scaups, scoters, Northern Shoveler, Redhead, Oldsquaw, Red-breasted Merganser, Osprey, Bald Eagle, and Bonaparte's and Iceland Gulls. Point Folly's most recent birding surprise was an Eared Grebe spotted in North Bay in 1988.

In fall and spring, Point Folly is a good spot to watch interactions between gulls and kingfishers. Ring-billed Gulls keep an eye on Belted Kingfishers foraging over the pond. When a kingfisher snatches a fish, gulls often harass the kingfisher until it drops the fish, which a gull intercepts in mid-air. This behavior is termed pirating and is also commonly seen in Bald Eagles and Ospreys.

After birding Point Folly, check the view from the Litchfield Town Beach and boat launch. Access to this area is restricted to town residents during the summer months but open during the rest of the year. To get to the town beach, backtrack along North Shore Drive 0.4 miles and turn right on a dirt road just before a gray barn. Follow the dirt road about 100 yards and take a 90 degree right turn (the first immediate right is private property) after passing the barn on your left. Follow the road 0.2 mile to the lake, then park and explore the area. To the north and east is a shrubby growth of button bush and willow intruding into the water along with pickerelweed and water lily. Waterbirds, especially herons, ducks, and geese may be spotted feeding near and among the vegetation.

Route 63 Picnic Area. Stands of white pine, mixed hardwoods, hemlock, upland and bottomland woods, clear-cuts, and forest edge predominate at the Route 63 Picnic Area which is located on Route 63, south of the center of Litchfield. To reach this site from the junction of Bissell Road and Route 202, follow Bissell Road east 0.8 miles to White Woods Road, turn right and continue on White Woods Road south 0.3 miles to Wheeler Road. Turn left and follow Wheeler Road 0.9 miles to Route 63. Turn right and continue 0.4 miles on Route 63 to the picnic area on the right. The picnic area lacks tables but does have a pull-off in which to park on the west side of Route 63.   Permanent residents usually seen or heard throughout most of the year are Pileated Woodpecker, Ruffed Grouse, Red-breasted Nuthatch, Brown Creeper, Black-capped Chickadee, and Tufted Titmouse.   Northern Goshawk and Cooper's Hawk are possible in the pine woods or edge habitat.

From May to August, nesting species include all the permanent residents noted above plus Broad-winged Hawk (nests in the crotch of large and medium sized trees), Great Crested Flycatcher, Winter Wren (represented by a small breeding population that is absent in some years), Veery, Hermit and Wood Thrushes, Solitary and Red-eyed Vireos, Scarlet Tanager, and a host of warblers including the Pine, Black-throated Green, Blackburnian, Black-and-white, and Yellow-rumped (occasional). The White-throated Sparrow intermittently nests in the denser woody undergrowth, usually beneath a log, tree stump, or in a thick growth of blueberry stems. Both Louisiana and Northern Waterthrushes may be found in early summer, hiding their moss-lined nests in holes beneath tree stumps or under overhanging stream banks. Look for the Louisiana Waterthrush along the small streams and the Northern Waterthrush in and around swampy bottomlands.

In winter, Dark-eyed Junco and White-throated Sparrow forage in the forest understory while the Golden-crowned Kinglet works the canopy for food. Winter finches are generally represented by the Purple Finch, Pine Siskin and, occasionally, Evening Grosbeak.   During winter finch years, Pine Grosbeak, and Red and White-winged Crossbills are sometimes observed. Of these, Pine Siskin and Purple Finch have nested in these woods among the branches of the mature pines.

Bantam River Canoe Trip.   A canoe trip down the Bantam River at daybreak offers good birding. This trip puts you in the midst of otherwise inaccessible habitat and provides a close look at a variety of wetland birds.   The bridge at the junction of White Woods and Bissel Roads makes an ideal canoe launch site on the river midway between Little Pond and Bantam Lake. A trip from here to Bantam Lake and back is about 3 miles in length while a trip to Little Pond and return is approximately 2 miles in length.

Paddle slowly and quietly down the river, checking the natural nooks and crannies of the bank and overhanging vegetation for birds and wildlife. Beaver and muskrat are normally seen along this route and the alert naturalist may catch a glimpse of a mink or river otter. This is a great way to observe elusive marsh dwellers (herons, rails, and maybe bitterns), several species of waterfowl, and shorebirds. In spring (mid to late May), and fall migration (August into September), the Olive-sided Flycatcher perches atop dead snags. The waterside thickets can be bursting with songbird activity in May. Two good birds that regularly occur but are normally difficult to find include Wilson's (uncommon) and Mourning (rare in late May to early June) Warblers.

Both species prefer the shrubby alder and willow thickets along the river. In addition, the stretch of river between White Woods Road and the iron footbridge (part of the Little Pond loop) is one of the best locations for Sora.

2 MOUNT RIGA AREA

Salisbury

Located in the extreme northwestern corner of the state, the Mount Riga area offers birders an opportunity to study the birdlife of Connecticut's northwestern highlands. Most of the land in this area is owned by Mount Riga Inc., a family-owned corporation. Public use of the land is prohibited with a few exceptions, including the roadways and the Bald Peak Trail. Access to Mount Riga is provided by a dirt road, which winds up Mount Riga through deciduous and mixed woodlands as it parallels Wachocastinook Creek for most of the way. As the road ascends from the creek, you get a great view of the beautiful hemlock ravine and a picturesque waterfall formed by the downcutting stream.

The Mount Riga area can be good during spring migration (mainly in May) and in summer when the higher and cooler elevation harbors many interesting species such as Winter Wren, Solitary Vireo, Black-throated Green, Black-throated Blue and Canada Warblers, Dark-eyed Junco, and White-throated Sparrow. The 2,010 feet high Bald Peak offers a panoramic view of Connecticut, Massachusetts and New York. The peak can also be a great spot for a picnic and a fall hawk watch.

DIRECTIONS

Take Route 8 to Winsted and follow Route 44 west to the center of Salisbury. Turn right at Washinee/Factory Street (Town Hall on corner) and turn left 0.7 miles onto Mt. Riga Road (no street sign is present, but a small sign points the way toward Mt. Riga). Immediately after turning, bear right at the Y and continue 0.5 miles to where the road becomes dirt and gravel. Set your odometer at the beginning of the dirt road. The road is usually closed in winter after the first snow storm.

BIRDING

The trip from the beginning of the dirt road to the parking area on Bald Peak is about 3.0 miles in length and rises almost 1,000 feet in elevation. Be careful when birding from the dirt road; although the road is generally in good condition, it can be narrow in spots. It is best to park in the pull-offs and walk along a section of the road. Also, be

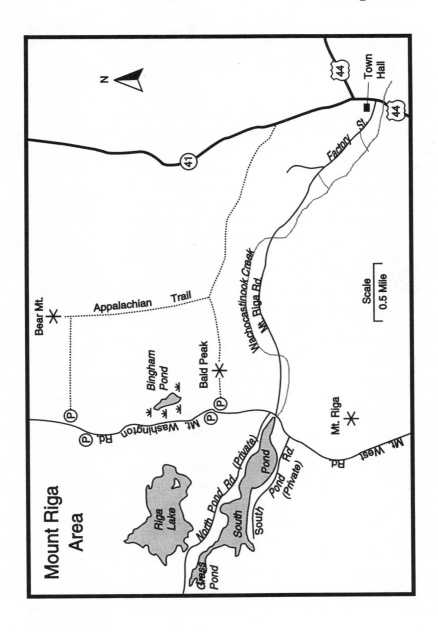

Mount Riga
Area

N

Bear Mt.

Appalachian   Trail

Bingham
Pond

Bald Peak

Mt. Riga

Wachocastinook Creek

Mt. Riga Rd.

Scale
0.5 Mile

Town
Hall

Factory   St.

44

44

41

Mt. Washington Rd.

Mt. West Rd.

Riga
Lake

South
Pond

North Pond Rd. (Private)

South Pond Rd. (Private)

Grass
Pond

aware that most of the property is private, so please respect the rights of the landowners.

As you proceed up the dirt road, stop occasionally and listen for the unique songs of Louisiana Waterthrush and Winter Wren which frequently resonate from along the stream. The Louisiana Waterthrush has a loud and ringing song which starts with two or three clear notes followed by a cascading jumble, while the Winter Wren's song consists of a series of high-pitched seemingly jumbled notes that ramble on and end in a high trill. Both species arrive about mid-April and breed in the area. Their songs are welcome sounds after a long winter.

At the bridge (0.3 miles), watch for Eastern Phoebe which nests on the ledges and abutments beneath the bridge. For much of its length, the stream is shrouded by eastern hemlocks which offer excellent habitat for many boreal migrants. Cape May, Bay-breasted, and Blackpoll Warblers are regular migrants, and Black-throated Green, Blackburnian, and Yellow-rumped Warblers remain in the area to nest. Solitary Vireo is an uncommon but regular breeder mainly found in the hemlock habitat between the bridge and waterfall area.

About 0.7 miles up the hill, a small spring (on the left) feeds into a large, carved-out log resembling a water trough. Park in the pull-off on the right, just beyond the spring. Upland habitat in this area consists of oak hardwoods which host the usual compliment of Connecticut breeding species. Typical woodland breeding birds include Ruffed Grouse, Barred Owl, Great Crested Flycatcher, Eastern Wood-Pewee, Red-eyed Vireo, Black-throated Blue and Black-and-white Warblers, Ovenbird, American Redstart, Scarlet Tanager, and Rose-breasted Grosbeak. The Dark-eyed Junco occasionally nests here and at higher elevations in the area.

Continue along the road to the pull-off on the right, near the top of the hill (0.8 miles). This is a good spot to view the waterfall in the ravine below. From spring into fall, the musical melodies of four thrush species (American Robin, Veery, Wood, and Hermit Thrushes) often radiate from the hillside and ravine. Swainson's Thrush has been heard singing in late May. The woodlands harbor a compliment of woodpeckers: Downy, Hairy, and Pileated are found year-round, while Yellow-bellied Sapsucker and Northern Flicker occur during the breeding season. Red-bellied Woodpecker is occasional in the lower elevations. Other species that may be found between the waterfall area and the parking lot for Bald Peak include Blue-winged, Yellow, and Chestnut-sided Warblers.

At the "T" junction (0.7 miles) turn right onto Mt. Washington Road. Park and scan South Pond, which can produce herons, waterfowl (Mallard, American Black Duck, Wood Duck, and occasionally Common Merganser), Belted Kingfisher, and Tree Swallow during summer. Return to the car and proceed along Mt. Washington Road, which can be a little rough in spots. The trailhead to Bald Peak is on the right at 0.5 miles. You can park on either side of the road, although the parking area to the left is better to avoid being blocked in by other vehicles.

The hike to Bald Peak is short (less than 0.2 miles), but fairly steep and rocky. The trail traverses a mountain laurel thicket that harbors breeding Black-throated Blue and Canada Warblers, American Redstart, and Eastern Towhee. At the top the panoramic view of the Berkshire Hills is magnificent; three states (New York, Massachusetts and, of course, Connecticut) are visible from this point.

The relatively flat top of Bald Peak also provides a great lookout for hawk watching in fall. September and October are generally the best months for hawk watching at Bald Peak. A good day should produce Turkey Vulture, Broad Winged (mainly in September), Red-tailed and Red-shouldered Hawks. Accipiters move through in smaller numbers. Two species, the Northern Goshawk and Cooper's Hawk nest in nearby woodlands. Both Bald (September through November) and Golden (usually October-November) Eagles have been seen from this lookout. Check the crows closely for Common Raven, which is a permanent resident of this remote area.

From the overlook you can also frequently spot migrant flocks of passerines. Regularly observed migrants include Blue Jay, Cedar Waxwing, Black-capped Chickadee, American Robin, and American Goldfinch. In late October and November, small flocks of winter finches sometimes drift by. Check for Evening Grosbeak, Purple Finch, Pine Siskin, or the occasional group of crossbills.

If you continue north along Mt. Washington Road both vegetation and birds remain fairly consistent. The road is narrow, sometimes rough, and lacks sufficient pull-offs. The swampy edge of Bingham Pond offers a different birding habitat. No good pull-off exists at the pond

edge, so park in the pull-off on the right at 0.7 miles and walk down the road 300 yards to the pond. In summer, the wet area and surrounding habitat can produce nesting Eastern Kingbird, Tree Swallow, Gray Catbird, Cedar Waxwing, Yellow Warbler, Common Yellowthroat, Northern Waterthrush, Common Grackle, and Swamp and White-throated Sparrows.

If you feel like exploring more of this area, continue north on the road another 1.7 miles to a parking area on the right. The clearly marked trail on the right leads to the Appalachian Trail and eventually to Bear Mountain.

3 UNDER MOUNTAIN ROAD
Canaan

Under Mountain Road has consistently produced interesting species in winter. Under Mountain Road junctions with and parallels Route 63 for approximately 4.9 miles before merging with Route 7. The trip along this scenic road bisects a variety of habitats including white pine forest, open farmland, marsh, reverting field, and mountainous terrain.

Under Mountain Road can also be an interesting raptor site. Bald and Golden Eagles and a variety of hawks occur in winter. Common Raven, a fairly rare species elsewhere in the state, nests in the area and frequently overwinters in good numbers. Winter birding along the road has also yielded the rarer Northern Shrike.

DIRECTIONS

From Route 8 take Exit 44 (Routes 4 and 202, Downtown Torrington) and follow Route 4 west for 6.5 miles to the Route 63 junction at the rotary. Turn right onto Route 63, heading north for 7.7 miles and turn right onto Under Mountain Road (a blue sign marked "Rustling Wind Stables" is posted at the corner). Property along this road is private, so please respect the landowners and do not trespass without permission.

BIRDING

Under Mountain Road passes through a white pine woodland which can yield Pileated Woodpecker (uncommon), Black-capped Chickadee, Red-breasted Nuthatch, Brown Creeper, and occasionally Pine Siskin and other winter finches. After 0.5 miles or so, the road breaks out of the woodland to more open habitat. Canaan Mountain is the impressive mountain ridge visible to the northeast (right). Stop periodically along the road and scan the craggy mountain ridge. The rugged woods that clothe Canaan Mountain support resident breeding pairs of Red-tailed Hawk, Northern Goshawk, and Great Horned Owl. The Northern Goshawk is an uncommon and local nesting species in Connecticut, requiring large tracts of secluded woodland available in only a few localities such as the wooded slopes of Canaan Mountain.

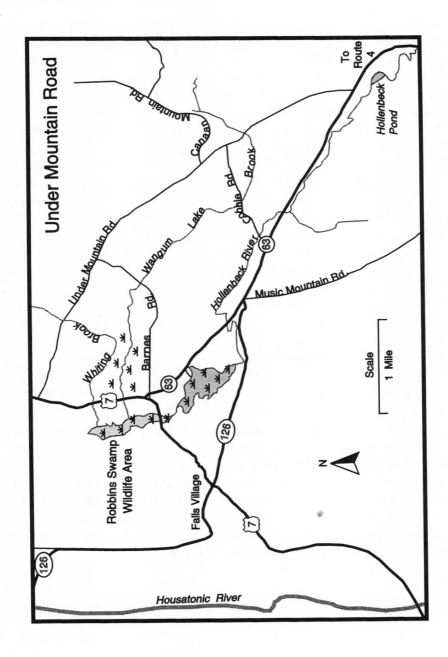

On sunny winter days (especially in January and February), raptors can frequently be seen catching the up-drafts along the ridge. Red-tailed Hawk is usually observed, but Golden Eagle has occurred during four of the past six winters (1991-1996)! Bald Eagle has accompanied Golden Eagle on occasion. This is an excellent locale to observe the soaring and cavorting antics of the Common Raven. Up to 18 Common Ravens have been sighted at one time engaged in pre-courtship aerial maneuvers or just harassing the raptors.

Cobble Road (1.5 miles from Route 63) is always worth a quick check. Turn left, and study the open field and wetland areas down to the small bridge crossing Wangam Lake Brook (this road continues back to Route 63). The field and wetland near the bridge are good for wintering American Robin, Eastern Bluebird, Cedar Waxwing, Northern Mockingbird, Northern Cardinal, and American Tree Sparrow. During winter, carefully examine the open habitats for Northern Shrike, a species periodically observed in the area. When present, the Northern Shrike is usually spotted along Cobble Road or Barnes Road to the north. American Kestrel is an irregular winter visitor to the open farmland throughout this area.

If you did not spot any raptors along Under Mountain Road, take some time to study the mountain from Cobble Road, which offers a good overview of the area. Frequently you can see raptors up above the mountain top which were not visible from Under Mountain Road.

Return to Under Mountain Road, turn left and continue north. At 1.8 miles Barnes Road veers off to the left and returns to Route 63. This road bisects farm fields and wetland and should produce the same assortment of species as seen along Cobble Road. Examine the field edges closely for Wild Turkey an elusive, but fairly common resident of the northwestern hills. After crossing Wangam Lake Brook, Barnes Road skirts an extensive shrub swamp to the north. The dead trees make ideal roosting sites for raptors and other birds.

4 AMERICAN LEGION AND PEOPLES STATE FORESTS

Barkhamsted and Hartland

The American Legion State Forest and Peoples State Forest are located along the state's northern border, primarily in Barkhamsted. The two state forests are bisected by the West Branch of the Farmington River. American Legion State Forest occupies 782 acres along the river's west bank, while the 2,954 acres of Peoples State Forest are situated on the eastern side of the river. A network of forest roads and trails are available for hiking and exploring. Both state forests have facilities for picnicking, hiking, camping (group camping by permit only in Peoples State Forest) and other outdoor recreation. Habitats in the forests are mainly deciduous and mixed coniferous uplands cut by small streams that discharge into the West Branch Farmington River. Conifer stands planted in various areas throughout the forests offer additional birding habitats.

If you are visiting the area on a weekend from July through early October stop at the Stone Museum on Greenwoods Road to view the displays on natural history, Indian culture and artifacts, and exhibitions of local artists. A slide-lecture program on the local fauna, flora, or colonial history is presented every Friday evening during July and August.

Birding the woodlands of the two state forests is best during the nesting season (May through July) when the dawn chorus of flycatchers, thrushes, vireos, warblers, and other songsters provide a welcome challenge to your birding skills. Both forests host a variety of nesting species including Yellow-bellied Sapsucker, Winter Wren, Solitary Vireo, Black-throated Blue, Black-throated Green, Blackburnian and Canada Warblers, and Dark-eyed Junco. Migration can be good for raptors and songbirds. Winter harbors mostly permanent residents and a handful of winter visitors, except during winter finch years.

DIRECTIONS

Take Route 8 north from Winsted and turn right onto Route 20. Follow Route 20 east for 2.3 miles through the village of Riverton to the bridge

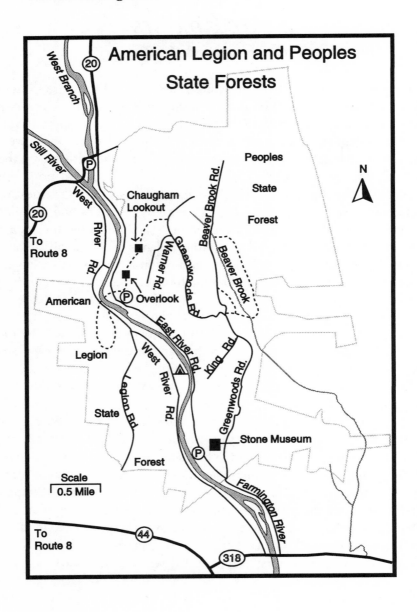

American Legion and Peoples State Forests

crossing the West Branch Farmington River. Immediately before the bridge, turn right into the small town park.

BIRDING

A good way to bird the state forests is to travel along East River Road and West River Road, stopping occasionally to check the river and adjacent uplands. An interesting array of species can be tallied along the way. A side trip up Greenwoods Road offers excellent birding and will take you into the heart of Peoples State Forest. A number of trails intersect these roads, offering the opportunity to explore the forest interior.

East River Road. From the town park, walk over to the bridge and check the river and adjacent habitats. During the breeding season you can usually spot Chimney Swifts in the area immediately around the bridge. Warbling Vireo, Rose-breasted Grosbeak, and Baltimore Oriole sing from the large sycamores and maples along the river edge. A small colony of Cliff Swallows formerly nested under the bridge (through 1994) but have been displaced by bridge repair work; hopefully the swallows will return.

Return to the car and drive over the bridge. Turn right onto East River Road. Set your odometer at this location. Follow East River Road south from the intersection. At 0.5 miles, a pipeline right-of-way crosses the river and road, allowing an open view of the river, hillside, and adjacent field. Scout the hillsides and overhead for raptors. Turkey Vulture and Red-tailed Hawk are the most commonly seen, but Cooper's and Broad-winged Hawks also nest in the area. Other typical species include Eastern Kingbird, House Wren, and Blue-gray Gnatcatcher. Nest boxes in the field provide homesites favored by Tree Swallow and Eastern Bluebird for rearing young.

Continue along East River Road through a diverse upland woodland habitat of hemlock, white birch, oaks, and hickories which harbor a fine assortment of species. You can stop and bird anywhere along the road, but a good pull-off is located about 0.5 miles from the pipeline. At the pull-off look for waterfowl on the river and a variety of passerines such as Wood Thrush, Veery, Black-throated Green Warbler, Ovenbird, and other species in the bordering trees and shrubs. At 0.2 miles a sign announces the entrance to "Peoples State Forest Whittemore Recreation Area" (just beyond the fish hatchery). Park near the picnic area which also contains rest room facilities.

From the picnic area, a trail parallels the riverbank, passing through a mature white pine and hemlock plantation. The mix of habitats along this streamside locale can produce a variety of birds. From spring through summer, look and listen for Red-breasted Nuthatch, Yellow-throated and Warbling Vireos, Yellow, Yellow-rumped, and Pine Warblers, American Redstart, and Cedar Waxwing. During migration, the area should also host Golden-crowned and Ruby-crowned Kinglets, a variety of thrushes and warblers, and White-throated Sparrow. The edge habitat around the parking areas and fields can yield Brown-headed Cowbird, Common Grackle, Chipping Sparrow, and American Goldfinch.

Return to East River Road and drive south to a pull-off opposite the Jesse Gerard trailhead on the left (0.4 miles). Typical birds found in the wet hollow near the river are Pileated Woodpecker, Yellow-bellied Sapsucker, Ruby-throated Hummingbird, Common Yellowthroat, Yellow and Black-and-white Warblers, Red-eyed Vireo, and a variety of resident species. You can take the Jesse Gerard trail (steep ascent) up to the overlook or access this site later from Greenwoods Road.

Continuing south on East River Road you will pass the Agnus Bowen trailhead on the left (0.6 miles) and come upon a hemlock and white pine stand (0.3 miles). Check the conifers for Solitary Vireo, Red-breasted Nuthatch, and nesting warblers. At 0.4 miles the Matthies Grove part of Peoples State Forest begins. Matthies Grove has a pavilion, picnic tables, toilets, and a ball field and can attract a large crowd of people in summer. An entrance fee is collected from Memorial Day to Labor Day. At other times entry is free. Species found here are similar to the Whittemore area discussed previously.

Greenwoods Road. Turn left onto Greenwoods Road at 0.2 miles. This road goes up through the heart of the forest and takes you away from most of the summer crowd.

> **Note: Greenwoods Road is a state forest road with a barrier gate. If you attempt to travel the road by vehicle prior to 8:00 am the gate may be closed.**

Greenwoods Road winds uphill and at 0.2 miles the Stone Museum is on the left. If you are birding on a weekend, stop and visit the museum or explore one of the many trails that pass through the woodlands. Proceeding north along Greenwoods Road check the James Stocking Recreation Area (0.5 miles). The white pine plantations on both sides of the road harbor many passerine species during summer including Wood Thrush, Veery, Red-breasted Nuthatch, Pine and Black-throated Green Warblers, and Brown Creeper.

Beaver Swamp. Continue along the forest road. At 0.7 miles you will notice the Charles L. Pack Trailhead on the right. Park at the pull-off on the left a little further down the road, immediately before King Road (dirt). By following a combination of trails and roadways for approximately 2.0 miles you can bird the habitats surrounding Beaver Swamp--- an area normally teeming with wildlife.

Take the Charles L. Pack Trail (yellow trail) counterclockwise around Beaver Swamp to the picnic area along Beaver Pond Road. From here you can turn left and follow the road back to the car (bear left at the Greenwoods Road junction). Alternately, follow Beaver Pond Road a short distance bearing left at the Agnus Bowen trail (orange) which parallels the swamp and crosses the yellow trail. Turn right at the yellow trail and return to the car. This loop can be very productive for birding during summer and also in spring and fall migration. Breeding species associated with the wetlands are Green Heron, Wood Duck, Virginia Rail (probable), Eastern Kingbird, Cedar Waxwing, Tree Swallow, Yellow and Chestnut-sided Warblers, Common Yellowthroat, Red-winged Blackbird, Common Grackle, and Swamp Sparrow.

Some of the species nesting in the pine, hemlock, and deciduous woods around the swamp include Broad-winged Hawk, Ruffed Grouse, Barred Owl, Yellow-bellied Sapsucker, Pileated, Downy and Hairy Woodpeckers, Eastern Wood-Pewee, Great Crested Flycatcher, Winter Wren, Veery, Wood, and Hermit Thrushes, Solitary and Red-eyed Vireos, Ovenbird, Yellow-rumped, Black-throated Blue, and Black-and-white Warblers, as well as and many of the warblers discussed earlier.

Overlook Area.   Return to the car and drive to the intersection of Greenwoods Road and Beaver Brook Road (0.3 miles).   Bear left and follow Greenwoods Road to the Big Spruce Recreation Area (1.2 miles). Periodically check the mountain laurel thickets enroute to the Big Spruce Recreational Area for Canada Warbler, an uncommon breeder in this forest. In summer, Dark-eyed Junco and Magnolia Warbler have occurred in and around Big Spruce Recreation Area.   Just past the picnic area is the Jesse Gerard Trailhead (yellow) on the left. A 1.2 mile hike along this trail takes you past Chaugnam Lookout and eventually to Overlook. The trail winds through a hemlock woodland interspersed with white pine. Make sure you bear left about 220 yards from the trailhead and follow the trail markers. Along this trail look for many of the same upland birds that were noted for Beaver Swamp area.

Chaugnam Lookout offers a fine northwestern view of the West Branch of the Farmington River and the small village of Riverton.   The view from the Overlook is truly spectacular---one of the best in the state. A mid-to-late October birding trip to this overlook rewards the nature enthusiast with visions of multicolored foliage as well as interesting birdlife. Overlook can be an ideal spot to picnic and study migrating raptors, which can be plentiful. Turkey Vulture, Sharp-shinned and Cooper's Hawks, Bald Eagle (foraging along the river), and Red-shouldered Hawk, along with Common Raven are all possible on a good fall day.

West River Road.   Return to your car and backtrack to East River Road, turn left and reset your odometer. Follow East River Road 0.8 miles to the stop sign, turn right and cross the bridge. Turn right again immediately after the bridge onto West River Road. At 1.2 miles the forest headquarters building is on the left. During working hours (Monday to Friday from 8:00 am to 4:30 pm) you may be able to obtain a map of the forest. A good pull-off along the river is at 0.2 miles. The riverine habitat here supports breeding Northern Rough-winged, Barn and Tree Swallows, Blue-gray Gnatcatcher, Warbling Vireo, Yellow Warbler, Baltimore Oriole, and various other species. A short distance (0.5 miles) further down the road is the campground set in a white pine woodland and supporting birdlife similar in composition to the areas east of the river.   From mid-May to early June, check the campground area for migrant Yellow-bellied Flycatcher (rare), and Blackpoll and Bay-breasted Warblers.

Continue along the road listening and watching for bird activity. The old bridge at 0.7 miles (opposite the Henry Buck Trail) is a good site to survey the birdlife along the river and adjacent upland. In spring (May) and fall (August and September) swallows can be plentiful. Check for Common Merganser during migration and summer; this species nests in quiet retreats along the river.

You can hike the Henry Buck Trail (about 1.3 miles in length) which leads up through a deciduous forest interspersed with conifer stands along the streams and ravines. The trail ascends the hillside to the ruins of a former cheese box mill then skirts along a cliff before looping back to the road 0.2 miles north of the starting point. Typical birds along this trail in summer are Great Crested Flycatcher, Eastern Wood-Pewee, Rose-breasted Grosbeak, Wood and Hermit Thrushes, Red-eyed Vireo, Canada Warbler, American Redstart, Black-and-white Warbler, and Ovenbird. Check the conifers for Brown Creeper, Blackburnian and Black-throated Green Warblers, and Solitary Vireo. Louisiana Waterthrush forage along the stream channel and Acadian Flycatcher (rare) occurs along the streams (the flycatcher has been seen along the trail about 0.3 mile from the trailhead, and just beyond the level section with mature hemlock and white pine where the trail ascends again).

Continue on West River Road to the gasline right-of-way cuts across the road at 1.0 miles. This scrubby area harbors edge and field species such as Northern Flicker, Indigo Bunting, and Field Sparrow. To return to Route 8 continue along West River Road to the stop sign, turn left and follow Route 20 south to Route 8.

In winter, the woodlands are less active but generally hold a few permanent residents and winter visitors. Residents regularly found include Ruffed Grouse, Barred Owl, Pileated Woodpecker, Hairy and Downy Woodpeckers, Blue Jay, Black-capped Chickadee, Tufted Titmouse, Red-breasted and White-breasted Nuthatches, Northern Mockingbird, Northern Cardinal, House Finch, and Song Sparrow. Winter visitors may include Golden-crowned Kinglet, Purple Finch, White-throated Sparrow, and Dark-eyed Junco. During winter finch years check the conifers for Red and White-winged Crossbills which feed on the cone crop. Look for Evening Grosbeak, Pine Siskin, Pine Grosbeak, and Common Redpoll in the woodland and edge habitats.

5 BARKHAMSTED RESERVOIR

Barkhamsted and Hartland

Owned by the Metropolitan District Commission, Barkhamsted Reservoir is located in the northwestern tier of the state near the Massachusetts border. The reservoir was formed in 1940 (upon completion of the Saville Dam) and it is approximately 8 miles in length and 1 mile at it's greatest width. Access to the property is restricted but good views along the length and breadth can be obtained from several vantage points described herein. In addition, the route along the reservoir abuts or bisects both Peoples State Forest and Tunxis State Forest which can also be accessed for birding.

In winter, Barkhamsted Reservoir can be a good site to view raptors, especially Bald Eagles and winter finches. Winter finches generally occur every year, even when these species are absent or scarce elsewhere in the state. Summer birding is highlighted by several interesting species which nest in the immediate vicinity of the reservoir. During migration, Barkhamsted Reservoir attracts a number of waterbirds and waterfowl, while Booth Hill in West Hartland is a good fall hawk watch location.

Rarer species recorded over the years include Golden Eagles, Rough-legged Hawk, Northern Saw-whet Owl, Common Raven, Red and White-winged Crossbills, and Pine Grosbeak. Since 1992, Bald Eagles have nested at the reservoir---the first Connecticut nesting records since the mid-1950's.

DIRECTIONS

Follow Route 8 north to Route 44 in Winsted (where Route 8 becomes a two lane road). Take Route 44 east for 3.6 miles to the junction of Route 318. Turn left and follow Route 318 east for 3.0 miles to the parking area on the east side of Saville Dam.

BIRDING

Begin birding at the parking area on the east side of the dam then cross over to the west parking lot. The parking lots and dam offer excellent views of the reservoir and surrounding hills. Scan the ridges for soaring Bald and Golden (rare) Eagles during winter. Common Raven may be

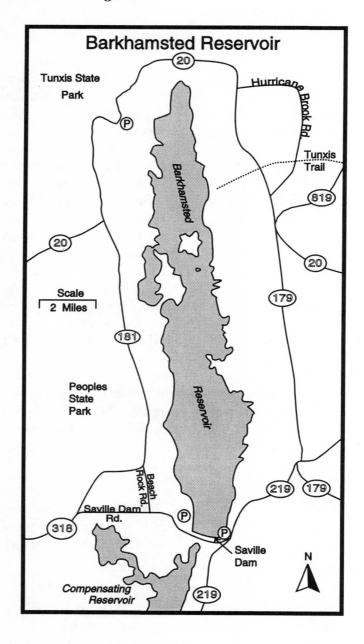

Barkhamsted Reservoir

Tunxis State Park

Hurricane Brook Rd.

Tunxis Trail

Barkhamsted

Reservoir

Scale
2 Miles

Peoples State Park

Beach Rock Rd.

Saville Dam Rd.

Saville Dam

Compensating Reservoir

N

conspicuous in winter and is an established, although uncommon, permanent resident. Deer sometimes wander out and die on the ice pack, so check carefully for any raptors, ravens, or coyotes feeding on dead carcasses.

During summer, other raptors frequent the area; scan the skies above the reservoir carefully for Turkey Vulture, Red-tailed (resident) and Broad-winged Hawks, all are fairly common. Northern Goshawk, Cooper's, and Sharp-shinned Hawks (rare) nest in the surrounding woodlands, but these accipiters are seldom observed unless you spend a lot of time surveying the ridges. Barn and Cliff Swallows nest under the foot bridge leading to the stone gate house. Other species that nest near the dam are Cedar Waxwing, Chipping Sparrow, American Goldfinch, and occasionally, Indigo Bunting and Purple Finch.

In fall and spring, check the reservoir for waterbirds and waterfowl, such as Common Loon, Double-crested Cormorant, and diving ducks (usually Ring-necked Duck and Common Merganser). Rarer species that have been spotted include Red-necked Grebe, Lesser Scaup, and Redhead.

From the parking lot on the western side of the dam, drive west on Route 318 (0.4 miles) and take the first right at Beach Rock Road. Beach Rock Road parallels the west side of the reservoir and along the way passes through conifer woodlands of white pine, spruce and eastern hemlock. Stop occasionally and explore the conifers by the roadside. In winter, Red-breasted Nuthatch, Brown Creeper (uncommon), Black-capped Chickadee, and Tufted Titmouse rove in small flocks. Winter is also the season to catch the nomadic winter finches in the conifers; look for Red and White-winged Crossbills, both species are rare to uncommon, but usually occur at least briefly each winter. Purple Finch and Pine Siskin are fairly regular, whereas Evening Grosbeak and Common Redpoll are more sporadic.

Summer birding along the western side of the reservoir should produce Hermit Thrush, Black-throated Green, Black-throated Blue, Blackburnian, and Yellow-rumped Warblers, and Solitary Vireo. Other typical woodland breeding species are Ruffed Grouse, Pileated Woodpecker, Veery, Wood Thrush, Red-eyed Vireo, American Redstart, Ovenbird, Scarlet Tanager, and Rose-breasted Grosbeak.

At the junction of Route 181 (0.8 miles from Route 318) continue straight on Route 181 heading north. Enroute to the junction with Route

20 (5.2 miles), Route 181 flanks Peoples State Forest (about 1.7 to 2.7 miles) on the left. The conifers along this area should be checked for winter finches or breeding species during the appropriate seasons. At the intersection with Route 20, continue straight ahead on Route 20, heading east to the village of West Hartland (0.9 miles). Feeders in the village occasionally attract finches, especially in winter months.

Continue east on Route 20 which shortly bisects Tunxis State Forest. The conifer woodlands in Tunxis State Forest may be the best location in the Barkhamsted area to find winter finches. Stop periodically to survey the roadside or wood roads leading into the forest. Birds found in late spring and summer include Dark-eyed Junco and Golden-crowned Kinglet, as well as the nesting species described above. Northern Waterthrush are regular breeders in the swampy areas toward the north end of the reservoir.

From West Hartland, continue 3.0 miles to a pull-off on the right (as you descend the hill and just beyond a sharp left corner) overlooking the reservoir. This high vantage point offers a fine view of the northern end of Barkhamsted Reservoir. Scan this area in winter for Bald and Golden (rare) Eagles, Common Raven, and winter finches. In winter, large flocks of Pine Siskin (sometimes numbering 500-1000 birds) have been seen feeding on birch catkins in this area. At the bottom of the hill (1.1 miles), a left turn will bring you into the Tunxis State Forest.

Winter birding can be very slow, but during the breeding season you can find an assortment of the woodland passerines previously listed for this site. The Tunxis Trail cuts across the road 3.2 miles further along. Take a hike if you feel like exploring the area.

To return to the starting point at the south end of the reservoir, you can retrace your route or continue along Route 20, bearing right on to Route 179 and right again at Route 219 south. This route will return you to Route 318.

Booth Hill Hawk Watch. Located 1.0 miles north of West Hartland on Route 20, Booth Hill can be a good hawk watch site in fall. The high, open farm fields around Booth Hill offer great views of the hills to the east and northeast. In September and October, members of the Hartford Audubon Society maintain a hawk watch at Booth Hill which can tally an impressive mix of migrant raptors. In September, good movements of Broad-winged Hawks takes place, along with small numbers of Sharp-shinned and Cooper's Hawks, Ospreys, American Kestrels, Red-tailed Hawks, and others passing along the ridge. On September 19, 1993, a movement of 25,000 Broad-winged Hawks was tallied at this locale.

6 NORTHEAST AUDUBON CENTER
Sharon

Also known as the Sharon Audubon Center, this 684-acre wildlife sanctuary is owned and operated by the National Audubon Society. The center features nearly 11 miles of trails and wood roads for hiking and nature walks. In addition to birding, attractions include native wildflower and herb gardens, a gift shop, and a book store. A wildlife and natural history interpretive area includes displays of local butterflies, bird, and mammals. Live exhibits of amphibians, reptiles, and raptors (Northern Saw-whet Owl and American Kestrel) are usually present. An impressive list of all bird species seen during the year is displayed in the interpretive building. The office is open Monday through Saturday from 9:00 am to 5:00 pm, and on Sunday from 1:00 pm to 5:00 pm. The nature center is closed on holidays but trails can be accessed from dawn to dusk. A small admission fee is required for non-Audubon Society members.

Migrants and summer breeding species highlight this area. Ford Pond, with its fringe of cattails, is particularly good for elusive marsh dwelling species and waterfowl during migration. Some of the species that may be found here include American and Least Bitterns, Northern Goshawk, Sora, Virginia Rail, Common Moorhen, Northern Saw-whet Owl, Olive-sided and Yellow-bellied Flycatchers, and a variety of warblers.

DIRECTIONS
From Interstate 84 take Exit 7 (Route 7 north) in Danbury, and follow Route 7 until it junctions with Route 4 at Cornwall Bridge. Travelers coming from the east can take Route 8 to Exit 44 (Routes 4 and 202, Downtown Torrington) in Torrington then follow Route 4 west to its junction with Route 7. At the intersection of Route 4 and Route 7 drive across the Cornwall Bridge and bear left on Route 4 for 5.7 miles to the Sharon Audubon Center on the left. After turning in to the center, bear right and follow the driveway around to the parking lot.

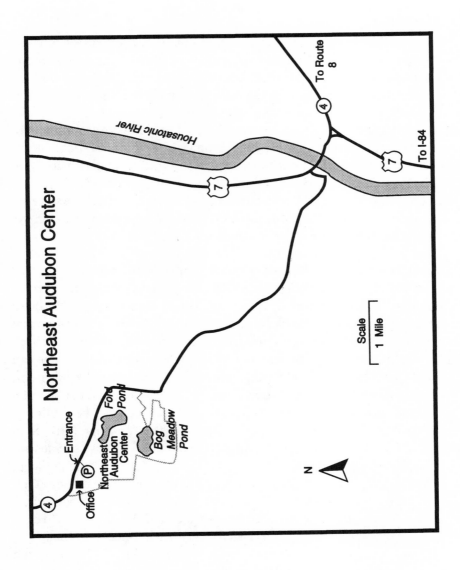

BIRDING

If the office is open, stop in and find out what's around of interest. Review the list of bird sightings posted on the board in the exhibit room. This list also notes the first date on which the species were first observed at the sanctuary. Obtain a trail map at the office. If the office is closed, check the information board near the parking lot. This board has a detailed map of the sanctuary and other tidbits of information. A brochure describing the sanctuary and trail system is available at the information booth. For an interesting loop trail through a variety of habitats take the main path to Ford Pond then hike along the Fern Trail to the Hendrickson Bog Meadow Trail. Follow the Hendrickson Bog Meadow Trail past Bog Meadow Pond and back around to Ford Pond. This hike is about 1.6 miles in length.

Ford Pond and Bog Meadow Pond. Between the Visitor Center and Ford Pond, the manicured grounds and gardens host a number of breeding species including Mourning Dove, House Wren, Northern Mockingbird, Gray Catbird, Northern Cardinal, Chipping Sparrow, and House Finch. Scan Ford Pond from a spot near the outlet to Herrick Brook. In late spring and summer, the pond and surrounding edge can yield Green Heron, Wood Duck, Spotted Sandpiper, Belted Kingfisher, Eastern Kingbird, Tree and Barn Swallows, Cedar Waxwing, Common Grackle, and Baltimore Oriole. Check the cattail edge at the south end of the pond for skulking species such as the Virginia Rail, Sora (uncommon), and Common Moorhen (uncommon). These species are often difficult to see, but can be quite vocal in May and June at dawn.

During migration, various species stop at the pond to rest and refuel. Look for Pied-billed Grebe, Least and American Bitterns (both rare), Snow Goose (uncommon), Green-winged and Blue-winged Teals, American Black Duck, American Wigeon, Ring-necked Duck, and Hooded Merganser. Mammals sometimes spotted on or around the pond include white-tailed deer, muskrat, and occasionally, river otter.

Fern Trail parallels the western edge of the pond and offers a closer view of the cattail border. As you hike the trail, listen and watch for the species previously listed plus Red-bellied Woodpecker, Least Flycatcher, Blue-gray Gnatcatcher, and Eastern Towhee. Along the trail, the large fern with the long cinnamon colored fronds (present in

May and June) is aptly named cinnamon fern.

When the Fern Trail merges with the Hendrickson Bog Meadow Trail, continue along Hendrickson Bog Meadow Trail to Bog Meadow Pond. This small pond surrounded by shrub swamp and rush hammock supports a nice assortment of birds and other wildlife. Nesting species of the woodland and wetland include Great Crested Flycatcher, Eastern Wood-Pewee, Willow Flycatcher, Wood Thrush, Veery, Red-eyed Vireo, Black-and-white Warbler, American Redstart, Ovenbird, Scarlet Tanager, and Rose-breasted Grosbeak. Other species seen at Ford Pond may also be present here.

In the open area around the pond scan the sky for raptors. Several hawks nest on or immediately adjacent to the sanctuary. Red-tailed Hawk and Northern Goshawk (uncommon) are permanent residents. Summer residents include Cooper's, Red-shouldered, and Broad-winged Hawks. Sharp-shinned Hawk and Osprey are regular during migration. Nocturnal raptors include Barred, Great Horned, Eastern Screech (uncommon), and Northern Saw-whet (mainly in winter) Owls. All the owls listed above have nested within or near the sanctuary.

Hal Borland Trail. To explore other habitats, return to the Visitor Center and hike the Hal Borland Trail. This 0.75 mile loop trail begins (and ends) behind the Visitor Center and winds along a rocky hemlock-clad ravine, a brook, and bramble thickets---all good for birding. Birds to look for during late spring and summer include Louisiana Waterthrush foraging along the brook, Winter Wren (uncommon), Black-throated Green Warbler, and Solitary Vireo. The thickets can hold Carolina Wren and Common Yellowthroat. With luck you may spot an elusive Pileated Woodpecker. In late May and again in September, be on the lookout for Yellow-bellied Flycatcher, a rare but regular migrant at the refuge.

The feeding station behind the Visitor Center is usually active. Species often found at the feeders include Hairy, Downy, and Red-bellied Woodpeckers, Blue Jay, White-breasted Nuthatch, Black-capped Chickadee, Northern Cardinal, House Finch, and American Goldfinch. Winter visitors may include Dark-eyed Junco, White-throated and American Tree Sparrows and a handful of winter finches, usually Purple Finch, Pine Siskin, and occasionally, Evening Grosbeak.

7 NORTHWESTERN HIGHLANDS TOUR
Sharon and Salisbury

Connecticut's Northwestern Highlands offer excellent spring and summer birding for upland and wetland species, especially during May and June. Following this tour takes the birder through mature deciduous and mixed woodlands, conifer plantations, wooded bottomland, streams, marshes, wooded wetlands, ponds, croplands, meadows, and secondary growth forests in the towns of Sharon and Salisbury. The tour begins at the covered bridge in West Cornwall and follows West Cornwall Road and White Hollow Road through the National Audubon Society's Miles Wildlife Sanctuary, the Housatonic State Forest, Roy Swamp Wildlife Area, and private farmland before ending at the infield track entrance to Lime Rock Race Track.

The best time to bird this tour is mid-May, when most breeding species are on territory and late migrants are still moving through. A variety of species can be found in other seasons as well. Winter birding is generally limited to resident species and a few winter visitors (including Bald Eagle), except during winter finch years.

DIRECTIONS
Take Route 8 to Exit 44 (Route 4 and Route 202, Downtown Torrington) in Torrington. Follow Route 4 west past the Route 63 intersection to the junction of Routes 4, 43, and 128 to a stop sign (12.1 miles). Continue straight across the intersection onto Route 128 west and follow to the village of West Cornwall (4.0 miles). Park near the covered bridge that spans the Housatonic River.

BIRDING
This tour is geared toward birding along the roadside. In many areas we suggest that you park the car and walk the road for a stretch before returning to the car. This birding protocol should yield the greatest variety of species.

Housatonic River. Check the riparian vegetation along the banks of the Housatonic River by the covered bridge. Typical summer species that occur along this stretch of river are Belted Kingfisher, Chimney

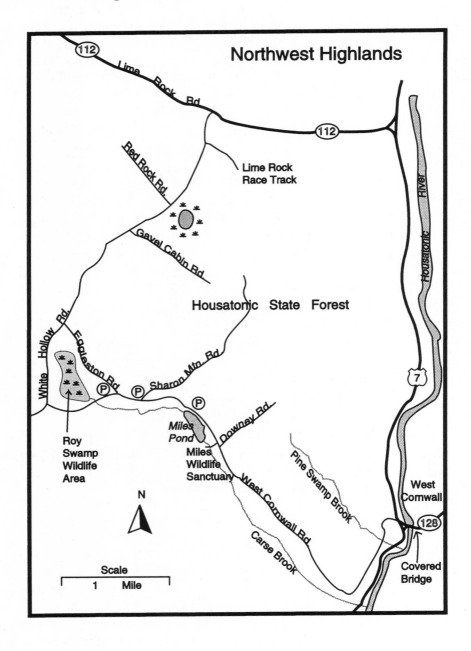

Northwest Highlands

Swift, Eastern Phoebe, Least Flycatcher, Warbling Vireo, and Northern Rough-winged and Cliff Swallows. Cliff Swallows regularly nest under the eaves of buildings in West Cornwall. Orchard Oriole has occurred sporadically and is always a possibility in the tall trees that line the river banks.

West Cornwall Road--Miles Wildlife Sanctuary. After birding the river area by the covered bridge, head west on West Cornwall Road, which begins just opposite the bridge where Route 128 junctions with Route 7 (heading north). West Cornwall Road is diagonally across Route 7 from Route 128. **Start recording mileage at this point.** West Cornwall Road first climbs a long, steep, winding hill, then follows more level terrain, paralleling a brook on the left. As you drive along West Cornwall Road stop at some of the streams which pass beneath or along the roadside to listen for the loud, babbling song of the Louisiana Waterthrush---three slurry whistles followed by a babble of jumbled notes. The small streams are the favorite haunts of this waterthrush.

About 2.2 miles (from the Route 7 junction) along West Cornwall Road, red signs posted on trees on either side of the road announce that you are in the Miles Wildlife Sanctuary. At 0.3 miles (2.5 miles from Route 7), check the beaver dam and small pond on the left for Wood Duck and Hooded Merganser, which may use the nest boxes placed along the swampy bottomland all along this stretch of West Cornwall Road between here and Roy Swamp. The alder and dogwood shrubs that border the beaver ponds and wetlands can be excellent for a number of nesting warblers (Blue-winged, Chestnut-sided, Yellow, and Common Yellowthroat), Swamp and Song Sparrows, blackbirds (Common Grackle and Red-winged Blackbird), and American Goldfinch. Black-billed Cuckoos call from the adjacent hillsides and can sometimes be spotted in the undergrowth. Cuckoos are regular breeding species in this area, but their abundance can fluctuate with the degree of gypsy moth infestation. Other nesting species to look and listen for on the wooded hillsides include Red-bellied Woodpecker, Great Crested Flycatcher, Winter Wren, Red-eyed Vireo, American Redstart, Black-and-white Warbler, Scarlet Tanager, and Rose-breasted Grosbeak. Rusty Blackbird is a regular migrant along this stretch during March and April.

Downey Road is on the right at 0.3 miles beyond the beaver dam.

Just beyond Downey Road, stop and scan the beaver ponds on the left and the small, grassy fields on the right (the fields are behind a bordering fringe of bramble and other shrubs). Eastern Bluebirds nest in the dead trees by the pond, and in nest boxes in the field. Eastern Kingbirds nest in the larger trees around the pond.   Northern Mockingbird, Gray Catbird, and Brown Thrasher (uncommon) are vocal breeding species.

The headquarters complex of Miles Wildlife Sanctuary is on the left, 0.2 miles further along West Cornwall Road. The headquarters consists of an impressive stone building and several outbuildings flanked by a row of Norway spruce and white pine near the roadside. Park and check the bird feeders placed in the yard. **Note: Miles Wildlife Sanctuary is a research center and is not open to the public unless permission is obtained.**   During most winters, Pine Siskin, Purple Finch, and Evening Grosbeak make an appearance in the conifer groves and at the feeders. During winter finch flight years, look for redpolls, crossbills, and Pine Grosbeak.   Permanent residents frequenting the feeders are Black-capped Chickadee, Tufted Titmouse, White-breasted Nuthatch, House Finch, and Northern Cardinal. The conifer grove can also attract a variety of warblers and vireos during spring and fall migration.

Miles Pond is on the far (west) side of the headquarters buildings but can be viewed from the road (a good pull-off is located 0.3 miles from Miles Sanctuary).   Check the pond for Great Blue and Green Herons which nest nearby. Other nesting waterbirds may include Canada Goose, Mallard, Wood Duck, and Hooded Merganser.

The pond edge and adjacent hillsides normally contain breeding Warbling and Yellow-throated Vireos. In winter, researchers at the sanctuary sometimes leave deer carcasses on the frozen pond to lure scavangers such as eagles and Common Ravens. The carrion feasts have attracted Bald Eagles---six eagles were observed feeding on a carcass in March, 1994.

Approximately 0.3 miles further, Sharon Mountain Road (unmarked) appears on the right. This dirt access road leads into the 3,030 acre Sharon Mountain Block of the Housatonic State Forest. To explore this state forest, follow the dirt road, but proceed with caution because the road can be rough in spots.

Shortly beyond Sharon Mountain Road, West Cornwall Road dips into a wetland hollow often teeming with bird activity. Park in the pull-off on the right (0.1 miles after the Sharon Mountain Road) and bird this wetland. A 0.5 mile walk along the road from here up the road to Roy Swamp can produce a good diversity of birdlife. Species composition is consistent with the variety encountered along the preceding section of roadway, but many birds are more prevalent and easier to find. Ruffed Grouse (drumming), Whip-poor-will, and Ruby-throated Hummingbird are regular and Northern Waterthrush breed in the wetland. During twilight hours, listen for the song of the nocturnal Whip-poor-will from the hillside. Willow and Alder (occasional) Flycatchers occupy the shrubby wetlands. During migration, Wilson's Warbler is also found in the wetland thickets.

This part of West Cornwall Road has traditionally been the best spot on the tour to find Golden-winged Warbler, a rare breeding species within the state. Blue-winged Warbler also occurs at this location, giving the birder an opportunity to compare its plumage and buzzy song, *beeee-bzzzzzz,* with the buzzy *bee-bz-bz-bz* song of the Golden-winged Warbler. Whenever breeding ranges of these two warblers overlap, interbreeding may occur, producing hybrid offspring (Lawrence's Warbler or Brewster's Warbler). A typical Brewster's Warbler looks like a Golden-winged with white underparts and sometimes a yellow chest patch. By comparison, a Lawrence's Warbler looks like a Blue-winged with yellow below but has a black throat patch. Check your field guide when viewing a suspect bird. In fact, it's always advisable to view a singing Golden-winged Warbler because Blue-winged Warbler (and hybrids) occasionally sing similar (*bee-bz-bz*) songs.

At least six species of woodpecker occur along West Cornwall Road: Downy, Hairy, Northern Flicker, Red-bellied, Pileated, and Yellow-bellied Sapsucker. The eerie territorial tapping of Yellow-bellied Sapsucker is a familiar sound at this site although the sapsucker does occur intermittently through the valley. The loud echoing of the Pileated Woodpecker's call can sometimes be heard resonating from the hillsides of the valley.

Roy Swamp Wildlife Area. About 0.4 miles further, Eggleston Road (dirt) bears off to the right, leading to White Hollow Road. Park and bird the tamarack (larch) grove near the junction of West Cornwall Road and Eggleston Road. During migration the tamarack grove can be an excellent migrant trap for kinglets and warblers (Blackburnian, Blackpoll, Cape May, Yellow-rumped, and Bay-breasted have been recorded in the tamarack grove). Other warblers found along West Cornwall and Eggleston Road include Magnolia, Canada, and American Redstart.

Walk up West Cornwall Road 0.1 miles and check the pond from the beaver dam. Scan the cattail and phragmites edge for elusive marsh birds. Some of the marsh birds may be difficult to see, but are usually vocal just prior to or immediately after dawn.

Species to look and listen for include Pied-billed Grebe, American and Least Bitterns (both intermittent breeders), Blue-winged Teal (probable breeder), Virginia Rail, Sora, and Common Moorhen (occasional). In May, Spotted and Solitary Sandpipers often forage along the pond edge. Swallows (Tree and Barn are the expected species) and Cedar Waxwing are conspicuous as they dart about in pursuit of insects. Swamp and Song Sparrows are common nesting species near this wetland habitat.

Eggleston Road. After birding the swamp and adjacent areas, continue along Eggleston Road (hike or drive to convenient lookouts along the road).

Common songbirds that occur along Eggleston Road include Eastern Wood-Pewee, Great Crested Flycatcher, Wood Thrush, Veery, Blue-gray Gnatcatcher, Red-eyed Vireo, Ovenbird, Baltimore Oriole, Scarlet Tanager, and Eastern Towhee. Worm-eating Warbler is fairly regular on the hillside. In late May, check the thrushes feeding along the sides of the dirt road for Swainson's and Gray-cheeked (uncommon).

The open areas along Eggleston Road and around Roy Swamp provide good vantage points to search for raptors which nest in the trees and snags that border the wetlands and on the wooded hillsides. Scan the ridges for Turkey Vulture, Red-tailed, Broad-winged and Red-shouldered Hawks, Northern Goshawk, and American Kestrel. Barred (3 or 4 pairs) and Great Horned Owls are often heard at dawn, calling from the hillsides or ridge tops. During spring and fall migration, Osprey and Sharp-shinned and Cooper's Hawks can frequently be sighted.

At 0.3 miles along Eggleston Road, the bramble thickets and field edge on the left have been reliable for Golden-winged Warbler. In the adjoining field (0.3 miles), American Kestrel nested in a dead tree for many years, but the tree fell victim to a storm in 1992. Hopefully the kestrels will remain in the area. The fields also harbor Bobolink and sometimes Eastern Meadowlark. In early morning, the gobbling calls of the Wild Turkey can be heard from the fields in this area, as well as around the corner on White Hollow Road.

White Hollow Road. At the junction of Eggleston Road and White Hollow Road (0.3 miles) turn right, heading northeast on White Hollow Road. Along this road, the combination of wet meadows and old fields on the right are attractive to Willow and Alder Flycatchers, Indigo Bunting, and Blue-winged Warbler, among others. The deciduous hillside on the left has produced Winter and House Wrens, and Worm-eating Warbler over the years.

At 0.7 miles along White Hollow Road the overgrown fields on either side of the road can yield Field Sparrow and other thicket species. Just past this area is a farm and Gavel Cabin Road (dirt) on the right. Drive down Gavel Cabin Road past the farm buildings and scope the pond and marsh in the hollow on the left. This marsh has produced Great Blue and Green Herons, bitterns, rails, Wood Duck, and Blue-winged Teal in the past. The fields around the farm contain Bobolink and Eastern Meadowlark (uncommon). Eastern Phoebe and Barn Swallow nest in the farm outbuildings.

Proceed 1.0 miles north on White Hollow Road past Red Rock Road (on left) and stop just before house 145 on the left. Behind the house is a saddle-shape mountain, the left side of which resembles a cone. The rocky ledges on this mountain have hosted breeding Common Raven since at least 1988. Breeding season for the Common Raven in Connecticut runs from approximately mid-March through May. After May, the ravens disperse throughout the valley and are not as easily located.

Check the white pine plantations that appear at 0.1 miles to 0.4 miles on both sides of the road. The conifers should produce breeding Brown Creeper, Solitary Vireo (sporadically), Pine and Black-throated Green Warblers, and possibly Blackburnian and Yellow-rumped Warblers.

Continue north on White Hollow Road. At 0.7 miles, the old fields on the left are reliable for Prairie Warbler, Field Sparrow, and sometimes, Indigo Bunting. The meadows on the right often have blackbirds, including Eastern Meadowlark and Bobolink. Slightly farther along the road (0.2 miles), the field on the right (just before the greenhouse and entrance sign to Lime Rock Park) has an American Kestrel nest box on the large American sycamore. A pair of kestrels have nested in this box for a number of years. In 1991, during late May, a Grasshopper Sparrow was heard singing from this field! The field also harbors a small population of nesting Savannah Sparrows.

This is the last stop on the birding tour. To return to the starting point you can retrace the route or continue another 0.3 miles to Lime Rock Road (Route 112), turn right and travel 1.4 miles to the junction of Route 7. Turn right at the junction and follow Route 7 (4.5 miles) back to West Cornwall.

8 MOHAWK STATE FOREST
Goshen and Cornwall

This large, heavily wooded state forest of 3,245 acres is a popular recreational area throughout the year. In summer, hiking and biking are common activities and the picnic tables are usually in demand, while in winter Mohawk Mountain becomes a ski resort for downhill and cross-country skiing. Fishermen try their luck at the ponds or along the streams almost any time of year. For hikers, the Appalachian Trail cuts through Mohawk State Forest.

The state forest takes its name from 1,683 foot high Mohawk Mountain. Legend suggests that the Tunxis and Paugussett Indians used the mountaintop to send smoke signals warning local tribes of the approach of Mohawk warriors entering Connecticut on raiding expeditions. Although Indian raids no longer occur, the mountaintop still provides spectacular views of the Catskill, Taconic, and Berkshire Mountains to the north and west.

This heavily wooded state forest includes conifer plantations, deciduous and mixed woodlands, old fields, and brushy growth. Upland habitat diversity is augmented by alder swales, hardwood swamps, a black spruce bog, marshes, brooks, and small ponds.

Over 150 species of birds have been recorded in the Mohawk State Forest area. During migration, some 28 species of warblers may pass through the area including Cerulean, Cape May, Worm-eating, Nashville and Mourning (rare). Yellow-bellied Flycatcher and Philadelphia Vireo are rare migrants. Northern Goshawk, Winter Wren, Hermit Thrush, Solitary Vireo, Yellow-rumped, Black-throated Blue, Black-throated Green, and Blackburnian Warblers, Northern Waterthrush, White-throated Sparrow, and Dark-eyed Junco are among the many interesting species that breed in Mohawk State Forest.

DIRECTIONS

Take Route 8 to Exit 44 (Routes 4 and 202, Downtown Torrington) in Torrington. Follow Route 4 west to Route 63 (6.5 miles) at Goshen. Continue west on Route 4 for 4.4 miles to the main entrance (Toumey Road) on the left, marked by a sign on the left. A trails map of Mohawk State Forest is located just inside the entrance, on the left.

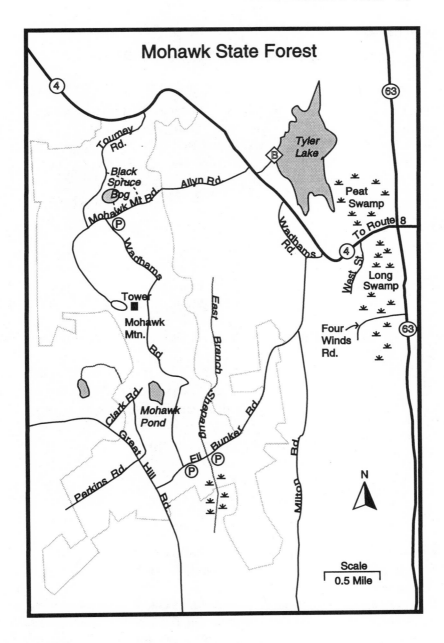

Mohawk State Forest

Toumey Rd.

Black Spruce Bog

Allyn Rd

Mohawk Mt Rd

4

B

Tyler Lake

Peat Swamp

Wadhams Rd.

To Route 8

4

West St

Long Swamp

63

Wadhams

Tower

Mohawk Mtn. Rd

East Branch Shepaug

Four Winds Rd.

63

Clark Rd

Mohawk Pond

Great Hill Rd

Eli Bunker Rd

Milton Rd

Perkins Rd

N

Scale
0.5 Mile

BIRDING

Park Entry. Stop at the scenic overlooks on the right side of Toumey Road. Turkey Vulture, Red-tailed Hawk, and other raptor species can often be spotted in the distance, soaring over the northern hills. At the third overlook (0.9 miles) park by the dirt road on the left. In spring and summer, a short walk down this dirt road through a hemlock and white pine stand should yield Brown Creeper, Red-breasted Nuthatch, Eastern Wood-Pewee, Black-throated Green and Nashville (uncommon) Warblers, Northern Waterthrush, and Solitary and Red-eyed Vireos. Barred Owl may respond to vocal imitation, especially by the black spruce bog further along the dirt road.

After birding the trail, continue on Toumey Road to the intersection with Mohawk Mountain Road (0.3 miles). Turn right and continue towards the summit. At 0.4 miles up from the intersection, the road bisects clear-cut areas. In summer, the logged areas may produce House Wren, Blue-winged and Golden-winged (rare) Warblers, White-throated Sparrow, and Eastern Towhee. The conifer stand immediately beyond the clear-cut areas usually harbors Winter Wren, Yellow-rumped Warbler and Purple Finch (uncommon).

Check the deciduous woods on either side of the road for common summer residents such as American Redstart and Black-and-white Warbler. Northern Flicker and Yellow-bellied Sapsuckers are regular from April to October, while Pileated, Downy, and Hairy Woodpeckers are resident here and elsewhere throughout most of the park. In May, Cerulean Warbler have been observed along the roadway. Near the summit (0.5-0.8 miles), the beautiful songs of the Hermit Thrush and Wood Thrush can be heard, giving you a chance to compare the subtle differences in their somewhat similar songs.

Summit. The scrubby growth at the summit makes for rather limited birding, but the panoramic view is splendid. Turkey Vulture and Red-tailed Hawk, are the most frequently spotted raptors during spring and summer. Least Flycatcher, Prairie, Blue-winged, and Chestnut-sided Warblers, Chipping and Field Sparrows, and Dark-eyed Junco nest near the summit and may be seen in the scrubby growth. In fall (September-November), the summit can function as a lookout for migrating raptors.

After birding the summit, backtrack to the junction with Toumey Road, but continue straight ahead on Mohawk Mountain Road for 0.2 miles, turn right onto Wadhams Road (dirt) and park in the lot on the left, by the buildings.

Black Spruce Bog. A sign on Mohawk Mountain Road points the way to the Bog Trail. The Bog Trail briefly winds through a small mixed woodland with an extensive mountain laurel understory. In June and July note how the white-flowered laurel within the wood gives way to pink-flowered tints in the open cut. As the trail descends into the boggy area, hardwoods are replaced by conifers; first red and white pine, then hemlocks, and finally black spruce and tamarack in the wettest and coolest part of the bog. A boardwalk provides access to the interior of the bog. Beneath the trees, black spruce seedlings and saplings spread over a carpet of ferns and sphagnum moss. The pitcher plant, sundew, and mountain holly are rare and fragile species that occur only in bogs. Stay on the boardwalk to prevent damage to these unique and fragile plants.

Black-throated Green, Blackburnian, Black-and-white, Black-throated-Blue, Chestnut-sided, and Canada Warblers, Ovenbird, and Northern Waterthrush are all possible along the Bog Trail. Other breeding species usually include Winter Wren, Cedar Waxwing, Veery, Wood and Hermit Thrushes, Black-capped Chickadee, White-breasted and Red-breasted Nuthatches, and Red-eyed and Solitary Vireos.

During May and August-September, the bog can be a good migrant "trap" if you catch the right combination of weather conditions On good days, the spruces and larches may teem with "northern species" such as Cape May and Bay-breasted Warblers, Ruby-crowned and Golden-crowned Kinglets, and the rarer Philadelphia Vireo and Yellow-bellied Flycatcher.

After birding the bog, check the large shagbark hickory and other trees and shrubs around the parking area for Eastern Phoebe and Barn Swallow, both of which nest in the building's eaves. The small pond across the road can be good for Least Flycatcher, Tufted Titmouse, Baltimore Oriole, Gray Catbird, House Finch, and Chipping and Song Sparrows. In the past, Yellow-bellied Sapsucker nested in the gray birches around the pond.

Clear-cuts, Tornado Paths, and Mohawk Pond. From the parking area, follow Wadhams Road for several miles through thick deciduous woods on either side. A number of marked trails lead into the woods on either side of the road, offering hiking and birding opportunities.

At the "T" intersection (2.8 miles), park and hike up the road to the right to a spruce grove. In late spring and summer, Golden-crowned Kinglet (uncommon), and Blackburnian, Black-throated Green, and Yellow-rumped Warblers may nest in the evergreens. After birding the spruce grove, continue up the road to the clear-cut area on the right (about 300-400 yards from the "T" intersection). This clear-cut has yielded Least Flycatcher, Golden-winged (rare) and Chestnut-sided Warblers, and White-throated Sparrow (May through July). To explore Mohawk Pond, return to the car and drive up the road past the clear-cut, bearing right onto Great Hill Road and right again onto Perkin Road. Mohawk Pond is down the road on the right.

East Branch Shepaug River and Shrub Swamp. After birding the spruce grove and clear-cut, return to the vehicle and turn left at the "T" intersection. Continue another 0.3 miles and park on the right, just beyond the bridge. The wetland was once a beaver pond, but the beaver dam was destroyed when the bridge was renovated in 1992, and the beavers have not returned. The wetland of scrubby willows and aquatic emergents forms part of the headwaters of the Shepaug River.

In spring and summer, Northern Flicker, Eastern Kingbird, Cedar Waxwing, and American Goldfinch roost on the dead snags. Ruby-throated Hummingbird are sometimes spotted and may nest in the area. Great Blue Heron, Pileated Woodpecker, Acadian Flycatcher (uncommon), Veery, Common Yellowthroat, Yellow Warbler, Scarlet Tanager, and Swamp Sparrow may also be tallied in and around the wetland. Barred Owls nest in the nearby woods and may respond to vocal imitations of their call.

From here, you can return to Route 4 by retracing your route through the park. Alternately, continue along the dirt road to its intersection with Milton Road. Turn left onto Milton Road which brings you back to Route 4.

1222

433444

Nearby Locations

Tyler Lake
To get to Tyler Lake from the junction of Route 63 and Route 4, drive west on Route 4 for 2.7 miles. Watch for the state boat launch sign for Tyler Lake and turn right onto Tyler Heights Road to the boat launch (0.1 miles). Park and scan the lake for waterfowl. Spring and fall species at Tyler Lake can include Common Loon, Great Blue and Green Herons, Mallard, American Black Duck, Ring-necked Duck, Wood Duck, Green-winged Teal, Common Merganser, and several swallow species. Rare birds observed at Tyler Lake include Black Tern and White-winged Scoter.

Long Swamp
To get to Long Swamp from the junction of Route 63 and Route 4 , follow Route 63 south and turn right on Four Winds Road (1.3 miles). Four Winds Road bisects the southern end of Long Swamp before ending at a farmhouse. Park along the edge of the road near the marsh.

Bird Long Swamp in the early morning hours to catch the dawn chorus of birds. Many elusive species frequent the marsh from spring through fall. Sora and Virginia Rail are fairly common and probably breed deep in the marsh. On a still May morning listen for American Bittern and Least Bittern, both are rare migrants (nesting?). Other species to look for include Blue-winged Teal, Wood Duck, Great Blue Heron, Eastern Kingbird, Least Flycatcher, Tree Swallow, Cedar Waxwing, blackbirds, Common Yellowthroat, and Swamp Sparrow. Both Willow and Alder (uncommon) Flycatchers occur during summer.

Peat Swamp
To get to Peat Swamp, from the junction of Route 63 and Route 4, head west on Route 4 for 0.6 miles. Park at the Goshen Oil Company lot on the left and cross Route 4 (observe caution) to bird Long Swamp, which begins just north of the road. The cover of rushes and sedges in Peat Swamp are shadowed by imposing snags, remnants of a long dead white pine forest which are still standing. These tall snags make ideal perches for Red-shouldered and Red-tailed Hawks and American Kestrel in

summer.   Downy and Hairy Woodpeckers and Northern Flicker may nest in the snags, along with an assortment of cavity nesting passerines such as Black-capped Chickadee and Tufted Titmouse. Green Herons forage in the swamp vegetation. The shrub thickets that border the swamp support breeding Willow Flycatchers. In 1992, Sedge Wrens (rare) were singing in the marsh grasses and may have nested.

9 *Nepaug Reservoir*
New Hartford, Canton, and Burlington

Owned by the Metropolitan District Commission, this reservoir is a public water supply. Most of the reservoir property is posted but a few areas are open for hiking and birding. Other parts of the reservoir can be viewed from town and state roads.

Habitat immediately around the reservoir consists of conifer stands of white pine, eastern hemlock, tamarack (larch), and spruces. Second growth hardwoods are replacing diseased red pine stands that were cut and burned to prevent further spread of the disease.

Nepaug Reservoir can act as a magnet for migrating waterbirds, waterfowl, and songbirds. Bald Eagle irregularly overwinters at the reservoir and are sometimes observed feeding on deer carcasses on the ice. The coniferous forest habitat around the reservoir provides nesting habitat for several species that prefer cooler and wetter climates.

DIRECTIONS

The reservoir and adjacent woodlands can be birded from several vantage points, roadways, and trails accessed from the roadways. To get to the first birding site at the reservoir, from Route 8 take Exit 44 (Route 4 and 202, Downtown Torrington) onto Route 202 east in Torrington. Follow route 202 east for 9.5 miles, where the reservoir appears on the right (south side of the road). Park in the parking area on the right immediately after crossing over a small section of reservoir bisected by the road.

BIRDING

Route 202. Scan the reservoir from the parking area. You can also walk through the gate and follow the access road around the northern part of the reservoir, crossing over the dam enroute. This roadway is about 1.1 miles in length (one way) and terminates at Torrington Avenue. From October through December (sometimes later depending on ice cover), and from March to May, the reservoir should be checked for waterbirds and waterfowl such as Common Loon, Double-crested Cormorant, Red-necked (rare) and Horned Grebes (uncommon to rare),

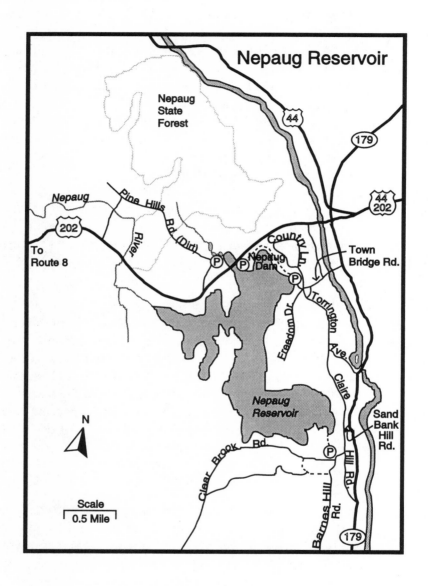

Nepaug Reservoir

American Black Duck, Green-winged Teal, Ring-necked Duck, Common Goldeneye (uncommon), Bufflehead, and Common and Hooded Mergansers. Other diving ducks which sporadically occur on the reservoir include Greater Scaup, Oldsquaw, White-winged and Black Scoters (an unprecedented 40 Black Scoters were recorded one October), and Redhead.

From late fall through April, gulls often frequent the reservoir. Common species include Herring, Ring-billed, and Great Black-backed, but check carefully for white-winged species; Glaucous Gull has been observed in January and April. Bald Eagle and Common Raven are also sometimes observed in winter. The conifers almost always harbor some winter finches; Pine Siskin and Purple Finch are annually recorded. During flight years check for Evening and Pine Grosbeaks and crossbills.

A walk along this trail in spring can be productive for many species of migrating passerines. Pine and Palm Warblers are regular and occasionally abundant in mid-April, usually occurring in mixed flocks with Golden-crowned and Ruby-crowned Kinglets, Yellow-rumped Warbler, and Solitary Vireo. Other interesting migrants that generally pass through from early to late May include flycatchers (Yellow-bellied and Olive-sided), Swainson's Thrush, and warblers (Tennessee, Northern Parula, Magnolia, Cape May, Bay-breasted, Blackpoll, and Canada).

At the parking area check the nesting boxes in the small field for Tree Swallow and Eastern Bluebird. In spring and summer, Eastern Phoebe, and Northern Rough-winged and Barn Swallows construct their nests on the structural elements comprising the dam, while Indigo Bunting and American Goldfinch nest along the woodland edge at the base of the dam.

An assortment of species nest in the coniferous and mixed woodlands around the reservoir. Typical nesters include Eastern Kingbird, Great Crested Flycatcher, Red-breasted Nuthatch, Wood Thrush, Veery, Solitary and Red-eyed Vireos, Scarlet Tanager, and occasionally, Purple Finch. The woodlands can produce numerous nesting warblers, including Blue-winged, Yellow-rumped (uncommon), Black-throated Green, Blackburnian, Chestnut-sided, Pine, Black-and-white, Ovenbird, Louisiana Waterthrush (along the river below the dam), and Common Yellowthroat. Great Horned Owl intermittently nest in the woods between the dam and Torrington Avenue. Occasionally the young owlets can be seen in the lower branches of the conifers along the roadway.

Pine Hill Road. To reach Pine Hill Road, backtrack west along Route 202 (from the parking area by the reservoir) for 0.4 miles and take the first right, an unmarked road. Follow the road for 0.2 miles until it terminates at a barrier. Park and bird along the dirt road to the left of the barrier which is Pine Hill Road. This woodland road leads to Nepaug State Forest. Hiking is permitted but don't stray away from the road or wander down the logging roads which are posted and have barrier gates.

Many of the same woodland birds seen in the trees around Nepaug Reservoir can also turn up here. Several woodpeckers are regular including Hairy, Downy, Northern Flicker, and the elusive Pileated. Other interesting breeding species include Eastern Wood-Pewee, Hermit Thrush, and Dark-eyed Junco. Barred Owl is resident and may respond to vocal imitations of its call. If you approach quietly, the small ponds near the parking area may yield Wood Duck, Belted Kingfisher and Green Heron.

Torrington Avenue. This area provides an open view of the north and northeastern section of the reservoir. To reach this site from Pine Hill Road, continue east on Route 202 for 1.7 miles to the junction with Route 179. Turn right (south) and follow Route 179 for 0.6 miles. Turn right onto Town Bridge Road for 0.5 miles (bear right at the Y) until it intersects with Torrington Avenue. Turn right and follow Torrington Avenue 0.1 miles. Park by the gate near the reservoir. Check the reservoir for gulls and other waterbirds and waterfowl previously listed.

Clear Brook Road. This area provides a view of the southern arm of Nepaug Reservoir. To get to Clear Brook Road, follow Torrington Avenue south and go straight onto Route 179 (1.0 miles). Proceed south on Route 179 for 0.6 mile and turn right onto Sand Bank Hill Road. Follow this road 0.1 miles bearing left at the Clair Hill Road junction. At 0.2 miles along Clair Hill Road take a right onto Barnes Hill Road and park immediately after making the turn, near the concrete building.

To view the reservoir walk to the top of the stairs behind the building. Scan the reservoir from the top of the dike. This site can produce similar waterbirds and waterfowl as the sites previously described. Indigo Bunting is a summer resident in this area.

After checking for birds from the dike, continue along Barnes Hill Road 0.2 miles, turn right and follow Clear Brook Road 0.5 miles, until the road parallels the reservoir. Park along the side of the reservoir and scout for birds.

From this site the southern end of the reservoir can be surveyed. Double-crested Cormorant and Common Loon are regularly observed in summer. The clear-cut area adjacent to the reservoir harbors a variety of species partial to thickets and second growth habitats. From late spring through summer, some of the regular breeding birds include Blue-winged and Chestnut-sided Warblers, Common Yellowthroat, and American Goldfinch. The conifers are also good for a variety of nesting species previously listed. Mourning Warbler was recorded twice in the past on the hillside opposite the reservoir--- look for this species in late May or early June.

The woodlands surrounding the reservoir support many nocturnal species. Owls are represented by Great Horned, Barred, and Eastern Screech Owls. Long-eared Owl is sometimes reported but most are likely migrants. A Long-eared Owl heard calling in May, 1992, may have nested. Northern Saw-whet Owl is an uncommon winter resident and also a potential breeder. Whip-poor-will is represented by a small nesting population and can sometimes be heard calling after dark from May into July at Clear Brook Road and other sites around the reservoir.

10 River Road

Kent

Natural strips of habitat linking increasingly fragmented woods, wetlands, and other preserves of wildlife habitat are called corridors. Corridors may range from narrow hedges and fence-rows to broader riparian habitats that border streams and connect dispersed woods and wetlands. These living landscapes act as biotic pipelines that promote the safe movement of birds and other wildlife through the mosaic of human habitats. Corridors thus enhance and conserve biotic diversity of wildlife.

A prime example of a corridor is found in a stretch of wooded landscape that borders the Housatonic River near Kent. Each spring, this riparian woodland corridor becomes a popular hot-spot for Connecticut's birders. During the peak warbler migration, a trip to this river corridor can yield 25 species of warblers plus a varied assortment of flycatchers, thrushes, and vireos. Other possible birds along the river include swallows, waterfowl, wading birds, and raptors. A good day's birding along this three-to-five mile stretch can result in 80 or more species of birds during the peak migration season.

Unusual warblers are the main birding attraction at River Road in Kent. Species consistently encountered include Cerulean, Golden-winged, Worm-eating, Mourning (rare), and Kentucky (rare) Warblers. Philadelphia Vireo is a rare migrant and Black Vulture is possible throughout the year. Within the last two decades, this area has attracted many noteworthy species as nesters. This is one of the best sites in the state to find nesting Acadian Flycatcher and Cerulean and Golden-winged Warblers. The state's first documented nesting record of Yellow-throated Warblers is also from River Road in Kent.

DIRECTIONS

On Interstate 84 take Exit 7 (Route 7, Brookfield and New Milford) and follow Route 7 north to Kent. At the junction of Route 7 and Route 341 in Kent turn left and take Route 341 west. Cross the bridge over the Housatonic River and take the first right onto Skiff Mountain Road (0.3 miles).

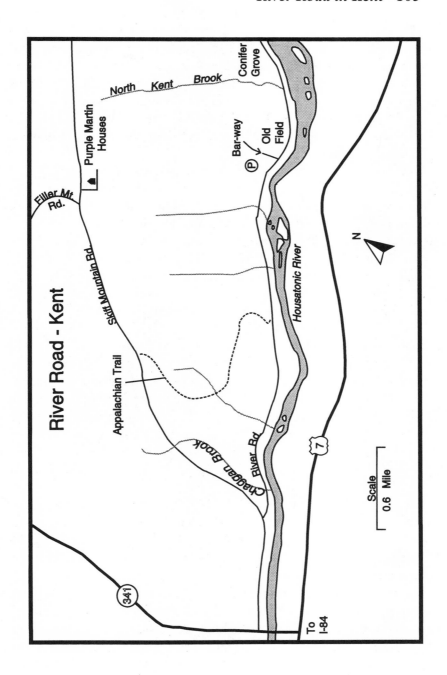

River Road - Kent

BIRDING

After crossing the Housatonic River on Route 341, turn right onto Skiff Mountain Road and park along the river's edge. Since 1993, Cliff Swallows have nested under the support beams of the bridge. Near the bridge, listen for the song of the Orchard Oriole, which sings from the trees along the river. From May through July, check the trees for Warbling and Yellow-throated Vireos, and along the river for swallows including the Purple Martin.

One or more raptor species can often be spotted overhead as they soar along the ridges or perch in trees on the ridges or by the river. On a good day, both vultures may be seen; Black Vultures are becoming regular but Turkey Vultures roost and nest on the high ledges of adjacent hillsides. Red-tailed and Broad-winged Hawks can be fairly common and one or more of the accipiters--Northern Goshawk, Cooper's, or Sharp-shinned Hawks, are occasionally spotted as well. Bald Eagles patrol the river for fish and waterfowl in winter, and migrating Ospreys forage over the deeper pools.

Proceed along Skiff Mountain Road. Check the roadside fields, orchards, and baseball fields for Killdeer, Eastern Bluebird, and Field and Song Sparrows. At 1.1 miles from Route 341 turn right onto River Road by the posted sign announcing the Appalachian National Scenic Trail. Follow River Road northward. The road is paved for a few hundred yards, then becomes dirt and goes through a stretch of typical deciduous woodland dominated by oak, maple, and hickory. If hiking is your theme as well as birding, you can hike from this point along the road for the best birding. If time is short, you can drive from spot to spot.

The hillside habitat to the left of the road is broken by small, steep, wooded ravines dominated by eastern hemlock. As you pass these ravines, stop briefly to listen and look for Winter Wren, Acadian Flycatcher, and Louisiana Waterthrush, all of which hunt along the brooks that cascade down to the river.

The right side of the road is lined by tall elms, ashes, and giant sycamores that border the river. About 0.9 miles north of Skiff Mountain Road there are two small islands in the river. In May, stop and check the islands for Spotted and Solitary Sandpipers, which often forage along the water's edge. Waterfowl that may be spotted along the river include Mallard, Canada Goose, Wood Duck, American Black

Duck, and Common Merganser. Great Blue and Green Herons hunt in the shallows. Often, a variety of swallows--Barn, Tree, Bank, and Northern Rough-winged--may be seen hawking for insects over the river. You may start hearing the raspy call of the Cerulean Warbler which sings, feeds, and nests high in the tops of the sycamores and other trees along the river and on the lower hillsides. This warbler can be difficult to locate once the trees have leafed out.

From this point on you can encounter a tremendous variety of bird species, especially on peak migration days during the second or third weeks of May. Listen for flycatchers, including Eastern Phoebe, Great Crested Flycatcher, Eastern Wood-Pewee, Eastern Kingbird, and Least Flycatcher, which also are all common breeding species. Blue-gray Gnatcatchers are also present in good numbers. All of Connecticut's regularly occurring thrushes pass through this valley; Swainson's Thrush migrates during the third and fourth week of May, followed closely by Gray-cheeked Thrush in late May and early June. American Robin, Veery, Wood and Hermit Thrushes all nest in this area.
Breeding warblers include Common Yellowthroat, Yellow, Chestnut-sided, Blue-winged, Golden-winged, Worm-eating (on the drier hillsides), Black-throated Blue, Black-throated Green, Black-and-white, American Redstart, and Louisiana Waterthrush. Northern Parula and Canada Warblers are seen regularly during migration and may also nest along the river.

River Road is a great place to brush up on vireo songs. Philadelphia Vireo is a rare migrant from mid-to-late May while Warbling, Yellow-throated, Red-eyed, and Solitary (uncommon) Vireos all nest along River Road. Other interesting breeding species are Scarlet Tanager, Baltimore Oriole, Rose-breasted Grosbeak, and Yellow-billed and Black-billed Cuckoos (both cuckoos are irregular nesters).

Continue on River Road for another 0.8 miles to a sign on the left announcing the parking area for the Appalachian Trail. Here, the Appalachian Trail merges with River Road to work northward along the river. Scout the area for woodpeckers; Downy, Hairy, Red-bellied, and Pileated are all permanent residents and may usually be spotted or heard along the trail, the last usually requiring some effort. Northern Flicker is a common breeder; Yellow-bellied Sapsucker is an uncommon April migrant and breeder, while Red-headed Woodpecker is a casual migrant. Other possible nesting species include House and Winter

Wrens.

From the Appalachian Trail parking lot, it is about 1.0 miles north to where River Road ends at a bar-way. From here, it is most productive to bird the rest of River Road on foot. From late May through July, listen for the song of Acadian Flycatcher, which is regular along this section of roadway. They usually nest in the lower canopy above feeder streams.

At the bar-way, scout the field and powerline cut to the left. Golden-winged and Blue-winged Warblers are regularly seen or heard here, and both nest in the scrubby, secondary growth that borders the field. Prairie Warblers are sometimes heard along the hillside. Other noisy vocalists include Least Flycatcher, Warbling and Yellow-throated Vireos, and Baltimore Oriole. Check the river for swallows which frequently concentrate over pools or pick up mud along the sand bars for building their nests.

Beyond the bar-way, River Road continues north along the river as the Appalachian Trail. About 250 yards up the trail is an old field on the left, now partly overgrown with honeysuckle and azalea and guarded by ancient black locust trees. Goldenrod, milkweed, butterfly weed, and other old field herbs provide food and cover for a variety of seed eating birds. In May and June, the fragrant blossoms of honeysuckle and azalea attract Ruby-throated Hummingbirds which feed on the nectar. Hummingbirds nest along the field edge and can often be spotted perched on dead branches, surveying their territory. The thick bushes can harbor a number of warblers, including Magnolia, Mourning (rare in late May and early June), Canada, Wilson's, and American Redstart. The field edge is also ideal for Cerulean, Golden-winged, and Blue-winged Warblers. Eastern Towhee is common, and Brown Thrasher is an uncommon summer resident.

Since 1989, Yellow-throated Warbler has been spotted in the woodland at the north end of the field, usually along the brook. Nesting was probable in 1990 and confirmed in 1991. Listen for their song and try to spot the male high in the sycamores. The birds are somtimes hard to spot, so be patient. **Don't disturb these birds by using playback of tape-recorded song to attract them--everyone wants to enjoy this new breeding species to Connecticut.**

Return to the trail and walk north another 100 yards to the brook. Beyond the brook is a conifer woodland of hemlock, red pine, and white pine. The red pine is now diseased and dying. When birding the conifers, avoid stepping on the white pine and hemlock seedlings tucked in their protective screens; they represent the future generation of this evergreen woodland. The Yellow-throated Warblers may also be found here as well. From mid-to-late May, Bay-breasted, Blackpoll, and Cape May Warblers are usually encountered in these conifers. Black-throated Green and Blackburnian Warblers are common but intermittent breeders in the grove. Tufted Titmouse, White-breasted Nuthatch, and Blue Jay are fairly common here while Brown Creeper and Red-breasted Nuthatch are occasionally seen.

On the wooded hillside, Ruffed Grouse can be heard drumming in spring and may be "scared up" almost any time of year. Barred and Great Horned Owls are permanent residents that nest on the hillside, the former mostly in deeper woods and the latter almost anywhere a suitable Red-tailed Hawk's or American Crow's nest can be appropriated. Barred Owl may respond to vocal imitations of its song during the day almost anywhere in the mixed conifer woods along the northern end of the road and trail, but this method of locating the owls is not encouraged. Northern Saw-whet Owls have also been reported in this area and may nest. They are most responsive to vocalizations in March and April. Eastern Screech-Owl nests and roosts in the sycamores and other mature trees along the river.

If you have not yet observed Purple Martins, check the small colony located along Skiff Mountain Road. To reach this colony, return to Skiff Mountain Road, turn right and drive uphill about 1.8 miles (0.1 miles beyond Fuller Mountain Road on the left). On the right is a small farm with two Purple Martin nest boxes immediately beyond the house. Park and scan the boxes and adjacent fields for the birds.

11 STEEP ROCK RESERVATION
Washington

In the southern tier of the Northwest Highlands, the Steep Rock Association manages two large tracts of undeveloped land; the Steep Rock Reservation and Hidden Valley Reservation. Both reservations are located in the town of Washington and have been set aside to protect and preserve the beauty of these natural areas. Dominated by the 380 foot high Steep Rock from which the preserve takes its name, the two reservations encompass the spectacular scenery and wildlands of the Shepaug River Valley and surrounding hillsides. The varied habitats include steep hillsides of hemlock and white pine which give way to dry deciduous growth toward the hilltops. The hemlock stands are rapidly succumbing to woolly adelgid infestations, and their destruction may adversely affect bird species diversity and distribution. The southern end of Steep Rock Reservation includes a shrubby powerline cut.

Birding at Steep Rock Reservation is best for spring and fall migrants and summer nesting species. Summer birding highlights include breeding Northern Goshawk, Winter Wren, Hermit Thrush, Solitary Vireo, and Blackburnian, Canada, and Black-throated Green Warblers. Other interesting species that nest on the preserve are Common Merganser, Spotted Sandpiper, Barred Owl, Pileated Woodpecker, and Acadian Flycatcher.

DIRECTIONS

From Interstate 84 take Exit 15 (Route 67, Southbury) and head north 9.3 miles on Route 67 into Roxbury, and turn right on Route 199 north. Follow Route 199 for 4.6 miles to Route 47, turn left, and drive 1.0 miles to the center of Washington Depot. Just before the junction of Route 47 and Route 109 turn left onto River Road. Follow River Road for 0.2 miles, turn left at the stop sign and continue on River Road. When River Road bends sharply right (1.2 miles) turn left onto a dirt road and immediately turn left again, crossing a bridge over the Shepaug River. Park in the lot by the horse riding field.

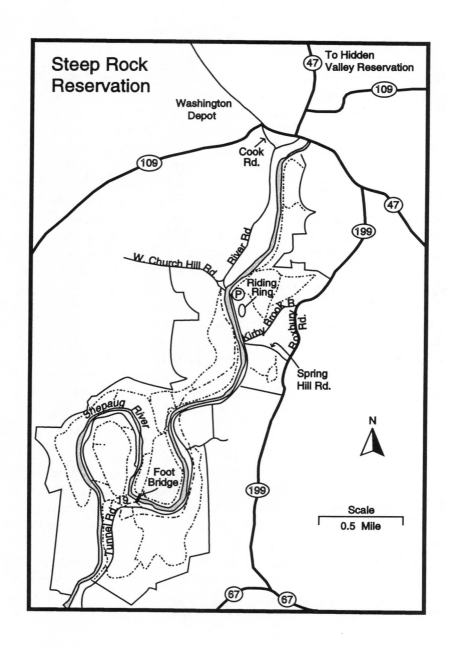

Steep Rock Reservation

To Hidden Valley Reservation

47

109

Washington Depot

Cook Rd.

109

47

199

River Rd.

W. Church Hill Rd.

Riding Ring

P

Kirby Brook R.

Roxbury Rd.

Spring Hill Rd.

N

Shepaug River

Foot Bridge

199

Tunnel Rd.

Scale
0.5 Mile

199

67

67

BIRDING

Steep Rock Reservation

An information board with a park map that outlines the trails and other features of Steep Rock Park is near the parking lot. To bird the reservation you can either drive or walk south along Dugway Tunnel Road, stopping frequently to bird along the roadside or venture along the trails. If you plan to bird the reservation on a summer weekend get an early start because the road often becomes congested with runners, hikers, bikers, and fishermen by mid-morning.

Parking Lot and Horse Riding Ring Area. The parking lot abuts a horse riding ring, open field and edge habitats as well as the river itself. From late spring through summer, the maples and sycamores along the riverside should yield Least Flycatcher, Warbling and Yellow-throated Vireos, Blue-gray Gnatcatcher, American Redstart, and Yellow Warbler. Along the field and woodland edges look for Mourning Dove, Gray Catbird, Blue-winged Warbler, American Goldfinch, and Chipping Sparrow. Check the nest boxes in the field for Tree Swallow and Eastern Bluebird. From the bridge, Belted Kingfisher is often seen or heard and Cedar Waxwing flocks frequent the riverside trees.

Michael Harwood Birdwalk. This one mile trail loop begins at the parking lot. The birdwalk is dedicated to the memory of Michael Harwood, a long time Connecticut birder, conservationist, and author of *The View from Hawk Mountain,* and other birding books. The Michael Harwood Birdwalk samples a variety of habitats including floodplains, fields, thickets, and woodlands. Downy Woodpecker, Tufted Titmouse, Hermit and Wood Thrushes, House Wren, Ovenbird, and Black-and-white, Worm-eating and Black-throated Green Warblers, and many other common birds of field and woodlands can be turned up along this trail during spring and summer.

Dugway Tunnel Road. To bird the rest of Steep Rock Reservation, set your odometer and head south on Dugway Tunnel Road, which parallels the east side of the Shepaug River. At 0.3 miles along the road two side roads on the left lead out of the park and back to Route 199. A 100 yard hike up these side roads reveals an overgrown field which hosts nesting Ruby-throated Hummingbird in summer. In fall and spring the field can also be good for migrant warblers.

Between 0.2 and 0.5 miles the road narrows and the hemlock covered hillsides descend steeply down to the river. The hemlocks here and throughout the reservation should be checked for Veery, Wood and Hermit Thrushes, Solitary Vireo, and Black-throated Green and Blackburnian Warblers. Eastern Phoebe nests on ledges above the river in this area.

At 0.2 miles the river broadens and deepens to form a large pool called Mitchell Hole. If the river isn't crowded with fishermen, Common Merganser, Green Heron, Spotted Sandpiper, and Louisiana Waterthrush are some of the better birds possible here. This stretch of the Shepaug River can also be counted on to yield Belted Kingfisher, Northern Flicker, Eastern Kingbird, Northern Rough-winged Swallow, Yellow-throated and Warbling Vireos, Common Yellowthroat, Common Grackle, and Baltimore Oriole. From spring through fall, Osprey regularly patrol the river.

On the left 0.3 miles further is a road which has been blocked off. Park here and walk south along the former railroad bed, turn left (220 yards) and follow a path along a small stream and up into the hemlocks. Acadian Flycatcher and Winter Wren have been seen along the small stream, while Worm-eating Warbler occurs in the open woodlands nearby.

After birding the trail, backtrack to Dugway Tunnel Road and continue driving south to a pull-off on the right at 0.4 miles. From here it is a short walk to the wooden suspension bridge over the Shepaug River. Erected in 1991, the 150 foot long bridge offers a commanding view of the river and bankside habitats. Check the river for Spotted Sandpiper, swallows, Louisiana Waterthrush, Cedar Waxwing, and other species. Mink can sometimes be spotted in the early morning or late evening hours. Just downstream from the bridge is a sharp bend in the river which forms part of a geological structure known as the Clam Shell. If time permits, cross the bridge and hike along one of the trails that meander through the hemlock and white pine woods along the west side of the river. In late spring and summer, Brown Creeper, Winter Wren, and Pine (uncommon), Blackburnian, and Black-throated Green Warblers are all possible along the trail. In winter, Golden-crowned

Kinglet, White-throated Sparrow, and the erratic Pine Siskin, grosbeaks, and crossbills can sometimes be tallied. Pileated Woodpecker is an uncommon woodland resident that may turn up in any season of the year.

Return to Dugway Tunnel Road and continue south. At 0.2 miles park on the right. This is picnic site 19. Just beyond the picnic area the road cuts steeply uphill and becomes increasingly difficult to drive. From picnic site 19, you can hike up the hill to the Clam Shell Trail or, alternatively, hike through the old railroad tunnel. You can also take the path that leads through the picnic site to an overlook for a sensational view of the river and part of the Clam Shell.

A nice hiking loop (about 1.8 miles in length) is to take the railroad bed through the tunnel, turn right and follow the river bank or Clam Shell Trail back to picnic site 19 from the south side of the tunnel. To get to the old railroad tunnel, take the trail that begins across the road from the picnic area for about 100 yards to the old railroad bed, turn right and the tunnel entrance is directly in front of you. The tunnel was dug through the "neck" of the Clam Shell to avoid constructing the railroad around the two mile long giant meander of the Shepaug River. The 180-foot long tunnel is dark and damp with wet footing in spots, but passable.

If you want to explore the Clam Shell without hiking through the tunnel, take the trail on the south side of the picnic site 19 where the road bends sharply left and ascends the hill. Follow the trail uphill a short distance and turn right at the intersection which leads through hemlock and white pine woods to a spectacular vista high above the river. From here you get a great view of the river and opposite hillside. The trail eventually leads down to the river and around the Clam Shell. In summer, the squeeks and chips of chipmunks and red squirrels along the trail add to the music of bird songs. The hemlock woods should harbor an assortment of woodpeckers, thrushes, vireos, and warblers. Yellow-bellied Flycatchers regularly migrate through this area and Acadian Flycatchers are fairly common in summer. Common Ravens also occur and may nest on the hillside or in the cliffs above the river. Other species likely seen in the conifers include Red-breasted Nuthatch, Winter Wren, Solitary Vireo, and Blackburnian, Black-and-white (mainly in the understory), Black-throated Green, and Worm-eating (along open areas near the river) Warblers.

Powerline Section.   To drive or hike to the powerline from picnic site 19, continue along Dugway Tunnel Road another 0.3 miles through an oak-hickory woodland to reach the powerline right-of-way at the southern edge of the reservation.   The shrubs and thickets along the powerline swath add to the park's habitat diversity.   Typical birds breeding in or along the shrubs include Brown Thrasher (uncommon), Chestnut-sided, Blue-winged, Prairie, and Yellow Warblers, Common Yellowthroat, Eastern Towhee, and Indigo Bunting.   In winter, the thickets can reveal many of the park's permanent residents, and Purple Finch and Eastern Bluebird.   The powerline allows an unobstructed view of the valley and far hillside that is ideal for spotting raptors such as Turkey Vulture, Red-tailed and Broad-winged (spring and summer) Hawks, and an occasional accipiter.

Hidden Valley Reservation
Hidden Valley offers additional birding opportunites plus the chance to examine geologically interesting structures called glacial kame terraces. To explore the Hidden Valley portion of Steep Rock Reservation, return to the junction of Route 47 and Route 109 in the center of Washington Depot and follow Route 47 north for 1.2 miles.   Park on the right just beyond the bridge which crosses over the Shepaug River.   A wooden footbridge across Bee Brook (a tributary of the Shepaug River) leads into the reservation.

   An extensive network of trails provides access to most of the hemlock and hardwoods slopes of Hidden Valley.   A map of the trail system is posted at the trailhead, near the foot bridge.   The same woodland birds likely seen at Steep Rock Reservation may also be be spotted at Hidden Valley. A number of interesting permanent residents make the reservation their home.   Species that may be encountered year-round include Ruffed Grouse, Hairy, Downy, Pileated, and Red-bellied Woodpeckers, Blue Jay, Tufted Titmouse, Black-capped Chickadee, White-breasted and Red-breasted Nuthatches, and Northern Cardinal. Whip-poor-will is an uncommon, but regular summer resident that can be heard calling its name from the hillsides adjoining the river.   Barred Owl occurs along the hemlock hillside and Northern Goshawks have nested in this area for many years. Some typical summer species of the deciduous and mixed woodlands in this reservation area include Wood and Hermit Thrushes, Red-eyed and Solitary Vireos, Black-and-white Warbler, Ovenbird, American Redstart, Scarlet Tanager, and Rose-breasted Grosbeak.

12 NEW MILFORD TOUR
Bridgewater and New Milford

This birding tour includes the former New Milford landfill, Sunny Valley Farm, and several other locations along the Housatonic River Valley in the New Milford area. In recent years, the area has become a hot spot for winter rarities. The proximity of the old landfill to the Housatonic River made this an ideal location to find a variety of gulls, which used the river as a dispersal corridor to and from Long Island Sound. The gulls formerly foraged and rested at the landfill, along the river, and in adjacent fields. The river can also host an assortment of waterfowl in winter. Nearby Sunny Valley Farm offers good birding throughout the year for migrants and many open field species.

Noteworthy species that may be observed during this tour include Redhead, Bald and Golden Eagles, Northern Goshawk, Rough-legged Hawk, Peregrine Falcon, Lesser Black-backed, Glaucous, and Iceland Gulls, and American Pipit.

DIRECTIONS

Begin the tour at the former New Milford Landfill. To get there from Interstate 84 take Exit 7 (Route 7, Brookfield and New Milford) and follow Route 7 north to the junction of Route 7 with Route 25 in Brookfield. Start your mileage reading at this point. Continue north on Route 7 until you reach a large shopping plaza on the left at 4.8 miles. The access road to the old landfill is along the southern end of the plaza and looks more like an alleyway behind the store than a road. Drive down the road and through the gate until you arrive at the scale house. Stop here and ask permission to enter the site. **Note: since the landfill has closed it may not be possible to access this site.**

BIRDING
New Milford Landfill
Closed since mid-1995, this landfill located by the Housatonic River Valley formerly attracted a variety of gulls. Stragglers may still appear along with an assortment of crows, vultures, and other open field species. Birding at the landfill has been excellent since the late 1980's,

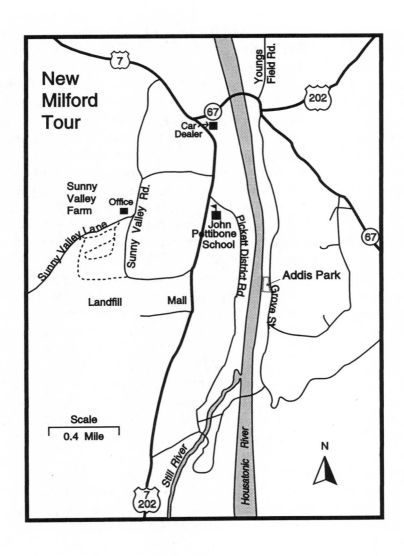

but undoubtedly, the landfill closure will impact species variety and numbers in the future. The landfill is private property but the company has been very accommodating to the needs of the birding community. Visitors to the landfill are welcome and usually granted access during normal working hours. However, visitors wishing to bird the landfill must first check in at the office or weigh station to secure permission and receive instructions for parking. Please adhere to the rules of the owners, so that other birders will be welcome. **Note: getting access to the landfill may be difficult since the site is now closed.**

In late fall and winter (late November through March), large concentrations of gulls formerly visited the landfill. These gull flocks contained thousands of individuals, mostly Ring-billed, Herring, and Great Black-backed Gulls. When the landfill was active, Lesser Black-backed, Glaucous, and Iceland Gulls were regular visitors (white-winged gulls were absent during the winter of 1994-95).

From the landfill area, scan the ridges and fields abutting the landfill for raptors and vultures: Turkey Vultures roost on the hillside behind the landfill and the birds require close scrutiny to find the rarer Black Vulture. In past winters up to 20 Black Vultures have been spotted at the New Milford Landfill or the adjacent Sunny Valley Farm. (Note: the state of the vulture roost remains uncertain since the landfill closed).

Common Ravens have also been heard "croaking" from the hillside. Hawks are represented by the Red-tailed (resident), Sharp-shinned (occasionally observed chasing the starling flocks foraging on the landfill), American Kestrel, and rarely, a Bald Eagle near the river.

Sunny Valley Preserve: Sunny Valley Farm
Owned by The Nature Conservancy, Sunny Valley Preserve consists of 1,850 acres of agricultural and natural areas located in the towns of Bridgewater and New Milford. A 400-acre parcel of the preserve includes Sunny Valley Farm which abuts the former landfill to the north. To get to this part of the Sunny Valley Preserve, return to the junction of the landfill road and Route 7 (at the mall), and follow Route 7 north for 0.4 miles. Turn left onto Sunny Valley Road and continue 0.8 miles and take the first left onto Sunny Valley Lane (may not be marked). The Sunny Valley Preserve office is on the right. Check in at the office and inquire about birding, special conditions, and restrictions. The preserve's current director is an avid birder and should

be able to provide updated information regarding unusual species and other pertinent facts concerning the property.

Sunny Valley Preserve is an active farm with livestock, orchards, field crops, and vegetable crops, therefore, certain areas may be restricted to visitors. First, check the office feeder for Red-bellied Woodpecker, Red-breasted Nuthatch, and other birds. The corn fields and open meadows have attracted many of the landfill rarities. During migration and also during mild winters American Pipit, Horned Lark, and Savannah Sparrow are fairly regular in the fields. American Pipit flocks of 50-100 birds are frequently found in fall.

Several trails are located to the south of Sunny Valley Lane. A trail system consisting of two loop trails connected by a shorter trail traverse the farm and permit a fairly close approach to the landfill property. The Yellow Trail starts opposite the office on Sunny Valley Lane.

During winter, check the fields along Sunny Valley Road and Sunny Valley Lane for resting gulls which often use the fields to congregate after feeding at the landfill or on the river. The power lines make good observation posts for Turkey Vulture, Red-tailed Hawk, and the occasional, American Kestrel. With luck you may spot a Black Vulture or a Rough-legged Hawk. Recently, Golden Eagle and Peregrine Falcon have been spotted here. From the southern section of the trail system, called Bird Lane, you can see the landfill, but it's about 0.5 miles off so a scope is required. For a closer look, walk through the field to the edge of the landfill property, **but don't enter the landfill property without permission**.

The fields and hedgerow along the trails can be productive for Eastern Bluebird, sparrows (White-throated, American Tree, Field, and Song), and Eastern Meadowlark (occasionally overwinter, spring migrants in late March). Fall migration also brings White-crowned and Lincoln's Sparrows.

Some species that nest on or adjacent to Sunny Valley Farm include Wild Turkey, Red-bellied and Pileated Woodpeckers, Cooper's Hawk, Eastern Wood-Pewee, Carolina Wren, Scarlet Tanager, and Rose-breasted Grosbeak. Nesting boxes located on the preserve attract breeding Tree Swallow, Black-capped Chickadee, Eastern Bluebird, House Wren, and American Kestrel. Cliff Swallows have nested on the barns behind the office. Since 1993, Fish Crows have occurred throughout the year around the preserve, although nesting has not yet been confirmed. Cooper's Hawk sometimes stoop for pigeons around the barnyard, so watch for panic-stricken pigeons.

Sunny Valley Preserve's properties in Bridgewater include several upland fields used by Eastern Meadowlark, Bobolink, and other field species. Extensive forests along Lake Lillinonah provide nesting habitats for Cerulean and Worm-eating Warblers, Northern Goshawk, and other woodland species. Pick up a copy of the Preserve's brochure and map at the Sunny Valley Farm office.

Steel Bridge

This bridge is a good spot to bird the Housatonic River near New Milford. To reach the steel bridge, follow Sunny Valley Road back to Route 7, turn left and head north on Route 7 for 0.8 miles. Just before the intersection of Route 7 and Route 67, stop and bird the Housatonic River south of the steel bridge (from the south end of Southworth's Dodge). To check the north side of the bridge continue into the intersection, bear right, and follow Route 67 across the river and take an immediate left onto Young's Field Road. Park and scout the river for waterfowl and gulls. Birding is best when the river is frozen and pockets of open water exist to attract and concentrate an assortment of species. In recent winters, waterfowl lingering in this area, include Green-winged Teal, Wood Duck, Ring-necked Duck, Redhead, and Hooded and Common Mergansers. The rarer gulls (Iceland, Glaucous and Lesser Black-backed) may turn up here as well.

Addis Park

To access this park from the steel bridge, continue south for 0.6 miles on Route 67 (through the center of town) and turn right onto Grove Street (past the junction where Route 67 and Route 202 split). Follow Grove Street 1.2 miles until you reach Addis Park on the right. Along the way, the road follows the river which can be viewed from many areas. **Be careful when birding from the roadside because the road is heavily traveled and lacks good parking areas.** Park near the small, town-owned boat launch. The boat launch can be recognized by the gravel driveway and parking lot identified by a park sign. This is the last driveway to the river heading south along this section of the road. All other driveways are private property, so please respect the landowner's posted signs.

Birdlife in this area is consistent with the sites previously discussed, basically including waterfowl, gulls, and an occasional Bald Eagle. Gulls frequently congregate along the river or on the ice if the river is frozen. From the boat launch or along the roadway scan the river for gulls. If the river remains open the area can host diving ducks (mainly Common Merganser, but Common Goldeneye, Bufflehead, and Canvasback occasionally occur). During summer, vireos (Warbling and Yellow-throated), warblers (Yellow, Common Yellowthroat, and Blue-winged), and blackbirds are common breeding species along this stretch of river. Willow Flycatcher and Orchard Oriole also nest along the river.

13A NORTHEAST UTILITIES SKIFF MOUNTAIN WILDLIFE MANAGEMENT AREA

Sharon

This 711-acre highland area set just west of the Housatonic River consists of a variety of habitats including high field, upland woodland, shrub and wooded swamps, marsh, thickets, and Peck Pond. Birding can be good for migrant raptors, waterbirds, and songbirds and summer nesting species of fields and woodlands

DIRECTIONS

From Interstate 84 take Exit 7 (Route 7, Brookfield and New Milford) and follow Route 7 north to Route 341 in Kent. Turn left heading west on Route 341 for 0.3 mile and turn right onto Skiff Mountain Road. Travel along Skiff Mountain Road and continue straight on West Woods Road when Skiff Mountain Road bears right at the Kent School (4.3 miles). Continue on West Woods Road (which becomes Skiff Mountain Road in Sharon) for 1.8 miles to the parking lot on the right, just beyond Peck Pond.

BIRDING

In late spring and summer, the fields and wetland habitats host a nice mix of birds. Check the high field abutting the parking lot for nesting Tree Swallow, Eastern Bluebird, and House Wren in the nest boxes, and Bobolink in the grasses. The reverting fields on the north side of the parking lot contain Blue-winged and Chestnut-sided Warblers, Field Sparrow, and American Goldfinch, while the shrub thickets and trees surrounding Peck Pond are good for Northern Flicker, Eastern Kingbird, Warbling Vireo, Common Yellowthroat, Yellow Warbler, Red-winged Blackbird, Common Grackle, and Baltimore Oriole.

From the adjacent woodlands Least Flycatcher, Eastern Phoebe, Eastern Wood-Pewee, Yellow-throated and Red-eyed Vireos, American

Redstart, Scarlet Tanager, and Rose-breasted Grosbeak are common vocalists.

Peck Pond is good for migrant waterfowl and waterbirds including Pied-billed Grebe, Wood Duck, American Black Duck, Ring-necked Duck, and Common and Hooded Mergansers, among others. Species nesting on the pond are Canada Goose, Mallard, Wood Duck and occasionally, Hooded Merganser. Green and Great Blue Herons are regular in spring and summer.

The fields offer a fine vantage point to scan the sky for raptors. A few species can be seen year-round (Turkey Vulture, Red-tailed Hawk and the rarer Northern Goshawk), but fall migration brings the best variety and number of individuals. Hawks regularly observed in fall include American Kestrel, Sharp-shinned, Cooper's, Broad-winged, and Red-shouldered Hawks.

13B MACEDONIA BROOK STATE PARK
Kent

Located in the northwestern corner of the state, Macedonia Brook State park consists of 2,294 mostly wooded acres bisected by Macedonia Brook. Birding habitats include stands of upland deciduous, coniferous and mixed woodlands, fields, thickets, edge, small feeder streams, Macedonia Brook, and red maple swamps. The park also includes two hill top peaks nearly 1400 feet in elevation with excellent views of the Catskill and Taconic Mountains to the west and northwest. An extensive trail system provides access to much of Macedonia Brook State Park. Part of the Appalachian Trail also runs through the park. Picnic and camping facilities are available for birders that want to spend more time here. Birding at the park is best for spring migrants and woodland nesting species.

DIRECTIONS
From Interstate 84 take Exit 7 (Route 7, New Milford and Brookfield),

and follow Route 7 north to Route 341 in Kent. Turn left onto Route 341, heading west for 1.7 miles, then turn right onto Macedonia Brook Road and continue to the park entrance. Follow the road, which becomes dirt, to the office building on the left (2.5 miles). Maps of the park and campgrounds are available at the office building.

BIRDING

In late spring and early summer, the upland woodlands provide habitat for such common and widespread woodland nesting species as the Red-eyed Vireo, Wood Thrush, Ovenbird, and Scarlet Tanager. The vegetation along the trails and woodland edges around campgrounds may harbor Blue-winged Warbler, Baltimore Oriole, Chipping Sparrow, American Goldfinch, as well as other possible species.

Woodland woodpeckers are well represented by Downy, Hairy, and Red-bellied Woodpecker, and Northern Flicker. Yellow-bellied Sapsucker and Pileated Woodpecker both occur in limited numbers. Louisiana Waterthrush nest along Macedonia Brook.

The deeper and more remote mixed woodlands may hold nesting Cooper's Hawk and Northern Goshawk. Owls are well represented in the park. Try for Barred Owl around the swamps and in the more extensive woods. Eastern Screech-Owl is more likely found along woodland edge habitat and around the campgrounds.

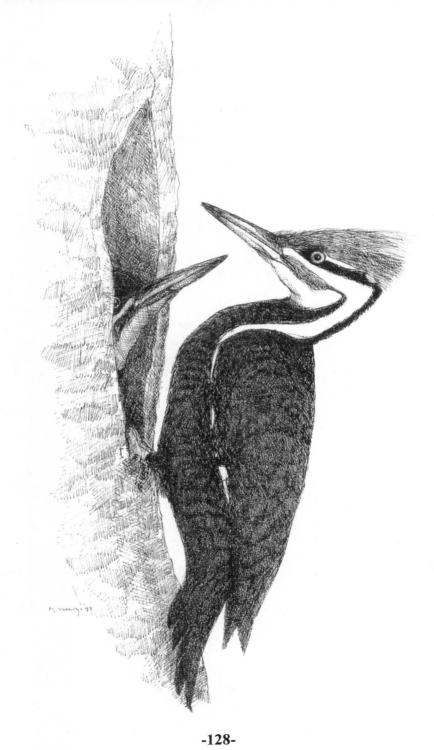

Western Hills

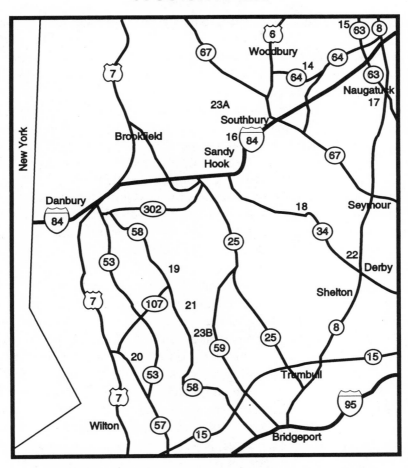

14. Flanders Nature Center
15. Sperry Park
16. River Road in Southbury
17. Naugatuck State Forest
18. Stevenson's Dam

19. C.P. Huntington State Park
20. Devil's Den Preserve
21. Valley Road
22. Osbornedale State Park
23A. Southbury Training School Pond
23B. Aspetuck Reservoir

14 FLANDERS NATURE CENTER
Woodbury and Middlebury

This privately-owned nature preserve consists of 24 sanctuaries totaling about 1200 acres scattered in the towns of Woodbury, Middlebury, Southbury, and Bethlehem. The two major components of the Flanders Nature Center, the Van Vleck Farm, and the Whittemore Sanctuary offer several miles of trails for birding and other outdoor activities.

The Van Vleck Farm has a nature shop, museum, wildlife exhibits, and interpretative trails among its attractions. The farm also features an annual (February and March) maple syrup harvest; maple sap is collected, cooked, and processed by the traditional method to produce maple syrup. A network of trails bisect the 200-plus acres at the Van Vleck Farm, providing the birder access to marsh, upland deciduous woods, old fields, farm fields, a Christmas tree plantation, pond, and stream. A wildflower garden attracts many visitors to the sanctuary. On weekends from mid-April thru May, bird walks are lead at the Van Vleck Farm by nature center staff or by members of the Western Connecticut Bird Club. These tours normally start at 7:00 am, and last for several hours in the morning.

Habitat at the 700-acre Whittemore Sanctuary consists mostly of coniferous and mixed woodlands, a wooded pond, and a bog featuring pitcher plants, bog cranberry, sundew, and other unique bog flora.

Both the Whittemore Sanctuary and Van Vleck Farm are best birded during spring and fall migration when a variety of flycatchers, swallows, thrushes, vireos, warblers, and sparrows are moving through. Summer is good for observing bird breeding behavior but species diversity is reduced. Uncommon but regularly occurring species located during spring and fall include Pied-billed Grebe, Green-winged and Blue-winged Teals, Hooded Merganser, Northern Goshawk, Cooper's Hawk, Pectoral Sandpiper, Common Snipe, Yellow-bellied Sapsucker, Olive-sided Flycatcher (rare), Swainson's Thrush, Mourning (rare), and Wilson's Warblers, Lincoln's Sparrow, Rusty Blackbird, and Orchard Oriole.

Over 90 species nest within the sanctuary, including Green Heron, Red-shouldered Hawk, American Kestrel, Barred, Eastern Screech and Great Horned Owls, Whip-poor-will, Ruby-throated Hummingbird,

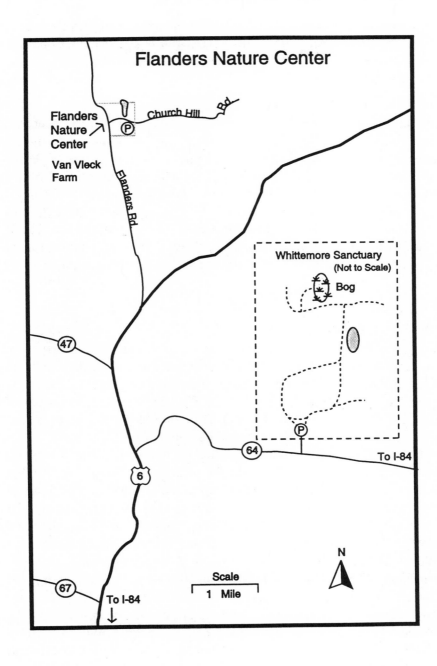

Pileated and Red-bellied Woodpeckers, Louisiana Waterthrush, Black-throated Green, Pine, Prairie, and Yellow-rumped Warblers, Bobolink, Eastern Meadowlark, and Swamp and Field Sparrows.

DIRECTIONS

To access Van Vleck Sanctuary, take Interstate 84 to Exit 15 (Route 67, Southbury) and follow Route 67 north. When Route 67 turns left toward Roxbury (1.5 miles) continue straight ahead on Route 6. At the junction of Route 6 and Route 64 (2.2 miles) continue east on Route 6 for 1.8 miles to Flanders Road. Turn left onto Flanders Road for 3.0 miles and bear right onto Church Hill Road. The Nature Center Headquarters is the large colonial house on the corner at the junction of Flanders Road and Church Hill Road. To get to the parking area, follow Church Hill Road for 0.2 miles to the parking lot on the right.

BIRDING

Van Vleck Farm

Cross the road and review the bulletin board showing the trail system. Six trails---Wildlife Habitat Trail, Wilderness Trail, Wildlife Luncheon Trail, Botany Trail, Plant Succession Trail, and Geology Trail provide access to most of the birding habitat. To find the greatest variety of species hike the Wildlife Habitat Trail that skirts the pond to the powerline cut then return by one of the upland trails.

The Wildlife Habitat Trail (also called the Edmund L. Briggs Wildlife Habitat Trail) begins just beyond the information board. A few feet down the trail, take the short spur trail to the left, which jogs down to the pond's earthen dam. From the dam you can look north across the pond, which features a large beaver lodge. In April and May, the pond may yield Green Heron, Pied-billed Grebe, ducks (American Black and Wood Ducks both nest, Green-winged and Blue-winged Teals, American Wigeon, and Hooded Merganser occur during migration), and Solitary and Spotted Sandpipers. Rusty Blackbirds are uncommon migrants during March and October. Spring and summer breeding species at the pond or along the edge include Eastern Kingbird, Eastern Phoebe, Willow and Least Flycatchers, Common Yellowthroat, and Yellow Warbler. The cattail marsh invariably holds a raucous Red-winged Blackbird nesting population. Northern Rough-winged, Tree, and Barn Swallows regularly forage just over the pond.

Return to the Wildlife Habitat Trail which works through the second growth deciduous woodland with the pond visible through the trees on the left. At trail marker #8, a spur trail on the left leads down to a bird blind which offers a view of the pond. From here, check the scrubby vegetation bordering the pond for Wood Duck.

Return to the Wildlife Habitat Trail and continue to the powerline. Check the powerline cut for breeding Prairie, Chestnut-sided and Blue-winged Warblers, Field Sparrow, and Indigo Bunting. Hawks are often seen overhead at this location. At the powerline, the trail jogs right and gradually curves back toward the parking area. As the trail enters the woods you can select several alternate trails (Plant Succession Trail, Geology Trail), all of which provide good habitat access and all of which return back to the Wildlife Habitat Trail or to the information board.

The mix of woods and fields along these trails is likely to produce a variety of thrushes (all pass through in migration, both Wood Thrush and Veery nest), vireos (all occur even the rare Philadelphia), warblers (30 species are possible during migration, many of which nest on the farm property), and sparrows.

Mid-May is the best time to observe the greatest variety of warblers; a sample of warblers that migrate through the sanctuary include Tennessee, Northern Parula, Magnolia, Cape May, Black-throated Blue, Blackpoll, Palm (late April and early May), Louisiana Waterthrush (along the brook north of the powercut), Northern Waterthrush, Mourning (rare late May/early June), Canada, and Wilson's. Nesting sparrows include Chipping, Swamp, and Song, while White-throated, White-crowned (uncommon), Lincoln's (uncommon), and Fox Sparrows are found as migrants.

A variety of hawks breed on or adjacent to the sanctuary. Scout the area for Red-tailed, Red-shouldered and Broad-winged Hawks, and American Kestrel. All the accipiters pass through during fall and spring migration. On occasion, normally in April-May or September-October, an Osprey can be spotted hovering over the pond in search of bass or other suitable prey.

After birding the Wildlife Habitat Trail, try the Botany Trail, a short loop trail that begins on the other side (south) of the parking lot. This trail works past a Christmas Tree Farm and field, around a small pond, and then back through upland and wet woodlands. The tree farm and field are excellent for Tree Swallow, House Wren, and Eastern Bluebird (which all nest in the boxes), and Northern Mockingbird. Other common permanent residents possible along the woodland and wet areas include Red-bellied, Downy and Hairy Woodpeckers, Blue Jay, Black-capped Chickadee, Tufted Titmouse, Northern Cardinal, and American Goldfinch. This trail is also very popular with wildflower enthusiasts. Many of Connecticut's native wildflowers, including some of the rarer species, have been cultivated and thrive along this trail.

Whittemore Sanctuary
To reach the Whittemore Sanctuary follow the directions for the Van Fleck Farm, but at the junction of Routes 6 and 64, turn right on Route 64, heading east. Take Route 64 for 2.5 miles and turn left onto a dirt road marked by the Flanders Nature Center sign. The parking area is on the left at 0.1 miles.

At the Whittemore Sanctuary, the trail to the bog provides a good mix of birds and birding habitat. The Bog Trail begins on the left (marked by a sign "Bog" tacked to a tree). The trail first climbs a hill, working through hardwoods, then bears left at a "T" junction. For most of its length, a brook and its associated wetland area parallels the trail on the left. A mixed woodland with white pine flanks the trail to the right.

Along the trail, listen for Louisiana Waterthrush from April into July. The loud, ringing song of this waterthrush is usually heard well before it can be spotted, flitting up and down the brook. In spring and summer, warblers can be common in the pines. Check the canopy for Pine, Black-throated Green, Blackburnian, and Yellow-rumped Warblers (all nest in limited numbers). Winter Wren and White-throated Sparrow are regular winter visitors and both linger into late spring and may occasionally nest.

In about 0.3 miles the trail comes to a small woodland pond at the top of the hill. From spring through early fall, the pond can be good for Common Grackle, Red-winged Blackbird, and Brown-headed Cowbird. Rusty Blackbird occurs during migration. Green Heron, Wood Duck, and Spotted Sandpiper (occasional) are possible here. Common summer nesting waterfowl include Canada Goose and Mallard, while Eastern Kingbird and Eastern Phoebe are regular in the trees and shrubs around the pond edge.

At the pond take the left trail, with the pond to your right. The trail shortly junctions with an old woods road, marked by a line of tall, ancient sugar maples which attest to an earlier time when the surrounding landscape was farm fields. Turn left, and follow the woods road 0.2 miles to a trail branching to the right, marked by a sign "Bog" tacked to a tree. In summer, some of the woodland birds possible along the trail include Ruffed Grouse, Great Crested Flycatcher, Eastern Wood-Pewee, White-breasted Nuthatch, Brown Creeper, Wood Thrush, Veery, Red-eyed Vireo, Ovenbird, Baltimore Oriole, and Scarlet Tanager. In winter, the species tally along the trail is less impressive, but look for woodpeckers (Downy, Hairy, Red-bellied, and Pileated), Golden-crowned Kinglet, Brown Creeper, Red-breasted and White-breasted Nuthatches, and White-throated Sparrow. Hermit Thrush occurs most of the year in limited numbers and is often heard practicing its lovely song during late spring and early summer somewhere along the trail.

Take a right turn onto the Bog Trail and continue a short distance to the bog. For much of its length the trail is lined with dense mountain laurel making birding difficult. The shrubs can harbor Eastern Towhee, Black-and-white Warbler, Common Yellowthroat, and Song Sparrow. At the bog a delapidated walkway allows partial access. Check out the carnivorous pitcher plants with their long, funnel-shaped leaves and the small, delicate sundew. Both plants are well adapted for survival in the nitrogen-deficient bog environment by catching and devouring insects which provide their nitrogen and other mineral needs. Tupelos border the bog. Also known as sourgum, the tupelo is an uncommon tree which is near the northern end of its range in Connecticut.

In spring and summer, the trees and shrubs around the bog may hold Northern Flicker, Ceder Waxwing, Gray Catbird, Yellow, Hooded (uncommon) and Canada Warblers, Northern Waterthrush (which may nest), Scarlet Tanager, Rose-breasted Grosbeak, Northern Cardinal, and Swamp Sparrow. Scan the sky for Turkey Vulture, Broad-winged, Red-tailed and Red-shouldered Hawks, and Northern Goshawk (rare).

After birding the bog, backtrack along the trail to the pond. At the trail junction, take the Eagle Path which works through the white pine woodland and down a steep hill. At the base of the hill the trail comes to a "T". Turn right and then take a quick left to return to the parking area.

15 SPERRY PARK
(JUNIPER HILL NATURAL AREA)
Middlebury

Formerly owned by The Nature Conservancy, this small nature preserve was transferred to the Middlebury Land Trust in 1979. Comprised of 147 acres of wetlands and woodlands, Sperry Park is best known to regional birders for the wintering Boreal Owl, a rare Connecticut record discovered in January, 1992. Sperry Park birding habitats include upland deciduous and mixed conifer woodlands, conifer plantations of white pine and Norway spruce, shrub swamps, and wooded swamps.

Sperry Park offers good spring birding for songbirds and some waterfowl species but the variety of wintering owls that normally can be found in the park is the main attraction. In spring, two or three owl species nest in the park. Other interesting species recorded at the park include Green Heron, Hooded Merganser, Northern Goshawk, Red-shouldered Hawk, Virginia Rail, Solitary Sandpiper, American Woodcock, Swainson's Thrush, Pine, Blackburnian, Blue-winged and Chestnut-sided Warblers, Rusty Blackbird, and Fox Sparrow.

DIRECTIONS
Eastbound on Interstate 84 take Exit 17 (Route 63, Watertown and Naugatuck), turn left at the bottom of the exit ramp and follow Route 63 north for 1.8 miles. From Interstate 84 westbound take Exit 17 (Routes 64 and 63, Middlebury and Watertown) to Route 64. Head west on Route 64 for 0.4 miles and turn right onto Route 63 heading north. Continue for 1.3 miles and park on the right side of the road. The entrance to Sperry Park is on the left (west), flanked by stone pillars connected by a guard chain.

BIRDING
A trail begins at the entrance to Sperry Park and continues westward through a small conifer grove, then along an elevated walkway separating ponds on either side. At the west end of the ponds the trail comes to a "T". The main trail goes to the right and skirts the pond before winding uphill, while the trail to the left works a short distance

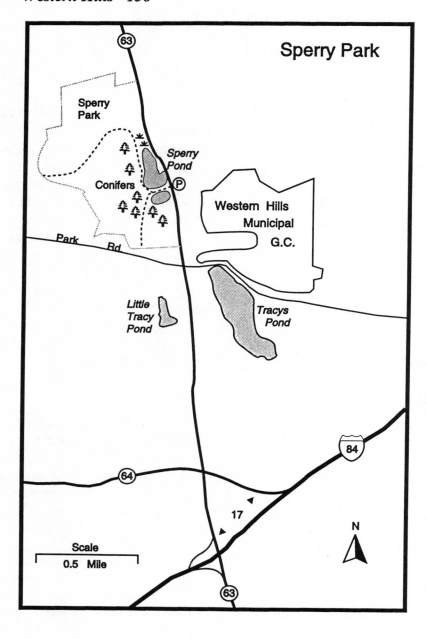

Sperry Park

into several small conifer stands. These conifer stands, along with the small conifer grove by the park entrance are the most likely places to find wintering owls. Check the conifers for fresh whitewash along the trunk and branches and the ground beneath for pellets that roosting owls have regurgitated. The whitewash and pellets signal the presence of an owl. **Northern Saw-whet Owls can be exceptionally tame and tolerent of human presence, but take care to avoid disturbing them or any other roosting owl that you may discover. Avoid photographing roosting owls with flash and strobes and do not cut or move branches to obtain a better view. Frequent visits and undue disturbance may alert potential diurnal predators such as hawks and cats to the owl's location.**

In winter, the small hemlocks and spruces along the edge of the pond and the Norway spruce grove to the west and south of the pond have proven good sites for Northern Saw-whet Owl. The Boreal Owl was found in the south end of the Norway spruce grove. Great Horned Owl has been recorded in the spruce, as well as in the hillside white pine stand northwest of the pond. From December through March, Great Horned Owls can be heard announcing their territorial claims to the area. Eastern Screech-Owl is another occasional resident of the park. They are sometimes seen sunning at the entrance of the Wood Duck nest boxes, especially in the late afternoon and early evening hours. Barred Owls have been recorded in the park but are irregular; they roost in the more inaccessible wooded swamp at the northern end of the pond. In early spring (March and April), check the ponds for Pied-billed Grebe, Great Blue Heron, Blue-winged Teal (uncommon), Wood and Ring-necked Ducks, Hooded Merganser, and swallows (mainly Tree and Northern Rough-winged). Other spring migrants may include Winter Wren, Hermit Thrush, Ruby-crowned and Golden-crowned Kinglets, Palm and Pine Warblers, Rusty Blackbird, Pine Siskin, and White-throated and Fox Sparrows. During peak migration periods (normally the second and third week of May), look for transient warblers such as Tennessee, Nashville, Northern Parula, Magnolia, Black-throated Blue, Yellow-rumped, Black-throated Green, Blackburnian, Blackpoll, Northern Waterthrush, Wilson's, and Canada.

From May through July, nesting waterbirds along the pond include Green Heron, Mallard, Wood Duck, and Virginia Rail. Other typical breeding species found in the wetland thickets and around the pond's

edge are Eastern Kingbird, Least and Willow Flycatchers, Eastern Phoebe, Gray Catbird, Cedar Waxwing, Warbling Vireo, Swamp and Chipping Sparrows, and Baltimore Oriole.

Check the wooded hillsides for nesting Red-tailed and Broad-winged Hawks, Ruffed Grouse, Pileated Woodpecker, Great Crested Flycatcher, Eastern Wood-Pewee, Yellow-throated and Red-eyed Vireos, Scarlet Tanager, and Eastern Towhee.

Breeding warblers can also be an attraction at Sperry Park. Scout the area for Worm-eating (on the drier hillsides), Blue-winged, Yellow, Chestnut-sided, Black-and-white, American Redstart, Ovenbird, Louisiana Waterthrush (along the stream), and Common Yellowthroat.

16 River Road

Southbury

River Road in Southbury is one of the best places in the state to find wintering Bald Eagles. Southbury River Road also features a variety of migrant waterfowl and wintering gulls. In summer, the area is good for species that nest in bottomland woods.

This birding tour will work north along the eastern bank of the Housatonic River in Southbury. Mixed deciduous and coniferous woods line the hillsides that face the river, and hemlock stands predominant on the north-facing slopes. The woodlands are interspersed with farmlands along the northeastern portion of the River Road birding site. Two major hydroelectric stations intercept the Housatonic River in this region. The southernmost of these is Stevenson's Dam which forms the eight-mile long Lake Zoar that parallels River Road. North of Southbury, the Housatonic River flow is interrupted by Shepaug Dam, which forms Lake Lillinonah.

A small population of Bald Eagles winters in the vicinity of Shepaug Dam, generally from November through March. Recently the winter eagle population peaked at about 30 individuals. The much rarer Golden Eagle has been seen here infrequently. Other irregular wintering species include Lesser Scaup, Blue-winged Teal, Cooper's Hawk, Northern Goshawk, and Iceland Gull.

In summer, the riparian woodlands along the river host a variety of nesting species including Wood Duck, Red-tailed and Broad-winged Hawks, Barred, Great-horned, and Eastern Screech Owls, Ruby-throated Hummingbird, Cliff Swallow, Eastern Bluebird, and Orchard Oriole.

DIRECTIONS

Westbound on Interstate 84 take Exit 14 (Route 172, South Britain). At the end of the ramp turn right and take a quick left at the traffic light onto Main Street which parallels Interstate 84 for one mile then turns left, crossing over Interstate 84. Immediately after crossing the bridge turn right at the stop sign onto Fish Rock Road. Follow Fish Rock

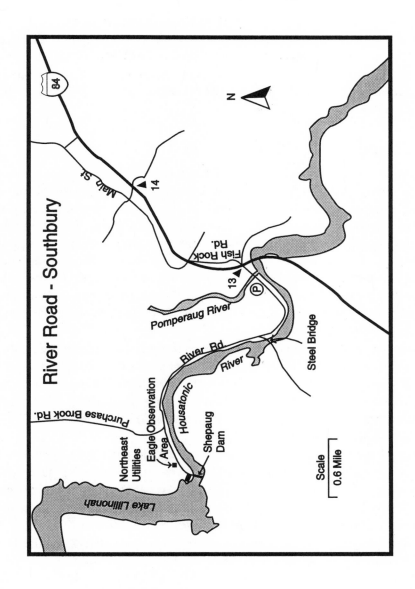

River Road - Southbury

Road 0.4 miles and then continue straight when Fish Rock Road turns left. This becomes River Road (at this point you will again cross over Interstate 84). Continue 0.3 miles and park on the right after crossing the Pomperaug River Bridge. Eastbound on Interstate 84 take Exit 13 (River Road), turn right at the end of the ramp and drive 0.5 miles to the parking area descibed above.

BIRDING

Bird the river and the delta formed at the confluence of the Pomperaug and Housatonic Rivers. In fall and spring, scan the emergent marsh vegetation, (phragmites and cattail stands) for herons and dabbling ducks and the open water for diving ducks. Common Snipe are also possible during migration. From May through August, this spot is good for Barn, Tree, and Bank Swallows. Northern Rough-winged and Cliff Swallows may also be spotted; both species nest under the bridge over the Pomperaug River. In summer, listen for the songs of Warbling Vireo and Baltimore Oriole which nest in the cottonwoods here and elsewhere along the river.

Continue along River Road. There are no good parking areas until you reach the steel bridge (0.9 miles) which crosses over the river. Bear right and stay on River Road at the bridge. Park near the steel bridge and scout the cove on the west side of the river. In winter, waterfowl and gulls can be found in this area. In 1990, an albino Ring-billed Gull was observed here.

Bird along River Road, which parallels the river for the next two miles, stopping periodically at suitable roadside parking spots to scan the river. You can also walk part of the way. If the river is not frozen, waterfowl can be abundant during migration and in winter, especially Canada Goose, Ring-necked Duck (large concentrations in March), and Common Merganser. Check the Canada Goose flocks for the less common Snow Goose (including the blue morph) and the very rare Greater White-fronted Goose. Other waterfowl to look for include Tundra Swan (rare), American Black Duck, Canvasback, Green-winged Teal, Greater and Lesser (uncommon) Scaups, Wood Duck, Bufflehead, and Hooded Merganser. In late winter this birding area can be great to catch the courtship behavior of several of these waterfowl species.

From spring through fall, warblers, vireos, and other songbirds can

M. SZANTYR '91

turn up anywhere along the river, adjacent hillsides, and in the scrub growth of the gasline swath. The Eastern Bluebird winters in this area and in the farm fields further north. The marshy area across the river from the gasline can yield migrant Great Blue Heron, American Coot (occasional), and Pied-billed Grebe.

About 1.4 miles above the steel bridge is a small pond on the right, adjacent to the field. In spring and fall, migrant shorebirds often forage along the pond's edge or in the fields. Check the field and pond for Killdeer, Common Snipe (usually found between September-October and March-April), Greater and Lesser Yellowlegs, Spotted and Solitary Sandpipers (normally found in May), and American Woodcock, the last is best observed at dusk from mid-March through June. Waterfowl, including dabbling ducks, also frequent the pond. Scan the emergent vegetation along the back of the pond carefully for Blue-winged Teal and Wood Duck.

Across from the pond, the river generally harbors a variety of waterfowl and gulls during winter. Study the gulls carefully for white-winged varieties such as Glaucous and Iceland Gulls. This portion of the river is open and offers a reasonably clear view of the Shepaug Dam.

From November through March, look upriver for Bald Eagles soaring or perched in the trees along the river's edge. From fall to spring, Red-tailed Hawk, Rough-legged Hawk (uncommon to rare) and sometimes an accipiter--- Northern Goshawk, Sharp-shinned and Cooper's Hawks---can be spotted in the trees or soaring overhead. Cooper's Hawk and Red-shouldered Hawk have nested nearby. Look for American Pipit along the river edge and in the cornfield during October. From October-November or March-April, the Rusty Blackbird may be observed in the cornfield or along the forest edge. From early May through July, Orchard Orioles can often be heard singing from the trees along the river.

The junction with Purchase Brook Road (1.8 miles from the steel bridge) is just past the farm house on the right. From December through March, travel on the remaining section of River Road is restricted unless you have a reservation to visit the Bald Eagle Observation Site. This restriction helps to minimize disturbance to the wintering Bald Eagles. The cornfields and river's edge can be good for migrating species especially in spring but also rewarding during the fall migration season. The field between the road and farm (and behind the barn) has been productive for sparrows. Look for White-crowned, Vesper, Lincoln, Savannah, Fox, and Swamp Sparrows, and Dickcissel, which is rare, but may sometimes be seen in September through November. Trespassing on the field is forbidden but it never hurts to ask the farmer for permission to bird the field.

Operations at the hydroelectric power station keep reservoir waters from freezing, providing a food source for the annual population of wintering Bald Eagles that congregate in the vicinity of the Shepaug Dam. Fish kills resulting from fish driven through the turbines also offer an easy and rather reliable food source for the eagles. The best spot to observe Bald Eagles is at the Bald Eagle Observation Area which is located near the dam. This observation post is open from about mid-December until mid-March, but reservations are required. Contact the Connecticut DEP--Wildlife Division at 860-424-3011 for reservations. Mid-January through February is the most opportune time to observe this magnificent species. The proximity of the observation station to the dam virtually guarantees spectacular views of Connecticut's wintering Bald Eagles. A naturalist is normally at the observation station and will assist visitors in finding eagles and describing their behavior.

17 NAUGATUCK STATE FOREST
Naugatuck, Beacon Falls, and Oxford

The Hunter's Mountain block of Naugatuck State Forest includes 2,200 acres of mixed hardwoods, pine plantations, laurel thickets, swampy areas, streams, and a hemlock ravine. Early this century, this locale was a popular recreational area called High Rock Park. Trains of the New York, New Haven, and Hartford Railroad stopped near Spruce Brook to drop off passengers for a day of picnics, hiking, or fishing. Today, much of Naugatuck State Forest is crisscrossed with hiking trails and unimproved roadways. Incredibly, the state sanctioned the construction of a rifle range within the forest, so be prepared to hear the "booms" of high-powered rifles as you hike along the trails.

Diverse landscapes of woods, ponds, and streams coupled with a beautiful ravine and 165 species of birds highlight birding in Naugatuck State Forest. The spring migration may show 25 species of warblers (including Hooded, Blue-winged, Worm-eating, Canada, and Wilson's), and Olive-sided Flycatcher.

The steep-sided hemlock ravine provides a cooler microclimate that attracts several interesting nesting species such as Hermit Thrush, Solitary Vireo, Winter Wren, and Black-throated Green Warbler. Rare species that have occurred include Upland Sandpiper, Black Vulture, Bald Eagle, Northern Goshawk, Red-headed Woodpecker, Connecticut and Mourning Warblers, and Golden-crowned Sparrow.

DIRECTIONS

Take Route 8 to Exit 26 (Route 63, South Main Street and Bethany) and follow Route 63 north over the Naugatuck River to Scott Street at the second light (0.3 miles). Turn left onto Scott Street and drive to the top of the hill and take the second left (0.1 miles) onto Lewis Street (the first and second left occur almost simultaneously). Follow Lewis Street to a stop sign (0.3 miles). Going straight, Lewis Street becomes Hunter's Mountain Road which ascends a steep hill passing several houses clustered towards the hilltop. Continue past a metal gate on the right (0.8 miles). The state forest boundary begins just down the road.

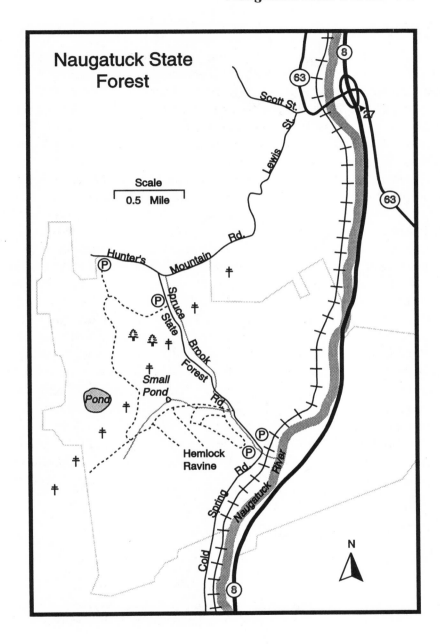

BIRDING

Hunter's Mountain Road. Continue slowly along Hunter's Mountain Road (after passing the former landfill entrance), stopping frequently to bird the adjacent habitats. In summer, the brushy fields to the left can produce House Wren, Brown Thrasher, and Chestnut-sided, Yellow and Blue-winged Warblers. By late summer, the brushy fields may host a variety of butterfly species. During winter, flocks of American Robin, Cedar Waxwing and occasionally, Evening Grosbeak feed in the overgrown apple trees which still persist. In fall, migrant Red-headed Woodpecker and Upland Sandpiper have been observed here.

Continue down the roadway to a white pine stand on the left (0.2 miles beyond the gate to the landfill). Ruffed Grouse, Brown Creeper, Northern Goshawk, Pine Warbler, and Hermit Thrush have occurred in this woodlot. Continue downhill past the paved forest road (0.3 miles) on the left and then uphill to a gravel parking area on the left (0.3 miles).

Park and scan the fields to the right (north) of the road for American Kestrel and Eastern Bluebird, both permanent residents. The grassy fields were once regularly mowed, but are now being invaded by sumac, rose, and other shrubs which provide food and cover for resident birds (Northern Mockingbird, American Goldfinch, and House Finch), and migrants (Cedar Waxwing, Purple Finch, and sparrows).

From the parking lot, walk back down the road about 70 yards and turn right onto a blocked path between a spruce grove and an old apple orchard. Some permanent residents along the path include Ruffed Grouse, Hairy and Pileated Woodpeckers, and Field Sparrow. White-throated and Fox Sparrows are regular winter visitors.

Forest Road Loop Trail. Return to the car and backtrack down Hunter Mountain Road to the paved forest road (0.3 miles), turn right, and drive 0.3 miles to where a gravel road begins on the right. The gravel road is blocked by large rocks to prevent vehicle entry (if you come to a powerline cut you are 0.1 miles too far). You can park here and bird a trail loop, about 2.4 miles in length. The trail bisects a wide variety of habitats and offers a good diversity of birds.

Before starting up the trail, check the mature trees along Spruce Brook (just across the road) which can be good for migrants, especially warblers. In spring and summer, Yellow-throated and Red-eyed Vireos, Common Yellowthroat, Blue-winged, Chestnut-sided and Black-and-white Warblers, and other common woodland nesting species are all possible.

The trail first ascends a moderately steep hillside featuring a mixed spruce grove on the right (200 yards). Between May and July, this trail section can be good for Hooded Warblers. They nest nearby, so use caution while searching for these birds. From mid-to-late May, scan the tops of the spruces for migrant Cape May, Bay-breasted, and Blackpoll Warblers. Ruby-crowned Kinglets are usually numerous in spring and fall. In 1985 a Golden-crowned Kinglet spent the summer here and may have nested.

Continuing uphill, the trail skirts a blackberry thicket which produced Mourning and Kentucky Warblers---late May into June is the best time to spot these rarer birds. Other possibilites along the trail include Wild Turkey, Ruffed Grouse, Eastern Towhee, American Redstart, and Scarlet Tanager. The trail tops out at a "T" intersection (about 800 yards from the trailhead). Go left at the "T". In summer, Canada Warbler has been recorded in the mountain laurel thickets that border the trail. Blue-wing/Golden-wing Warbler complex, including the Brewster's hybrid are possible along this trail. Field Sparrow and Rose-breasted Grosbeak are often common. Brown Thrasher was once common, but is now declining as the habitat reverts to woodland.

A pond is on the right, about 0.3 miles down the trail. The open area around the pond provides an opportunity to scan just above the treetops for Northern Goshawk and overhead for Red-shouldered and Red-tailed Hawks and the occasional Osprey. Turkey Vultures soar on warm summer days after departing nest sites on ledges overlooking the Naugatuck River. Check the tops of the dead trees and snags in and along the edges of the pond for Eastern Bluebird at any season, and in summer for Northern Flicker, all of the swallows, blackbirds, and Olive-sided Flycatcher. Eastern Phoebe nest in the up-turned root systems of fallen trees and Eastern Kingbird nest in the taller trees around the pond's periphery. Depending on the season and water level, wading birds might include Great Blue and Green Herons, the latter has nested. Spotted, Solitary, Least, and Semipalmated Sandpipers occur during spring and fall migration. Ducks often spotted at the pond include

Mallard, American Black and Wood Ducks. Least Flycatcher nest in the woodlots near the pond.

After birding the pond, continue along the trail, bear left at the "Y" and head toward the powerline (about 100 yards). If time is tight, you can follow the powerline downhill to emerge at the paved forest road (about 0.4 miles) back near the trailhead. Be careful along this route as many sections are wet, muddy, and slippery. From spring through fall, the shrubby habitat along the powerline can be ideal for Prairie and Yellow Warblers, Indigo Bunting, Field and Song Sparrows, and American Goldfinch. During winter, search the trailside vegetation for Purple Finch, Dark-eyed Junco, White-throated, and Fox Sparrows.

If you continue along the main trail (instead of taking the powerline back to the road), be alert for Chestnut-sided and Nashville Warblers, and both cuckoos (irregular). The woodland along the left side of the trail has produced American Woodcock as late as December. From this point to the sharp right curve about 500 yards further along, the area abounds with wild grape. In season, both the grape and insects they attract provide a food source for Ruffed Grouse, Gray Catbird, Veery, Wood Thrush, Northern Cardinal, Rose-breasted Grosbeak, and a host of other species. Hooded Warblers also occur here regularly. Both Olive-sided Flycatcher and Gray-cheeked Thrush have been observed during fall migration.

If time permits, take the trail on the right which appears about 275 yards along. This trail leads through a red maple shrub swamp to a hemlock and white pine "canyon" (about 400 yards). From spring through summer, this trail supports Eastern Wood-Pewee, Great Crested Flycatcher and Worm-eating Warbler. In the lower "canyon" a river otter was once observed scurrying in and around the rocky ledge as it headed into a small stream.

Return to the main trail and continue downhill to where a small stream parallels the trail. In late spring and summer, Louisiana Waterthrush is common and nest nearby. Northern Waterthrush occurs sporadically during migration. Continue to the small pond on the left where Ruby-throated Hummingbirds have been recorded in the apple trees along its edge. Baltimore Oriole, Scarlet Tanager, Common Yellowthroat, and many other species will be conspicuous (spring-fall) in the vegetation around the pond.

The pine grove beyond the pond can be a good spot for Pine Warbler,

Brown Creeper, and the uncommon Pileated Woodpecker. Broad-winged Hawks have nested in the vicinity in recent summers. Permanent residents in the dry deciduous woods along this trail are Downy and Hairy Woodpeckers, Black-capped Chickadee, Tufted Titmouse, and White-breasted Nuthatch. Wood Thrush, Red-eyed and Yellow-throated Vireos, and Ovenbird are common species from spring to fall. After birding the pond, pine grove, and decidous woods, continue downhill along the trail. The white pine grove on the left, about 150 yards further along the trail, may also yield Pine Warbler. The trail continues down a narrow ravine, paralleling a small brook on the right, then goes over a footbridge into an open bottomland of hemlock, birch and beech. Acadian Flycatcher has been observed along the brook near the foot bridge.

From spring through fall, the open bottomland between the steep ravine slopes can be teeming with bird life. Blue-winged and Chestnut-sided Warblers, American Redstart, Common Yellowthroat, Solitary and Red-eyed Vireoes, Veery, Wood Thrush, and Northern Cardinal are all likely species in this area.

The trail junctions with the paved forest road. To get back to the car, turn left and hike about 0.5 miles back to the parking area. On the way, check the wooded slopes on the right for Worm-eating Warbler, if you have not yet seen or heard one. The more open areas along the way may hold Olive-sided Flycatcher in late May and late August into early September.

To the left of the road is a shooting range (as you may have already heard!). It is difficult to understand why the state sanctioned the construction of a shooting range in the middle of a state forest, especially since the Naugatuck State Forest has traditionally been a major recreational location in the Naugatuck Valley. Between the shooting range and the powerline, the Hooded Warbler can often be located, first by its song and, with persistence, by sight. At the powerline cut check for hawks, Pileated Woodpecker, Gray Catbird, Brown Thrasher, Prairie and Chestnut-sided warblers, Field Sparrow, Indigo Bunting, Baltimore Oriole, and Rose-breasted Grosbeak, before proceeding to your car, which is a further 0.1 miles up the road.

Naugatuck River and Spruce Brook Ravine. To continue birding Naugatuck State Forest, drive down the forest road past the shooting range (that you had just hiked by a few minutes earlier) to the Naugatuck River (0.6 miles) at the bottom of the steep hill. **Note: During winter the forest road is frequently blocked off at the shooting range due to ice conditions.** At the bottom of the hill, park in the lot on the right, just where the forest road makes a sharp right.

From spring into fall, scope the hillsides, rock ledges, and along the river for Turkey Vulture, Northern Goshawk (rare), Cooper's and Sharp-shinned Hawks, Bald Eagle (rare in winter), Broad-winged and Red-tailed (resident) Hawks, and Osprey. Check along the river for waterfowl and gulls. Fish Crows can frequently be heard calling as they fly above the river valley. Common Raven nest further up the Naugatuck River Valley and have been spotted in this area. It should be only a matter of time before ravens start nesting on the secluded ledges high above the Naugatuck River.

A hike north along the railroad track will considerably increase your chances of spotting raptors, as well as waterfowl and other riparian species. **Note, this is a busy railroad, so be careful when hiking near the tracks.** Some of the species that nest, forage, or migrate along the river corridor include Belted Kingfisher and Common Merganser. In late afternoon impressive numbers (30 to 50 birds) of Turkey Vulture thermal above the river valley. Check the soaring birds closely for Black Vulture, another recent visitor to the forest.

After birding along the railroad bed, return to the car and continue along the forest road over Spruce Brook Bridge. About 0.1 miles up the road a sharp right leads to a parking lot. At the back of the lot (northeast corner) is a trail leading to Spruce Brook and into the ravine. The trail follows the brook uphill, deeper into the ravine. The waterfalls and deep pools along the brook are exceptional at any time of year, but are especially stunning in winter, when icefalls and ice ledges are plentiful. Along the trail be on the lookout for Eastern Phoebe, which nests on the moss covered rock outcroppings. Louisiana Waterthrush darts up and down along the banks. It also nests here. This trail is rocky and slippery along its length, so hike with caution.

The 0.3 mile trail along the brook is refreshingly cool even on a hot summer day. The water is clear and cold. The occasional striped maples along the trail reflect the colder microclimate in the ravine. About 200 feet before the trail terminates at Spruce Brook, a small trail branches off to the left and at first slowly, then steeply ascends the north-facing slope of the ravine. Hike this trail for 0.2 miles to where it intercepts a major trail, turn left to return to the car (0.4 miles). You may want to turn right and walk about a quarter mile to a small feeder stream before returning to the car. Birding can frequently be good near the stream.

Climbing from the brook you enter the north facing slope of Spruce Brook Ravine. Bisected by the river, the north slope of this beautiful east-west oriented ravine forms a cool, moist conifer-forested microhabitat. Watch for Winter Wren, Black-throated Green Warbler, Solitary Vireo, and Hermit Thrush. One July day a Northern Saw-whet Owl was heard calling by the feeder stream.

The trail back to the car is steep, but fortunately it's all downhill and in good condition. The bank slopes steeply to the brook 300 feet below along parts of the trail. Past the steep area, the ravine opens up and habitat changes to a mixed woodland. In spring and summer, Worm-eating Warbler, Eastern Wood-Pewee, Great Crested Flycatcher, Veery, Wood Thrush, and Ovenbird are fairly common along here.

Return to the car and continue slowly south along the gravel road which parallels the railroad tracks on the left. Stop occasionally and listen for Worm-eating Warbler along the bedrock slopes and for Warbling Vireo in the cottonwoods and sycamores that line the river. Killdeer and Spotted Sandpipers nest along the small islands and gravel banks of the river. About 0.2 miles from the parking lot, check the sand banks on the right for the round nesting holes of Belted Kingfishers. When the paved road is reached (0.4 miles), continue 0.5 miles to a stop sign. Turn left, cross a railroad overpass and turn left again crossing a steel bridge over the Naugatuck River to arrive at the former Route 8. To access Route 8 north, turn left towards Naugatuck. To head south, turn right and continue towards Seymour.

Twilight and Nocturnal Birding. The forest hosts a variety of nocturnal species: Eastern Screech, Great Horned, Barred, and Northern Saw-whet Owls all have been recorded and are probably permanent residents (although the Saw-whet is rare). Undoubtedly, the Eastern Screech-Owl is the most common owl in the state forest. It can likely be heard calling along Hunter's Mountain Road, especially in the forest-field habitat at the park boundary and along the paved park road near the powerline right-of-way. Great Horned and Barred Owls range throughout the forest and have been seen or heard on Hunter's Mountain Road and along the Naugatuck River. Barred Owl has recently nested near the white pine stand on Hunter's Mountain Road. American Woodcock are common along Hunter's Mountain Road and from April to June can be observed at dusk performing their courtship ritual. Whip-poor-will are fairly common from late-April to August and can be heard along Hunter's Mountain Road, by the park boundary; near the forest loop trailhead; and along the dirt road leading into Spruce Brook Ravine. Common Nighthawks are ironically uncommon, but can be observed performing their aerial maneuvers in pursuit of insects along the Naugatuck river from late May to June. From mid-August to mid-September nighthawks are sometimes abundant, especially on overcast evenings. The nighthawks apparently use the river valley as a migratory corridor.

18 STEVENSON'S DAM

Oxford and Monroe

The flow of the Housatonic River is blocked between the towns of Oxford and Monroe by a large dam known as Stevenson's Dam. This hydroelectric generation station can be accessed from Route 34 which passes directly over the dam. The dam created a large body of water known as Lake Zoar, which can be good from late fall through winter for waterbirds, waterfowl, gulls, and raptors, including Bald Eagle.

DIRECTIONS

From Route 8 take Exit 15 (Route 34 Derby/New Haven) and drive north on Route 34 for 7 miles. Park on the right, just before the road makes a sharp left to cross over the dam.

BIRDING

Walk across the road (Route 34) and scan the base of the dam. **Note: Route 34 is a busy highway so use caution when crossing.** The river at the base of the dam usually harbors a few species of waterfowl including Canada Goose, Mallard, and Common Merganser, but be on the lookout for other species. In early fall and late spring, Double-crested Cormorant is fairly regular and during winter Great Cormorant is occasional. The high vantage point is an ideal site to check for Bald Eagles: Carefully scan the eastern cottonwoods lining the riverbanks for roosting birds and the ridges along the lake and river for soaring eagles. Red-tailed Hawk, Turkey Vulture (scarce December and January), and an occasional accipiter are also possible. Swallows are frequently in abundance during migration and Cliff, Barn, and Northern Rough-winged all nest on the dam or adjacent structures.

Drive over the dam and turn right (0.3 miles) into the Town of Monroe Boat Launch (a pedestrian cross walk sign marks the turn). This area is posted for resident use only but during the off-season no one will bother you. From the boat launch you get a good view of Lake Zoar. Scope the lake for an assortment of regular waterfowl including Mute Swan, American Black Duck, and the species noted above. Less common species to check for on the lake are Common Loon, Horned and Pied-billed Grebes, Snow Goose, American Wigeon, Wood Duck,

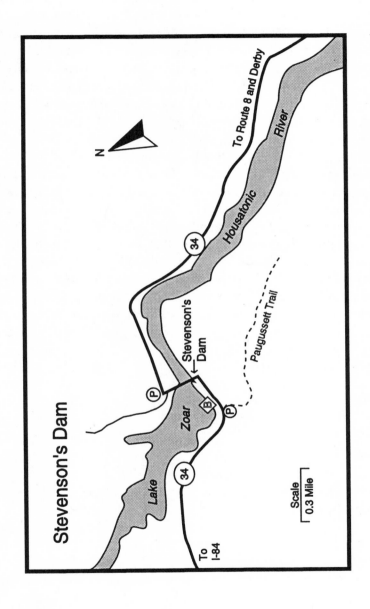

Canvasback, Ring-necked Duck, and Common Goldeneye.

During winter, large concentrations of gulls are found on the ice flows just above the face of the dam. The gulls use the river as a daily migration corridor, traveling between Long Island Sound and inland locations. The gull flocks have yielded an assortment of species. Regular gull attendees include Herring, Ring-billed, and Great Black-backed Gulls, but with close study and a little luck you may find an Iceland, Glaucous, or Lesser Black-backed Gull. All these uncommon gulls occur on an annual basis.

If you have time, hike along the Paugussett Trail which works through the hillside woodlands to the west of the road. The trailhead begins in a parking area located northwest across Route 34 from the boat launch parking area exit. The trail winds toward the south along the western ridge of the Housatonic River and offers splendid views of the river valley from selected lookouts. Species that may be found along the trail from fall to spring include Northern Goshawk (uncommon), Ruffed Grouse, Pileated Woodpecker, and many of the other permanent residents. In summer, Black-and-white Warbler and Eastern Towhee nest beneath the mountain laurel tangles along the trail.

19 COLLIS P. HUNTINGTON STATE PARK

Redding, Bethel, and Newtown

The Collis P. Huntington State Park consists of 878 acres of scenic beauty located primarily in Redding. The park property was gifted to the state by Archer and Anna Hyatt Huntington in memory of her stepfather, Collis P. Huntington, a railroad builder and transportation millionaire. Anna Huntington was a world famous sculptor and also designed the sculptured bears and wolves at the entrance to the park.

Habitat at Huntington State Park mainly consists of upland deciduous woodlands interspersed with wet bottomlands of red maple swamps and shrub thickets. Small streams interconnect the uplands and bottomlands throughout the area. Five ponds, several small conifer plantations, and field edge embellish the limited habitat. This is an undeveloped state park where activities are restricted to nature study, hiking, mountain biking, horseback riding, and the like.

Birding is good during spring and fall migrations. In late spring and summer the park also hosts an assortment of breeding species. Several species with localized distribution in Connecticut nest in this state park including Hooded, Canada, and Black-throated Blue Warblers, and Northern Waterthrush. Some other breeders include Pileated Woodpecker, Barred Owl, White-eyed Vireo, and Worm-eating Warbler. The fall hawk migration (September and October) can be quite impressive on a good day with northeast winds. At these times, members of the Western Connecticut Bird Club and the New England Hawk Watching Association watch for hawks from the field near the park entrance.

DIRECTIONS

From the Merritt Parkway (Route 15) take Exit 45 (Route 58, Redding). Northbound travelers turn right onto Route 58 north (also called Black Rock Turnpike); southbound traffic must take a left at the end of the ramp, drive 0.1 miles and turn right onto Route 58. Follow Route 58 north for 10.8 miles as it winds along the Hemlock and Aspetuck Reservoirs to the junction of Sunset Hill Road on the right. Turn right and drive 0.7 miles to the park entrance on the right.

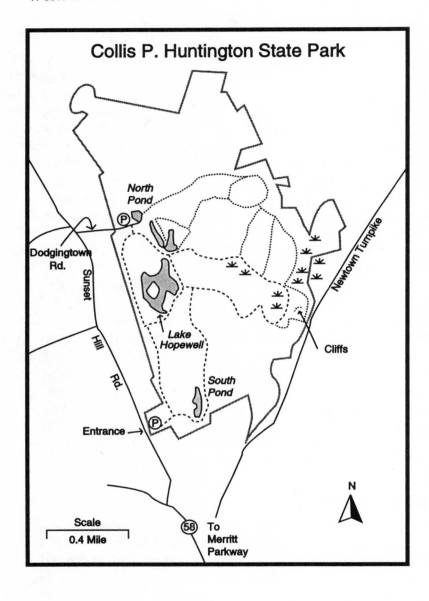

Collis P. Huntington State Park

North
Pond

P

Dodgingtown
Rd.

Sunset

Hill

Rd.

Lake
Hopewell

South
Pond

P

Entrance →

Newtown Turnpike

Cliffs

N

Scale

0.4 Mile

58 To
Merritt
Parkway

Note: Enroute to this locale you drive by two other sites identified in this book: Aspetuck Reservoir (good during fall) and Valley Road (best in spring and summer). Birding these areas may also be coupled with your visit to Huntington State Park.

BIRDING

Approximately eight miles of trail and wood roads traverse the property. Many trails form loops, however the trail marking system at present is poor and it is easy to get "lost" for a period of time. If you have plenty of time you may want to spend the entire day checking most of the trails, if not, we offer the following suggestions. The park can be birded effectively from two areas; (1) from trails that begin near the main entrance or (2) from trails that begin near the north end of the park, off of Dodgingtown Road.

Main Entrance. The parking lot abuts the field used for hawk watching in fall. During September and October, scan the sky for migrants. In 1994, more than 2,000 hawks were observed in 48 hours of watching. The majority of these species were Broad-winged Hawk interspersed with an occasional American Kestrel, Sharp-shinned Hawk, Osprey, Northern Harrier, and a few other raptors.

Walk east through the field to the trail at the base of the hill. Turn left and follow the trail north. This trail skirts fields (private property) and thickets along the park's western boundary. By hiking this trail north for 0.4 miles or so and returning you should find several species that are unlikely elsewhere in the park. Breeding species found along this route include Mourning Dove, Carolina Wren, Northern Mockingbird, White-eyed Vireo, Chestnut-sided and Blue-winged Warblers, Northern Cardinal, Field Sparrow, Indigo Bunting, and Eastern Meadowlark. Hooded Warbler occurs in the section of woodland overlooking Lake Hopewell (also known as Huntington Pond) to the east. Sparrow flocks can be numerous during fall migration. Check the flocks for the regular Dark-eyed Junco, Song, Chipping, Swamp, and White-throated Sparrows, and the less common White-crowned, Lincoln's, and Fox Sparrows.

Dodgingtown Road Section. To get to this part of the park from the main entrance, turn right and continue north on Sunset Hill Road to Dodgingtown Road (1.0 miles), turn right and park along the left side of the road (0.2 miles) by the conifers and slightly before North Pond, also on the left. Walk across the road to where a couple of well-worn paths begin. The paths connect to the main perimeter trail (which is the same trail that continues from the main entrance). Follow the connector path for about 100 yards to the main trail and turn left. This area can turn up Hooded Warbler in summer, and Kentucky Warbler has occurred in the past. Listen for the loud ringing song of both species as you traverse the area. The trail continues through an open deciduous woodland and along the edge of a long pond surrounded by mountain laurel before crossing a wooden bridge between two ponds (Lake Hopewell is on the right). A trail junction is straight ahead.

From spring into fall, check the ponds for Green Heron and Wood Duck. Ring-necked Duck is often spotted during spring migration (March and April). In summer, Eastern Phoebe and Eastern Kingbird foray along the pond's edge in search of aerial insects and Belted Kingfisher stalk fish from perches above the water. During migration, swallows commonly hunt over both ponds. Look for the occasional Northern Rough-winged and Bank among the more numerous Tree (nest) and Barn Swallows.

To bird a two-mile loop-trail (which starts and ends at the trail junction by the ponds), take the left fork and continue straight when a spur trail turns left at the east side of the pond (about 100 yards). From here, the trail parallels a small stream and descends through deciduous woodland dominated by oaks, maples, and birches. Louisiana Waterthrush (migrants and breeder) forage along the streams and bottomlands throughout the forest. Other breeding species found in the deciduous woodlands and shrubby understory are Hairy, Downy, and Red-bellied Woodpeckers, Great Crested Flycatcher, Eastern Wood-Pewee, Wood Thrush, Veery, Red-eyed Vireo, Black-and-white Warbler, Ovenbird, Scarlet Tanager, Rose-breasted Grosbeak, and Eastern Towhee.

At about 0.6 miles along the trail (after passing two other trails to the left) you approach a main trail junction (a trail marker is located at the junction, but all the colors are faded) with a shrub swamp on the right and a small grove of immature hemlocks. From this junction you will eventually turn right to complete the loop back to Lake Hopewell but first bear left and walk over the small knoll to another junction. Turn left and check out the large red maple and shrub swamp that flanks the path. This extensive wetland can yield an assortment of migrants and summer residents. Typical breeding species found in the wetland or the adjacent wood margin are Ruffed Grouse, Tufted Titmouse, Gray Catbird, Common Yellowthroat, Yellow Warbler, American Redstart, Common Grackle, and Song Sparrow. Hooded Warbler and Winter Wren are uncommon, but regular nesters. Several species with localized breeding distributions in the state that may occur here include Canada and Black-throated Blue Warblers and Northern Waterthrush.

Backtrack to the main junction and bear left (a right would retrace your initial route). This trail loops around a wetland surrounded by rock outcroppings. Bear right at the next intersection which will lead back to Lake Hopewell (about 0.5 miles). The open woodland dominated by American beech along this route supports a small nesting population of Worm-eating Warbler. Listen for the Worm-eating Warbler's song----a dry trill with an insect-like quality. Bear right at the next intersection and continue a short distance to the lake, turn right and hike over the hill to where you started the loop walk. Turn left to return to the car. In winter, the pine and spruce groves flanking North Pond to the west and north has held roosting owls. Check the conifers for Great Horned, Barred, and the occasional Northern Saw-whet or Long-eared Owls. Except for the Long-eared Owl, all of these species plus the Eastern Screech-Owl have nested in or adjacent to the park, although the Northern Saw-whet Owl is the rarest of the nesting owls.

20 Lucius Pond Ordway--
(Devil's Den)--Preserve
Weston and Redding

Better known as Devil's Den, this 1720-acre sanctuary is owned by The Nature Conservancy. Devil's Den features over 20 miles of trails that provide access to most of the property. Habitats at the den include extensive tracts of upland hardwoods, hemlock and pines copses, and rocky wooded hilltops. Swamps, mountain laurel thickets, streams, the West Branch Saugatuck River, and Godfrey Pond add habitat diversity. The preserve is open from dawn to dusk throughout the year. Admission to the preserve is free but contributions are appreciated.

Devil's Den can offer good birding during spring and fall migration. Spring is best for migrant passerines while fall migration yields a return of songbirds and also raptors. The preserve hosts a fine assortment of breeding birds. Two breeding species of special interest include the Hooded and Worm-eating Warblers. Both species can be difficult to find within the state, but are fairly common at the preserve.

DIRECTIONS

From the Merritt Parkway take Exit 42 (Route 57, Westport and Weston). Go north on Route 57 for 5 miles and turn right (east) onto Godfrey Road. Follow Godfrey Road 0.5 miles and turn left onto Pent Road, which ends at the parking area for Devil's Den Preserve.

BIRDING

A trail map can usually be obtained at the shelter near the parking lot. If unavailable, check the display map and write down the names of the trails that you plan to bird in the preserve. The many miles of interconnecting trails offer many birding possibilities for each visit. Herein, we offer a hike of about 3-4 miles that encompasses a good portion of the preserve and its variety of habitats. Along this route you should be able to find Hooded and Worm-eating Warblers.

To bird the preserve, take the Laurel Trail to Godfrey Pond. This trail begins at the parking lot. Laurel Trail works through mixed woodlands and past an historic charcoal site and winds downhill to

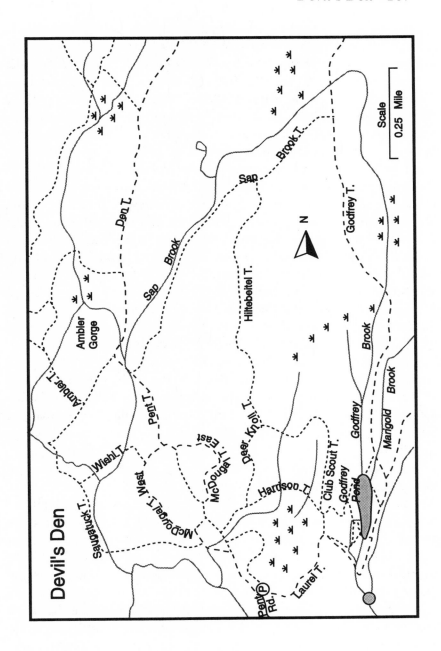

Devil's Den

Godfrey Pond. The open woodlands along this trail and elsewhere throughout much of the preserve offer chickadees, titmice, nuthatches, and several woodpeckers---Downy, Red-bellied, and Hairy throughout the year. In season, check Godfrey Pond for Green and Great Blue Herons, and Belted Kingfisher. Mallards, American Black Duck, Wood Duck and Canada Geese are the most commonly seen waterfowl on the pond. In spring and fall, migrant Osprey may stop briefly at the pond to snare a fish. In early morning and evening hours, the pond can be good for thrushes and sparrows in the brush along the water's edge.

By the pond, turn left on Godfrey Trail which skirts the eastern side of the pond. At the north end of the pond, Godfrey Trail works through a swamp area and crosses Marigold Brook and Godfrey Brook, then continues through wooded bottomlands that can be good for Louisiana Waterthrush in spring and summer. Continue through the woods on Godfrey Trail to just beyond the portable sawmill on the right, then turn left onto Sap Brook Trail (marker 39).

Sap Brook Trail climbs up and down hill through open woodlands with mountain laurel shrubs. From May into June, breeders that can turn up along Godfrey Trail and Sap Brook Trail include Eastern Wood-Pewee, Eastern Phoebe, Great Crested Flycatcher, Veery, Ovenbird, American Redstart and Black-and-white Warbler. Brown Creeper and Winter Wren are often heard in late spring and possibly nest. Worm-eating and Hooded Warblers and Scarlet Tanager sing from the wooded hillsides. Wild Turkey and Ruffed Grouse occur year-round throughout the sanctuary.

Sap Brook Trail junctions with Pent Trail. If you have had enough hiking, a left turn onto the Pent Trail takes you back to the parking lot. To continue birding for another mile or so, turn right onto Pent Trail and take the second left (marker 44) onto the Ambler Trail which loops around Ambler Gorge to the Saugatuck Trail. At this trail junction, turn right and follow the Saugatuck Trail along the floodplain of the West Branch Saugatuck River. A narrow boardwalk provides footage through the worst of the wet spots. The swampy area along the Saugatuck Trail hosts nesting Cedar Waxwings. Connecticut Warbler (rare) has been seen in September near the southern end of the Saugatuck Trail, while Yellow-rumped and Palm Warblers are regular spring migrants. In the breeding season, Wood Thrush, Red-eyed and Yellow-throated Vireos, Ovenbird, and Rose-breasted Grosbeak should be found along the woodland trail.

At the junction of the Saugatuck Trail with the West McDougal Trail, turn right and continue a short distance to the Pent Trail. A right turn onto Pent Trail takes you back to the parking lot. The low, swampy area to the right of Pent Trail is part of the Saugatuck Wildlife Refuge. From spring through summer, Red-winged Blackbirds, Common Grackles, various ducks and Eastern Kingbirds can be heard in and about the trailside wetland. The open area around the snags can also hold breeding Eastern Bluebird.

Raptors found at Devil's Den throughout the year are Great Horned Owl (open woodlands) Barred Owl (in wooded wetlands along the Aspetuck Trail and northern sections of the preserve), and Eastern Screech-Owl (open woodlands near parking lot). Broad-winged Hawk (summer) and Red-tailed Hawk are possible almost anywhere in the open woodlands while Red-shouldered Hawk may nest in the larger tracts of wooded swamp. From the preserve's vistas, Turkey Vultures are usually a common sight. In fall, birders use these overlooks for hawk watching.

In winter, Devil's Den is pretty quiet, but can yield mixed foraging flocks and sometimes Winter Wren. In spring and fall, many migrating warblers, vireos, and thrushes stop over to pause and rest before resuming their journey.

North Section. The northern part of the Devil's Den Preserve should also be checked for birds. Leave the main parking lot and follow Pent Road back to Godfrey Road. Turn left onto Godfrey Road and continue 0.5 miles to Route 53. Turn left at the traffic light onto Route 53 north for 3.7 miles and take a left turn onto Tudor Road. Follow Tudor Road for 0.3 miles and take the first right onto Dayton Road and park in the parking area on the right (0.1 miles).

To bird this area, cross Dayton Road and walk up the driveway to the Pinchbeck Trail, which leads to the Great Ledge Trail. Vistas along the Great Ledge Trail offer spectacular views of the Saugatuck Reservoir. To explore this section, it is best to have a map because there are many side trails that you can get lost on.

A variety of woodland breeding species may be heard and seen in the northern part of the preserve throughout the late spring and summer. Hermit Thrush breeds in the deciduous and mixed woodlands while

Solitary Vireo (uncommon) and Black-throated Green Warbler are closely associated with the hemlock stands. Pine Warbler occurs in the white pine stands near Great Ledge and further south along the trail.

21 VALLEY ROAD

Easton and Redding

Valley Road can be one of the best birding sites in the Western Hills for the spring songbird migration. In summer, Valley Road holds an assortment of woodland and wetland breeding species such as Eastern Screech, Barred, and Great Horned Owls, Pileated Woodpecker, Willow Flycatcher, and Worm-eating Warbler. Fall migration is not as spectacular, but offers a fair selection of transient songbirds.

A two-mile section of road skirts the secluded Aspetuck River Valley and traverses a variety of habitats. Conifer plantations (mostly white pine, some mixed spruce), mixed deciduous woodland, riverine, and shrub swamp offer spring migrants assorted habitat to forage and rest.

DIRECTIONS

From the Merritt Parkway (Route 15) take Exit 45 (Route 58, Redding): northbound travelers turn right onto Route 58 north (also called Black Rock Turnpike); southbound traffic must take a left at the end of the ramp, drive 0.1 miles and turn right onto Route 58. Follow Route 58 north for 6.4 miles to Valley Road. Turn right and drive 0.8 miles to a dirt pull-off on the left (0.2 miles past the junction of Staples Road on the right).

BIRDING

The Bridgeport Hydraulic Company owns most of the property along Valley Road. Access is prohibited so restrict your birding explorations to the area along the public roadway. The white pine woodland and spruce grove near the roadside pull-off attracts migrant Ruby-crowned and Golden-crowned Kinglets, Brown Creeper, Solitary Vireo, and several warblers (Yellow-rumped, Black-throated Green, Blackburnian, and Blackpoll). In summer, Pine Warblers nest in the conifers and Louisiana Waterthrush and Eastern Phoebe breed along the nearby Aspetuck River.

After checking the river and conifers, continue north on Valley Road. At 0.7 miles, bear right at the Y and continue to the stop sign (0.1

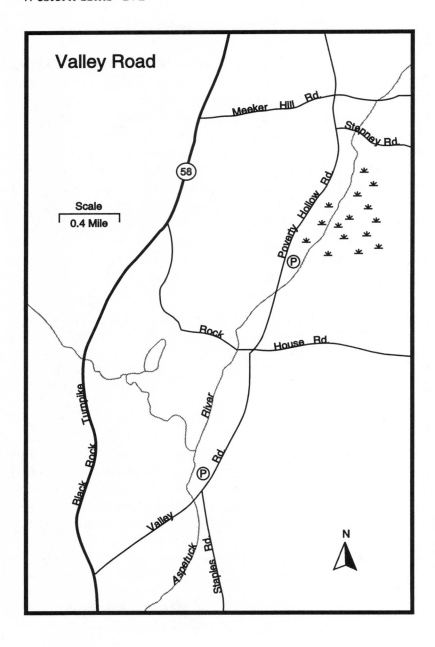

Valley Road

miles). Drive straight across the intersection where Valley Road now becomes a dirt lane. Just past a couple of houses, the road cuts through a deciduous woodland and descends to an open, shrubby wetland. Woodland species found here from mid-spring through summer are Eastern Wood-Pewee, Great Crested Flycatcher, Scarlet Tanager, Red-eyed Vireo, and Rose-breasted Grosbeak. Park before or after the bridge (0.4 miles from stop sign) and spend some time walking the roadway for 0.6 miles or so north, checking the swamp on the right.

The wetland consists of a mix of cattails and other emergent vegetation, shrubs, and scattered snags, and is a premier birding location along Valley Road. This wetland attracts a variety of spring migrants and early summer breeders. Check the open water for migrant waterbirds and shorebirds including Great Blue and Green Herons, Wood Duck (nests), Hooded Merganser (possible breeder), and Solitary and Spotted Sandpipers. In March and April, Rusty Blackbirds can sometimes be numerous as they forage in the swamp vegetation. Check the shrub thickets that line both sides of the roadway for migrant warblers including Wilson's, Mourning (rare migrant from late May to early June), and Palm (early migrant from April to early May). Northern Waterthrush occurs in the swampy areas during migration.

From late spring into summer, the swamp hosts nesting Willow and Least Flycatchers, Eastern Kingbird, Gray Catbird, Yellow and Blue-winged Warblers, Common Yellowthroat, Swamp Sparrow, Red-winged Blackbird, and Common Grackle. Cavities in the standing dead timber provide breeding sites for Northern Flicker, Hairy, Downy, Red-bellied, and Pileated Woodpeckers, Tree Swallow, Black-capped Chickadee, Tufted Titmouse, and Eastern Bluebird. Blue-gray Gnatcatcher, Yellow-throated and Warbling Vireo, Scarlet Tanager, and Baltimore Oriole prefer the live trees around the periphery of the swamp for breeding.

Scan the sky overhead periodically for raptors. Turkey Vulture and Red-tailed, Broad-winged, and Red-shouldered Hawks all nest in nearby woodlands. Accipiters (mainly Sharp-shinned and Cooper's Hawks) are more prevalent during fall migration, but both species also occur in spring and summer.

After birding the swamp, continue north to a deciduous slope just beyond the bridge (0.1-0.3 miles). In spring, the woods can be good for migrant Hermit, Swainson's, and Gray-cheeked Thrushes, and

Northern Parula, Yellow-rumped, Magnolia, and Tennessee Warblers. In late spring and summer, the woods host nesting Veery and Wood Thrush, American Redstart, Ovenbird, and Blue-winged, Black-and-white, and Worm-eating Warblers.

Nocturnal inhabitants along this roadway include Eastern Screech, Barred, and Great Horned Owls, all permanent residents. American Woodcock nest in the area and put on courtship displays from late March to June. Whip-poor-Will (uncommon) is an often vocal summer visitor. Northern Saw-whet Owl occurs sporadically during winter and has been heard calling as late as May. Is nesting a possibility?

To return to Route 58, follow Valley Road (actually Poverty Hollow Road after you entered Redding) north to the intersection with Stepney Road, bear left and take the next left onto Meeker Hill Road. Meeker Hill Road leads to Route 58. If you have time you may want to visit Collis P. Huntington State Park on Sunset Hill Road just off Route 58 a mile or so north of Meeker Hill Road.

22 OSBORNEDALE STATE PARK
Derby and Ansonia

This 350-acre state park is situated on the hills overlooking the Housatonic River near its confluence with the Naugatuck River. Osbornedale State Park offers a mosaic of habitats bisected by a network of trail systems. Habitats within the park include deciduous uplands, successional old fields, pasture and hay fields, hemlock slopes, wetlands, ponds, and brooks.

The best time to visit the park is from spring through fall. Winter is not quite as productive, but even in winter the thickets of rose, sumac, red cedar, and other shrubs provide suitable food that entice quite a good variety of avian species. The nearby Housatonic River affords birding for waterfowl, waterbirds, and swallows.

Within the decade, birding activity at Osbornedale State Park has increased dramatically, resulting in observations of many noteworthy species. Some birds recorded at this state park include Bald Eagle, Short-eared Owl, Pileated Woodpecker, Olive-sided Flycatcher, Fish Crow, Gray-cheeked Thrush, Kentucky and Worm-eating Warblers, Lincoln's Sparrow, and Orchard Oriole.

A checklist of birds and a map of Osbornedale State Park can be obtained at the Kellogg Environmental Center located at the southwest corner of the property. The center features exhibits, restrooms, picnic facilities, and a convenient parking lot. The Kellogg Environmental Center is open Monday to Friday from 8:30 am - 4:00 pm, but the trails are accessible every day from dawn to dusk.

DIRECTIONS

On Route 8 take Exit 15 (Route 34, Derby/New Haven). Follow Route 34 west through the center of Derby and turn right onto Cedric Avenue (1.5 miles). Continue on Cedric Avenue to the "T" junction (0.2 miles) and turn left onto Hawthorne Avenue. Follow Hawthorne Avenue for 0.3 miles to the parking lot entrance for the Kellogg Environmental Center on the left (marked by a sign, Kellogg Environmental Center).

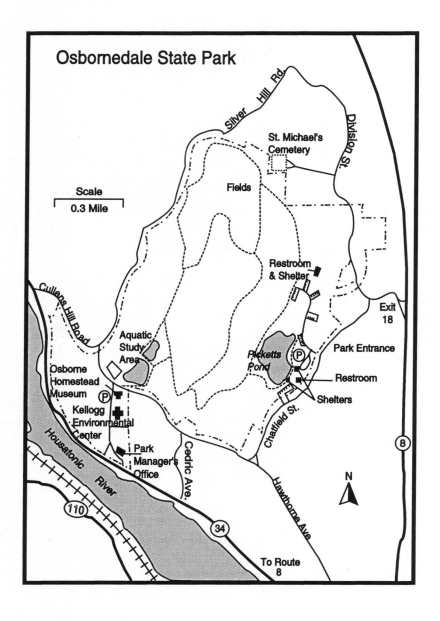

Osbornedale State Park

BIRDING

Kellogg Environmental Center. Park in the lot by the Environmental Center. Near the parking lot in late spring and early summer, listen for the songs of the Orchard Oriole (which nests in the tall trees near the Environmental Center), Brown-headed Cowbird, Carolina Wren, House Wren, Blue Jay, Warbling Vireo, American Robin, Northern Mockingbird, and House Finch. Eastern Bluebird often use the nest boxes placed along the edge of the field. Keep your visit to the Orchard Oriole nesting area brief to avoid disturbing the pair. This oriole is an uncommon nesting species in Connecticut. Ring-necked Pheasant, Killdeer, and Least Flycatcher all may nest in the fields, edge, and landscaped habitats around the Environmental Center or the Kellogg Estate's Gardens. Check the skies above the fields for foraging Chimney Swift. Great Horned Owl has nested in nearby conifers along the edge of the open fields.

Nature Trails. After birding the Environmental Center area, carefully cross Hawthorne Avenue to the trail which begins just across the road. The trail works along the eastern edge of the two Aquatic Study Ponds.

In March, the chorus of spring peepers is enlivened by songs of Red-winged Blackbird and Eastern Phoebe as they proclaim territories around the ponds. By May, the bullfrogs and green frogs provide the musical accompaniment as they "croak" for female attention (the green frog's voice is distinctive and sounds like plucking a banjo string). Scan the shallows along the pond's edge for Great Blue and Green Herons and American Bittern (rare). Likely waterfowl on the pond include American Black Duck and occasionally, Green-winged Teal. American Wigeon, Ring-necked Duck, Bufflehead, and Hooded Merganser are sometimes seen during spring and fall migration. The clumps of bulrush, cattail, and iris around the ponds can hold Solitary and Spotted Sandpipers during migration. At the second pond, an observation bench is available at the end of a short peninsula that juts into the pond. Check the Wood Duck nest boxes for occupancy. Young Wood Ducks are on the pond in late June and may be glimpsed as they follow the adults through the weedy pond vegetation. Barn, Tree, and Northern Rough-winged Swallows forage over the water. Tree Swallows often nest in the bluebird boxes that line the fields. Other species to look for around the two ponds include Eastern Kingbird, Warbling Vireo, Yellow Warbler, Common Yellowthroat, and American Goldfinch. The grassy field on the left (north) of the ponds is good for Ring-necked Pheasant and Field Sparrow. During migration, check the fields for Bobolink, Eastern Meadowlark, and Savannah Sparrow.

From the second pond, a well-maintained grassy trail veers to the right, skirting the pond edge and entering the woods where it junctions with the Red Trail. Turn left on the Red Trail, which first works through mixed hemlock-hardwoods on the hillside to the right and along a small stream. Woodland and edge species are often abundant here and along the stream bed. In summer, look for Eastern Phoebe in the low branches over the stream and Eastern Wood-Pewee, Scarlet Tanager, and Rose-breasted Grosbeak in the trees overhead. Spring and fall migrants include Yellow-rumped Warbler, Ruby-crowned and Golden-crowned Kinglets, and occasionally ,Yellow-breasted Sapsucker (more frequent in April). Listen for the deep, sonorous pounding of the Pileated Woodpecker, a permanent resident which also nests in these woodlands. The Red Trail gradually winds up the wooded hillside. The feeder streams are excellent for Louisiana Waterthrush which nest along the streamside banks.

At the wooden footbridge take the right trail (Yellow Trail) which crosses over the footbridge and continues up the steeper, dryer, wooded slopes. In late spring and summer, listen for songs of Great Crested Flycatcher, Red-eyed Vireo, Ovenbird, Worm-eating Warbler, Veery, and Wood Thrush. In fall and winter, the woods harbor mixed foraging flocks of chickadees, titmice, kinglets, nuthatches, and Brown Creeper (uncommon).

The Yellow Trail forks about 400 yards uphill; the right trail cuts across the hilltop through hemlock woods and eventually leads back to the Red Trail. Take the left trail, which works through dry oak-maple woods and then along an old field edge before junctioning with the Red Trail again. Turn left on the Red Trail which shortly emerges to cross open fields bordered by old stone walls sprouting shrubs and maples. The fields can be good for migrant Eastern Meadowlark and Bobolink, nesting Prairie Warbler, Field Sparrow, and Indigo Bunting. In fall, the hilltop fields are also good hawk watch sites from which to spot a variety of buteos and accipiters as they funnel down along the

Naugatuck and Housatonic river valley corridors that lie on either side of the ridge. The Red Trail reenters the woods and gradually winds back down the hillside past a red maple swamp. This trail section can be good for woodpeckers; Downy, Hairy, Red-bellied and Pileated Woodpeckers are resident species while Northern Flicker and Yellow-bellied Sapsucker (uncommon to rare) are migrants. Beyond the swamp, the Red Trail again passes the wooden footbridge (on the left) where the Yellow Trail began. Continue downhill on the Red Trail, retracing your steps back to the Aquatic Study Ponds. Near the ponds, you can take a trail on the right which crosses the old dam and continues through edge and thicket habitat to emerge on the west side of the ponds. In summer, the edge habitat along the trail can yield Blue-winged Warbler, Carolina Wren, Baltimore Oriole, and other species listed previously.

Picketts Pond. To get to Picketts Pond turn right as you exit the parking lot by the Kellogg Environmental Center. Continue on Hawthorne Avenue for 0.6 miles and turn left onto Chatfield Street. Continue 0.4 miles to the park entrance on the left marked by a sign, Osbornedale State Park. Drive in the entrance, bear left and park by the picnic area near the pond.

In summer, Picketts Pond often hosts a variety of activates; fishing is popular and children feed the Mallards and Canada Geese. Still, the pond is big enough to hold a few surprises and should be checked each time you bird the park. The thin stand of cattails that line parts of the pond are always good for Red-winged Blackbird. Scan the water and edge closely for Tree, Barn, Northern Rough-winged, and Bank Swallows, and Great Blue and Green Herons. In spring and fall, the pond may also harbor American Wigeon, Green-winged Teal, Ring-necked Duck, and occasionally, Hooded Merganser. Virginia Rail has been spotted here also, skulking in the pond-side reeds.

In May, a loop around Picketts Pond can yield an excellent assortment of migrating flycatchers, vireos, and warblers. The east-facing hillside in back of the pond warms up quickly on cool spring mornings and can be teeming with bird activity. To get to the hillside, take the grassy path to the left (south) of the pond by the spillway. The path first traverses a field and then joins the Red Trail by a fork. The left fork continues around the hill and back towards the Aquatic Study Ponds near the Kellogg Environmental Center. Take the right fork, which leads through rose thickets, then a scrubby red maple woodland and then along the wooded slope. Check the thickets carefully for migrant Wilson's and Mourning (rare) Warblers. Breeding species in the thickets and on the adjacent hillside may include Carolina Wren, Brown Thrasher (uncommon), Northern Mockingbird, Black-and-white, Hooded, Worm-eating, Yellow and Blue-winged Warblers, Common Yellowthroat, American Redstart, Ovenbird, and Northern Cardinal.

The trail continues along the backside of the pond and then forks. The right trail leads to a paved road which continues back down toward the picnic area. Follow the paved road downhill along the north end of Picketts Pond. During a good warbler movement the trees and shrubs along this roadway (and also in the picnic area) can produce Northern Parula, Tennessee, Nashville, Palm, Magnolia, Blackpoll, Black-throated Blue, Black-throated Green, Blackburnian, and Yellow-rumped Warblers. Uncommon species to search for include Cerulean, Cape May, and Bay-breasted Warblers.

Typical species that breed in the mix of woodland and edge habitats along this stretch are Least and Great Crested Flycatchers, Eastern Kingbird, Cedar Waxwing, Warbling and Yellow-throated Vireos, Chestnut-sided Warbler, Indigo Bunting, and Brown-headed Cowbird.

23A *SOUTHBURY TRAINING*
SCHOOL POND
Southbury

In recent years, the state owned property at Southbury Training School has drawn increased attention among birders during fall migration, especially in October and November. Each fall, large flocks of migrating Canada Geese are attracted to the pond and lawn habitats at the school by the presence of their more sedentary relatives. The pond is a safe haven from hunting and is also located in the midst of agricultural land the geese use for foraging. The extensive lawns on the property also represent an attractive food supply for the Canada Geese flocks. The large flocks regularly attract unusual stragglers.

DIRECTIONS

From Interstate 84 take Exit 14 (Route 172, South Britain) and follow Route 172 north for 3.1 miles to the Southbury Training School. The pond and ballfield are located on the right just past the power plant with the large smokestack. Turn right into the driveway which leads to the parking lot for the baseball field.

BIRDING

For birders, Southbury Training School is most productive during October and November when large flocks of Canada Geese pause here while migrating to their wintering grounds. The geese use the pond, ballfields and lawns on either side of Route 172 for foraging and resting. Don't be discouraged if the geese are not present when you arrive---wait awhile or return later in the day as the geese come and go on foraging jaunts throughout the day. Some of the flocks can be huge, numbering a thousand or more individuals during peak migration. Carefully study the flocks for Snow Goose (and the occasional blue morph of the Snow Goose) which are uncommon, but regular annual visitors. Rarities that have occurred within the past decade include Barnacle Goose (birds were possible escapees and, therefore, not accepted by the Connecticut Rare Records Committee) and Greater White-fronted Goose (almost annually during the last four years). Other waterfowl likely to be seen at the pond during fall migration include Mute Swan, American Black Duck, Green-winged Teal, American Wigeon, Wood Duck, and Hooded Merganser.

The pond normally freezes over during winter months but the spring thaw often brings a small flock of Ring-necked Duck. Canada Goose numbers are not as impressive in spring, resulting in few reports of rarities. Spring waterfowl variety includes many of the species observed during fall migration.

23B ASPETUCK RESERVOIR
Easton

Aspetuck Reservoir can host a fine assortment of migrant waterfowl especially during fall migration. Constructed in 1914, the reservoir consists of 60 narrow acres approximately 0.8 miles long at its greatest length. Bridgeport Hydraulic Company owns the property and access is prohibited, except near the aeration plant. However, a number of vantage points along the reservoir's length offers good views of the species using the site as staging and feeding grounds. Since 1992, this has been a reliable fall location for Eurasian Wigeon in the large flocks of American Wigeon.

DIRECTIONS
From the Merritt Parkway (Route 15) take Exit 45 (Route 58, Redding); northbound travelers turn right onto Route 58 north (also called Black

Rock Turnpike); southbound travelers must take a left at the end of the ramp, drive 0.1 miles and turn right onto Route 58. Follow Route 58 north as it winds along the Hemlock Reservoir enroute to the Aspetuck Reservoir. At 4.1 miles a small parking lot appears on the right as you approach Aspetuck Reservoir. A sign identifies the reservoir and the large aeration fountain is easy to spot.

BIRDING

Walk over to the reservoir by the aeration fountain. From here you get a good look at the southern end of the reservoir where many species of waterfowl seem to congregate. The initial scan of the water should reveal Mute Swan, Canada Goose, American Black Duck, and Mallard. Other species commonly seen are Ring-necked Duck, American Wigeon, and Common and Hooded Mergansers, the latter sometimes in flocks of 50 or more. Study the American Wigeon closely for its eastern counterpart, the Eurasian Wigeon. The drake Eurasian Wigeon is easily distinguished by its gray body with a red-brown head and buff crown, whereas the female Eurasian Wigeon is more difficult to separate from its western counterpart and requires careful study. In addition to waterfowl, the shrubs and conifers should be checked for migrant passerines including Cedar Waxwing, warblers, and kinglets.

Drive north on Route 58 for 0.5 miles to a pull-off marked by a sign with the elevation (225 feet). This site gives you a good view of the middle stretch of the reservoir, along which many of the same species observed earlier can be spotted. Another good observation site to investigate is at the north end of the reservoir. Drive north 0.2 miles, turn right at Center Road and park on the right near the reservoir. Walk up to where the road bisects the reservoir and check out the open water and adjacent shoreline on either side of the roadway. This site may also yield Wood Duck and Green Heron.

Central Valley

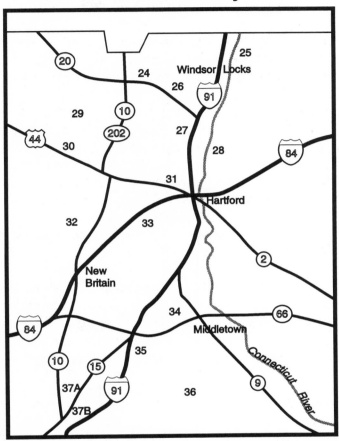

24. Quarry Road
25. Connecticut River in
    Enfield and Suffield
26. Bradley International Airport
27. Northwest Park
28. Station 43
29. Great Pond State Forest
30. Roaring Brook Nature Center
31. Talcott Mountain Reservoir Area

32. Farmington Meadows and
    Shade Swamp Sanctuary
33. Batterson Park Pond
34. Cromwell Meadows Wildlife
    Management Area
35. Black Pond and Bishop Pond
36. Durham Meadows
37A. Sleeping Giant State Park
37B. Quinnipiac River State Park

24 QUARRY ROAD
Granby and Suffield

Quarry Road has been a favorite spring birding haunt of the Hartford Audubon Society for many years. In spring and summer, a short walk along Quarry Road and the old railroad bed (a part of the former Farmington Canal towpath) can produce a nice assortment of migrants and breeding species. Quarry Road in Granby and Suffield is about as far north as you can bird in the state without being in Massachusetts. The road parallels the state line for a short distance before bending sharply around Manitook Mountain. After making the bend, Quarry Road tracks south, skirting the mountain. Manitook Mountain is a prominent traprock structure jutting 400 feet above the surrounding terrain. Evidently, this massive basaltic mountain towering above the surrounding landscape acts like a "magnet" and attracts migrant passerines on their northerly passage.

One interesting historic feature of Quarry Road is the remnants of the former Farmington Canal. You can view a portion of the canal near the intersection of Phelps Road. The canal was built between 1825-1835 to provide a trade route between New Haven and Northhampton, Massachusetts. Unfortunately, the canal proved to be a dismal failure and in 1847 a railroad line was laid over much of the former towpath.

DIRECTIONS
From Interstate 91 take Exit 40 (Route 20, Bradley International Airport) and follow Route 20 west to the intersection with Route 10 in Granby (9.1 miles). Turn right and take Route 10 and Route 202 north for 3.0 miles to Quarry Road at the blinking light. Turn right onto Quarry Road (Notch Road junctures at the same location, so after turning right bear left onto Quarry Road).

BIRDING
From Route 10 follow Quarry Road east for 1.0 miles. At this point you will notice a swampy wetland to the left owned by the Granby Land Trust. Park and bird this section of road for a few minutes. The wetland is interspersed with standing dead white pine that make ideal perches for

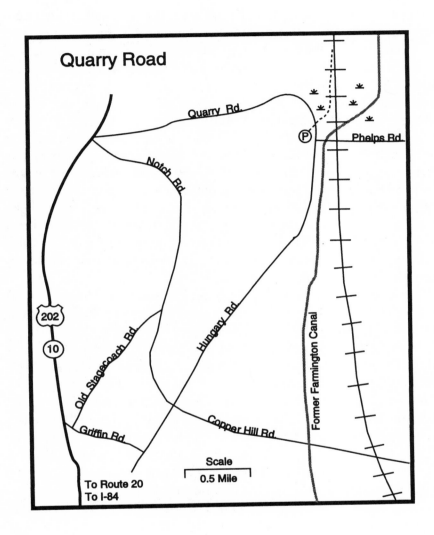

Quarry Road

Quarry Rd.

Phelps Rd.

Notch Rd.

202

10

Old Stagecoach Rd.

Hungary Rd.

Former Farmington Canal

Copper Hill Rd.

Griffin Rd.

Scale
0.5 Mile

To Route 20
To I-84

P

numerous species. Check the dead trees for Red-tailed and Red-shouldered Hawks, Northern Flicker, Eastern Kingbird, and Eastern Bluebird. Gray Catbird, Common Yellowthroat, Common Grackle, and Swamp Sparrow; all of these species nest in the marsh. The white pine grove 50 yards further along the road may support migrant Ruby-crowned and Golden-crowned Kinglets, Black-throated Green, and Blackburnian (probable nester) Warblers.

Continue east on Quarry Road for 0.7 miles and park on the left near the junction of Phelps Road. This stretch of roadway (approximately 0.4 miles south and 0.2 miles north from the parking area) and the old railroad bed are the premier birding sites on Quarry Road. Take note of Manitook Mountain with its jagged talus slope immediately to the right. The quiet river on the left is actually a fragment of the former Farmington Canal. Quarry Road received its name from the quarry which was once operated in this area. Do not venture into the quarry area because the property is posted.

Backtrack on Quarry Road for 0.1 miles and turn right onto a dirt road/trail leading to the former railroad bed. Breeding birds along this trail should include Blue-gray Gnatcatcher, Veery, American Redstart, Blue-winged and Yellow Warblers, and American Goldfinch. Follow the railroad bed north a short distance as it bisects a wetland marsh. Nesting species occurring along this stretch include Green Heron, Eastern Phoebe, Least Flycatcher, Tree Swallow, Tufted Titmouse, Eastern Bluebird, and Red-winged Blackbird. Migrant flycatchers (Olive-sided is rare in mid-to-late May), thrushes, and warblers can be found in late April through late May. Check the thickets along the stream for Palm (April and early May),Wilson's (uncommon), and the rarer Mourning Warblers (late May and early June).

After birding along the railroad bed return to Quarry Road and walk south. Common Raven has been spotted many times and may nest on the jagged cliffs, as does Great Horned Owl. The mixed woodland on the mountain slope supports breeding flycatchers, Wood Thrush, Red-eyed Vireo, Black-and-white Warbler, Scarlet Tanager, and Rose-breasted Grosbeak. The trees along the stream may contain Warbling and Yellow-throated Vireos, Louisiana Waterthrush, and Baltimore Oriole. Some interesting migrants spotted along this area include Yellow-bellied Flycatcher, and Cape May, Blackburnian, and Bay-breasted Warblers.

25 CONNECTICUT RIVER

Enfield and Suffield

A trip to the Connecticut River in Enfield and Suffield has become an annual winter pilgrimage for many state birders. Wintering Barrow's Goldeneye and Bald Eagle are the primary attractions at this locale, although gulls and other waterbirds are usually present. The Town of Enfield hosts the best areas for viewing birdlife along the river, but the Suffield Boat Launch can be a worthwhile stop.

DIRECTIONS

From Interstate 91 take Exit 46 (King Street/ Route 5) to Route 5 north. Take the first left onto Old King Street (0.3 miles) and continue 0.3 miles to Parsons Road, turn left, and travel 0.3 miles (just past railroad tracks) to where a sign announces Kings Island Wildlife Management Area on the left. Turn left into the boat launch parking area.

BIRDING

Kings Island WMA and Enfield Boat Launch

From the parking lot and boat launch you can get a good view of the Connecticut River and King's Island, just south (slightly down river) of the boat launch. Every winter the Connecticut River in the Enfield area harbors a small winter population of Bald Eagles. Scan along the river carefully for this raptor. When foraging, eagles can be spotted flying up and down the river stalking prey. When resting, the eagles are usually in the trees on the island and along the far shoreline.

When not looking for eagles, check the waterfowl. Waterfowl often on the river include Mallard, American Black Duck, Bufflehead, Common Merganser, and Common Goldeneye. Study the Common Goldeneye flocks for Barrow's Goldeneye, which has been observed annually since the winter of 1987-88. Gulls may also frequent the river.

Eastern Screech-Owl (red and gray phases have been observed) can sometimes be spotted sunning at the entrance to cavities in the red maple and sycamores around the boat launch area and especially along the north edge of the ramp. Red-tailed Hawk, Red-bellied, Hairy, and Downy Woodpeckers, Tufted Titmouse, White-breasted Nuthatch,

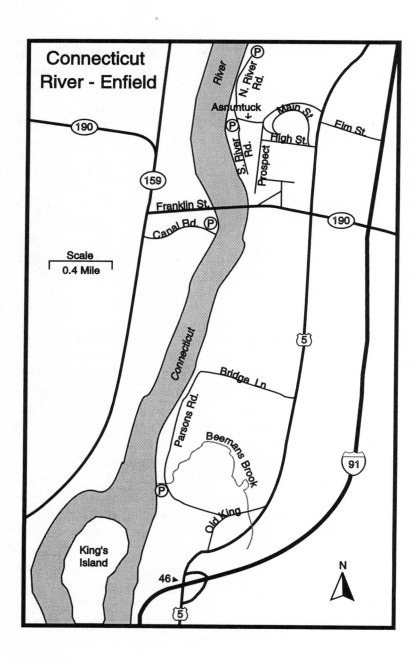

Carolina Wren, and Northern Cardinal can also be tallied in the trees and shrubs along the shoreline.

Thompsonville Boat Launch

If you can't find Barrow's Goldeneye or Bald Eagle at the Enfield Boat Launch, try further north along the river. To get to other sites, return to Parsons Road, bear left and follow the road 1.4 miles north to Route 5 (Parsons Street becomes Bridge Lane at the sharp right turn, crossing over the railroad tracks). Parsons Road parallels the river until it becomes Bridge Lane. Along the way, stop and scan the river at any likely overlook. Barrow's Goldeneye is sometimes spotted on the river along the north section of Parsons Road, before the road cuts across the railroad tracks.

At Route 5, turn left (north) and travel 1.6 miles, turn left at the light onto High Street. Take High Street until it ends (0.2 miles), turn right onto Prospect Street and take the first left at Asnuntuck Street. Follow Asnuntuck Street beneath the railroad overpass to the Thompsonville Boat Launch straight ahead (0.2 miles).

The boat launch provides an excellent view of the river. Common Goldeneye and other waterfowl can usually be observed on the river to the north of the boat ramp. Check the goldeneyes carefully for Barrow's Goldeneye. Ring-billed, Herring, and Great Black-backed Gulls are usually present. Close scrutiny of the gulls may also reveal a white-winged variety (Iceland or Glaucous), as both species have been reported from the area. Bald Eagle is also regular at this locale.

For another view of the river, return to the railroad overpass, turn left onto South River Street (which shortly becomes North River Street) and travel 0.5 miles to a cul-de-sac at a natural gas pumping station. This area overlooks the river and may include the same species listed previously. Unfortunately, trees obstruct the view of the river at this site, therefore, you have to move around to find the best view.

Suffield Boat Launch

The Suffield Boat Launch offers a view of the Connecticut River from the west. To get to this boat launch from North River Street, return to the junction of High Street and Route 5, turn right and follow Route 5 south 0.4 miles. At Route 190, turn right (west) and travel 1.0 miles across the bridge to Route 159, turn left, and left again (0.2 miles) onto Canal Street. Follow Canal Street down to the parking area near the river (0.4 miles).

From the parking area follow the dirt road toward the Route 190 Bridge. The dirt road leads to an unimproved boat launch beneath the bridge which provides a good vantage point to scope the river. Check for the same species listed for the Enfield side of the river.

From April through November, you can bird along part of the former Enfield Canal dike. The pathway along the dike begins about 100 yards south of the parking lot by the river. Access to the dike and canal area is restricted from December through March to protect the wintering Bald Eagles.

26 BRADLEY INTERNATIONAL AIRPORT
East Granby, Suffield, and Windsor Locks

The open habitat that surrounds Bradley International Airport attracts a variety of grassland birds, especially since most of the state's natural grasslands have fallen victim to urban development as well as natural processes of ecological succession which convert them into deciduous woodlands.   The airport's maintained grasslands offer nesting habitat for two of Connecticut's rarer species, the Upland Sandpiper and Grasshopper Sparrow.   Other interesting grassland species that nest at the airport include Savannah Sparrow, Horned Lark, Bobolink, and Eastern Meadowlark.

During migration the open grasslands around the airport have attracted such rarities as Western Kingbird and Scissor-tailed Flycatcher.   Fall migration can be productive for sparrows along the grassland and edge habitats.   With good hawk migration weather, in September and October, a variety of hawks may be spotted.

DIRECTIONS
From Interstate 91 take Exit 40 (Route 20, Bradley International Airport) onto Route 20 and follow the road west toward the airport for 2 miles.   Take the Route 75 exit, turn right and follow Route 75 north for 2.8 miles.   This road parallels the eastern boundary of the airport. As you approach the end of the airport look for the New England Air Museum sign on the left.   Turn left onto Perimeter Road, which is just past the sign.   The 1.8 mile stretch of road to the New England Air Museum is the best area for birding at the airport.

BIRDING:
Airport---North End. Set the odometer when you turn onto Perimeter Road.   While this stretch of road can be excellent for the specialty species, parking is restricted, so it is best to park at the Connecticut Fire Academy (1.5 miles) and walk back along the road a mile or so toward Route 75.   The grassland south of the road is the best area for Upland Sandpiper and Grasshopper Sparrow.   You may also elect to park at the New England Air Museum (1.8 miles) and hike west along the road. If you bird from the car or park along the road in restricted areas,

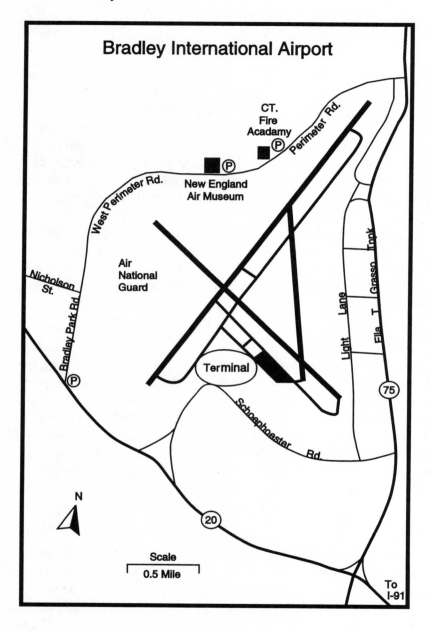

Bradley International Airport

security will come by periodically and prompt you to move along.

Upland Sandpiper generally arrive on their breeding territories in late April.   Once the species has established territory it is easier to locate; listen for the eerie but beautiful courtship song (mainly heard at dawn and shortly thereafter) as you drive or walk the road.   From May through July, listen for the faint, almost insect-like song of the Grasshopper Sparrow which consists of two short introductory notes followed by an insect-like buzzing *pi-tup-zeeeeeeee*.   The somewhat similar *tsit-tsit-tsit,tseeee-tsaaay* song is that of the Savannah Sparrow, which also nests in the airport grassland.

The knoll (0.8 miles from Route 75) is a good area to find the Grasshopper Sparrow and Upland Sandpiper.   You can usually park just beyond the knoll, in the gravel area on the right, for a short period of time without drawing attention to yourself.   Another good location for Upland Sandpiper is at 0.3 miles from the knoll, where the perimeter fence juts at a sharp angle to the left.   Brown Thrasher may also occur at this location.

Scout the fields and edge for sparrows, Bobolink, and Eastern Meadowlark in late spring and summer.   During fall migration (October/November), sparrows (Savannah, Field, White-crowned, White-throated, Swamp, and occasionally, Vesper) can be encountered.

In the breeding season a nice mix of species occurs here.   Check the grassland and woodland edge for Eastern Kingbird, Willow Flycatcher (occurs in the wet area with small willows located 0.6 miles from Route 75), warblers (Blue-winged, Yellow, Chestnut-sided, American Redstart, and Common Yellowthroat), Swamp Sparrow, Baltimore Oriole, and blackbirds.   Red-tailed Hawk and American Kestrel are sometimes spotted in the trees along the airport edge or soaring overhead.

Airport---South End.   If you have not yet located Upland Sandpiper or Grasshopper Sparrow, two other sites at the airport are worth checking. From the New England Air Museum, drive west on Perimeter Road to the stop sign (0.7 miles), then continue straight through on West Perimeter Road to the next stop sign (0.4 miles) at the entrance to the Connecticut Air National Guard.   Turn right, and then take an immediate left (0.1 miles) onto Bradley Park Road to the traffic light at

Route 20 (0.5 miles). Turn left onto Route 20 and continue 0.3 miles to a dirt parking area on the left. Parking is permitted at this site.

From the parking lot you can scan the short grass area near the runway for the Grasshopper Sparrow and Upland Sandpiper. Another uncommon state nesting species at this location is Horned Lark. Formerly Vesper Sparrow nested here, but breeding has not occurred for several years. Occasionally, Vesper Sparrow can be found during spring and fall migration.

Airport---East End. If you still haven't spotted a Grasshopper Sparrow or Upland Sandpiper try the eastern side of the airport (you already drove by this area enroute to the north end). To get to the east end of the airport, take Route 20 east for 1.6 miles and exit at Route 75. Follow Route 75 north for 0.7 miles, turn left onto Schoephoester Road and take an immediate right onto Light Lane. Birding along this lane which runs between the airport and Route 75 has also yielded Grasshopper Sparrow and Upland Sandpiper. The beginning stretch of Light Lane cuts across the aircraft approach zone, therefore, lingering here in a car or on foot is strictly prohibited. It is best to drive slowly along, looking for the birds. Once outside the approach zone (about 0.3 miles), you can stop briefly and scout the area from your car.

Grasshopper and Savannah sparrows have been spotted near the beginning of Light Lane (between 0.2 and 0.4 miles from Schoephoester Road). The field to the left, past the first stop sign (0.5 miles from Schoephoester Road) has been fairly consistent for Upland Sandpiper in late July and August. Mourning Dove and Killdeer also nest and forage here and elsewhere on the airport grasslands.

27 NORTHWEST PARK

Windsor

Northwest Park is a 473-acre recreational park owned and operated by the Town of Windsor. The park contains a Nature Center open Monday-Thursday from noon to 5:00 pm, and Saturday from 10:00 am until 4:00 pm. In July and August, the center is open from Monday to Friday from 9:00 am to 5:00 pm. Within the Nature Center are seasonal exhibits, live animals, a nature library, and gift shop. Other features of the park include an animal barn, sheltered picnic areas, a maple sugar house and an impressive trail network. Picnicking, hiking, cross-country skiing, and biking are favorite past times at the park. Maps, self-guided trail brochures, and additional information are available in the Nature Center.

Another interesting feature of the park is the Gordon S. Taylor Tobacco Museum, established in 1991, by the Connecticut Valley Tobacco Historical Society, in cooperation with the Town of Windsor. The tobacco museum is open Tuesday, Wednesday, Thursday, and Saturday, from noon until 4:00 pm (except holidays), from March 1 to December 15. The museum and archives provide a glimpse of the culture and history of the tobacco industry that once dominated this part of the Connecticut Valley.

Northwest Park has eight miles of well marked and maintained trails. The trail network traverses a diversity of scenic habitat including former tobacco fields, reverting fields, deciduous and coniferous woodlands, a small hemlock ravine, pond, shrub swamps, wooded swamps, brooks, and the Farmington River (Rainbow Reservoir). Trails at the park are open from dawn to dusk.

The varied habitat at the park can provide good birding throughout the year. Spring migration offers the best birding but the park also hosts a nice assortment of specialty breeding species such as Eastern Bluebird, Grasshopper and Field Sparrows, Indigo Bunting and Orchard Oriole. Northwest Park is relatively unknown to the birding community and has received limited coverage in the past; however, the park's birding potential has been highlighted with the discovery of singing Clay-colored Sparrow and Blue Grosbeak in late-May and June 1995.

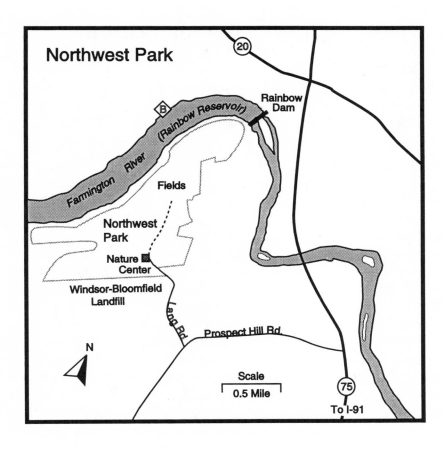

Northwest Park

DIRECTIONS

Northbound on Interstate 91 take Exit 38 (Route 75, Poquonock), turn right and follow Route 75 north for 1.6 miles to Prospect Hill Road on the left. Traveling southbound on Interstate 91 take Exit 38A and 38B (Poquonock and Windsor) and bear right as the exit splits. Turn right at the end of the exit ramp and continue north on Route 75 for 1.3 miles to Prospect Hill Road. Turn left, and follow Prospect Hill Road to the rotary (1.1 miles), bear right, and continue on Lang Road to where it deadends at the park.

BIRDING

From the parking lot walk north and follow the gravel path past the information board and Elan Pond to the Nature Center (a red, refurbished tobacco barn). If open, you can obtain a trail guide and other literature in the center. If the center is closed, trail maps and park brochures are available in the information stand just left of the front door.

You can start birding right at the center. In late spring and summer, the shade trees around the nature center and private residence contain Eastern Kingbird, Northern Mockingbird, House Finch, Chipping Sparrow, and Orchard and Baltimore Orioles. Eastern Bluebirds are plentiful in the area due to the active nest box program. Check the nest boxes around the center and in the nearby fields for bluebirds, as well as Tree Swallows, House Wrens, and House Sparrows which all utilize the boxes for rearing young.

The fields north of the nature center contain a variety of interesting breeding species. To bird the fields walk north along the gravel road past the animal barn. Some of the birds that breed in the scrubby fields on either side of the gravel road include Brown Thrasher, Blue-winged and Prairie Warblers, Red-winged Blackbird, Field Sparrow, Indigo Bunting, and American Goldfinch. A small population of Grasshopper Sparrow nest in these fields. This species, identified as endangered by the Connecticut DEP, is a rare breeder in the state. In late May and early June of 1995, a Clay-colored Sparrow was found singing in this area. Blue Grosbeaks occurred in June, 1995, and nested in the summer of 1996 for the state's first breeding record. A pair of Dickcissels probably nested here in 1996.

In fall (mainly October), check the fields and edges for migrating sparrows including Savannah, Song, Swamp, White-throated, Chipping, and American Tree (fall and winter), and the less common, but regular White-crowned and Lincoln's Sparrows.

The Rainbow Reservoir Trail starts near the northeast corner of the last field to the northeast and flanks a small hemlock ravine before skirting deciduous forest along the Rainbow Reservoir. Louisiana Waterthrushes reside in the ravine during summer and in late May you may get lucky and find a migrant Yellow-bellied Flycatcher in this area. Other species found during the breeding season along this trail and throughout the deciduous and mixed woodlands of the park are Great Crested Flycatcher, Eastern Wood-Pewee, Eastern Phoebe, Wood Thrush, Veery, Red-eyed and Yellow-throated Vireos, Ovenbird, American Redstart, Scarlet Tanager, and Rose-breasted Grosbeak.

The Softwood Forest Trail at the north end of the park traverses a mature stand of white pine and eastern hemlock. Pine Warbler and Brown Creeper nest in this area, as well as the elusive Pileated Woodpecker. This is also a good area to check for Great Horned and Barred Owls, both are permanent residents. The owls are regularly seen in this area and along the Hemlock Trail in the southwest corner of the park. During spring, look for migrant Golden-crowned and Ruby-crowned Kinglets, warblers, and thrushes in this woodland.

In the southwest corner of the park, the Bog Trail encircles a small, but active shrub swamp. This thicket and surrounding edge harbors breeding Gray Catbird, Cedar Waxwing, Common Yellowthroat, Yellow Warbler, Common Grackle, and Northern Cardinal while Palm and Wilson's Warblers and Northern Waterthrush occur during migration.

Permanent residents found year-round include Ruffed Grouse, Mourning Dove, Downy, Hairy, Pileated (uncommon), and Red-bellied Woodpeckers, Blue Jay, Carolina Wren, Black-capped Chickadee, Tufted Titmouse, White-breasted Nuthatch, Northern Mockingbird, Eastern Bluebird, Northern Cardinal, American Goldfinch, and Song Sparrow.

Windsor-Bloomfield Landfill. This landfill abuts the southwest region of Northwest Park and can be accessed from the Bog Trail (also referred to as the Brail Trail). Take the Bog Trail (clockwise) about half-way around the wetland---upon climbing a slight hill along the trail you will encounter an opening that leads to the left. This path leads to the landfill, where numerous species of gulls frequent the landfill from fall through spring. Check the gulls for rare stragglers, such as Iceland and Lesser Black-backed, both of which occurred in April, 1995. Turkey Vulture and Fish Crow are usually present in the area throughout the year.

28 STATION 43

South Windsor

Members of the Hartford Audubon Society praise Station 43 as one of the premier birding locations in north-central Connecticut. This unique locale has produced an outstanding assortment of rarities throughout the years primarily due to an array of extensive wetlands and its strategic location along the Connecticut River, a prime bird migration artery through the state's interior.

Birding habitats at Station 43 include deciduous woodlot, shrub wetland, old fields, agricultural land (predominately corn and potato fields), meadows, magnificent freshwater marshes, sedge pockets, small ponds, the river, and its flood plain. The wetlands provide important nesting habitats and also function as post-breeding dispersal areas for many wetland species.

The Hartford Audubon Society owns about 10 acres of the wetland habitat (primarily a pond and adjacent wetland formed by the sluggish flowing Newberry Brook) north of Newberry Road at Station 43. Vibert Road can be accessed by vehicle and terminates at a state boat launch on the Connecticut River. Most of the property at Station 43 is private land but local farmers permit access to birdwatchers. Hunting begins after the third Saturday in October, and it is advisable to wear bright clothing during the hunting season.

Least Bittern, Sora, King (rare) and Virginia Rails head the list of specialties for Station 43. Some of the rarities seen include American White Pelican, Wood Stork, Tundra Swan, Barrow's Goldeneye, Black Vulture, Golden Eagle, Purple Gallinule, Sandhill Crane, Buff-breasted and Stilt Sandpipers, Whimbrel, Wilson's Phalarope, Western Kingbird, Northern Shrike, Yellow-headed Blackbird, and Clay-colored Sparrow.

Spring is good for waterfowl and other wetland species while fall migration brings a return of waterfowl, along with shorebirds, passerines, and a variety of hawks and owls. Station 43 also supports an interesting array of breeding species that have localized breeding distributions in the state. Midsummer is often good for post-breeding families of marsh and waterbirds which become more visible as the young learn how to ply their trade while the adults watch anxiously nearby.

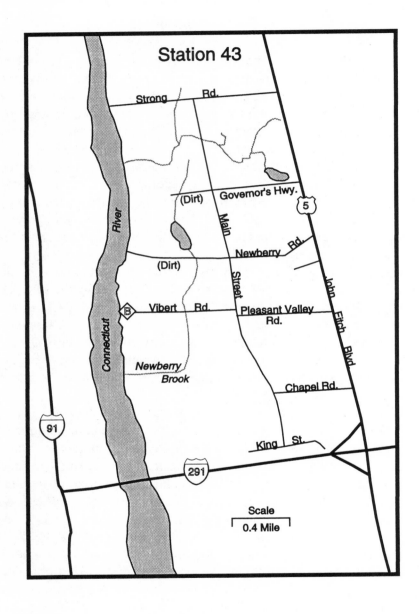

DIRECTIONS

From Interstate 91 northbound take Exit 35A - 35B (Interstate 291, South Windsor) and bear right on Exit 35A. Southbound traffic on Interstate 91 take Exit 35A (Interstate 291, Bissel Bridge). Both exit ramps merge with Interstate 291. Follow 291 about 2.4 miles to Exit 4 (Route 5, John Fitch Blvd.). At the bottom of the exit ramp turn left and follow Route 5 (northbound) 1.6 miles to Newberry Road (0.3 miles past MacDonald's). Turn left at Newberry Road and proceed 0.6 mile to the stop sign at Main Street. Newberry Road continues straight ahead as a dirt road directly across the intersection.

BIRDING

Station 43 can be birded by using a variety of strategies depending on the amount of time you have available. Two methods seem to work best: you can walk down Newberry Road to the pond and/or the field edge and return (about 0.8 miles round-trip) to your car and explore Vibert Road. Alternately, take a loop walk by following Newberry Road to the Connecticut River, bear left and hike the river bank south for 0.4 miles, then pick-up Vibert Road and return to Main Street (this loop trip is about 2.4 miles). If time permits, plan to bird Governor's Highway and Strong Road. Both of these roadways are just to the north of Newberry Road and can also be accessed from Main Street.

Newberry Road. To bird Newberry Road, park near the intersection of Newberry Road and Main Street and walk along the dirt roadway west toward the river. Do not block the road, as it is often used by local farmers. Due to the wet conditions at this locale (especially in spring and fall), it is advisable to wear protective footgear. Along the way, the road bisects hedgerows and wet thickets that can be productive throughout the year but provide good habitat for sparrows during fall migration (primarily October and early November). Sparrows to look for here include Savannah, Field, Song, Lincoln's (uncommon), Swamp (nest), White-crowned, White-throated, Fox (uncommon), and American Tree (mid-October throughout winter). Several unusual sparrows sometimes occur in the flocks; Saltmarsh Sharp-tailed and Clay-colored have been spotted. When birding the road from mid-

September through mid-October check the thickets carefully for Connecticut Warbler, a species that has occurred sporadically over the years. Typical summer species of the thicket and hedge areas include Eastern Phoebe, House Wren, Carolina Wren, Tufted Titmouse, Northern Mockingbird, Northern Cardinal, and Chipping Sparrow among a variety of others.

About 0.3 miles down the dirt road you will come upon a black willow grove on the right. Beyond that to the right (north) is a short marsh of pickerelweed surrounding a small open pond which is in turn surrounded by shrub swamp of buttonbush. On the left (south) side of the road is a tallgrass marsh habitat of purple loosestrife---gorgeous in flower--- and cattails interspersed with scattered clumps of tall wild rice. This varied combination of wetland habitats can host an attractive variety of species. Green Heron, Least Bittern, Wood Duck, Common Moorhen (species sporadic was more regular in the past), Sora, Virginia Rail, Willow Flycatcher, Marsh Wren, and Swamp Sparrow are all likely. All of these species nest or have nested here in recent years. The elusive King Rail occurs during migration and sometimes in the breeding season as well. From late May into July, the drab green and brown marsh vegetation is accentuated by small scattered patches of blue flag and yellow flag. Take a few minutes to study and enjoy these lovely flowers.

During spring and fall migrations, check the pond for Snow Goose (uncommon), American Black Duck, Green-winged and Blue-winged Teals, Northern Pintail (uncommon), Northern Shoveler (uncommon), American Wigeon, Ring-necked Duck, and Hooded Merganser. Tundra Swan and Eurasian Wigeon are rarer species that have occurred here. The Pied-billed Grebe has also proven a regular visitor during this period. Spring migration brings a nice compliment of shorebirds; look for Common Snipe (March and April), American Woodcock (courting from late March until July), Killdeer, and Pectoral, Spotted, and Solitary Sandpipers, and Greater and Lesser Yellowlegs. In fall, many of the same shorebirds return. In addition, the rarer Buff-breasted and Upland Sandpipers and American Golden-Plover sometimes make an appearance in the adjacent farm fields.

Beyond the wetlands, the road continues through farm fields, meadows, and small woodlots as a tractor path for another 0.4 miles to the river. The property becomes private after leaving the wetland, but the local farmers allow access to birders. Please respect the right of the property owners. Breeding species along this path include Northern Flicker, Red-bellied Woodpecker, Eastern Kingbird, Ceder Waxwing, Gray Catbird, Wood Thrush, Yellow Warbler, Common Yellowthroat, Field Sparrow, Common Grackle, Bobolink, and Eastern Meadowlark.

Raptors are usually present throughout the year. Permanent residents include Red-tailed Hawk, American Kestrel (uncommon) and Great Horned and Eastern Screech Owls. During winter, the meadow and cropland harbor Sharp-shinned Hawk (uncommon), and occasionally, Northern Harrier or Rough-legged Hawk. Bald Eagle is an uncommon to rare winter visitor usually observed foraging along the river. Spring and fall raptor migrations often produce Osprey, Broad-winged and Red-shouldered (both nest nearby) Hawks, Merlin, Cooper's Hawk, and sometimes, Peregrine Falcon.

Vibert Road Section. Also known as Station 39, this area takes its name as a stop on the former trolley line. From the intersection of Main Street and Newberry Road, follow Main Street 0.4 miles south and turn right onto Vibert Road. Vibert Road is paved for the first 0.3 miles, then becomes dirt at the town's water pollution control plant and remains a dirt/gravel road to the boat launch. The birdlife along this road is similar in composition to the species found at Newberry Road. Bobolink nest in the field across the road from the wastewater treatment plant.

At 0.4 miles from Main Street the road crosses Newberry Brook, a slow flowing stream supporting a cattail marsh north of the bridge and tussock sedge habitat south of the bridge. During spring and fall, this area is good for locating the same species of waterfowl and shorebirds as mentioned above. In addition, Blue-winged Teal occurs regularly during migration and may nest in the marsh. Scout the field edges for Ring-necked Pheasant and Wild Turkey, both species like to feed on residual corn left behind by the farmers. Also, in October, scan the cornfields closely for American Pipit which can be difficult to see when they are in the furrows.

Park in the lot on the left at the end of the road. Check the river for waterfowl and gulls. In winter, Common Goldeneye (uncommon) and Common Merganser occur on the river and with good luck you may find a Barrow's Goldeneye. During summer, the silver maples and undergrowth that line the riverbank provide cover for Least Flycatcher, Warbling Vireo, American Redstart, and Baltimore Oriole. Walk the dirt road between the riverbank and farm fields north for about 0.3 miles to a river overlook. This area is good to view swallows (Tree, Barn, and occasionally, Northern Rough-winged). Belted Kingfishers and Bank Swallows have nested in the riverbank along here.

Governor's Highway. To get to Governor's Highway follow Main Street from Newberry Road 0.5 miles north and park near the intersection of Governor's Highway. Cross the street and walk down the dirt road between the house and horse corral. The road is posted with no trespassing signs but is open to birders.

The road passes between a wooded area good for all of the woodland species mentioned above. At about 0.2 miles there is a marsh on both sides of the road. The open water marsh on the right (north) of the road is ringed by cattail and tussock grass with a shrubby buttonbush border.

The low marsh to the left (south) is comprised of pickerelweed with its showy blue-purple flowers in summer. Again, this area is good for post breeding dispersal in summer. Some of the birds likely to be seen here in midsummer include Willow Flycatcher, Black-crowned Night-Heron, Great Blue Heron, Swamp Sparrow, Belted Kingfisher, Wood Duck, and American Black Duck.

Strong Road. From Governor's Highway, Strong Road can be reached by travelling north on Main Street for another 0.6 miles. Strong Road is on the left, toward the river. Like Newberry Road and Governor's Highway, Strong Road is a farmer's access way, so don't block the roadway.

Habitats along Strong Road include a small scrubby woodland and farm fields. Check the woodlot for woods and edge species listed previously. In fall the plowed fields are good for American Pipet (mainly October) and shorebirds such as Killdeer. In spring, seasonal rain pools in the fields hosts good numbers of Common Snipe. Cattle Egret have also been spotted in these fields. Strong Road concludes your birding tour of Station 43.

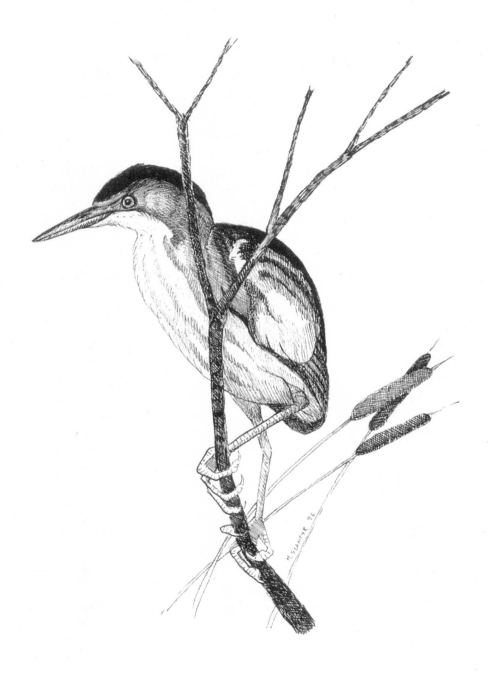

29 GREAT POND STATE FOREST
Simsbury

This 281-acre state forest was donated to the state by James L. Goodwin, an early and enthusiastic Connecticut conservationist, and for many years, the director of the Connecticut Forest and Park Association. The Great Pond State Forest is a managed woodland habitat and was for years part of the Connecticut Tree Farm system. Early forestry practices involved replacing most of the hardwoods that originally surrounded the pond with pine stands; some of which have fallen victim to disease and blight.

Great Pond offers a good mix of habitats including pine plantation (primarily white pine), red maple and shrub swamp, mixed hardwood and conifer woodland, scrubby second growth, and the pond with its fringe of marsh. This blend of habitats offers seasonal birding for waterfowl at the 25-acre pond and a variety of summer breeding species including Blackburnian, Black-throated Green, and Black-throated Blue Warblers. Rarer species that have turned up at Great Pond include Northern Goshawk, Greater White-fronted Goose, Brant (locally rare), and Snowy Owl. Nature enthusiasts will enjoy the variety of wetland wildflowers, ferns, and other vascular hydrophytes, as well as the rhododendron thicket which flowers in early July.

DIRECTIONS

From Interstate 84 take Exit 39 (Route 4, Farmington) to the light at the end of the long exit ramp. Continue straight and follow Route 4 west to its junction with Route 10 (0.9 miles), turn right and follow Route 10 north to Route 44 (4.9 miles). Turn left onto Route 44 west (and Route 10 combined) and continue to the center of Avon (0.7 miles). Turn right and follow Route 10 north to the junction of Route 167 (4.7 miles). Turn left on Route 167 for 0.2 miles and turn right on Firetown Road. At 0.7 miles bear left on Great Pond Road and follow it for 1.6 miles to the entrance on the right (marked by a sign "Great Pond State Forest"). A dirt road about 0.3 miles long leads to the parking lot.

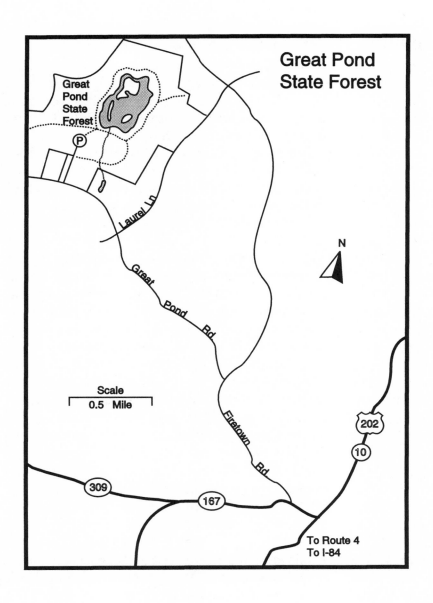

BIRDING

Check the trail map display at the northwest corner of the parking lot before proceeding. A hike around the 1.5 mile-long loop trail that encircles Great Pond provides good birding through a variety of habitats. In addition, you can explore the side trails which lead into the western and southeastern sections of the forest.

At the northeast corner of the parking lot three trails merge: The left trail makes a sharp left and continues west to the powerline right-of-way and the western section of the forest. The center and right trails form the loop trail. Take the trail to the right, which goes through a conifer stand and out to the pond on the left. The pond's outflow supports a scrubby wetland on the right.

In spring and fall, scan the pond for flocks of Bufflehead, Ring-necked Duck, and Common Merganser. Other waterfowl may include Canada Goose, Mallard, American Black Duck, and Green-winged Teal. Check the emergent vegetation forming the islands at the north end of the pond for the shyer and more elusive Wood Duck and Hooded Merganser. Belted Kingfisher is regularly seen and heard as it flies noisily from perch to perch while Osprey and Double-crested Cormorant make irregular visits during migration. In fall, check the pond's edge for small flocks of migrant Pectoral Sandpipers. Migrant Canada Geese flocks should be closely scanned because Snow Goose occurs periodically and Greater White-fronted Goose (very rare) has occurred.

The trail continues over the dam and turns left, flanking the eastern side of the pond and a clear-cut area reverting to scrubby secondary growth. Typical summer breeding species in the scrubby growth include Blue-winged and Chestnut-sided Warblers, Common Yellowthroat, Northern Cardinal, American Goldfinch, Eastern Towhee, and Song Sparrow.

Further down the trail you come to an extensive rhododendron thicket nestled beneath a Scotch pine grove. The trail turns left through this area. In July, the flowering rhododendrons are spectacular. Take a few minutes to admire the beautiful pink blooms. From this point on the trail continues around the north end of the pond through deciduous woodland and over a boardwalk that works through a red maple swamp.

Early spring migrants (April) in this area may include Blue-gray Gnatcatcher, Palm Warbler, Rusty Blackbird, and Eastern Bluebird (the latter also nests in tree cavities around the pond). Red-shouldered Hawks can be vocal and are sometimes spotted circling just over the treetops; this species nests in the wet woodlands.

Breeding species in the woodlands along the north end of the pond include Northern Flicker, Eastern Kingbird, Eastern Phoebe, Tree Swallow, Gray Catbird, Cedar Waxwing, Yellow Warbler, American Redstart, Black-throated Blue Warbler, Common Grackle, and Red-eyed and Yellow-throated Vireos.

After the trail leaves the swamp and turns south you will come upon a good location to view the north end of the pond. Again, check the emergent vegetation on the island and northern shore closely for waterbirds including Green Heron, a regular nesting species. Proceeding south, the trail reenters mature white pine woodlands which in April should harbor migrant Ruby-crowned and Golden-crowned Kinglets, Brown Creeper, and Red-breasted Nuthatch (also nests). From mid-to-late May, look for Yellow-bellied Flycatcher (rare) and Bay-breasted, Cape May, and Blackpoll Warblers. Species breeding in the conifers are Veery, Solitary Vireo, and Pine, Black-throated Green, Blackburnian, and Yellow-rumped Warblers.

If time permits, explore the spur trail that starts near the parking lot and leads to the western section of the forest. In summer, the scrubby growth along the powerline right-of-way should yield Prairie and Blue-winged Warblers, Indigo Bunting, and Field Sparrow. Northern Goshawks have nested in the vicinity of the right-of-way and Cooper's Hawk has occurred here during summer.

The mixed deciduous woodland beyond (west) the powerline contains breeding Great Crested Flycatcher, Eastern Wood-Pewee, Wood and Hermit Thrushes, Ovenbird, Scarlet Tanager, and Rose-breasted Grosbeak. Permanent residents found throughout the forest include Ruffed Grouse, Hairy, Downy, Red-bellied, and Pileated Woodpeckers, Blue Jay, American Crow, Black-capped Chickadee, Tufted Titmouse, and White-breasted Nuthatch. Barred and Great Horned Owls are resident species that nest in or adjacent to the forest.

30 ROARING BROOK NATURE CENTER

Canton

The Roaring Brook Nature Center and the adjacent state-owned Werner Woods Preserve offers the birder and nature enthusiast over 100 acres to explore. Approximately 6 miles of nature trails maintained by the nature center meander through an interesting array of habitats including riverine, hemlock forest, second growth hardwoods, pine plantations, and fields. More than 160 species have been recorded on this small sanctuary. An active wildlife feeding station allows visitors an opportunity to study and photograph numerous species at close quarters.

Roaring Brook Nature Center has an interpretive building with a replica of an Indian longhouse, wildlife dioramas, seasonal exhibits, and trails. The remnants of a 19th century quarry can be viewed along the Quarry Trail. A highlight for many visitors is the live raptor exhibit featuring Bald Eagle, Red-tail Hawk, and Long-eared, Eastern Screech, and Northern Saw-whet Owls. The raptors on display have sustained permanent injuries and can never be returned to the wild, but are still valuable for nature education. Roaring Brook Nature Center is open from Tuesday-Saturday from 10:00 am to 5:00 pm, Sunday from 1:00 pm to 5:00 pm, and on Monday during July and August. Trails are open daily from dawn until dusk. A trail map, self-guiding trail guide, and bird checklist can be purchased at the visitor center gift shop. There is a nominal entrance fee for visitors.

Birding at Roaring Brook Nature Center is best during spring and, to a lesser extent, fall migration. A nice assortment of breeding birds can be located during a field trip from May through July; over 70 species have nested. In winter, the feeding station draws most of the permanent residents as well as winter visitors. Rare or unusual species that have been observed on the property include Merlin, Long-eared Owl, Red-headed Woodpecker, and Northern Shrike. Some interesting breeding species include Wild Turkey, Barred Owl, Pileated Woodpecker, and Winter Wren. Sharp-shinned Hawk formerly has nested at the nature center.

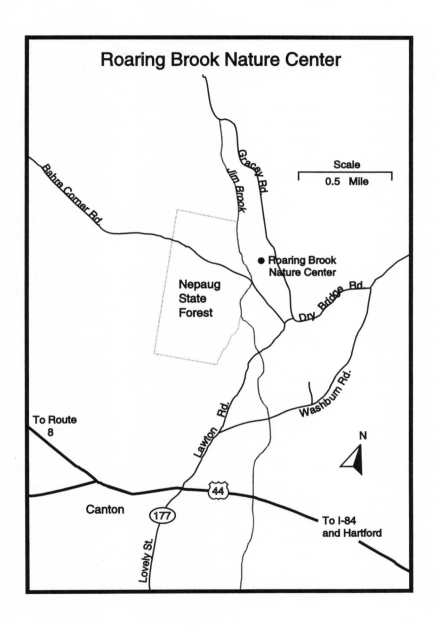

Roaring Brook Nature Center

Scale

0.5 Mile

Gracey Rd.

Jim Brook

Babra Comer Rd.

● Roaring Brook
Nature Center

Dry Bridge Rd.

Nepaug
State
Forest

Washburn Rd.

To Route
8

Lawton Rd.

N

Canton

44

177

To I-84
and Hartford

Lovely St.

DIRECTIONS

Follow Route 44 east from Route 8 in Winsted or west from Hartford.
At the junction of Route 44 and Lawton Road in the center of Canton,
turn north onto Lawton Road. Bear left at the first stop sign (0.3 miles),
staying on Lawton Road. Continue to the next intersection (1.0 miles),
turn right and take an immediate left, onto Gracey Road, then travel 0.5
miles to the nature center on the left.

BIRDING

If you arrive during office hours, obtain a trail map from the gift shop.
A map will assist your explorations of the trail network which includes
five longer (from 0.5 to 1.5 miles) loop trails, two shorter loops (about
0.25 miles each), and several crossing trails.

   First, check the wildlife feeding station on the south side of the
interpretative building. The feeder can produce many of the permanent
residents, such as Mourning Dove, Red-bellied, Downy, and Hairy
Woodpeckers, Blue Jay, Black-capped Chickadee, Tufted Titmouse,
White-breasted Nuthatch, Northern Cardinal, American Goldfinch, and
House Finch. Winter visitors include Red-breasted Nuthatch, Purple
Finch (uncommon), Dark-eyed Junco, and White-throated, American
Tree (occasionally) and Fox Sparrows. In good winter finch years,
Evening Grosbeak, Pine Siskin, and Common Redpoll can be seen at the
feeders. All of the activity around the feeders sometimes attracts
accipiters in search of easy prey. Northern Goshawk, Sharp-shinned,
and Cooper's Hawks have all raised havoc with the songbirds at this
feeding station. In April, male Wild Turkeys strut about the feeding
station trying to impress the local females. Barred Owl often nest near
the interpretative center and in summer the young are frequently seen
along the trails in the area.

   A hike along the Werner Pond Trail (red trail) and the Hillside Trail
(dark blue trail) with a short jaunt into the field is about 1.5 miles, and
will take you through a nice mosaic of habitat (hemlock forest,
deciduous woodland, white pine plantation, field, thicket, riverine, and
pond). The varied habitat can produce a fine assortment of species.

   Take the Werner Pond Trail, a loop-trail starting near the rear of the
parking lot and ending at the interpretive building. The trail goes

predominately through a hemlock woodland bisected by Jim Brook and around Werner Pond. In April and May, the area along the trail can yield migrating thrushes (Hermit, Swainson's, and the occasional Gray-cheeked), Ruby-crowned and Golden-crowned Kinglets, Solitary Vireo, and a variety of warblers (Yellow-rumped, Black-throated Green, Blackburnian, Blackpoll, and the uncommon Bay-breasted). Look for Louisiana Waterthrush foraging along Jim Brook, this species is a migrant as well as a breeder. Additional nesting species to scout for along the trail are Ruffed Grouse, Eastern Phoebe, Wood Thrush, Veery, and Ovenbird. An early morning trip to the pond during migration often yields Wood Duck.

The Hillside Trail (dark blue) veers to the right off of the Werner Pond Trail, ascends a deciduous woodland and traverses a white pine plantation before breaking out into a field. Breeding woodland and field edge species found along this route include Northern Flicker, Eastern Kingbird, Great-crested Flycatcher, Eastern Wood-Pewee, Yellow-throated and Red-eyed Vireos, Black-and-white Warbler, American Redstart, Scarlet Tanager, and Rose-breasted Grosbeak. Be on the lookout for Sharp-shinned Hawk, a species that has nested along the trail at least twice in the past.

Before returning to the Werner Pond Trail (hillside trail ends near its starting point on the red trail) scout the field and thickets. During fall migration this area can yield a variety of sparrows (Song, Chipping, Field, White-throated, American Tree, and Dark-eyed Junco), some thrushes, and an occasional American Kestrel. White-crowned or Lincoln's Sparrow are sometimes spotted. Species nesting in the habitats along this trail include Least Flycatcher, House Wren, Northern Mockingbird, Common Yellowthroat, Prairie, Blue-winged, and Chestnut-sided Warblers, Field Sparrow, Eastern Towhee, Indigo Bunting, Baltimore Oriole, and American Goldfinch. Nesting boxes in the fields draw Eastern Bluebird and Tree Swallow as occupants.

If you have more time, hike one or more trails (Quarry, Orchard, and Plantation) on the south side of Bahre Corner Road. Habitats along these trails consist mostly of hemlock hillside and mixed deciduous growth and a couple of small fields and white pine plantations. Worm-eating Warblers nest near the property boundary on the Orchard Trail.

31 Talcott Mountain Reservoir Area

West Hartford and Bloomfield

Owned by the Metropolitan District Commission (MDC), the Talcott Mountain Reservoir area is located along the Metacomet Ridge; a long traprock ridge that runs north and south through Connecticut's central valley. The Talcott Mountain Reservoir area features deciduous and conifer woodlands, wetlands, and several reservoirs. Reservoir 6, approximately 1.6 miles in length, is the largest and most accessible water body. Trails and paved and dirt roads provide access to much of the reservoir complex, but some areas are restricted. The Metacomet Trail, a former Indian trail, runs the length of the Talcott Mountain Ridge and is frequently used by hikers and birders.

Reservoir 6 and the surrounding habitat has been a favorite birding haunt of the Hartford Audubon Society during spring and fall migration. This area is especially good for spring migrants which funnel northward along the ridge line. In fall, the reservoir provides a safe haven for migrant waterfowl which stop for brief periods.

Talcott Mountain Reservoir Area encompasses a large tract of land, therefore, we suggest that you obtain a map from the MDC before venturing too far away from the beaten track. A map can be purchased for a nominal fee from: The Metropolitan District Commission, Engineering and Planning, 555 Main Street, Hartford, CT. Maps are also posted on information boards at the main parking area and near the parking lot by the treatment facility at the northeast corner of the reservoir.

Specialities of this site include migrant songbirds, especially warblers, and to a lesser extent, waterfowl and other waterbirds. Some of the noteworthy birds recorded at this site include Common Loon, Greater White-fronted and Snow Geese, Bald Eagle, Northern Goshawk, Acadian and Olive-sided Flycatchers, Cape May and Lawrence's (hybrid) Warblers, and Red and White-winged Crossbills.

DIRECTIONS

From Interstate 84 take Exit 39 (Route 4, Farmington) to the light at the end of the long exit ramp. From the light follow Route 4 west to the intersection of Route 10 (0.9 miles). Turn right and follow Route 10 north to the intersection of Route 44 (4.9 miles). Turn right, and

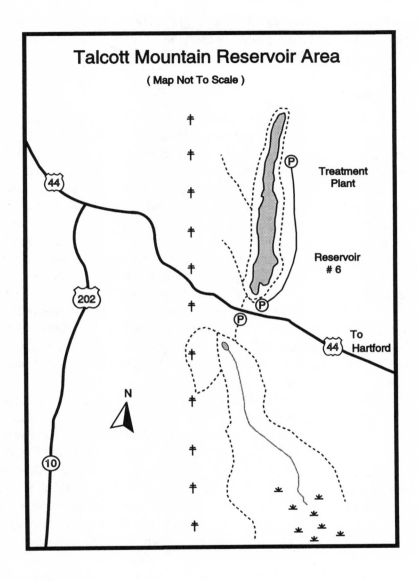

Talcott Mountain Reservoir Area

(Map Not To Scale)

proceed east on Route 44 (2.3 miles) to the reservoir parking area on the left side of the road (sign posted; Reservoir 6 Water Treatment Plant for the Metropolitan District).

BIRDING

Talcott Mountain Reservoir often attracts an assortment of outdoor recreational enthusiasts, so get an early start to avoid the crowds. In spring and summer, some of the best birding can be found along the Metacomet Trail, which can be accessed at the north end of the parking lot. Take the gravel road that bears to the left (the paved road continues to the treatment plant near the north end of the reservoir). The Metacomet Trail follows the western border of the reservoir for about 1.5 miles. Ambitious birders may want to hike around the reservoir which is about 3.5 miles in total length. The trail is flanked by a conifer belt of pines and spruces. The hillsides support an oak hardwoods community that includes chinnapink oak. Some typical boreal species that migrate through this area include Red-breasted Nuthatch, Gray-cheeked and Swainson's Thrushes, Golden-crowned and Ruby-crowned Kinglets, Philadelphia Vireo (rare), and Tennessee, Cape May, Black-throated Green, Blackburnian, Bay-breasted, Yellow-rumped, and Blackpoll Warblers.

You can bird the upland woodlands along almost any of the spur trails that branch off to the left from the Metacomet Trail. Likely woodland nesting species include Red-tailed and Broad-winged Hawks, Ruffed Grouse, Red-bellied Woodpecker, Eastern Wood-Pewee, Great Crested Flycatcher, Veery, Wood Thrush, Yellow-throated and Red-eyed Vireos, American Redstart, Ovenbird, Black-and-white Warbler, Scarlet Tanager, and Eastern Towhee. In the thickets or along the water edge, check for Spotted Sandpiper, Gray Catbird, Yellow Warbler, and Common Yellowthroat; all migrate through the area and also nest nearby.

Return to the car and drive to the treatment plant at the end of the paved road. Nest boxes in the fields near the treatment plant harbor breeding Tree Swallow, Eastern Bluebird, and occasionally, House Wren. Other species breeding in the area include Eastern Kingbird, Northern Mockingbird, Cedar Waxwing, Northern Cardinal, Chipping Sparrow, and American Goldfinch. Pine Warbler nest in the white pine plantation near the reservoir. The dike above the reservoir provides a vantage point to view the reservoir and surrounding hillsides. Check for Common Loon, Double-crested Cormorant, waterfowl, and gulls during fall and spring. Scan the Canada Geese for the occasional Snow Goose and the very rare Greater White-fronted Goose; both have occurred during migration.

Flood Control Dike. The flood control dike and powerline cut south of Route 44 provide additional birding habitat. To get to this area which is located about 0.1 miles west of the main parking lot described above, return to Route 44 and turn right, heading west. Continue for 0.1 miles, turn left and park in the small dirt parking area adjacent to the road. Alternately, you can walk across the street or hike south along the Metacomet Trail (pick up the trail near the north end of the main parking lot as described above, but bear left and follow the trail uphill). The trail winds through a deciduous woodland for about 0.1 miles before crossing Route 44 and continuing to the dike.

Walk to the top of the flood control dike and scan Welles Pond. This small pond is fringed with narrow-leaf cattail and frequently contains Green Heron, sandpipers (Spotted and Solitary), and waterfowl during migration. The elevated dike provides a good view of the surrounding habitat. By following the dike to the left (southeast) you bypass the deciduous forest and come upon a field with a shrub swamp and some open water to the right (about 0.5 miles). Along this route check for Red-shouldered Hawk, Eastern Kingbird, Blue-gray Gnatcatcher, Cedar Waxwing, Yellow-throated and Warbling Vireos, and many of the species previously described.

The field may harbor Eastern Meadowlark and Bobolink during migration. Scan the dead timber in the swamp carefully for Olive-sided Flycatcher (rare) during late-May and late-August into September.

At the end of the wetland a trail branches off to the right into a mixed deciduous woodland which parallels the swamp. If you feel adventurous, you can eventually loop back to Welles Pond by taking a series of right turns starting at the field-swamp interface along the east side of the swamp and then over a dike at the south end of the swamp and then finally through a mixed woodland. However, if you take this loop it is advisable to have a map, since the entire loop is about 3.3 miles.

Metacomet Trail and Powerline Loop.   From Welles Pond you can take a mile long hike which follows the Metacomet Trail south and returns by way of the powerline cut.   This loop trail bypasses a nice blend of habitats and can produce a fine assortment of species during migration and early summer.   To follow this loop, walk west (right) along the dike and turn left, following the Metacomet Trail south along a gravel road.   The Metacomet Trail bisects a mixed oak-maple hardwoods which should be checked for thrushes (Wood, Veery, Hermit, Swainson's, and, rarely, Gray-cheeked) in the understory and on the forest floor.   Check the forest canopy for warblers and vireos during spring migration.   The more open woodland may yield Worm-eating Warbler, an uncommon breeder.

The trail crosses and then parallels a small stream (containing Louisiana Waterthrush during summer) and eventually turns right (where the gravel road changes into a deteriorated paved road).   The trail continues about 220 yards, crossing the stream again, before breaking out to the powerline cut.   Turn right and follow the powerline trail back to the dike.   Typical breeding species found along the powerline are Prairie, Blue-winged, and Chestnut-sided Warblers, Field Sparrow, American Goldfinch, and Indigo Bunting.   A Lawrence's Warbler (Blue-winged x Golden-winged hybrid) has been seen several times over the years along this corridor.

32 FARMINGTON MEADOWS AND SHADE SWAMP SANCTUARY
Farmington

Farmington Meadows is predominately flood plain habitat set aside by the Town of Farmington as open space. This site lies along the flood plains of the Farmington and Pequabuck Rivers and is used for recreational and agricultural purposes. In the area along the south bank of the Farmington River, the meadow is comprised of about 300 acres of property contiguous with the state-owned Shade Swamp Sanctuary. Habitat at Farmington Meadows consists of meadow, cropland (corn, pumpkin, and various other crops), red maple swamp, and edge thickets.

Birding is best in fall (September and October) and to a lesser degree in spring and summer. Summer also hosts a variety of breeding species. Due to the small size of the area, the site can be birded in an hour or two which makes it convenient for birders with limited time. It is also possible to launch a canoe from Meadow Road with the options of paddling upstream into Shade Swamp Sanctuary or downstream to the Farmington River.

While in the area you can visit Shade Swamp Sanctuary property owned by the State of Connecticut and managed by the Department of Environmental Protection. This 800-acre sanctuary consists of two distinct parcels located along Route 6, east and west of New Britain Avenue, respectively.

DIRECTIONS

From Interstate 84 take Exit 39 (Route 4, Farmington) to the light at the end of the long ramp. From the light, follow Route 4 west (0.9 miles) to its junction with Route 10 in the center of Farmington. Turn left and travel south along Route 10 for 0.9 miles. Turn right and follow Meadow Road 0.4 miles. After passing over the Pequabuck River, cornfields appear on the right. You can park along the roadside in this area or near the Farmington River at the community garden's dirt parking lot a short distance down the road on the right.

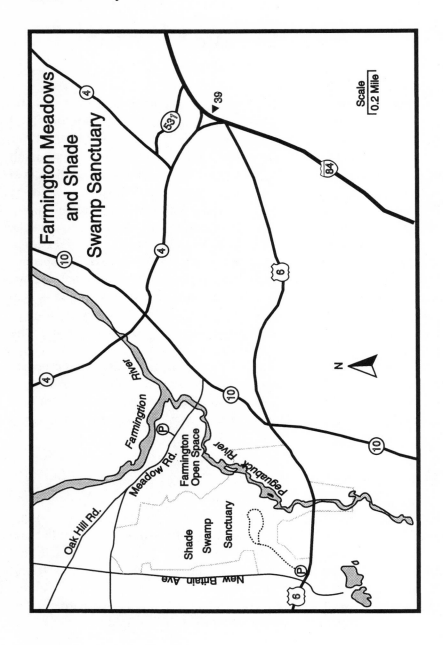

Farmington Meadows
and Shade
Swamp Sanctuary

Scale
0.2 Mile

N

BIRDING

Farmington Meadows

During fall migration, the cropland and field areas usually harbor Killdeer, Mourning Dove, Palm Warbler, Red-winged Blackbird, Common Grackle, Brown-headed Cowbird, and Savannah, Vesper (uncommon), American Tree (late October through winter), Chipping, Field, White-crowned, Swamp, and Song Sparrows.

In October, the meadows are very good for American Pipit which occur regularly in the stubble remaining from the harvested corn fields and pumpkin patches. Lapland Longspur has also been observed in the meadows in October. A flock of 10 American Golden-Plover was observed in September 1993! The large flocks of migrating Canada Geese should be checked for the occasional Snow Goose (mainly October and April). The woodland edge can be productive for Eastern Phoebe, Hermit Thrush, Ruby-crowned and Golden-crowned Kinglets, Ceder Waxwing, and a variety of sparrows---mainly White-throated, Fox (uncommon), and Lincoln's (uncommon). The edge habitat between the cornfield and wet woodland often harbor Rusty Blackbird during this period. Connecticut Warbler has been seen in the scrubby thickets in late September.

Migrating hawks often seen include Red-tailed, (also a permanent resident), Broad-winged, Sharp-shinned, American Kestrel, and Osprey (usually found foraging along the Farmington River). Bald Eagles are occasionally observed during winter hunting along the river.

In summer, a search of the riparian growth along the river will yield many breeding species including Green Heron, Wood Duck, Common Merganser (suspected), Spotted Sandpiper, American Woodcock, Belted Kingfisher, Eastern Kingbird, Eastern Phoebe, Least and Willow Flycatchers, a variety of swallows, Wood Thrush, Veery, Warbling Vireo, American Redstart, Yellow Warbler, Common Yellowthroat, Cedar Waxwing, Indigo Bunting, Common Grackle, and Baltimore Oriole. Eastern Bluebirds breed in the nest boxes near the bridge crossing the Pequabuck River.

The area further west along Meadow Road is another good birding site. Follow Meadow Road to the vegetable stand, bear left at the Y junction (0.3 miles), and park along the roadside before you reach the woodland. The farm field and woodland edge on the south side of the road can be teeming with activity during fall. Check this area for the same birds listed above.

Shade Swamp Sanctuary

To reach Shade Swamp Sanctuary continue along Meadow Road to the stop sign at New Britain Avenue, turn left, and follow New Britain Avenue 1.2 miles to the junction of Route 6. Turn left (heading east) on Route 6 for about 200 feet from the junction and park on the left side of the road in a small lot between the bus stop (the wooden, somewhat delapidated structure) and New Britain Avenue.

The trailhead to Shade Swamp Sanctuary is directly behind the bus stop, but may be difficult to locate (especially during summer) so look for the cages of a former zoo--- the trail runs through the center of this area. Once you find the trail (about 0.8 miles round-trip) it is fairly easy to follow and it terminates on the terrace overlooking the marsh and swamp below. Along the way, the trail passes through mixed woodlands of oaks, pines, and hemlock and then crosses over a foot-bridge and skirts a red maple swamp before ending at the marsh. In spring and fall, the varied habitat along the trail can be good for an assortment of flycatchers, nuthatches, thrushes, vireos, and warblers.

Interesting permanent residents include Great Horned Owl, Northern Goshawk, Pileated Woodpecker, and Ruffed Grouse. The thickets of young hemlock have produced Northern Saw-whet Owl in winter. Summer residents include many of the same species found along the woodland and edge habitats at Farmington Meadows, plus Black-and-white Warbler, Scarlet Tanager, and Swamp Sparrow.

To explore the western part of Shade Swamp Sanctuary, exit the parking lot and head west for 0.3 miles along Route 6. A sign announcing the State of Connecticut, Department of Environmental Protection--Farmington Headquarters is visible on the north (right) side of the road. Drive between the two stone pillars and park by the pond on the left. If the road is blocked, park near the gate and walk in. A loop trail (designated as the white trail) about 1.8 miles in length passes through varied habitats including pond, deciduous and mixed coniferous woodlands. Species composition in this area is consistent with woodland birds found at the eastern preserve and Farmington Meadows.

33 BATTERSON PARK POND
Farmington and New Britain

Located on the periphery of a metropolitan area, Batterson Park Pond is a favorite waterfowl birding area for members of the Hartford Audubon Society. The majority of the pond is situated within Farmington; however the southwestern part of the pond is in New Britain. Birding is best during fall (October/November) and spring (March/April) waterfowl migration. Occasionally, other waterbirds and gulls make brief appearances at the park.

DIRECTIONS

From Interstate 84 take Exit 37 (Fienemann Road), at the end of the exit ramp turn right onto Fienemann Road and drive 0.2 miles (northbound) or 0.4 miles (southbound) to Alexander Road. Turn left and continue 0.1 miles and bear left into a driveway as Alexander Road bends to the right. The access road leads to a parking lot which offers a good view of the pond. If the driveway is barricaded, park here and walk down to the parking lot, or continue another 0.1 miles and pull-off on the side of the road and scope the pond from the elevated bank.

BIRDING

This large pond attracts a variety of waterbirds during fall and spring. Species to anticipate include Pied-billed Grebe, American Coot, and several species of dabbling ducks (Mallard, American Black Duck, American Wigeon, Green-winged Teal, and occasionally, Wood Duck). In the deeper water, a few species of diving ducks occur such as Ring-necked Duck, Bufflehead, and Common and Hooded Mergansers. Ruddy Duck usually make a brief appearance during fall (October is good) but is very scarce in spring. Always be on the lookout for scoter, scaup, Common Goldeneye, and Canvasback; all of which have occurred. A few species of gull, mainly Herring, Ring-billed, and Great Black-backed are generally in the area. Other waterbirds occasionally seen on the lake are Horned Grebe (rare) and Double-crested Cormorant. The thickets around the parking lot can harbor migrating warblers and sparrows during fall and spring.

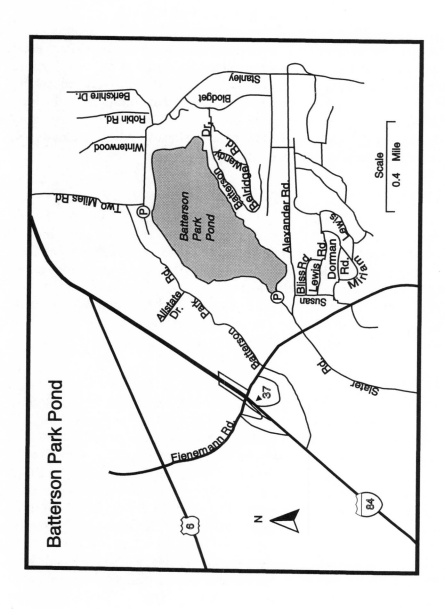

Batterson Park Pond

To view the north end of the pond return to Fienemann Road, turn right and drive 0.2 miles, and turn right onto Batterson Park Road. Follow Batterson Park Road for 1.0 miles to a stop sign, turn right and take an immediate right onto the park road. The gate may be locked from late fall through winter, so park along the access road and walk down to the water's edge. The lawns in this area have attracted large flocks of Canada Geese in fall and spring. Check the flocks carefully for stragglers. Occasionally, Snow Goose, and very rarely Greater White-fronted Goose have occurred within the geese flocks.

34 CROMWELL MEADOWS
Cromwell and Middletown

Cromwell Meadows Wildlife Management Area consists of 496 acres of state-owned property which are primarily managed for game species. Located near the confluence of the Mattabesset and Connecticut Rivers, the wildlife management area is comprised predominately of wetland habitats including rush, cattail, and sedge marsh, and shrub swamp. Smaller segments of upland habitats of field, old field, and small woodland parcels are also represented. The extensive tidally influenced freshwater wetland system has limited hiking access but can be readily explored by canoe.

Cromwell Meadows can be productive for elusive marsh dwellers like bitterns (irregular), rails, and waterfowl. Also, the close proximity of the former Middletown landfill makes the site attractive to gulls. If birding during hunting season, from approximately mid-October through January (except Sundays), be careful and wear bright clothing. This site is extensively used by hunters.

DIRECTIONS
From Route 9 northbound take Exit 18 (Route 99, Cromwell, Rocky Hill) onto Route 99 north and proceed 0.4 miles. Turn left and follow South Street 0.9 miles, turn left (directly across from Diane Drive), and follow the access road beneath the highway to the parking area. Heading southbound on Route 9, take Exit 19 (Route 372, West Street, Cromwell). Turn left on West Street (Route 372), for 0.3 miles, turn right onto Hicksville Road and continue 1.0 miles (at 0.8 miles Hicksville Road becomes South Street at the stop sign) to the meadow's access road on the right (across from Diane Drive).

BIRDING
Access to Cromwell Meadows is essentially along a narrow sliver of upland surrounded by wetland habitats. One trail approximately 0.7 miles in length bisects the limited upland habitat and deadends at the marsh. A major spur trail splits off to the right from the main trail about 0.2 miles from the parking lot. The spur trail deadends at a good overlook of the marsh and a cove of the Mattabesset River. A few other

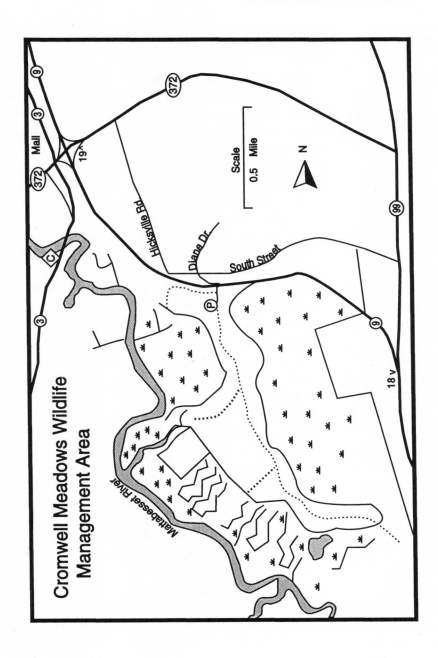

Cromwell Meadows Wildlife Management Area

spur trails (most made by hunters) diverge from the main trail, all deadend or return to the main trail.

In May through July, the upland woodland, edge, and field habitats host a variety of breeding species including Eastern Kingbird, Least and Willow Flycatchers, House Wren, Gray Catbird, Brown Thrasher, Blue-gray Gnatcatcher, Ceder Waxwing, Red-eyed, Yellow-throated, and Warbling Vireos, Blue-winged, Chestnut-sided, and Yellow Warblers, Ovenbird, Common Yellowthroat, Eastern Towhee, Chipping and Field Sparrows, Common Grackle, and Baltimore Oriole. During this period the wetland may harbor Green Heron, Least (rare, irregular breeder) and American (rare migrant) Bitterns, Wood Duck, Virginia Rail, Sora (irregular), Marsh Wren, Red-winged Blackbird, and Swamp Sparrow. Raptors that are regular during summer are Red-tailed and Broad-winged Hawks, Osprey, and Kestrel (formerly common but now uncommon to rare during this period).

In fall, waterfowl migrate into the marsh and adjacent waterways. Regularly occurring species include American Black Duck, Green-winged and Blue-winged (uncommon) Teals, Gadwall, Ring-necked Duck, and Hooded, and Common Mergansers. Check the blackbird flocks (normally consisting of Red-winged Blackbird and Common Grackle) carefully for Rusty Blackbird, which is a regular fall (October/November) and spring (March/April) migrant. Northern Harrier occurs regularly during fall and spring migration and sometimes in winter. Rough-legged Hawk and Bald Eagle have been sighted during winter.

You can view the marsh and Mattabesset River from a different vantage point by walking west along the dirt road which parallels Route 9 to an open field. This road junctions with the access road to Cromwell Meadows between the parking lot and the Route 9 overpass. The hike along the dirt road passes by thickets and an immature conifer plantation before coming to the field. The combination of thickets, field, and marsh in this area can be good during peak sparrow migration in October; look for Swamp, White-throated, Savannah, Field, Chipping, American Tree (winter resident), and the uncommon Fox, Lincoln's, and White-crowned Sparrows. Eastern Meadowlark and Bobolink (sporadically) have nested in the field in past years. From late fall into spring a search of the conifers may yield a roosting owl.

Canoeing. A great way to explore the meadows is by canoe. This normally gives the birder a chance to view many elusive marsh dwellers up close. The best time to canoe the riverine and marsh habitats is from mid-May through early October; June and July are prime times to locate breeding species.

A canoe can be launched from the bridge on Route 3. To access this area take Exit 19 (Route 372, West Street, Cromwell), head west on Route 372 and take an immediate left onto Route 3 south. Follow Route 3 south for 0.4 miles through the traffic light to the Mattabesset River Bridge (a sign indicates Sebethe River). Cross over the bridge and park on the right.

Be aware that the river is tidally influenced in this area, therefore, the water level can rise and fall a foot or more. **Do not venture too far up shallow creeks or inlets when the tide is receding or you may become stranded.** By canoe it is about a mile to the meadows. The trip to the meadows is extremely picturesque as the river meanders along flood plains lined with graceful Silver Maple; this voyage is reminiscent of a more southern latitude.

Birdlife along the river is similar to the species described at the meadows; however, during May, August, and September shorebirds are frequently encountered such as Spotted and Solitary (normally in May) Sandpipers, Greater and Lesser Yellowlegs, Common Snipe, and occasionally, Pectoral Sandpiper. With a little luck, when searching the nooks and crannies of the marsh you may spot a rail or bittern.

35 BLACK POND AND BISHOPS POND
Meriden

These two birding sites are located within two miles of one another just off Interstate 91 in Meriden and may conveniently be birded together. Both offer good seasonal birding for waterbirds during migration.

Black Pond is located on the Meriden/Middlefield boundary at the foot of the talus slope of the Metacomet Ridge. The unique geological features of the Metacomet Ridge at Black Pond offer the visitor a scenic and interesting backdrop while birding. The best area for birding the pond is from the state-owned boat ramp, unless you bring along a canoe. The pond is a good place to check quickly when enroute to another birding site or when time is limited. Birding is best during waterfowl migration in spring and fall. Summer may bring a few surprises, especially if you bird by canoe along the emergent and floating vegetation at the southern end of the pond.

Local birders consider Bishops Pond a worthwhile stop for viewing waterbirds and waterfowl during spring and fall. Research Parkway bisects these two small ponds which are located in the midst of an industrial park and bordered by Interstate 91 to the west. Both ponds are small and can be birded quickly. The western pond fringed by phragmites and cattail is usually most productive and can yield many species of waterfowl.

DIRECTIONS

To get to Black Pond from Interstate 91 southbound take Exit 17 (Wilbur Cross Parkway, East Main Street) and bear right onto Exit 67 (East Main Street) where the exit ramp divides. Follow the exit ramp to East Main Street. Turn left and proceed along East Main Street 1.3 miles. Traveling north on Interstate 91 take Exit 16 (East Main Street) which terminates at East Main Street. Turn right and follow East Main Street about 1.1 miles. Travel along East Main Street to the point where the street appears to becomes an access ramp onto Routes 66 and 691. Just past the Middlefield Town Line sign, turn right then quickly bear left (sign, Black Pond) and follow the pond's access road to the boat launch and parking lot.

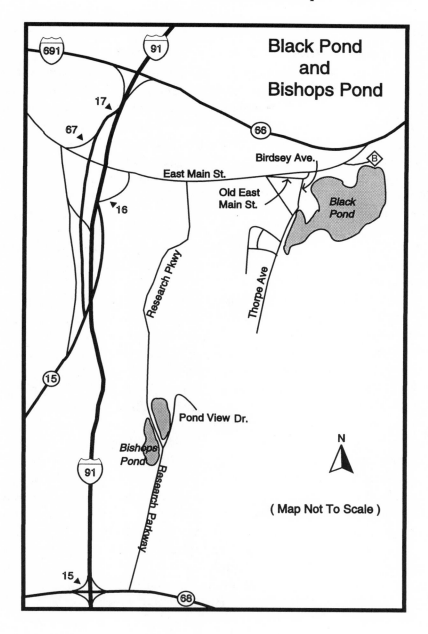

Black Pond
and
Bishops Pond

(Map Not To Scale)

BIRDING

Black Pond

Birding is best during fall migration when waterbirds and waterfowl are enroute to southern wintering grounds. During fall, check along the shoreline vegetation at the southern end of the pond for Great Blue and Green Herons, and the open waters for Pied-billed Grebe, Mute Swan, Canada Goose, Mallard, American Black Duck, Green-winged and Blue-winged (uncommon) Teals, American Wigeon, Wood Duck, Ringed-necked Duck, and Common and Hooded Mergansers. Also during this season (mainly September and October), be on the alert for migrating hawks following and taking advantage of the updrafts produced by the nearby ridge. Raptors frequently sighted above the ridge during good movements include Sharp-shinned, Red-tailed (permanent resident), and Broad-winged Hawks, Osprey, and American Kestrel.

The shallow pond often freezes over in winter; therefore, avian activity is limited to a handful of permanent residents foraging in the woodlands along the pond's edge. The March thaw brings along the Ring-necked Duck, a harbinger of spring. Following shortly thereafter are Wood Duck and most of the species that were seen in fall.

Some summer residents include swallows (Barn, Tree, and Northern Rough-winged), Belted Kingfisher, warblers (Yellow, Black-and-white, Ovenbird, and Common Yellowthroat), blackbirds (Red-winged, Common Grackle, and Baltimore Oriole), and sparrows (Swamp, Chipping, and Song).

To view the west end of Black Pond, return to East Main Street, turn left, take the first left (0.1 miles) onto Old East Main Street, bear left (0.1 miles) and follow Birdsey Avenue 0.2 miles to a stop sign. Turn left onto Thorpe Avenue and park along the road to survey the pond.

If you plan to bird Bishops Pond, return to East Main Street via Thorpe Avenue (0.2 miles). Turn left and follow East Main Street to Research Parkway (0.3 miles) on the left. Drive for 1.3 miles along Research Parkway until you reach Bishops Pond, which is on both sides of the road.

Bishops Pond

To get to Bishops Pond from Interstate 91 take Exit 15 (Route 68,

Durham and Yalesville) and follow Route 68 east to the first left (0.2 miles from southbound ramp, 0.1 miles from bottom of northbound ramp) which is Research Parkway. Continue on the parkway for 1.9 miles until Bishops Pond is encountered on both sides of the road.

Birding at Bishops Pond is best in spring and fall. The two halves of Bishops Pond offer safe havens for waterfowl during hunting season. The pond along the west side of Research Parkway is more secluded and, therefore, generally best for birding. Waterfowl (mainly dabbling ducks) and marsh species use the protective cover provided by the emergent vegetation found around the periphery of the west pond. During fall and spring closely scan the ponds and edges for Pied-billed Grebe, Great Blue and Green Herons, Mute Swan, Canada Goose, Mallard, American Black Duck, Green-winged and Blue-winged (uncommon) Teals, Wood Duck, Ring-necked Duck, and Hooded Merganser.

Large flocks of American Wigeon (sometimes numbering a hundred or more) occur in fall. Check these flocks for the rarer Eurasian Wigeon. Less common species that periodically turn up at Bishops Pond include Northern Pintail, Gadwall, and American Coot.

36 DURHAM MEADOWS
Durham

Much of Durham Meadows is a 500-acre state-owned wildlife management area consisting of two distinct land parcels segregated by Route 68 west of Durham center. The area is predominately marshland, open wet meadow, and shrub swamp with several small deciduous woodlots comprised mostly of red maple swamps. The wetlands and farmlands contain a variety of species with localized breeding distribution in the state.

Access is difficult due to the wet nature of much of the area throughout the year. The only available trail is a short, somewhat overgrown deadend. Consequently, much of the area must be birded from roadways or across trailless areas. The northern section is best accessed by canoe. An early morning canoe trip into the meadows can reward the birder with a diversity of marsh species.

Rails and bitterns are the major attraction of this superb wetland. Least and American Bitterns both nest in the marsh. Rails present include; Virginia, Sora, and King, which is rare. Common Moorhen also occurs but its status varies from year to year. Uncommon waterfowl include migrant Blue-winged Teal, Northern Pintail, Gadwall, and Northern Shoveler. Durham Meadows can also be good for a variety of raptors (Great Horned Owl, Eastern Screech-owl, Red-tailed Hawk), and wintering raptors (Northern Harrier, Rough-legged Hawk, and rarely, Long-eared Owl), and Northern Shrike (rare).

DIRECTIONS
To access the southern section of Durham Meadows Wildlife Management Area from Interstate 91 take Exit 15 (Route 68, Durham and Yalesville) and follow Route 68 east for 5.2 miles to its junction with Route 17 (at Durham center). Turn right and follow Route 17 south 1.5 miles and park in one of the dirt pull-offs on the right before or just after the small bridge.

BIRDING
South Section. Follow the path north that parallels the small river. The path is the only "trail" that leads into the meadows and follows the

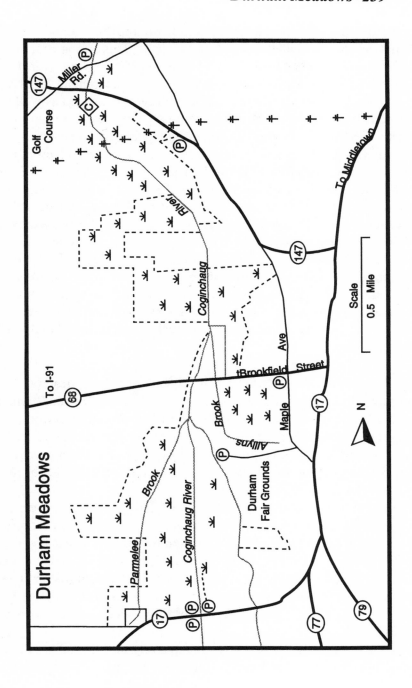

Durham Meadows

east side of the river through a shrub swamp bordered by marsh comprised predominately of sedge and rush. This site is best birded during early morning in spring and summer. Sora, King (rare), and Virginia Rails occur here and can be quite vocal and territorial in May and June. American Bittern has been recorded in this area as well but, unfortunately bittern are elusive and normally only heard. Listen for the bittern's peculiar "pumping" sound emanating from the marsh on a quiet May morning. Other species to search for include Green Heron, Red-tailed Hawk, American Kestrel, Ring-necked Pheasant, Belted Kingfisher, Northern Flicker, Eastern Kingbird, Willow, Least, and Olive-sided (late May or early September migrant) Flycatchers, Gray Catbird, Brown Thrasher, Blue-gray Gnatcatcher, Ceder Waxwing, White-eyed Vireo, Blue-winged, Yellow, and Chestnut-sided Warblers, Common Yellowthroat, and Northern Waterthrush. Red-winged Blackbird and Swamp Sparrow are both common. Both Black-billed and Yellow-billed Cuckoos have been recorded in this wetland but their abundance is related to the extent of gypsy moth and tent caterpillar infestation. Northern Shrike has occasionally been recorded in this area during winter.

North Section. To get to the North Section of Durham Meadows from the junction of Route 68 and Route 17 in Durham, follow Route 17 north 0.6 miles to the junction of Route 147. Turn left onto Route 147 and proceed 0.9 miles to a dirt pull-off on the left beneath the powerline. If you intend to canoe, continue 0.5 miles to the small bridge crossing over the Coginchaug River, park at the small pull-off (left side of road) and launch the canoe.

The area by the powerlines has a makeshift trail that leads you closer to the marsh. However, due to thick vegetation, this area is best birded by song and call rather than sight. Listen for all the species identified above plus Least Bittern, King Rail (rare), and Marsh Wren. Other common breeding birds include Killdeer, Belted Kingfisher, Great Crested Flycatcher, Eastern Phoebe, Tree Swallow, Blue-gray Gnatcatcher, Ceder Waxwing, Warbling Vireo, and American Goldfinch.

Canoeing is really the best way to effectively bird this area. Put the canoe in at the bridge and paddle south into the marsh. This will give you a splendid opportunity to explore the area and view the tremendous diversity of wildlife. Most of the elusive rails and bitterns can be seen by birding in this manner. In addition, waterfowl (American Black Duck, Wood Duck, and occasionally, Gadwall) can usually be located and observed during summer. Blue-winged Teal is a rare breeder.

Miller Road. To reach this area travel 0.8 miles north of the powerline stop on Route 147 and turn right onto Miller Road. Drive along Miller Road to the parking area next to the Coginchaug River (0.4 miles). Birding along the road from the Route 147 junction down to the bridge crossing the Coginchaug River can be interesting and rewarding any time of the year.

In winter, the shrub swamp and wet meadow on the south side of the road have produced Northern Shrike for several concurrent years. Permanent residents include woodpeckers (Downy, Hairy, Red-bellied, and Northern Flicker), Carolina Wren, Northern Mockingbird, Northern Cardinal, and Eastern Meadowlark (usually a small flock overwinters). Another permanent resident is Eastern Screech-Owl which can sometimes be seen roosting in the cavities of the old sugar maples along Miller Road.

The slightly higher elevation along the road provides a good vantage point to survey the wet area and river. Both can be excellent for waterfowl and Common Snipe. In late March and April, scan the emergent vegetation along the canal closely for Gadwall, Blue-winged and Green-winged Teals, American Black Duck, Northern Shoveler (occasionally), Northern Pintail, Wood Duck, and the cryptically colored Common Snipe. During this season, as many as 40 Common Snipe have been observed forging in the mud and shallow water in search of invertebrates and other food items. At dusk, the "peenting" and aerial display of the American Woodcock can be witnessed from this locale, as well as in the areas previously mentioned.

In spring and summer, many of the same passerine species will be found here but the deciduous woodland and edge habitat near the river can also harbor Eastern Phoebe, Tufted Titmouse, Wood Thrush, Red-eyed and Yellow-throated Vireos, Common Grackle, and American Goldfinch.

Route 68 Wet Meadow and Pond and Durham Fair Grounds.
From the junction of Route 17 and Route 68, take Route 68 west for 0.2
miles to a dirt parking area adjacent to a pond on the left. The pond,
grassy wetlands, wet thickets and tree lines around this area are always
worth a quick check. Durham Fair Grounds form the southern part of
this area.

During spring and fall migration, the pond and wet meadow near the
parking area often attract a variety of shorebirds (Greater and Lesser
Yellowlegs, Spotted, Solitary, and Least Sandpipers). Green and Great
Blue Herons also are regular along the pond edges and in the deeper
waters of the wetland. Breeding species include Killdeer, American
Woodcock, Red-winged Blackbird, Common Grackle, Brown-headed
Cowbird, Eastern Meadowlark, Bobolink, Baltimore and occasionally,
Orchard Orioles, and Swamp and Song Sparrows. Savannah Sparrows
are sometimes heard singing on their territory and may nest. A singing
Grasshopper Sparrow has occurred at this location (breeding?) in the
past.

To bird the Durham Fair Grounds exit the pond parking lot, turn right
and follow Route 68 east. Take an immediate right onto Maple Avenue
and follow this road 0.3 miles to the Durham Fair Grounds. Turn right
onto a gravel road at the northern edge of the fair grounds. Follow the
gravel road down the hillside through the fields to the flood plain and
wet meadow below. This area has a few scattered picnic tables which
offers the birder a fine stop to rest and watch for the same birds noted
above.

Raptors are often conspicuous inhabitants of these wetland locales.
In winter, Red-tailed Hawk, American Kestrel, and the occasional
Northern Harrier and Rough-legged Hawk are found throughout the
area. March (and periodically during winter) brings the return of the
Red-shouldered Hawk, which is a vocal breeding resident that can be
heard and observed hunting in the red maple swamp at the fair grounds.
Red-tail Hawk and Great Horned Owl are permanent residents--both
species have nested in the small woodlot between the fair grounds and
Route 68, and along Miller Road. Eastern Screech-Owls nest in several
areas and Long-eared Owls have been reported during winter and spring
near Miller Road.

37A SLEEPING GIANT STATE PARK
Hamden

This state park of 1,331 acres features more than 30 miles of hiking trails. Habitats include extensive stands of upland hardwoods, small stream-carved ravines with hemlock, ledge and talus slopes, and riparian wetlands along the Mill River. Recreational activities peak in spring and summer, but the more isolated trails offer good birding for nesting species. Many of Connecticut's upland woodland species can be turned up as migrants or breeders.

DIRECTIONS
From Interstate 91 take Exit 10 (Route 40, Hamden) and follow the Mt. Carmel Connector to Route 10 north (2.6 miles). Turn right onto Route 10 north, continue 1.4 miles, and turn right onto Mt. Carmel Avenue at the traffic light. The park entrance is 0.3 miles on the left. There is a seasonal fee for entry into this state park.

BIRDING
Trail maps of Sleeping Giant State Park may be obtained at the park entrance and also at the park information bulletin board located next to the main park road just within the park. Some of the more remote trails in the park are less traveled and for that reason should produce a wider variety of birds. A late spring or summer hike along the park's wooded trails should produce a variety of nesting vireos, flycatchers, and thrushes. Ovenbird, Veery, and Eastern Wood-Pewee are common and widespread nesting species. Hawks and owls are well represented on the more remote wooded hillsides; Great Horned and Eastern Screech Owls and Red-tailed and Cooper's Hawks all nest at Sleeping Giant State Park. Woodpeckers are well represented with Hairy, Downy, Red-bellied, and Pileated all possible throughout the year.

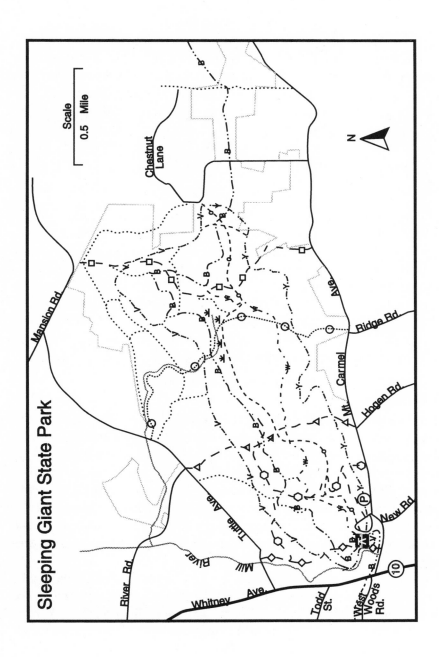

Nearby Attractions

Clark's Pond

Created by damming the Mill River, this small pond is located within easy walking distance of the entrance to Sleeping Giant State Park. To get to Clark's Pond, turn right when exiting Sleeping Giant State Park and then take the first left (0.1 miles) onto New Road. Continue 0.5 miles and park on the right, just before the bridge. The pond attracts an assortment of waterfowl, herons, swallows, and shorebirds during migration and is usually worth a quick check.

The Fat Robin

Located near the junction of Routes 22, 10, and 40 at 3000 Whitney Avenue (Route 10) in Hamden, this wild bird and nature shop is open for business seven days a week. Birders may stop and browse for optics, nature gifts, books, tapes, videos, bird feeders, bird seed, and other nature related supplies.

37B QUINNIPIAC RIVER STATE PARK

Hamden and North Haven

Located next to the Wilbur Cross Parkway in North Haven, this 340-acre state park is a narrow, linear strip of fields and floodplain forests that lies between the Quinnipiac River on the east and the Wilbur Cross Parkway on the west. In fall, this state park is hunted for white-tailed deer, cottontails, grouse, and pheasant. The south end of the park was once a housing development, long since flooded out, but vestiges of roads, driveways, and foundations survive along with many trees and shrubs originally planted as ornamentals but now providing a diverse vegetation attractive to birds.

North of this old housing area is a mixed bag of habitats; small white pine stands, red maple swamps, red cedar stands, grasslands, and mixed hardwoods. The Quinnipiac River streambelt functions as a central valley migration corridor in spring and fall.

DIRECTIONS

From Wilbur Cross Parkway southbound take Exit 63 (Route 22, North Haven), go left at the end of the exit ramp and take an immediate left at the traffic light onto Route 22, heading east. Follow Route 22 east for 0.2 miles and turn left onto State Street, heading north. Continue for 0.2 miles and turn right onto Banton Street and follow it to the end of the road. Park at the end of Banton Street, behind the service area. Entrance to the state park is just beyond the barricade. If northbound on the parkway, take Exit 63 (Route 22, North Haven) and take a right at the end of the exit ramp onto Route 22. Take the first left (0.1 miles) onto State Street and continue as described above.

BIRDING

To bird this state park, walk along the former roadway which begins just north of the service station. In winter, the small stands of Norway spruce, white pine, and red cedar have been good for Northern Saw-whet Owl. These small owls are best located by checking the ground beneath the conifers for recent sign, e.g., pellets and whitewash, then searching the branches above for the owls.

When the asphalt road ends, look for the blue trail markers which follow a dirt road. The blue trail continues northward through the park, winding between the Quinnipiac River to the right and the Wilbur Cross Parkway to the left. In spring and fall, look for an assortment of flycatchers, thrushes, vireos, and warblers migrating through the riparian area. Throughout the year, the taller white pines harbor roosting Great Horned or Barred Owl. In winter, the red cedar stands and even the occasional solitary red cedar may shelter a Northern Saw-whet or Long eared Owl. In late spring and summer, the varied habitats also attract an interesting variety of field, edge, and woodland nesting species.

Eastern Hills

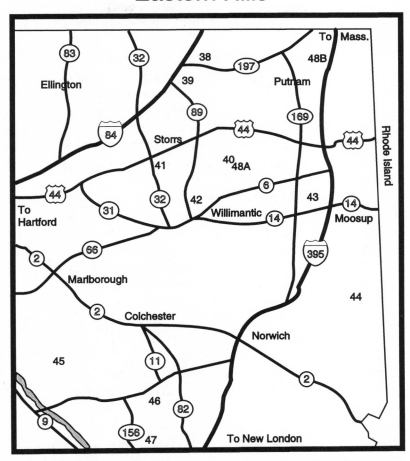

38. Bigelow Hollow State Park
39. Boston Hollow and Yale Forest
40. Natchaug State Forest/
    James L. Goodwin State Forest
41. Storrs Area Tour
42. Mansfield Hollow State Park
43. Quinebaug River Wildlife
    Management Area

44. Pachaug State Forest
45. Devil's Hopyard State Park
46. Hartman Park
47. Nehantic State Forest
48A. Trailwood
48B. West Thompson Dam

38 BIGELOW HOLLOW STATE PARK

Union

This 513-acre state park located in the northeastern corner of the state is situated in a natural hollow that has a colder and wetter climate, even in summer. The cold hollow produces a habitat of mature hemlock woodlands with an admixture of white pine and hardwoods that surround the cold, clear waters of Bigelow Pond and Mashapaug Pond. The combination of conifers and cool microclimate serves as a natural habitat island for several nesting species that are usually found further north in summer.

Both Bigelow Pond and Mashapaug Pond are popular boating and fishing ponds. The two ponds are connected by a marshy brook. The ponds are drained by Bigelow Brook, a distant tributary of the Thames River. The two ponds support good populations of largemouth bass and brown trout along with an abundance of sunfish and golden shiners. The fish attract fishing birds as well as fishermen to the pond.

Bigelow Hollow State Park is a popular state park in almost every season of the year. Hot summer days typically bring out good numbers of picnickers and hikers, while fishermen regularly haunt the two ponds in spring and fall, and ice fish in winter. Throughout most of the year, the best birding times are generally early in the morning or late in the evening, before recreational commuters arrive in numbers at the park and after they leave.

Birding specialties at Bigelow Hollow include several nesting species that have a localized nesting distribution within the state such as Blackburnian, Yellow-rumped, Black-throated Green, and Black-throated Blue Warblers, Red-breasted Nuthatch (occasional), Dark-eyed Junco, and White-throated Sparrow. Nesting raptors may include Broad-winged Hawk, Northern Goshawk, Cooper's Hawk, and Barred and Great Horned Owls.

DIRECTIONS

On Interstate 84 take Exit 73 (Route 190). Follow Route 190 eastbound for 1.9 miles to its junction with Route 171. Turn right and follow Route 171 east for 1.5 miles. The park entrance is marked by a sign on

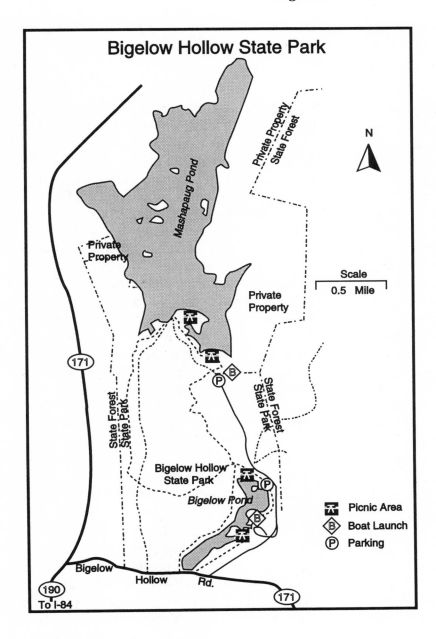

Bigelow Hollow State Park

Mashapaug Pond

Private Property / State Forest

Private Property

Private Property

N

Scale
0.5 Mile

171

State Forest / State Park

State Forest / State Park

Bigelow Hollow State Park

Bigelow Pond

Picnic Area

Boat Launch

Parking

190
To I-84

Bigelow Hollow Rd.

171

the left at the bottom of a long hill, just after the road crosses over Bigelow Brook.

BIRDING

Bigelow Pond. The 20-acre Bigelow Pond can be accessed by a number of trails on the left, just inside the park entrance. You can park here and walk the Yellow Trail north or continue along the main park road for another 0.3 miles (from the park entrance). Stop at the Hiker Information Board on the right for park information and a trail map.

Just beyond the Information Board turn left onto a dirt road that leads a short distance to the boat launch for Bigelow Pond. Park near the boat launch and check out Bigelow Pond for waterbirds. Great Blue and Green Herons are often early morning regulars in summer, hunting fish among the emergent vegetation around the pond's margin. Other fishing waterbirds may include migrant Common and Hooded Mergansers, and Pied-billed Grebe. Waterfowl possible during migration include Ring-necked, American Black, and Wood Ducks. From spring through fall, Tree Swallows and Belted Kingfisher patrol just over the water or perch on limbs projecting over the water. Wood Duck have nested in the nesting boxes placed around the perimeter of the pond. Other nesting waterfowl may include Canada Goose and Mallard.

From the boat launch you can access the Yellow Trail which loops around Bigelow Pond and is 1.6 miles in length. A short hike of about 100 yards along the Yellow Trail to the left (south) leads to an unmarked trail that cuts sharply right, guarded by a barricade of poles. This trail cuts straight west across a narrow spit of land and out to an island which affords a good view of the north and south end of Bigelow Pond. Again, check the pond for waterbirds and waterfowl. From here you can also scan the sky for an occasional Turkey Vulture or Red-tailed Hawk and call Barred Owl, which sometimes respond from the wooded hillside beyond the pond. The hemlock and white pine woodlands and woodland edge here and throughout the park are good in summer for Red-breasted Nuthatch, Brown Creeper, Solitary Vireo, and Blackburnian, Black-throated Green, Yellow-rumped, and Black-throated Blue Warblers. Common permanent residents include the Blue Jay, Black-capped Chickadee, Tufted Titmouse, and White-breasted Nuthatch. Summer breeders in the open area surrounding the boat launch include Chipping and Song Sparrows, and possibly Dark-eyed Junco.

To the right (north) of the boat launch the Yellow Trail leads along the northeastern edge of the pond to the picnic area. Alternately, you can drive to the picnic area and Mashapaug Pond.

Picnic Area. To get to the picnic area from the boat launch return to the paved road and turn left. Continue for another 0.3 miles to the picnic area parking lot on the left. A second Hiker Information Board is located just across from the picnic area.

For birders, the picnic area affords a good view of the northern end of Bigelow Pond which can be checked for the waterbirds previously listed. From the picnic area, you can take a 1.5 mile loop by hiking northward for 1.0 miles along the Blue over White Bar Trail and returning via the park road. This trail initially crosses two small footbridges over the brook and swampy area before coming to a junction. At the junction, turn right (a left turn will start you on a five mile loop) and follow the trail along the hillside between Bigelow Pond and Mashapaug Pond to the north.

The habitat along the trail attracts a variety of birds throughout the year. Vireos, warblers, and thrushes are especially common during spring migration. Veery, Hermit, and Wood Thrushes, Red-eyed Vireo, Yellow Warbler, Common Yellowthroat, and American Redstart are some of the common nesting species. Less common nesting species possible are the Canada Warbler and White-throated Sparrow. Downy, Hairy, and Pileated (uncommon) Woodpeckers may be found in any season of the year. Both waterthrushes nest in the park and occur along the brook; Northern works the marshy areas, whereas Louisiana prefers the stretches of fast moving water. Acadian Flycatcher has occurred by the footbridge and along the road about 0.1 miles north of the picnic area. Dark-eyed Junco is regular in summer along the hike.

Mashapaug Pond. You can get to Mashapaug Pond by hiking the Blue and White Bar Trail, as above, or by driving another 0.5 miles north from the picnic area to the parking lot by the boat launch. Since the boat launch area is usually busy, the best way to bird the lake is to take the forest road by the bar-way which begins just to the left of the boat launch. In 120 yards, the forest trail intersects the Blue with White Bar Trail. A left at this junction leads back to Bigelow Pond (1.0 miles) while a right continues towards Mashapaug Pond, skirting the shoreline for a mile or so before returning to Bigelow Pond via a longer route. Take the right trail which winds along the southern end of Mashapaug Pond through evergreen woods interspersed with attractive white birch before looping back through mixed woodland.

Spring migrants and summer nesting warblers are possible anywhere along the trail. Scan the upper canopy and listen for Yellow-rumped, Black-throated Green, and Blackburnian Warblers. Winter Wrens and Dark-eyed Juncos nest in rocky areas on the hillsides while Solitary Vireos and Black-and-white Warblers nest in the vicinity of the laurel thickets. Other breeding species in the mixed woodland include Eastern Wood-Pewee, Great Crested Flycatcher, Red-eyed Vireo, and Scarlet Tanager. Ruby-crowned and Golden-crowned Kinglets are common migrants and the latter is a possible breeder. In fall, check the pond for Common Loon, Common Merganser, and diving ducks. Osprey occurs during migration and occasionally in summer.

The quieter and more secluded areas of the park support several species of hawks and owls. Try calling Northern Saw-whet in early spring and Barred Owls throughout the year. In late fall and winter, the conifers offer the possibility of roosting Northern Saw-whet or Long-eared Owls. The best way to locate roosting owls is to check around the base of the conifers for pellets and whitewash which indicate the presence of a roosting owl in the canopy above. Some raptors that may nest in the more secluded conifers include Northern Goshawk, Red-tailed and Broad-winged Hawks, and Great Horned Owl.

39 BOSTON HOLLOW AND YALE FOREST
Ashford and Union

Located in the northeastern corner of the state, the Yale Forest occupies more than 7,000 acres of steep hilly terrain ranging in elevation from 600 to 1,200 feet. A mosaic of habitats can be found in Yale Forest, including ravine, upland deciduous and coniferous woodlands, swamp, river, and pond. The higher elevations and resulting cooler climate attracts an assortment of more northerly nesting species. A wooded ravine within the Yale Forest known as Boston Hollow provides excellent spring birding with over 30 species of warblers regularly occurring during migration.

A May or June car tour beginning at Boston Hollow and proceeding north through Yale Forest to Kinney Pond can yield an assortment of birdlife. Some noteworthy nesting species found at Boston Hollow include Acadian Flycatcher, Common Raven, Winter Wren, Cerulean, Blackburnian, Black-throated Green, Black-throated Blue, and Yellow-rumped Warblers, Dark-eyed Junco, and White-throated Sparrow. This is also a classic location to observe both Louisiana and Northern Waterthrushes which nest along the local streams.

DIRECTIONS
To reach Yale Forest from Interstate 84 take Exit 72 (Route 89, Westford and Ashford) and travel 4 miles south on Route 89 to the center of Westford. When Route 89 makes a sharp (90 degree) right turn in Westford (across from the church) continue straight ahead onto Boston Hollow Road. At this junction start your mileage reading.

BIRDING
The best strategy for birding the forest is to drive slowly, stopping frequently to bird along the roadside and the trails that cross the road. From the Route 89 junction, follow Boston Hollow Road north. Stop at the first house on the left (0.1 miles) and take a quick look at the feeding station. Several resident species frequent the feeder most of the year. In winter, check for seasonal visitors including winter finches.

Boston Hollow Road becomes dirt at the junction with Eastford Road (0.3 miles). Continue straight at the junction, entering the ravine known

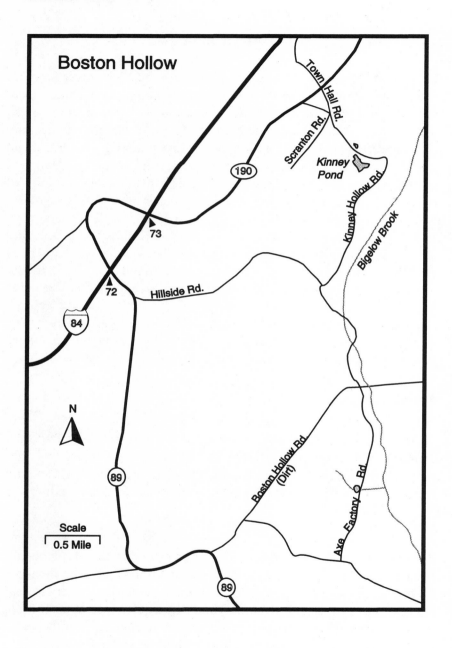

Boston Hollow

as Boston Hollow. The ravine is actually a fault scarp cleft through part of Connecticut's eastern hills. Further along (0.1 miles), the road skirts a swamp and sluggish stream on the left which are flanked by hardwoods of birches, oaks, and maples. In late spring and summer, Eastern Wood-Pewee, Great Crested Flycatcher, Eastern Phoebe, Veery, Wood Thrush, Common Yellowthroat, both species of waterthrush, and Rose-breasted Grosbeak usually can be found in this immediate area. The standing dead timber in the swamp is attractive to various cavity nesting species including Hairy, Downy, Red-bellied, and Pileated Woodpeckers (all resident). Northern Flicker occurs from April through fall.

As you continue the roadside swamps give way to brooks which in turn broaden to produce swamps. These contrasting wetlands provide an excellent locale to compare the habitats of Northern Waterthrush and Louisiana Waterthrush. The secretive Northern Waterthrush prefers a swampy habitat and can be very difficult to observe as it forages methodically in the dense vegetation of the swamp, but patience and a little luck should enable you to catch a glimpse of this waterthrush. The Louisiana Waterthrush normally occurs along flowing brooks or streams that lack substantial emergent vegetation and shrub thickets. The Louisiana Waterthrush is generally easier to see as it darts up or down the waterways. Look for its clear throat and white eyeline that widens behind the eye and continues almost to the nape.

Just beyond the swamp the road enters the hemlock ravine. From this section onward during the nesting season, look and listen for Winter Wren, Red-eyed and Solitary Vireos, Ovenbird, and Blackburnian, Black-throated Green, Canada, and Black-throated Blue Warblers. Three species of thrushes (Veery, Wood, and Hermit) nest in the hollow; listen for the subtle vocal differences between the songs of the Hermit and Wood Thrushes. At 0.9 miles Acadian Flycatcher is fairly regular (although it can be found throughout Boston Hollow). This small, nondescript flycatcher is usually found along streams and brooks in the open understory beneath a dense canopy of conifers. Blue-gray Gnatcatcher and Dark-eyed Junco are also possible along the road. With a little luck, maybe a Barred Owl can be coaxed into calling. Northern Goshawk is a rare but regular breeder here.

The Nipmuck Trail (blue-blazed) crosses the road (0.2 miles) and ascends steeply out of the ravine. If time permits explore the woodlands along the trail. Woodland species that may be found along the trail during the breeding season include Scarlet Tanager, Worm-eating Warbler, American Redstart, and many others. The hollow can be quiet during winter and the road is frequently snowbound. However, winter finches do turn up sporadically, even in non-finch years. Species most consistent include Pine Siskin and Purple Finch, but watch closely for grosbeaks and crossbills, especially the White-winged Crossbill, which has occurred even in summer.

At 0.2 miles the dirt road on the left (large rocks block vehicle access) leads up to a gravel bank where Common Raven has nested. This is private property, so listen and watch for the ravens from the main road. Winding slightly downhill, the road soon exits the ravine. Continue for 0.3 miles and turn left onto Axe Factory Road (dirt). Near the corner, Least Flycatcher is regular during summer. An interesting array of species can usually be tallied along the wetland habitat for the next few hundreds yards or so. It is best to park and survey the habitat on foot. Be on the lookout for breeding species such as Eastern Kingbird, Tree Swallow, Cedar Waxwing, Gray Catbird, and Swamp Sparrow. Ruby-throated Hummingbird is a regular nester and can be seen resting high on dead snags surveying its territory. Raptors often patrol the sky, so be on the alert for Turkey Vulture, Red-tailed and Red-shouldered Hawks, and Northern Goshawk.

Axe Factory Road parallels Bigelow Brook for the next mile or so, weaving through habitats of open fields, wet bottomland, hemlock slopes, and streams. As you bird along the area listen for Black-and-white Warbler, Ovenbird, Hermit Thrush, and Field Sparrow.

The road crosses (0.7 miles) and then recrosses (0.1 miles) Bigelow Brook. Park in this area and explore the wetland habitat. In May, you should spot migrant Solitary and Spotted Sandpipers foraging along the sluggish flowing water or wet pools. Many wetland associated species found at the beginning of this road also occur here.

Go north on Axe Factory Road for 0.5 miles and continue straight onto Kinney Hollow Road at the junction. This road soon becomes paved as it crosses into the town of Union (0.1 miles). The next 0.2 to 0.3 miles along the road is a picturesque hemlock stand enhanced by a forest floor carpet of ferns. This evergreen woodland harbors nesting

Brown Creeper, House Wren, Black-throated Blue and Black-throated Green Warblers, and Hermit Thrush. During spring migration, the hemlocks should produce a variety of thrushes, warblers, and vireos. For the next mile the road passes through deciduous and coniferous woodland which can harbor Pileated Woodpecker, Eastern Wood-Pewee, Least and Great-crested Flycatchers, Red-breasted and White-breasted Nuthatches, Solitary and Red-eyed Vireos, Canada and Pine Warblers, Scarlet Tanager, Baltimore Oriole, and Dark-eyed Junco. A small spruce grove at 1.0 miles is worth investigating for boreal species, however, the property is posted, so please explore the site from the road. Check the stand for nesting Blackburnian and Yellow-rumped Warblers. Golden-crowned Kinglet is a potential breeder here.

Kinney Pond (0.3 miles) is the last stop along this tour. This picturesque pond fringed by hemlock and white pine creates an image of a more northern setting. The pond can produce Wood Duck and Solitary and Spotted Sandpipers during migration, as well as a variety of swallows (Tree, Barn, and Northern Rough-winged nest in the area). A scan of the sky may produce Broad-winged, Red-tailed, or Red-shouldered Hawks, all of which nest in the immediate area.

To return to Interstate 84, continue north along Kinney Hollow Road and go straight through the intersection with Scranton Road and Town Hall Road (1.2 miles). Turn left at Route 190 south. Follow Route 190 about 1.5 miles back to Interstate 84. If you want to visit Bigelow Hollow State Park, turn right at the intersection described above onto Town Hall Road and continue to Route 190 north. Follow Route 190 north (0.5 miles), turn right at Route 171 and travel 1.5 miles to the park entrance on the left.

40 NATCHAUG STATE FOREST

JAMES L. GOODWIN STATE FOREST

Chaplin, Eastford, and Hampton

The 12,448-acre Natchaug State Forest is located in the Eastern Hills primarily within the town of Eastford. Natchaug is an Indian name meaning the land between the rivers, which refers to the land that lies between the confluence of the Bigelow River and Still River. This state forest offers a variety of habitats--waterways, upland woodlands, conifer plantations, marshes, and wooded swamps interlaced with numerous trails and dirt roads that collectively provide excellent birding and hiking opportunities.

Birding at Natchaug is best during the nesting season but good passerine movements can occur during spring and fall migrations. Due to the large size of the forest, the best birding strategy is to do a car tour that loops through the forest. This birding tour will hit all the major habitat and birding spots, but along the route be prepared to spend some additional time exploring the various side trails and dirt roads.

DIRECTIONS

From Interstate 84 take Exit 69 (Route 74 to 44, Providence) and follow Route 74 east 7.5 miles to the intersection of Route 44. Turn left on Route 44 east for 5.2 miles, then turn right and follow Route 198 south to the forest entry (2.6 miles) on the left.

BIRDING

Natchaug State Forest

Enroute to the state forest entrance, stop and check the large Bank Swallow colony (active from May to July) on the west side of Route 198 (2.2 miles from Route 44). The colony is in a sand bank about 200 yards from the road. The property is private, so please observe the birds from the roadside. Belted Kingfisher also nests in burrows in this sand bank.

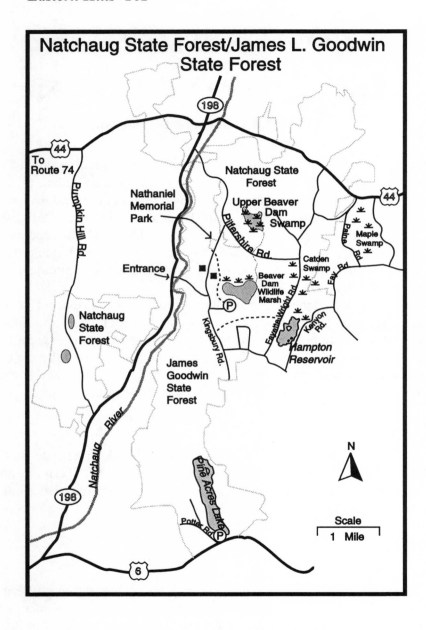

Natchaug State Forest/James L. Goodwin State Forest

Park Headquarters. A forest map can be obtained at the state forest headquarters, which is 0.8 miles from Route 198. You can bird along the way to the headquarters or you may elect to check this section on your way out again. In any event, set the odometer to zero at the state forest entrance.

To begin birding, park in the large pull-off on the right just as you enter the forest. The white pine plantation on both sides of the road are usually good for Red-breasted Nuthatch and Pine Warbler during the breeding season. Listen for the high-pitched call note and warbler-like song of the Brown Creeper; this interesting little species is frequently heard before it's observed. The Brown Creeper nests under the loose bark of the white pine and other suitable trees.

Follow the park road downhill 0.2 miles toward the Natchaug River. About 100 yards before the bridge take the dirt road on the left which leads through a delightful picnic area along the river's floodplain before it deadends. Breeding species found along the watercourse include Belted Kingfisher, Eastern Phoebe, Warbling Vireo, American Redstart, Louisiana Waterthrush, Baltimore Oriole, and a host of other common birds.

After birding the river, return to the forest road and continue as it ascends from the river valley. The steep-sided hemlock ravine on the right at 0.2 miles has harbored Acadian Flycatcher and Winter Wren in summer. At the fork (0.3 miles), bear left onto Kingsbury Road and continue another 0.1 miles to the Natchaug State Forest Headquarters. Stop and pick up a map at the map booth which is across from the flagpole and the sign for Natchaug State Forest.

The habitat around the headquarters consists of open lawn and field. During the nesting season, Mourning Dove, Barn Swallow, Northern Mockingbird, Chipping Sparrow, House Finch, and House Wren can be found here.

Beaver Dam Wildlife Marsh. Make a U-turn at the headquarters and retrace your route for 0.1 miles, then bear left at the fork (a right would return you to the park entrance) as the forest road (Kingsbury Road) turns to dirt. Drive 0.1 miles before making a left turn to the Beaver Dam Wildlife Marsh parking area. This large marsh surrounded by deciduous and coniferous woodlands is attractive to wildlife.

Species that nest in this area include Great Blue and Green Herons, Wood Duck, Northern Flicker, Yellow-billed and Black-billed Cuckoos (irregular, numbers fluctuate with extent of gypsy moth infestation), Eastern Kingbird, Willow Flycatcher, Tree Swallow, Yellow and Blue-winged Warblers, Common Yellowthroat, Common Grackle, and Swamp Sparrow. Virginia Rail may also nest in the marsh.

During migration, scan the open water carefully for waterfowl, especially Green-winged and Blue-winged Teals. You can pick up the Natchaug Trail along the left side (as you face the marsh) of the parking lot. This trail skirts the western edge of the marsh and will bring you closer to the shy residents that inhabit the far side of the wetland. In spring, Rusty Blackbirds are regular along the margin of the swamp.

Hampton Reservoir. Return to Kingsbury Road, turn left and drive 1.1 miles. This road takes you through deciduous forest interspersed with pine plantations. Along the way from mid-May through July, listen and watch for Eastern Wood-Pewee, Great Crested Flycatcher, Wood Thrush, Red-eyed Vireo, Ovenbird, and Scarlet Tanager in the deciduous woodland. In April and May, listen for the drumming of Ruffed Grouse and the loud, resonant tapping of the Pileated Woodpecker. At 1.1, miles bear left at the Y, then continue 0.7 miles turning left again onto Fayette Wright Road (not marked). A large stand of Norway Spruce and pine on the left, prior to and after the turn, can produce nesting Red-breasted Nuthatch, Black-throated Green and Blackburnian Warblers, and Solitary Vireo. These species can be found throughout the forest wherever suitable conifer patches occur.

Fayette Wright Road skirts along the west side of Hampton Reservoir through deciduous woodland which can reveal an assortment of species. Cerulean Warbler has slowly extended its breeding range into the eastern part of the state and can now be found quite regularly along this stretch of road. Between 0.4 and 0.5 miles along Fayette Wright Road is a small path leading to Hampton Reservoir. Take the path and check the reservoir for waterfowl, herons, and swallows, as well as other species. Continuing along the road be sure to scan the marsh from the small overlook (0.5 miles from junction); Swamp Sparrow and Common Yellowthroat are regularly found in this marsh.

Catden Swamp.   At 0.8 miles, Fayette Wright Road bisects Catden Marsh. The main portion of the marsh lies to the east (right).   Catden Swamp is an extensive palustrine environment containing a rich assortment of wetland birds. The swamp harbors nesting Virginia Rail, Willow Flycatcher, Blue-winged and Yellow Warblers, and various species of blackbirds. During late May and September, check the snags for migrating Olive-sided Flycatcher and other songbirds. Additional species found in this area will be similar to those around Beaver Dam Wildlife Marsh.

Upper Beaver Dam Marsh.   Continue north along Fayette Wright Road passing the gasline and turn left at Pilfershire Road (0.3 miles from Catden Swamp). This road traverses deciduous woodland interspersed with conifer plantations. At 0.7 miles stop and scan the Upper Beaver Dam Marsh. Check this picturesque marsh in summer for Wood Duck, Great Blue and Green Herons, Cedar Waxwing, American Goldfinch, and Swamp Sparrow. Be alert---if lucky you may encounter a Sora, Virginia Rail, or American Bittern in the vegetation along the edge of the emergent vegetation.

Nathaniel Lyon Memorial.   To complete the loop follow Pilfershire Road another 0.7 miles and turn left onto Kingsbury Road (unmarked, narrow, paved road displaying a sign marked "unit headquarters").   At 0.4 miles along the road is the Nathaniel Lyon Memorial and picnic area on the right.   A large stone fireplace and chimney is all that remains of the birthplace home of this distinguished figure. General Nathaniel Lyon was the first Union General killed in the Civil War. He was credited with saving Missouri for the Union and lost his life during the Battle of Wilson's Creek. To return to the main entrance on Route 198 follow Kingsbury Road by the headquarters and turn right (0.9 miles)--- this is the entrance road.

Pumpkin Hill Road.   To reach this section of the forest from the junction of Route 198 and the forest entrance road, go south on Route 198 for 3.0 miles. Turn right onto Pumpkin Hill Road, where a sign on the right announces the "Pumpkin Hill State Wildlife Area". Follow this road for 0.4 miles to a wood road on the left. The dirt road passes through a mature deciduous woodland. This site is noted for spring migrants and summer residents. A hike along this road from late April through May can produce a variety of migrants including flycatcher, vireos, warblers, and thrushes. Worm-eating and Cerulean Warblers are summer residents in this woodland. Other summer residents include many of the species listed above.

Continue along Pumpkin Hill Road and look for Canada Warbler, which is regularly observed during summer along the roadside before you reach the next birding stop. At 0.8 miles is a small stand of red cedar on the left toward the bottom of the hill just before a small pond. In many winters this cedar thicket has produced Northern Saw-whet Owl. The pond can be attractive to waterfowl in spring and fall and Wood Duck nest at the pond in summer. Be sure to check the other small pond on the right (0.6 miles) for wetland associated species.

Maple Swamp. To access Maple Swamp follow Route 44 west from the Route 198 intersection. Shortly after passing the Pomfret Town Line sign turn right (3.3 miles) onto Paine Road (gravel road). Follow Paine Road 0.3 miles to the swamp on the left. Maple Swamp is a large expansive palustrine habitat consisting predominately of marsh and swampland. Scan the cattail and sedges for elusive wetland species: Virginia Rail nests and American Bittern is occasionally observed during migration and in summer. Great Blue Heron nest in the trees on the west side (right) of the road between the small wetland and Catden Swamp farther west. Other breeding species to watch for are Least Flycatcher and Swamp Sparrow.

James L. Goodwin State Forest
To get to the James L. Goodwin State Forest from the entrance road to Natchaug State Forest follow Route 198 south to Route 6 (3.5 miles), turn left and follow Route 6 east for 3.0 miles. Turn left onto Potter Road and drive 0.1 miles to the nature center (on the left) and parking lot which is to the right.

Located in Hampton and Chaplin, The James L. Goodwin State Forest consists of 2,171 acres of mixed deciduous woodland interspersed with conifer plantations of white pine and mixed spruces. Aquatic habitats include several small streams and Pine Acres Lake.

Natchaug State Forest adjoins James L. Goodwin State Forest to the north. A number of trails and wood roads crisscross the property and provide access to the assorted habitats. A conservation center, museum, and arboretum provide insight into all the forest practices common in Connecticut. An information booth near the parking lot displays a map and offers additional information about the forest.

Drive or walk down to the boat ramp overlooking Pine Acres Lake. This large and shallow lake is littered with standing and fallen dead timber which provide numerous nooks and crannies for waterbirds and waterfowl to forage and hide. Wood Duck and Hooded Merganser (suspected breeder) are summer residents that nest in tree cavities. Other summer visitors include Great Blue and Green Herons. Migrants include Pied-billed Grebe, Common Merganser, and an occasional Olive-sided Flycatcher, as well as dabbling ducks. Nesting raptors are Barred Owl, and Red-tailed, Red-shouldered, and Sharp-shinned Hawks.

The numerous conifer plantations harbor many of the same species described for Natchaug State Forest including Red-breasted Nuthatch, and Pine and Black-throated Green Warblers. During winter, the conifer cone crops may yield winter finches, especially during incursion years.

41 STORRS AREA TOUR
Mansfield

The Storrs region offers a number of interesting sites for birders who want to work the interior of eastern Connecticut. Mainly rural and residential, much of the area consists of mowed and cultivated fields, thickets, and scrub, interspersed with woodlands. Many species of birds common to open fields and croplands can be found throughout the year, but the area is best for spring and fall migrations.

DIRECTIONS
To get to the first birding site---the "W" Parking Lot on the University of Connecticut campus---take Exit 68 off Interstate 84 (Route 195, Tolland and Mansfield). Head south on Route 195 (Storrs Road) for 6.7 miles. The parking lot entrance is on the right, just north of the university water towers.

BIRDING
During classes the parking lot is restricted to University of Connecticut students, but it is generally open at other times. It is also best to bird the campus on weekends or early in the morning before student activity picks up. Permits to park and a campus map can be obtained at the W Lot traffic booth. Don't be tempted to park illegally because the traffic police are notoriously vigilant when classes are in session.

University of Connecticut Campus
"W" Parking Lot. Habitats at the back side of the parking lot include cultivated fields to the north and west, thickets, a small pond and large areas of mowed grass. A dirt road provides foot access around the edge of the farm field and into the woods and thickets. The pond can be checked from the edge of the parking lot. This mix of habitats has proved exceptional for attracting migrants, especially in fall.

In summer, the thickets and trees around the pond can produce Eastern Kingbird, Northern Mockingbird, Gray Catbird, Cedar Waxwing, Yellow Warbler, Common Yellowthroat, and American Goldfinch--all nest nearby. The list of fall migrants includes Bobolink, Philadelphia Vireo (rare), Yellow-breasted Chat (rare), several sparrows

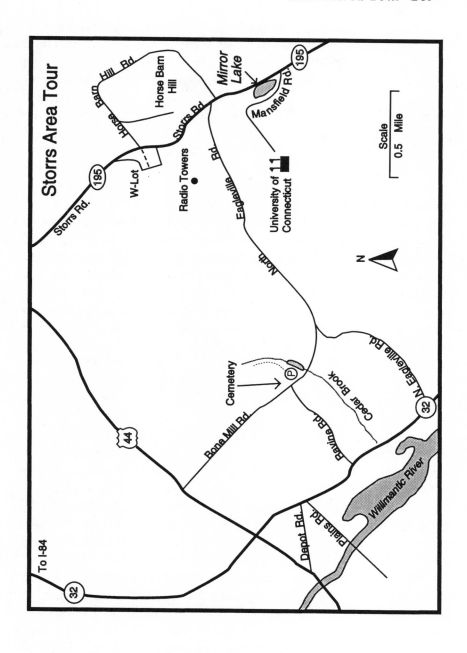

Storrs Area Tour

such as the Savannah, White-crowned, Field, Lincoln's and the rarer Grasshopper and Clay-colored. Both Mourning and Connecticut Warblers have been found in September mainly at bird banding locations but both are rare and move through the area quickly. Snow Bunting flocks have occurred in November and December. In late fall the cornfields are also good for American Pipit, Horned Lark, and the occasional Lapland Longspur. Other rare migrants reported from this area include Whimbrel, Gyrfalcon, Northern Shrike, and Greater White-fronted Goose.

Horse Barn Hill Road. Exit the "W" Parking Lot and cross Route 195 to Horse Barn Road (directly opposite the center of the lot). Named after a former horse barn and an equestrian area, Horse Barn Hill Road makes a broad loop to the right, returning to Route 195 a short distance further south. Horse Barn Hill is part of the campus; the fields and buildings are for raising cows, chickens, sheep, pigs, and horses and the fields are cultivated for food to feed the animals. Take care to avoid disturbing farm animals---close all gates and don't walk through the crop fields in spring and summer. The low marsh on the right of this road can support a variety of shorebirds, gulls, and geese and is famous for a Glossy Ibis flock in 1958. The first right after the dairy barn is a dead-end road that provides central access to bird the fields and wet areas along the road side.

The fields attract a variety of open habitat species throughout the year; in summer, American Kestrel, Eastern Bluebird, Barn, Northern Rough-winged and Tree Swallows, Killdeer, Savannah, Chipping, and Field Sparrows, Eastern Meadowlark, and Bobolink all nest. Fall migrants that frequent the fields and grassy areas include Horned Lark, Savannah Sparrow, and American Pipit which may also linger into winter. In winter, the fields often host large flocks of Canada Goose which should be carefully checked for stragglers such as the occasional Snow Goose and the much rarer Greater White-fronted Goose and Barnacle Goose. Here, and at Mirror Lake (below), are good spots to check the Canada Geese flocks for individuals of the smaller Richardson's race. Scan the gull flocks for the rarer Iceland and Lesser Black-backed Gulls. Red-tailed Hawk (resident) and American Kestrel are also regularly seen in fall and winter. Merlin is a regular but uncommon migrant and Peregrine Falcon (rare) is occasionally spotted. Northern Harrier sometimes hunt over the fields in fall and winter. In summer, the pig barns and pig ponds are always worth checking for swallows, sparrows, Indigo Bunting, and blackbirds. On the eastern slope a red fox has denned for the past several years.

Mirror Lake. From the south end of Horse Barn Hill Road turn left, heading south on Route 195 for 0.4 miles and turn right onto Mansfield Road. The lake is on the right. Although small, Mirror Lake usually holds flocks of waterbirds and some wetland edge species. In winter, the flocks of mallards spill over onto the nearby campus lawn as they hunt for acorns. Check the ducks, gulls, and geese for occasional rarities such as Iceland Gull and Greater White-fronted Goose. Double crested Cormorant is regular in fall. Other waterfowl which make an occasional appearance include Wood Duck, Green-winged Teal, and Northern Pintail. In fall and winter, Canada Geese roost on the lake at night. These birds should be checked for the same stragglers previously listed at Horse Barn Hill.

Pink Ravine
Visit this site in May, when pink phlox is in full bloom and spreads across the cemetery. From Mirror Lake turn left on Route 195, heading north. Take the first left (0.5 miles) onto North Eagleville Road. Follow North Eagleville Road for 1.6 miles and turn right onto Bone Mill Road (as North Eagleville Road takes a sharp left). Continue on Bone Mill Road 0.3 miles to a parking area on the right, just after crossing a small bridge. The cemetery is on one side of the parking area and a pond on the other. You can hike the trail along the edge of the pond and along the brook into the woods. The site is good for Red-shouldered Hawk, Yellow-rumped, Black-throated Green, and Pine Warblers, American Redstart, Louisiana Waterthrush, and Blue-gray Gnatcatcher, all of which nest along the brook.

You can also hike along Ravine Road which begins on the other side of Bone Mill Road and parallels the hemlock ravine for awhile. Pine and Black-throated Green Warblers, and Yellow-throated Vireo are summer residents in the wooded areas while Brown Thrasher and Prairie Warbler can be turned up in thicket and scrubby growth. Bird the woods, fields, and thickets along Bone Mill Road and Ravine Road from the roadside only, **as trespassing on private property is strictly prohibited here.** A Cattle Egret was spotted in the fields here in 1993. Northern Bobwhite was once regular along the road but is now scarce; listen for them in spring.

Plains Road

Follow Ravine Road (directly opposite the parking area) downhill to Route 32, turn right onto Route 32 for 0.3 miles and then left onto Plains Road (the dirt road just before Depot Road). Plains Road goes between a field on the left and an overgrown field and deciduous woodlot on the right, crosses an active railroad line, then continues to the Willimantic River and its marshy floodplain (0.2 miles). Park along the roadway near the bridge and check the river habitats. Again, stick to the road as all of the land is private. Check the fields, wetlands, and riverside trees for nesting Gray Catbird, Warbling Vireo, Yellow and Blue-winged Warblers, and Common Yellowthroat. In spring and fall, a variety of other warblers and sparrows migrate through the river valley. Eastern Meadowlark is a regular breeder in the field habitat.

42 MANSFIELD HOLLOW STATE PARK
Mansfield and Windham

This 2300-acre state park is good for landbird migrants and grassland birds in spring, summer, and fall. It is also one of the best locations in northeastern Connecticut for shorebirds during summer and fall. The state park includes the 500-acre Naubesatuck Lake (also known as Mansfield Hollow Lake), which was created in 1949 by the U.S. Army Corp of Engineers as a flood control reservoir. Today, the park is jointly managed by state and federal agencies to develop and promote a variety of recreational facilities and activities including hiking, boating, and fishing. Birdwatchers benefit from the mix of habitats that are protected and managed.

The park offers a number of trails including the Nipmuck Trail, which work through mixed hardwoods, fields, brushy marsh, lakeside vistas, pastures, and old orchards. Summer recreational activity in the park can be high, so plan to bird in the early morning hours, before the park begins to fill up with people.

DIRECTIONS

To access the park take Exit 68 (Route 195, Tolland and Mansfield) off Interstate 84 and go south on Route 195 for 12.1 miles, turning left at the traffic light onto Bassetts Bridge Road. Follow this road for 0.4 miles and turn right onto Mansfield Hollow Road. Continue straight at the stop sign (0.2 miles) along Mansfield Hollow Road for another 0.2 miles to a parking lot just below the dam.

BIRDING

Mansfield Hollow Dam. From the parking lot you can scan the area at the base (west) of the dam, which features a small pool and runoff-sculpted stream bottom habitat into which intrude cattails and other wetland plants. Painted turtles are usually abundant in summer, sunning lazily at the edge of logs or boulders while the occasional snapping turtle can make an appearance almost any time but is most likely seen in spring and fall.

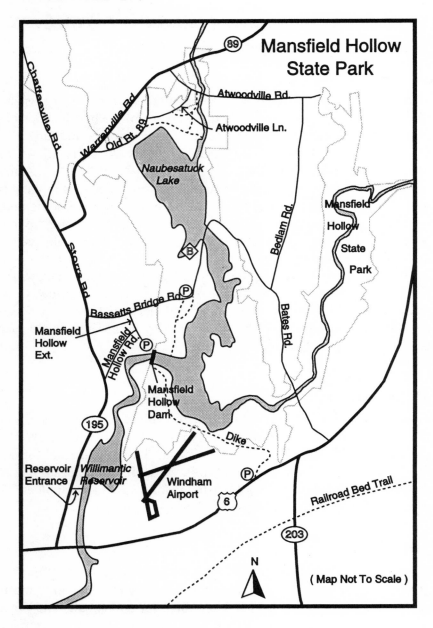

Mansfield Hollow State Park

(Map Not To Scale)

In spring and fall, swallows can be abundant, especially Barn, Tree, and Bank. The shoreline, sandy spots, and wetlands can hold shorebirds. Check for Solitary Sandpiper during migration and for Spotted Sandpiper from spring into fall. In summer, Wood Duck and Mallard swim the pools or hide among the vegetation while Green Heron forage in the shallows.

The wetland attracts a variety of breeding birds so check for Gray Catbird, Red-winged Blackbird, and Yellow Warbler. The shade trees and lawns near the dam may yield Northern Mockingbird, Warbling Vireo, American Robin, Eastern Bluebird, Northern Cardinal, House Finch, and Chipping Sparrow.

After checking the area by the dam, climb the stairs to the top of the dam and check out the impoundment below. Small flocks of Snow Bunting have been spotted from this location in late fall.

Sandy Bottom. Backtrack along Mansfield Hollow Road and turn right onto Bassetts Bridge Road for 0.5 miles to a parking lot on the left. Park here and cross the road to the trail which first goes through a mature white pine grove, then comes out on an access road leading to the lake. Turn left and hike down the dirt access road with the mowed field on your right and pine woods on the left. The fields and edge are generally good for Eastern Meadowlark, Killdeer, and Eastern Bluebird.

The white pines provide nesting habitat for Downy Woodpecker, Tufted Titmouse, and Pine Warbler, while Baltimore Oriole, House Wren, and Red-eyed Vireo are invariably in the immediate vicinity of the scrubby edge. Other residents possible throughout the year include Ring-necked Pheasant, Ruffed Grouse, and Northern Bobwhite.

The road ends on a pleasant pine-clad bluff that overlooks Naubesatcuk Lake below and a grassy field off to the right. Check the lake for waterfowl and the shoreline for herons and shorebirds.

To return to the car, backtrack a short distance along the road to a trail leading off to the right, through a mixed woodland and beneath a powerline. The trail ends at Bassetts Bridge Road a short distance below the parking lot, which is to your left. As before, the mixed woods along the trail are good for migrating warblers, vireos, sparrows, and thrushes. Along the way, check the powerline scrub growth for Prairie and Blue-winged Warblers, Eastern Towhee, and Brown Thrasher which nest here in summer.

Boat Launch. From the parking lot, turn left onto Bassetts Bridge Road and continue for 0.5 miles to the boat launch on the left. Park and check the water's edge and open water on both sides of the road for gulls, cormorants, waterfowl, and waders. The lake is best birded for waterbirds from fall to spring. Regular species include Common Loon, American Black Duck, Ring-necked Duck, and Common Merganser. In fall, check cormorants for the occasional Great Cormorant which is a rare inland migrant; it has been found several times from mid-October to mid-December. Osprey is a regular visitor to the lake in spring. Both Barred and Great Horned Owls have been heard calling from the pine-covered hillsides on the other side of the lake. In summer, Pine Warblers sing from the pines adjacent to the parking lot.

Turnip Meadow. This is the premier spring migrant trap in the Storrs area. To get to Turnip Meadow, follow Bassetts Bridge Road back to Route 195, turn right and head north on Route 195. Turn right at 0.5 miles onto Route 89 (Warrenville Road) and head east. Continue on Route 89 for 1.5 miles, and take a sharp right onto a narrow old road (the former Route 89). Drive down the road for 0.3 miles and park near the barricade.

The trail to Turnip Meadow is to the left, about 130 yards beyond the barricade. A short walk down the former highway beyond the trailhead gives a good view of the relatively quiet waters of the north end of the lake. On warm, sunny days in spring this place is great for spring migrants. In fall and winter, check for waterfowl and waterbirds, especially dabbling ducks and mergansers. After birding the roadway and lake, backtrack up the road and take the trail on the right. This is a ski trail which works through overgrown fields, thickets, woodlands, swamps, and lake overlooks; the whole providing good birding opportunities throughout the year. In spring and fall, the trees and thickets along the trail can be loaded with vireos and warblers. In summer, Wood Thrush, Veery, Blue-winged and Yellow Warblers, Common Yellowthroat, Ovenbird, House Wren, Veery, and woodpeckers can be common along the trail. Winter foraging flocks of Northern Cardinal, Dark-eyed Junco and American Tree, White-throated, Field, and Song Sparrows are often encountered along the trail.

The trail continues along the edge of the lake or through bordering wetlands. Another trail branches off to the right into an impressive and soon to be impassible swamp, which is an ideal place to find Swamp Sparrows in summer and Northern Waterthrush during migration.

After birding the swamp, backtrack to the ski trail, turn right and continue to follow it through the hardwoods, birding for Red-eyed and Yellow-throated Vireos, Blue-gray Gnatcatcher, Louisiana Waterthrush (along the stream), American Redstart, and Black-and-white and Worm-eating Warblers. Additional songbirds are always possible along the trail during spring migration.

The first trail branching off to the left goes a short distance and then passes along the edge of a private yard before ending at a paved road. Your car is to the left and down the road a short distance. Alternately, you can continue birding the ski trail which follows along the Mount Hope River, then crosses Atwoodville Road. To get back to the car turn left on Atwoodville Road and hike about 100 yards to Atwoodville Lane on the left, which leads to the car (about 0.3 miles).

Nipmuck Trail. Famous among hikers and birders, this old Indian trail starts in southern Mansfield and continues into Massachusetts. The trail is accessible from several points in the Mansfield area. It can be accessed just north of the picnic area in Mansfield Hollow State Park, on Warrenville Road (Route 89) across from the South East School, and at the Chaffeeville Road Bridge (1.7 miles north of Route 195). Along its length, the Nipmuck Trail winds through a variety of woodland and scrub habitats, around part of Naubesatuck Lake and along a portion of the Fenton River.

The Grist Mill Trail section of the Nipmuck goes through hemlock and red maple woodlands along the Fenton River from the Chaffeeville Bridge to the Grist Mill and is often good for spring birding. To reach the Chaffeeville Road Bridge, head north on Route 195 from Route 89 (Warrenville Road) to Chaffeeville Road (0.5 miles). Turn right and drive 1.7 miles to the bridge and park beyond the river. Look for blue blaze trail markers which follow the river to the north (toward the Grist Mill) and south. Along the trail, look for the same woodland and edge species listed previously.

Additional Birding Sites

Willimantic Reservoir
This reservoir is one of the better sites in the Mansfield area for migrant waterfowl. To get to Willimantic Reservoir from the junction of Route 195 and Warrenville Road (Route 89), follow Route 195 south for 1.9 miles and turn left into the reservoir entrance marked by a sign "Town of Windham Water Works." While driving south on Route 195, you will bypass an open field on the left (1.7 miles) overlooking the Willimantic Reservoir. This property, owned by the town of Mansfield, is open to the public and provides a good view of the reservoir. To survey the reservoir from this site, continue south on Route 195 to the reservoir entrance, turn around and backtrack (0.2 miles) and park on the right side of the road. Scan the reservoir from the field or walk downhill for a closer view.

From fall through spring, check the shoreline and open waters for waterfowl and waterbirds that frequent the reservoir. Waterfowl regularly seen include Canada Goose, Ring-necked Duck, Common Goldeneye, Bufflehead, Ruddy Duck, and Common Merganser. Pied-billed Grebe and American Coot frequently occur during fall migration.

Windham Airport and Dike
To access this spot from the reservoir driveway, follow Route 195 south for 1.1 miles and then turn left and head east on Route 6. Follow Route 6 east for 2.5 miles and park on the left, near the eastern end of the airport. Walk around the barricaded road (old Route 6) and bear left up to the top of the dike which forms an elevated walkway that continues in a great curve around the north side of the airport and the southern section of Naubesatuck Lake. From the dike, the airport fields are to the left and a marsh to the right, behind which is a red maple swamp. The dike provides a great spot to scan these habitats. A scope is handy when birding from the dike since some birds are frequently seen at a distance.

The mowed grasslands around the runway can be great for a wide variety of species, including Eastern Meadowlark, Eastern Kingbird, Chipping and Field Sparrows, and Killdeer. In summer, the marsh is consistently good for Swamp Sparrow, Red-winged Blackbird, Common

Grackle, Belted Kingfisher, and Great Blue and Green Herons. Bank, Barn, Tree, and Northern Rough-winged Swallows are regular from spring to September and Purple Martin in early fall. Grasshopper Sparrows have been found in summer several times and are considered rare breeders. Look for the sparrows in the taller grass at the north side of the airport. Check from the top of the dike, as public access to the airport is restricted.

From July into autumn, this is also a great place to spot shorebirds and gulls. The rarer Baird's, Upland, and Buff-breasted Sandpipers have occurred in the grassland, while Pectoral, Solitary, Semipalmated, Least, and Spotted Sandpipers, and Greater and Lesser Yellowlegs are regular in the pool and marsh at the base of the dike. Check the peeps carefully for White-rumped Sandpiper, an occasional fall migrant. In July, 1995, an extremely rare Long-billed Curlew spent a week at the airport and in September, 1995, two immature Sabine's Gulls stopped briefly on the lake for a first state record.

Atlantic White Cedar Swamp and Railroad Bed Trail

This recently discovered birding locale in Windham is slated to become part of the property managed by the Joshua's Tract Conservation and Historical Trust. To access this location from the airport area, continue east on Route 6 to Route 203 south (0.5 miles). Turn right, drive 0.1 miles, and park on the right by a dirt trail leading up an embankment. A sign "closed to motor vehicles" signals the start of this trail.

The railroad bed trail begins at the top of the embankment. Although relatively new as a birding site, this location appears to have good potential for migrants. A mile-long hike along the railroad bed in early May can produce a variety of migrating thrushes, vireos, and warblers in the woods to either side. Birding can be especially good for canopy species, which can be spotted nearly at eye level along the elevated railroad bed.

From late April through May, the walk may produce several thrushes (Wood, Hermit, and Veery), warblers (Black-and-white, Blue-winged, Northern Parula, Cape May, Yellow-rumped, Blackpoll, Yellow, and American Redstart), Baltimore Oriole, and Rose-breasted Grosbeak.

In the cedar swamp and marsh fringe listen and look for Northern Waterthrush and Swamp Sparrow. This location should also yield a number of interesting breeding species such as Red-shouldered Hawk,

Great Horned Owl, Black-billed Cuckoo, Winter Wren, and Prairie, Black-throated Blue, and Worm-eating Warblers. A winter search of the conifers may produce Northern Saw-whet Owl.

43 QUINEBAUG RIVER
WILDLIFE MANAGEMENT AREA
Canterbury and Plainfield

The Quinebaug River Wildlife Management Area is comprised of 1,219 acres of varied habitat consisting of fields, riparian woods, ponds, and thickets. This wildlife management area can be good for spring migrants that traverse the Quinebaug River valley corridor and breeding species of riparian, field, and thicket areas. In addition, the ponds and wetlands below the Quinebaug Valley Hatchery are known to harbor semi-hardy species into early winter.

An interesting feature of the site is the Quinebaug Valley Hatchery, the newest and largest of Connecticut's three fish hatcheries. The Quinebaug Valley Fish Hatchery is the largest fish hatchery in the Northeast. About 1.5 million trout eggs are fertilized annually and the production of fish for stocking in the state's streams amounts to some 500,000-600,000 brown, brook, and rainbow trout per year. The hatchery includes a visitor center (open 10:00 am to 6:00 pm) at the headquarters building where visitors can view the holding tanks located in the building. Hatchery operations are described via a series of live and static displays illustrating management procedures and fish ecology. Other features of the visitor center include attractive collections of mounted freshwater and saltwater game fish.

DIRECTIONS
On Interstate 395 take Exit 89 (Route 14, Sterling and Central Village) and follow Route 14 west for 1.1 miles to Cady Lane on the right (sign posted announcing the "Quinebaug Valley Hatchery"). Turn right and bear left onto Cady Lane. When Cady Lane turns left (0.2 miles) continue straight on Trout Hatchery Road through a bar-gate (0.4 miles) to the fish hatchery (0.1 miles) on the left.

BIRDING
The bar-gate just before the fish hatchery is open from 6:00 am 8:00 pm; if you arrive during off-hours you will need to hike in from the gate. Upon your arrival, check the white pine and deciduous woodland near

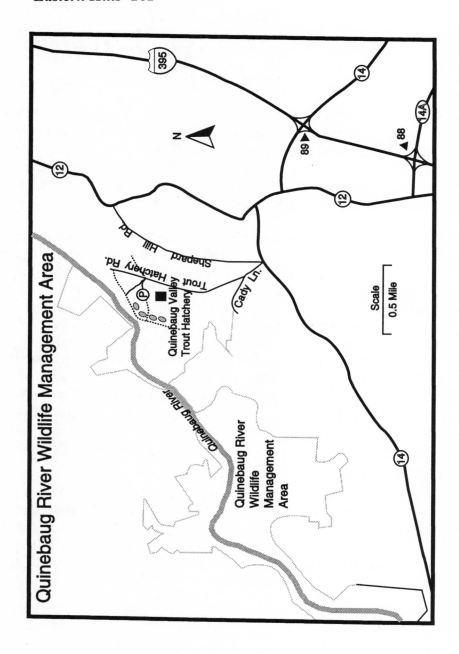

Quinebaug River Wildlife Management Area

395

14

14A

88

89

12

12

14

Shepard Hill Rd.

Trout Hatchery Rd.

Cady Ln.

P

Quinebaug Valley Trout Hatchery

Quinebaug River

Quinebaug River Wildlife Management Area

N

Scale
0.5 Mile

the gate for nesting Pine and Black-throated Green Warblers and Chipping Sparrow. This location offers the birder an opportunity to compare the similar trilling songs of both the Pine Warbler and Chipping Sparrow---the trill of the Pine Warbler is slower, softer, and more melodious than that of the Chipping Sparrow.

From the bar-gate continue 0.1 miles to the fish hatchery on the left. In late spring and summer, swallows are regularly observed pursuing insects overhead. Check for Northern Rough-winged, Barn, Bank and Tree Swallows, and Purple Martin. Purple Martins breed in the nest boxes surrounding the fish hatchery. Other species found in this area include Eastern Kingbird, Eastern Phoebe, and American Goldfinch.

To take a one-mile-loop hike that traverses a good mix of habitats, continue along Fish Hatchery Road 0.1 miles beyond the fish hatchery. Turn left by the pump house at the end of the paved road, then bear left and follow the dirt road slightly downhill to a parking lot. Hike along the dirt road at the opposite end of the parking lot working past the fishing pond for children on the left and along the side of a white pine woodland. The road continues to a slight bluff overlooking much of the hatchery grounds. Straight ahead and to the left (west and south) are broad fields and large holding ponds for stock fish. To the immediate right are two small ponds with marsh fringe and beyond them are grassy fields flanked by the Quinebaug River.

In spring, scan the fields for migrant Eastern Meadowlark, Bobolink, and Savannah Sparrow. The overlook is also a good spot to scan the sky for migrant Osprey, which pause to work the holding ponds for food. Other species taking advantage of the easy food include Great Blue and Green Herons. The small sandbank almost at your feet has held nesting burrows for Belted Kingfisher, and Bank Swallows are also possible.

Check the small ponds for nesting waterfowl (Mallard, American Black Duck, and Wood Duck) and Spotted Sandpiper; during migration Blue-winged (uncommon) and Green-winged Teals both occur.

Continue downhill and bear right between the two ponds. In late fall and early winter, these ponds and the ponds near the hatchery outflow have yielded a variety of semi-hardy species. Uncommon species found in the past include Great Blue Heron, Common Snipe, Eastern Phoebe, Palm Warbler, and Rusty Blackbird. Who knows what might turn up---an Iceland Gull was spotted on the 1994 Christmas Count!

After passing between the ponds bear right and head north through the field. In summer, the riparian woods, field edge, and marshy ponds along the Quinebaug River should yield Cedar Waxwing, Gray Catbird, Blue-gray Gnatcatcher, Warbling Vireo, Yellow Warbler, Common Yellowthroat, Baltimore Oriole, Red-winged Blackbird, and Common Grackle. A variety of species occur during migration. When hiking through the field periodically check the sky for the regularly seen Turkey Vulture and Red-tailed Hawk and the occasional Red-shouldered or Broad Winged Hawk.

About half-way through the field, the road bears right and returns to the parking lot. To continue the loop, bear left, and follow another road to the north end of the field and through the woodland before circling back to Fish Hatchery Road. From late spring through summer, the woodland may harbor Black-billed and Yellow-billed Cuckoos (both irregular), Eastern Wood-Pewee, Great Crested Flycatcher, House Wren, American Redstart, Ovenbird, Black-and-white Warbler, Scarlet Tanager, Rose-breasted Grosbeak, and Eastern Towhee.

The trail skirts thickets and fields of barberry and Russian olive just before emerging from the woods onto the paved road. The parking lot is to the right. Before you return to the car, take a short hike uphill into the field on the left beyond the barrier gate. This area should produce a nice assortment of breeding field and thicket species including Brown Thrasher, Blue-winged and Prairie Warblers, Indigo Bunting, and Field, Chipping, and Song Sparrows. Resident species found in the field and thickets include Wild Turkey, Northern Bobwhite (some are stocked birds), Mourning Dove, Carolina Wren, and Northern Mockingbird.

Typical species found throughout the year along the loop-hike are Red-bellied, Hairy, and Downy Woodpeckers, Blue Jay, Black-capped Chickadee, Tufted Titmouse, White-breasted Nuthatch, Northern Cardinal, and Song Sparrow.

44 *PACHAUG STATE FOREST*

Voluntown, North Stonington, and Griswold

This much fragmented state forest is comprised of more than 24,000 acres in six towns, making it Connecticut's largest state forest. Extensive tracts of mature and second-growth hardwoods, conifer stands, red maple swamps, creeks, and ponds represent the most common habitats within Pachaug State Forest. The coastal Atlantic white cedar swamp is reputed to be the finest wetland of this type in the state. Two additional attractions include the open cranberry heath along the Pachaug River and the Rhododendron Sanctuary. These unusual habitats are highly recommended to the nature enthusiast and botanist as well as the birder. Unfortunately visits by birders to this expansive state forest are infrequent and the potential of the area is yet to be fully explored.

The H. H. Chapman part of Pachaug State Forest, located north of Voluntown, has the widest variety of birding habitats. A small campground in this area makes an ideal base camp for birding activities.

Numerous trails, including the Pachaug, Nehantic, and Quinebaug Trails, and wood roads provide access to much of the H. H. Chapman Block. A map of Pachaug State Forest can be obtained at the state forest headquarters. The map is useful in identifying the major trails and dirt roads.

Birding is best during migration but the nesting season also yields an assortment of species.

DIRECTIONS

From Interstate 395 take Exit 85. Northbound travelers continue straight at the end of the exit ramp to the next traffic light and turn right onto Route 138. Traveling southbound, turn left at the end of the exit ramp onto Route 138. Follow Route 138 through Voluntown to the junction of Routes 138, 165, and 49 (about 6.6 miles). Turn left and head north on Route 49. At 0.6 miles turn left onto Headquarters Road (unmarked). Immediately in front of you and to the left is the parking area for Beachdale Pond.

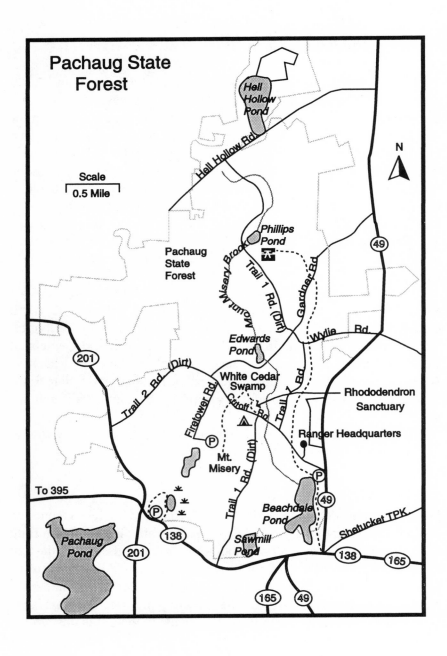

Pachaug State
Forest

BIRDING

Beachdale Pond and Nehantic Trail.   Beachdale Pond is a small pond with a scrubby border of alder and cattail.   From spring through summer scan the pond and surrounding habitat for Great Blue and Green Herons, waterfowl (Wood Duck and Mallard nest, while migrants include Green-winged and Blue-winged Teals and Hooded Merganser), Osprey, Belted Kingfisher, flycatchers (Eastern Kingbird and Eastern Phoebe), swallows, blackbirds, Cedar Waxwing, and warblers (Yellow, Common Yellowthroat, and American Redstart).   Virginia Rail can sometimes be heard or seen along the marshy edge.

After birding the pond, hike the Nehantic Trail which passes through the picnic area and continues north along the pond's eastern boundary for 0.5 miles before it crosses over Headquarters Road. This short section of trail wanders through a beautiful forest of white pine that contains breeding Red-breasted Nuthatch, Brown Creeper, Winter Wren, Pine, Black-throated Green, and Yellow-rumped Warblers, and Veery.   During migration periods various species of kinglets, vireos, warblers, and thrushes are possible.

Rhododendron Sanctuary and Atlantic White Cedar Swamp.
Follow Headquarters Road northwest from Beachdale Pond to a "Y" intersection (junction of Cutoff Road and Trail 1 Road) at 0.8 miles. Enroute you will pass (0.3 miles) a sign announcing the forest headquarters.   To obtain a map of Pachaug State Forest turn right and proceed to the headquarter's building. Maps are located in an information booth by the front door of the office. At the "Y", bear left onto Cutoff Road and continue 0.2 miles to the Rhododendron Sanctuary on the right, across from the field (do not bear left before the field). A sign along the right side of the road marks the trailhead to the Rhododendron Sanctuary.

The sanctuary trail is about 0.3 miles long with a small loop at the end. The Pachaug Trail and Nehantic Trail also merge with and follow the sanctuary trail part way through the area, but diverge from the loop to go deeper into the white cedar swamp.   If you decide to continue along the Pachaug Trail where it diverges into the swamp (near the loop), be aware that the footing becomes wet and tricky. However, the rough section is short (0.2 miles) and the trail soon joins with an abandoned forest road. Turn left and follow the forest road back to Cutoff Road. A trip through the Rhododendron Sanctuary is intriguing and mysterious. Overhead, tree and shrub branches form convoluted tangles, while beneath, the ground is covered by a luxuriant growth of mosses and ferns. A walk through the rhododendron thickets in early July will give the birder an opportunity to appreciate the lovely floral bloom of this magnificent shrub. Nearby is an equally impressive stand of Atlantic white cedar, a rare wetland habitat in Connecticut. Hiking the trails through these areas in summer can yield a variety of nesting species---most of which will be heard rather than seen. Look and listen for Brown Creeper, Hermit Thrush, Solitary Vireo, Black-throated Green and Canada Warblers, and Northern Waterthrush.

Campground and Field. To get to the campground continue along Cutoff Road for 0.1 miles and turn left into the camping area (diagonally across from the abandoned forest road returning from the cedar swamp). Birding habitat at the campground consists of hardwoods interspersed with tall white pines. The campground road makes a semicircular loop around a mowed field. Summer birding of these habitats should turn up Whip-poor-will, Eastern Kingbird, Eastern Phoebe, Red-breasted and White-breasted Nuthatches, House Wren, Chestnut-sided and Blue-winged Warblers, Ovenbird, Red-eyed Vireo, and Eastern Towhee. From late March into June, American Woodcock can frequently be observed performing it's courtship ritual in the field at dusk.

Mount Misery . A short hike (about 1.0 miles round trip) from Cutoff Road to the summit of Mt. Misery rewards the hiker with a panoramic view of the gentle rolling hillsides of eastern Connecticut. To reach the trail to Mt. Misery, continue along Cutoff Road about 0.1 miles beyond the campground entrance. A blue trail cuts across the road (this is the same Nehantic/Pachaug trail that transverses the white cedar swamp).

Park on the right and take the trail on the left side of the road. The trail cuts through hemlock woods and makes a steep ascent up the hill through a series of short switchbacks before making a final ascent to the overlook. Hilltop habitat consists of a shrubby cover of lowbush blueberry, scrub oaks, and a growth of saplings. In summer, some of the nesting species that can be turned up along the trail include Prairie and Black-and-white Warblers, Ovenbird, Gray Catbird, and Eastern Towhee. From the summit, the insect-like trill of Worm-eating Warbler can be heard from the hillsides below. On summer evenings, this is also a great spot to listen to the beautiful melodies of the Veery, Hermit, and Wood Thrushes. While at the summit check the sky carefully for raptors---often Turkey Vulture and Red-tailed Hawk can be spotted and sometimes Broad-wings as well. Red-shouldered Hawk also occurs, but is usually heard calling from the wet woodland in the valley.

You can also drive to Mount Misery by continuing along Cutoff Road 0.2 miles past the trail and turn left at Firetower Road. Follow the road 0.6 miles to its end. Park and follow the path up the hill a short distance to the overlook.

Trail I Road. At the "Y" junction of Cutoff Road and Trail 1 Road follow Trail 1 Road north. This forest road cuts through the Youth Group Camping Area. The mix of conifers stands, wetlands, and second growth hardwoods along the road can be birded productively.

From May to mid-July, the open areas and wetlands by the Youth Campground reveal many of the same species found near the family campground and also Mourning Dove, Northern Flicker, Northern Mockingbird, Cedar Waxwing, Common Grackle, Baltimore Oriole, American Goldfinch, and Chipping Sparrow.

Further along, the hemlock and pine conifer stands (between 0.3 and 0.9 miles from the "Y") are ideal for Red-breasted Nuthatch, Brown Creeper, Winter Wren, Solitary Vireo, Pine and Black-throated Green Warblers, and Ovenbird. The hardwoods are good refuge for a variety of breeding species including Ruffed Grouse (listen for the tell-tale drumming which initially sounds like an outboard motor that increases in tempo), Great Crested Flycatcher, Eastern Wood-Pewee, Veery, Wood Thrush, Red-eyed Vireo, American Redstart, and numerous warblers. Hermit Thrush nest in the hemlock stand between 1.3 and 1.5 miles along with many of the species noted above. Barred Owl and Northern Goshawk (rare) have been observed along Trail I Road and in woodlands elsewhere in the forest. During migration check the conifers for Ruby-crowned and Golden-crowned Kinglets, thrushes, vireos, and various species of warblers.

Route 138 Pond. To explore this locale take Route 49 south from the junction of Headquarters Road to the Route 138 intersection (0.6 miles), turn right and follow Route 138 east for 2.5 miles. As you approach the intersection of Route 201 park on the right by the Pachaug Trail sign.

Follow the Pachaug Trail north from the parking area to reach the pond and marsh. The trail cuts through a shrubby field that has grown in since the hardwoods were cut for timber. In summer, birding the field can yield Chestnut-sided and Blue-winged Warblers, Common Yellowthroat, American Goldfinch, and Field Sparrow among others.

About 0.3 miles along the trail you approach the pond. To obtain an unobstructed view of the pond, bear right and walk to the dike. The view from the dike should reveal a variety of wetland species. From late spring through summer, scan the area for Great Blue and Green Herons, Wood Duck, Belted Kingfisher, Eastern Phoebe, Eastern Kingbird, swallows, Cedar Waxwing, Red-winged Blackbird, Common Grackle, and Swamp Sparrow. The extensive marsh vegetation around the pond may harbor Virginia Rail and Sora.

During fall and spring, check the pond for migrating waterfowl and Pied-billed Grebe. With luck you may spot an American Bittern hiding within the vegetation. To return to the car continue across the dike and walk through the white pine plantation to the road.

Winter Birding. Winter birding at Pachaug State Forest may reveal an array of interesting winter visitors and permanent residents. During winter finch years, plan a tour through the forest that includes a number of conifer stands. These areas should be surveyed carefully for Red and White-winged Crossbills, Pine Siskin (normally occurs every year), and Pine and Evening Grosbeaks. Open weedy and secondary growth areas adjacent to the conifer woodlands may yield Common Redpoll and Purple Finch. Squeaking and pishing at or near the conifer stands may produce winter finches, and will certainly attract Red-breasted (sometimes in droves) and White-breasted Nuthatches, Golden-crowned Kinglet, Black-capped Chickadee, and, if you are a very fortunate birder---a Northern Goshawk or Barred Owl. The white cedars and rhododendron can be checked for Northern Saw-whet Owl, but don't stray from the trails in these unique and fragile habitats.

45 DEVIL'S HOPYARD STATE PARK
East Haddam

The unusual terrain of Devil's Hopyard has long been considered hallowed ground by the superstitious. Early New Englanders believed that land's wild and rugged beauty was a favorite haunting ground of the devil, who, it was said, had a great eye for strange natural features. This colonial folklore is reflected in the names given many of the Hopyard's striking landmarks, such as Devil's Pulpit, Devil's Kettle, Devil's Tombstone, and Devil's Oven .

A central feature of the 860-acre Devil's Hopyard is Chapman Falls, located near the main parking lot. The falls drop more than 60 feet over a series of steps in the Scotland schist stone formation. At one time, the falls supplied water power for Beebe's Mills, named after the original owner of the park. In addition to the falls, the park offers over 15 miles of trails through hemlock and hardwood forests, shrubby swamps, and small brooks. The park is bisected by Eight Mile River, a tributary of the Connecticut River.

The river and its riparian woods provide a natural migration corridor for birds and other wildlife. The conifer and mixed woodlands of Devil's Hopyard also host a variety of late spring and summer nesting species. Cooper's Hawk, Northern Goshawk, and Red-shouldered Hawk have nested here and Barred Owls can be called in almost every month of the year.

DIRECTIONS

Traveling northbound on Interstate 95 take Exit 70 (Route 156, Old Lyme). Turn left onto Route 156 and go west about 8.7 miles to the junction with Route 82. If southbound on Interstate 95, take Exit 70 (Old Lyme). At the light at the end of the exit ramp go straight ahead on Route 1 to the Route 156 junction (0.8 miles). Turn right onto Route 156 west and continue 8.5 miles to Route 82. Turn right onto Route 82 for 0.2 miles and turn left onto Route 434 (Hopyard Road). The park begins about 2.6 miles down the road on the right. Continue to the entrance to the main picnic area and parking lot on the right (3.2 miles from Route 82/Route 434 junction).

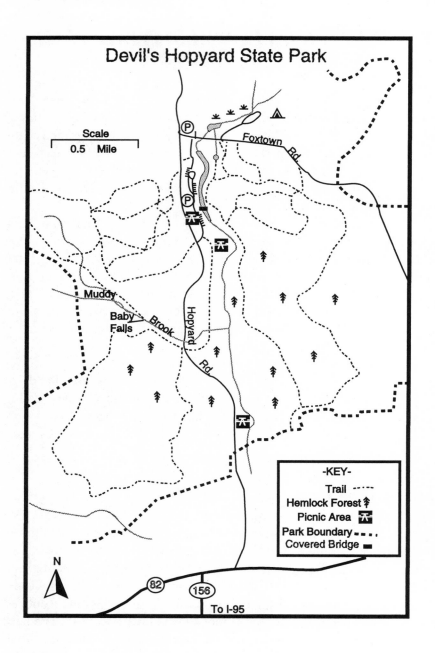

Devil's Hopyard State Park

Scale
0.5 Mile

Foxtown Rd.

Muddy
Baby
Falls
Brook

Hopyard Rd.

-KEY-
Trail --------
Hemlock Forest 🌲
Picnic Area 🎪
Park Boundary ....
Covered Bridge —

N

82
156
To I-95

BIRDING

Picnic Area.   Park at the main (upper) picnic area. The picnic area is shaded by tall oaks, beech, and hickory. To the right (east) of the picnic area is Eight Mile River, bordered by hemlock and birch.

In late May, the trees around the picnic area and along the river can yield a variety of warblers, thrushes, and vireos. In spring and summer, the tree tops are favorite nesting sites for Blue-gray Gnatcatcher, Cerulean Warbler, and Rose-breasted Grosbeak.   Other breeding species may include Baltimore Oriole, American Redstart, and Black-and-white, Blue-winged, and Chestnut-sided Warblers. The picnic area also attracts the usual assortment of the woodland and edge species.

Red Trail.   After birding the picnic area walk the Red Trail, which begins at the south end of the picnic area. The Red Trail parallels the river as it winds southward through a mature woodland of hemlocks interspersed with hardwoods. Undergrowth along the trail consists mostly of mountain laurel and large clumps of cinnamon fern and interrupted fern.

In spring, the trees along the river can be good for migrant warblers and vireos. Summer nesting species along the trail include Least and Acadian Flycatchers, Scarlet Tanager, and Red-eyed and Yellow-throated Vireos in the woodland canopy. Other common nesters include Tufted Titmouse, Ovenbird, White-breasted Nuthatch, Brown Creeper, and Downy Woodpecker. The shrubs and trees along the trail are good for Veery, Hooded Warbler, and Chipping Sparrow while Eastern Towhee and Song Sparrow forage through the forest floor litter.   The Red Trail crosses a small stream called Muddy Brook, which is a perfect spot for nesting Louisiana Waterthrush and Eastern Phoebe. If scared up, Louisiana Waterthrush sometimes put on a broken-wing show to lead you away from the nest. Keep moving as you check out this behavioral display to avoid disrupting the nesting pair or by calling attention to the nest site.

Shortly after crossing the brook, the Red Trail turns sharply right and crosses Hopyard Road, then continues on the other side through mixed woodlands of hemlock, oak, and birch. Shortly after crossing the brook near Baby Falls, the Red Trail junctions with the Yellow Trail. The Yellow Trail features a luxuriant witch hazel growth, good for Hooded

Warbler. Alternately, stay on the Red Trail which climbs a wooded slope and eventually works back to the picnic area. The mixed woodland along the Red Trail is excellent for nesting Black-throated Green Warbler and Solitary Vireo, both of which most likely will first be heard singing high in the forest canopy. Other species sure to turn up along this trail include the Scarlet Tanager, Wood Thrush, and Great Crested Flycatcher.

Vista Trail Loop. After birding the Red Trail return to the main picnic area parking lot. From here you can take the Vista Trail Loop which covers about two miles of steeply wooded hillside. The Vista Trail Loop begins across the covered bridge to the right (east) of the main picnic area. Just beyond the covered bridge on the right, is a trailside bulletin board displaying the Vista Trail Loop and other trails, as well as points of interest and local history.

The Vista Loop Trail first curves to the right, paralleling the east bank of Eight Mile River. In late spring and summer, the hemlocks by the river can produce Blue-gray Gnatcatcher and Acadian Flycatcher, especially along the river bank. Thrushes are also well represented along the trail, including Wood and Hermit Thrushes, Veery, and American Robin. Listen for Worm-eating Warblers which nest on the steep, rocky hillside to the left of the trail. Other summer birds along this section of the trail may include Eastern Wood-Pewee, Red-eyed Vireo, and Black-and-white Warbler.

In winter, the hemlocks attract foraging flocks of Black-capped Chickadee, Brown Creeper, Downy and Hairy Woodpeckers, and Winter Wren (uncommon). During finch irruptive years keep a sharp lookout for Pine Siskin, Evening Grosbeak, and crossbills.

After paralleling the river, the Vista Loop Trail cuts left and starts uphill, at times becoming steep, so watch your footing. The hemlocks gradually give way to a more open dry oak-hickory woodland. At the summit, the birder is rewarded with a beautiful view of the valley below. The vista is a good place to spot Red-tailed Hawk and Turkey Vulture in summer or perhaps a migrating Broad-winged, Cooper's, or Sharp-shinned Hawk in fall. From here, the Vista Loop Trail is all downhill through mixed woodland featuring huge American beech interspersed with oaks, maples, and birch. Toward the bottom on the hill hemlocks and red cedar again become more prevalent. In fall and winter, a check beneath the red cedars may yield pellets or whitewash that indicate the presence of a Long-eared or Northern Saw-whet Owl. The trail narrows as it passes through a mountain laurel thicket before returning to the covered bridge.

Chapman Falls. To get to Chapman Falls from the picnic area you can either walk or drive north along Hopyard Road for 0.2 miles. Turn right onto Foxtown Road and park in the lot on the left. Chapman Falls is just across the road from the parking lot.

Trails allow access to the upper and lower reaches of Chapman Falls. The potholes found at the base of the falls are some of the finest examples of pothole stone formations in the Northeast. Many are near-perfect cylindrical impressions in the rock ranging in size from a few inches to several feet in diameter and depth. These potholes were originally formed by the scouring action of small rocks that had been caught in the swirling eddies downstream of the falls. As the stones spun around and around they cut a depression in the rock. Eventually the stones were ground away but the depression they created trapped more stones which continued to enlarge the hole. The early settlers offered a different explanation for these perfectly round holes. They thought that the devil had got his tail wet when he passed by the falls. This made him so mad that he burned holes in the rocks with his hooves as he bounded away!

In summer, the area around the falls can yield Eastern Bluebird, which are usually near the bridge, American Redstart, Baltimore Oriole, and Chipping Sparrow. Swirling flocks of Tree, Northern Rough-winged (spring), and Bank (spring) Swallows hunt insects above the water while Eastern Kingbird and Eastern Phoebe catch emerging flights of mayflies and other aquatic hatches.   On the way back to the parking lot, bird the marshy area on the north side of Foxtown Road. In spring, the swampy area can host migrating Palm, and Wilson's Warblers. Hermit Thrush, and Canada, Yellow, and Chestnut-sided Warblers nest in the shrubby vegetation adjacent to the marsh. In fall, Yellow-rumped Warbler, and Song, Fox, and White-throated Sparrows are often common migrants. In the evenings during August and early September this can be a good spot to watch Common Nighthawks forage.

46 HARTMAN PARK
Lyme

This recreational park is considered to be a good area to catch spring migration in the eastern part of the state. An early morning walk along Gungy Road and through Hartman Park can provide a nice mix of migratory species (especially during May) and an assortment of breeding species during late spring and summer. Gungy Road is a short section of roadway starting just north of the Lyme-Salem town line in Salem. Traveling south from Salem into Lyme, the road bisects deciduous upland and skirts along the western border of the 302-acre, town-owned Hartman Park. Hartman Park is an undeveloped tract of varied habitat including upland deciduous, wet bottomland, beaver pond, open field, and a powerline right-of-way. The park is adjacent to Nehantic State Forest and features about 9 miles of hiking trails and wood roads, including a couple of trails that weave in and out of the adjacent forest. All major habitats in the park are traversed by the network of trails.

Birding highlights at this site include a variety of migrant flycatchers, thrushes, vireos, and warblers. Broad-winged Hawk, Whip-poor-will, Willow and Least Flycatchers, Eastern Bluebird, White-eyed and Yellow-throated Vireos, and Hooded, Worm-eating, and Cerulean Warblers are several of the interesting species that nest.

DIRECTIONS

From Interstate 95 take Exit 70 (Route 156, Old Lyme) northbound. Turn left at the end of the ramp and travel west on Route 156 to the second traffic light (0.2 miles, junction of Route 1) then follow the directions described below. Southbound on Interstate 95 take Exit 70 (Old Lyme) to the traffic light at the end of the exit ramp. Continue straight for 0.8 miles to the intersection of Route 156 and turn right. Follow Route 156 west to Salem Road (7.6 miles), turn right and proceed 3.0 miles to Darling Road, turn right and drive 0.1 miles to Gungy Road on the right.

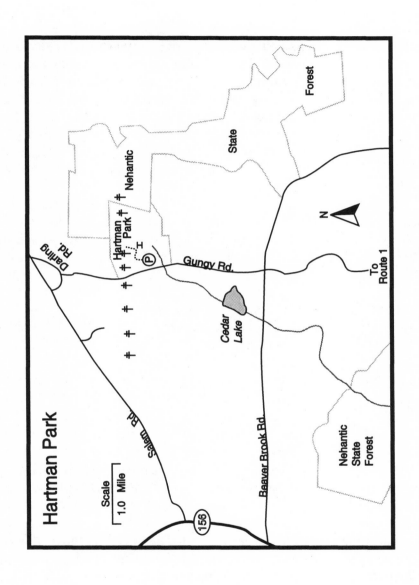

BIRDING

Start your mileage reading after turning right onto Gungy Road. Drive south along this route toward the Lyme town line. For the first half-mile or so the road cuts through a suburban neighborhood flanked by secondary growth deciduous woodland. At 0.9 miles, before reaching Hartman Park, stop and check along the roadside where from May through July you should find Red-eyed Vireo, Blue-winged and Worm-eating Warblers, Ovenbird, American Redstart, and Scarlet Tanager. On the right side of the road is a hillside with an open deciduous forest which is good habitat for Worm-eating Warbler.

After passing the Lyme town line (0.1 miles) you will notice two wood roads blocked by metal gates on opposite sides of the road (0.3 miles). Stop and hike down the wood road to the left (east) into the town park. The dirt road soon enters a small field with cherry trees and a few red cedars. Scan the field for nesting Eastern Bluebird, House Wren, and other cavity breeders which may occupy the nest boxes, as well as Cedar Waxwing and Chipping Sparrow.

Return to the car and stop at the powerline right-of-way (0.2 miles). This is an excellent spot to find birds of brushy field and shrub swamp habitats. If so inclined, a hike along the powerline road (to the east) should produce many birds. Breeding species to check for along this trail are Willow and Least Flycatchers, Northern Mockingbird, Brown Thrasher, White-eyed Vireo, Blue-winged, Prairie and Yellow Warblers, Common Yellowthroat, Northern Cardinal, Indigo Bunting, and Field Sparrow. Purple Finches have been spotted along the powerline in June and may occasionally nest. The nest boxes placed along the powerline road attract Tree Swallow, House Wren, and Eastern Bluebird. During summer evenings the unmistakable calls of the Whip-poor-will and Barred Owl emanate from the bottomland.

From the powerline, scan the sky for hawks. Red-tailed Hawk is common most of the year, whereas Red-shouldered and Broad-winged Hawks may be spotted during the breeding season.

After birding the powerline, walk down the road to look and listen for migrants and breeding species or drive down and park on the left side of the road at the main entrance to Hartman Park (0.4 miles from powerline). Take the dirt road on the left which meanders through a

M.S.SANIYR 93

bottomland and then along the edge of a former mill and pond before arriving at an information stand (about 0.2 miles) displaying a trails map and list of recent bird sightings.

Scan the pond. From spring through fall, Mallard, Wood Duck, Northern Flicker, Eastern Kingbird, Eastern Phoebe, Red-winged Blackbird, and Common Grackle are regular. During summer, Louisiana Waterthrush can be found in the small outlet stream below the dam. Check the maples for Blue-gray Gnatcatcher, Yellow-throated Vireo, Cerulean Warbler (uncommon) and Baltimore Oriole. The trails traversing the wetlands and deciduous hillside can produce breeding Ruffed Grouse, Red-bellied Woodpecker, Eastern Wood-Pewee, Great Crested Flycatcher, Wood Thrush, Veery, Black-and-white Warbler, American Redstart, Hooded Warbler (uncommon), Scarlet Tanager, and Rose-breasted Grosbeak. In spring migration, boreal forest passerines moving north may include Blackpoll, Tennessee, and Yellow-rumped Warblers, and Ruby-crowned and Golden-crowned Kinglets.

To get back to Route 156, head south on Gungy Road to the stop sign, turn right onto Beaver Brook Road and continue 2.6 miles to Route 156.

47 NEHANTIC STATE FOREST
Lyme

The Taney Hill tract of the Nehantic State Forest comprises more than 1,200 acres of mature and second growth hardwoods of oak and hickory, evergreens, laurel thickets, an extensive shrub swamp wetland, streams, and Norwich Pond and Uncas Pond.

The wetlands and adjacent woods of this state forest can be excellent in spring for migrant warblers and vireos, and the rarer Olive-sided Flycatcher. Nesting birds at Nehantic State Forest include Hooded and Worm-eating Warblers, Blue-gray Gnatcatcher, Red-shouldered Hawk, Barred Owl, Hooded Merganser, and Wood Duck. Birding the wetland thickets and adjacent habitats during fall can also yield an assortment of migrant songbirds and wetland species.

DIRECTIONS

Northbound on Interstate 95 take Exit 70 (Route 1 and Route 156, Old Lyme). Turn left at the exit ramp, going west on Route 156 to the second traffic light (0.2 miles) at the junction of Route 1, then follow the directions described below. Southbound on Interstate 95 take Exit 70 (Old Lyme) to the traffic light at the end of the exit ramp. Continue straight for 0.8 miles to the intersection and turn right onto Route 156. Head west on Route 156 for 3.8 miles to the entrance to Nehantic State Forest on the right. A sign marks the entrance.

BIRDING

Shrub Marsh and Adjacent Upland Woodland. The access road is narrow and rough riding. About 0.6 miles along, the road cuts through brushy marsh on both sides of the road. To bird the marsh park alongside the road about 100-150 feet further up from the culvert, on the left.

To the right of the road is a shrub swamp of buttonbush, alder, elderberry, willow, and poison sumac. White ash, grape, and bramble line the swamp edge. In spring, the shrub swamp can be a magnet for warblers, vireos, flycatchers, and thrushes which migrate northward up the Connecticut River Valley. At least 25 warbler species have been seen here from late April to early June, including Black-throated Green,

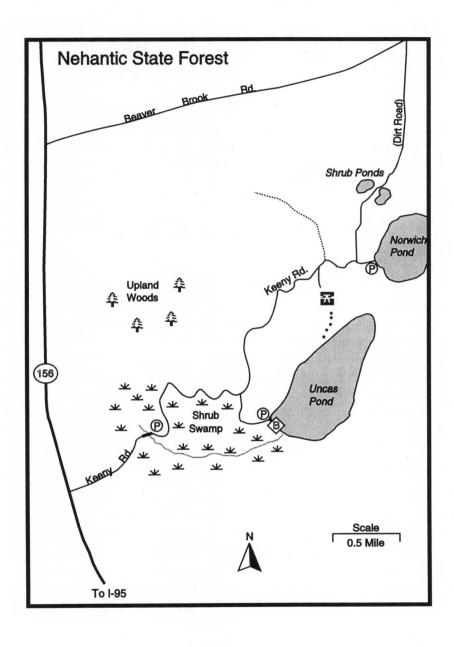

Nehantic State Forest

Black-throated Blue, Cerulean, and Northern Parula. This is also a good site to spot a variety of vireos including the Philadelphia (rare). Flycatchers can turn up in numbers and the Olive-sided Flycatcher (rare) moves through in late May-early June and again from late August into early September.

In spring and summer, the marsh and adjacent upland habitats hosts many cavity nesting species including Eastern Bluebird, Tufted Titmouse and an assortment of woodpeckers. Yellow Warbler, Rose-breasted Grosbeak, Common Grackle, Baltimore Oriole, American Goldfinch, and Least Flycatcher nest in the taller shrubs and trees along the marsh-upland border. In fall, the marsh can harbor an exceptional variety and abundance of sparrows. Four residents of interest include Red-shouldered and Broad-winged Hawks and Hooded and Worm-eating Warblers.

Uncas Pond and Adjacent Habitats. After birding the marsh and woodland, continue along the road for another 0.5 miles to a fork (1.2 miles from the state forest entrance). Signs at the fork provide distances to Uncas Pond and Norwich Pond. Take the right fork to the boat ramp at Uncas Pond. For most of its length, the road parallels the shrub marsh on the right, all the way to Uncas Pond. At Uncas Pond park alongside the road, taking care to not block access to the boat ramp.

Known locally as Hog Pond, Uncas Pond is a small, deep, natural body of water about 70 acres in size. It offers good fishing for brown and rainbow trout, bass, and the sea-run alewife. The clear and transparent waters also provide good fishing for Belted Kingfisher, Osprey, mergansers, and cormorants. In spring and fall, migrating Ospreys often stop to catch a meal before resuming their flight.

Spring migration brings a variety of swallows (Barn, Tree, Northern Rough-winged, Bank, and Cliff). Migrant songbirds may include Northern Waterthrush and Rusty Blackbird. During peak migration, both species can be fairly common but difficult to see as they skulk along the water's edge beneath the thick undergrowth. Common Merganser and Ring-necked Duck are less common but fairly regular spring and fall waterfowl migrants that often stop at the pond.

In summer, the thickets and shrubs along the pond edge and marsh usually shelter Blue-winged Warbler and Brown Thrasher (uncommon), Eastern Phoebe, Eastern Kingbird, Gray Catbird, White-eyed Vireo,

Common Yellowthroat, Yellow Warbler, and Northern Cardinal. Listen for their chorus in twilight hours of dawn and dusk throughout much of summer. Check the swampy areas for nesting Swamp Sparrow

Picnic Area and Norwich Pond. After birding Uncas Pond, backtrack to the fork and turn right, heading toward Norwich Pond. Worm-eating Warbler has been consistently found in the wooded hillsides along this stretch. At 0.8, miles a sign announces the picnic area on the right which can be accessed by a dirt road. The mixed woods around the picnic area have afforded good birding in the past. Two summer nesters to look for include the Blue-winged Warbler and Blue-gray Gnatcatcher. Some forest floor and undergrowth species likely seen between the fork and the picnic area include the Hooded Warbler, Ovenbird, Eastern Towhee, and Wood Thrush. The woods along the little brook that runs through the picnic area has hosted nesting Yellow-throated Vireo, Louisiana Waterthrush, Least Flycatcher, and Red-bellied Woodpecker. Barred Owls are resident and may respond to vocal imitation of their songs.

After birding the picnic area, continue along the road toward Norwich Pond. About 0.1 miles above the picnic area the Nayantaquit Trail begins on the left offering a hike through the scrubby, open woodland. About 0.3 miles further, a road to the right leads to Norwich Pond, a short distance to the east. This small 28-acre pond has a heavily wooded shoreline. Check the open water and pond edge for the species that were likely at Uncas Pond.

After birding Norwich Pond, return to the main road and turn right, continuing along the forest road which becomes dirt. Ruffed Grouse, Pileated Woodpecker, and other upland species are possible among the woodlands on either side of the road. About 0.9 miles, there is a dip in the road with wetlands on both sides. The wooded swamp on the right should be checked for Hooded Merganser and Wood Duck, both of which have nested here.

Further along, the road again becomes paved and a sign marks the state forest boundary. From here you can either retrace your path back through the forest or continue on a short distance to Beaver Brook Road. Several ponds along this stretch of the road are private, but may be worth checking for waterbirds from the roadway. At Beaver Brook Road a left brings you back to Route 156.

48A TRAILWOOD:

The Edwin Way Teale Memorial Sanctuary
Hampton

This property was purchased by the naturalist and writer, Edwin Way Teale in the late 1950's and immortalized in his book, *A Naturalist Buys an Old Farm*. Edwin Way Teale was a popular nature writer in the middle decades of this century. His books such as *North with the Spring* and *Autumn Across America* are timeless in their appeal. Trailwood is now owned and managed by the Connecticut Audubon Society.

Trail Wood is open for hiking and nature explorations from dawn to dusk. Edwin Way Teale's study in the old farmhouse is open on Saturdays by appointment (contact the Connecticut Audubon Society at 203-259-6305). A trail map and information display is provided in the outbuilding behind the house. The farm is preserved as a sanctuary and consists of about 150 acres of woodland, fields, a beaver pond, and brook. About 3.5 miles of trails provide access to most of the habitats. Birding is best during spring and fall migrations and from late spring and summer for nesting birds.

DIRECTIONS

From Interstate 395 take Exit 97 (Route 44, Woodstock, E. Putnam) and follow Route 44 west to its second junction with Route 97 (about 9.0 miles). Take Route 97 south to Kenyon Road on the right (4.0 miles). Follow Kenyon Road 0.5 miles to a gravel driveway on the left, marked by a sign "Trail Wood: The Edwin Way Teale Sanctuary of the Connecticut Audubon Society". Take the dirt/gravel driveway to the parking lot on the left (0.1 miles). From the parking lot, walk down the driveway to the former Teale farmhouse on the right.

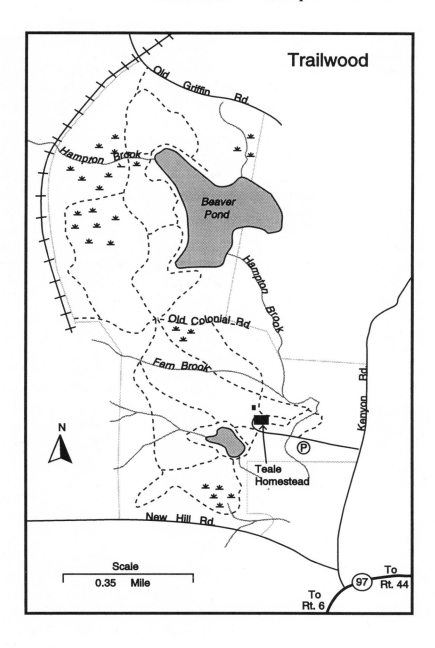

Trailwood

BIRDING

The birder has a choice of several trails which begin just beyond the buildings. Take the Fern Brook Trail to its junction with Old Colonial Road and turn left. Continue along the old road through the open woodland and turn right onto the Beaver Pond Trail which leads to the pond. In spring, this pond can be productive for Canada Goose, Mallard, Ring-necked Duck, Green-winged Teal, and Hooded Merganser. While birding the pond, keep an ear tuned for the rattle of Belted Kingfisher. During the nesting season, the trees that ring the pond should hold Northern Flicker, Red-bellied Woodpecker, Eastern Phoebe, and Eastern Kingbird.

The Beaver Pond Trail continues along the pond's western flank then turns left (west) through the Far North Woods which offer seasonal birding for thrushes, warblers, and vireos. Other trails traverse pastures and fields productive for Eastern Bluebird and sparrows throughout much of the year.

48B WEST THOMPSON LAKE
Thompson

Located in the northeastern corner of the state, West Thompson Lake was created by the U.S. Army Corp of Engineers. The 1,950 acres encompassed by this flood control area include the lake, the Quinebaug River north of the lake, fields, mixed hardwoods, conifer plantations, brushy swamps, and marshes. Birders can also explore the marsh and portions of the lake by canoe. The lake attracts waterbirds in spring and fall while from April through July the varied habitats hold an assortment of nesting species. In addition, September and October are good months to observe migrant hawks from the open vistas near the dam.

DIRECTIONS

To get to West Thompson Dam from Interstate 395, take Exit 99 (Route 200, N. Grosvendale). onto Route 200. Travel east on Route 200 for 0.6 miles and turn right onto Route 193 (Thompson Road). Follow

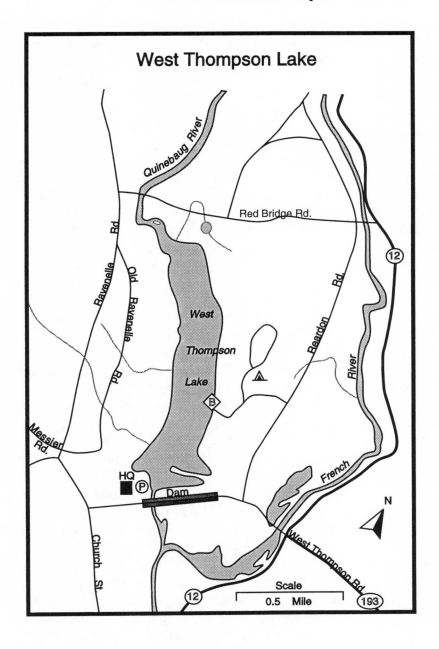

West Thompson Lake

Thompson Road another 1.7 miles to the junction with Route 12. Stay on Thompson Road, which continues straight through the junction and crosses the dam to the West Thompson Lake headquarters on the western side (0.9 miles). Park in the lot on the right, next to the headquarters building.

BIRDING

You can obtain a map of the West Thompson Lake area at the dam headquarters. From the parking lot at the dam scan the lake for waterfowl. Mallard, American Black Duck, Green-winged Teal, Ring-necked Duck, Bufflehead, and Common and Hooded Mergansers may be expected during spring and fall. Swallows (Barn, Northern Rough-winged, Tree, and Bank) and Eastern Phoebe are regular nesting species around the dam parking area and can also be seasonally common during migration periods.

To further explore the West Thompson Lake area, continue west on West Thompson Road and take the first right onto Ravenville Road, heading north. Many of the barricaded roadways and pathways along the right head down to the reservoir and are worth exploring.

To complete a circuit of West Thompson Reservoir, continue north on Ravenville Road to the first right onto Red Bridge Road. Stop near the bridge and bird the Quinebaug River. Both Red-shouldered Hawk and Warbling Vireo nest along the flood plain and adjacent uplands at the north end of the reservoir and along the river. Other nesting species found here include Common Yellowthroat, Yellow Warbler, and Baltimore Oriole.

From Red Bridge Road, a right onto Reardon Road will complete the circuit of the reservoir and take you back to the junction with West Thompson Road by the east end of the dam. The West Thompson Lake Campground is also located on Reardon Road about 0.5 miles north of the junction with West Thompson Road. The campground offers attractive campsites for birders that may want to spend a couple of days birding this part of northeastern Connecticut. The parking area near the boat launch and campground is an ideal spot to scan the lake for waterfowl or to launch a canoe to further explore the lake.

Southwestern Coastal

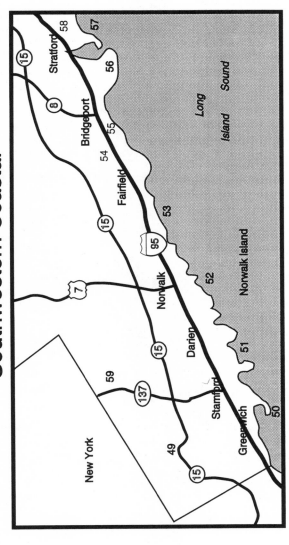

49. Audubon Center of Greenwich
50. Greenwich Point Park
51. Southwest Shoreline Tour
52. Norwalk Harbor Tour
53. Sherwood Island State Park
54. Connecticut Audubon Society Sanctuaries

55. Fairfield to Bridgeport Shoreline Tour
56. Great Meadows Marsh and Lordship Area
57. Milford Point
58. Gulf Pond
59. Laurel Reservoir

49 AUDUBON CENTER OF GREENWICH
Greenwich

Long considered one of the best birding locales in the southwestern part of the state, the Audubon Center in Greenwich is an educational facility owned and operated by the National Audubon Society. Another excellent birding feature at the center is the hawk watch site at Quaker Ridge, which ranks as one of the more spectacular fall hawk watch sites in southern New England.

The Audubon Center is comprised of 510 mostly wooded acres split into two major tracts; a 280-acre nature sanctuary---the Audubon Center---located at 613 Riversville Road and the 127-acre Audubon Fairchild Garden located on North Porchuck Road, about a mile south of the Audubon Center.

The Audubon Center is open from Tuesday through Sunday, 9:00 am to 5:00 pm. There is a nature center with a bookstore, a display gallery, and a bird-feeding station with observation windows and interpretive displays. About eight miles of trails provide access to most of the property which features a variety of habitats: mixed and deciduous woodlands, ponds, shrub and woodland swamps, and streamside habitats. Visitors who are not National Audubon Society members must pay a fee at the Nature Center Interpretive Building to walk the trails; a trail map is provided.

While the Audubon Center in Greenwich and Fairchild Garden are best for spring and fall bird migrations and hawk watches, summer birding offers a good selection of woodland and swamp nesting species.

Over 160 species of birds have been recorded at the Audubon Center, and for those birders with broader interests, there are more than 900 species of flowering plants and ferns.

Noteworthy species spotted at the Audubon Center through the years include Merlin, Peregrine Falcon, Yellow-throated (very rare), Prothonotary (very rare), and Cerulean Warblers, Summer Tanager, Blue Grosbeak, and American Bittern. Kentucky Warbler nests at the Fairchild Garden and Yellow-breasted Chat has nested in past years. Probably, the center's most spectacular bird was the Black-backed Woodpecker which put in an extended appearance around the old apple orchard in the early 1960's.

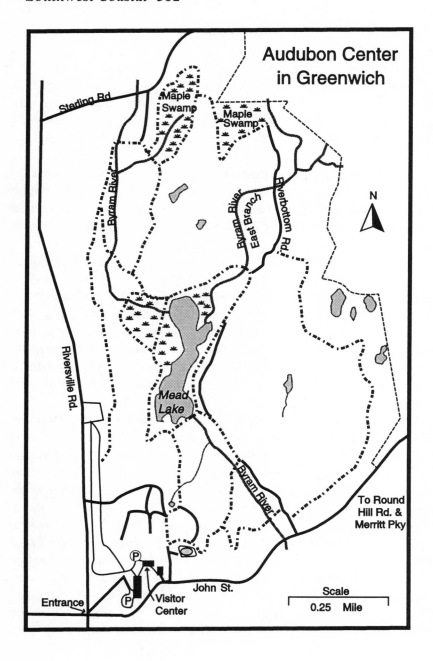

Audubon Center in Greenwich

DIRECTIONS

Take Exit 28 off the Merritt Parkway (Route 15) and follow Round Hill Road north for 1.4 miles to John Street on the left. Take John Street 1.5 miles to the stop sign at Riversville Road. The entrance to the Audubon Center in Greenwich is to the right.

BIRDING

A number of trails provide access to most of the habitats located within the Audubon Center at Greenwich. Most trails are named and many are well marked and maintained. Some, however, are unmarked and difficult to follow when snow or leaves blanket the ground. You can obtain a trail map at the Interpretive Center and check the trail signs which are provided at key junctions of trails throughout the property.

Nature Center and Quaker Ridge Area. Stop at the Interpretive Building to pay the fee and pick up a copy of the trail map. A large trail map is on display on the outside wall by the door. Feeders placed at strategic locations near the building attract resident and winter birds and should be checked. The roadside thickets are good for migrating sparrows and warblers. Summer nesting species of the thickets and the nearby old apple orchard north of the road include White-eyed Vireo, Blue-winged Warbler, and Carolina Wren. Check the bluebird nest boxes in the apple orchard and on Quaker Ridge for activity. During fall migration the open fields, thickets, and edge habitats here and along Quaker Ridge can produce a variety of birds. Sandhill Crane, Red-headed Woodpecker, Olive-sided Flycatcher, and Yellow-breasted Chat are rarer species seen here over the years. Flocks of winter finches, mainly Pine Siskin, are occasionally recorded. In 1993, no fewer than 76 Ruby-throated Hummingbirds moved through the area between 25 August and 29 September. Large flocks of Canada Geese, Snow Geese (including Blue Geese), and Brant can sometimes be common in October.

Discovery Trail to Mead Lake. To get to the Discovery Trail, follow the paved road leading down from the Interpretive Building to the bottom of the hill. Thickets of rose, forsythia, and grape tangles on either side are good for sparrows. Discovery Trail begins at the bottom of the hill, first winding around tiny Indian Spring Pond and then leading through wet woodlands of oak, maple, and American beech. At Mead Lake take the right fork along the eastern edge of the lake to the first of two tower bird blinds on the left of the trail. The first blind affords a view over the open water of Mead Lake, just beyond the sweet pepperbush and maple trees that provide cover for the blind. Scan the open water and scrubby vegetation along the edge for waterfowl, long-legged waders, and other species.

The second blind overlooks a shrub swamp of willow and sweet pepperbush. Ducks are regular, and Red-winged Blackbirds and Common Grackles nests in the tall grasses. Rusty Blackbird usually occurs here as an early spring (March and April) and fall (October and November) migrant.

After birding from the blinds, continue along the Discovery Trail. In summer, listen for Louisiana Waterthrush. This species nests along Byram River which parallels part of the trail to the left. The Discovery Trail junctions with Lake Trail, which cuts sharply to the left. The highlight of Lake Trail is an elevated boardwalk spur trail through the swampy end of Mead Lake. The well-maintained boardwalk cuts through poison sumac (so be careful), pepperbush, swamp rose, and red maple. The boardwalk is a good site for scanning the shrub swamp for waterbirds. The shrubs also provide good cover for birders wishing to check the open waters beyond for waterfowl. Canada Goose, Mallard, and Wood Duck nest around the lake. Spring migrants may include Hooded Merganser, Ring-necked Duck, Bufflehead, and Palm, and Yellow-rumped Warblers. Two common nesting species in the swamp include Yellow Warbler and Common Yellowthroat.

After birding Mead Lake, backtrack to Lake Trail and turn left. A short distance down the trail a sign points to Beech Hill Trail, which branches to the right. The aptly named Beech Hill Trail traverses an open woodland of American beech. Hairy, Downy, Red-bellied, and Pileated Woodpeckers can be turned up anywhere along this and the other woodland trails. Beech Hill Trail joins with the Maple Swamp Loop, which follows the edge of a maple swamp that lies in the extreme northern corner of the Audubon Center. Dominated by red maple, the swamp has a shrub strata of highbush blueberry, winterberry, and swamp azalea, and a substratum of hummock grasses and skunk cabbage. In late spring and summer, the swamp and surrounding woodland should yield Eastern Wood-Pewee, Red-eyed Vireo, American Redstart, Rose-breasted Grosbeak, and Scarlet Tanager.

The Maple Swamp Loop continues as the Hemlock Trail, which cuts through a mixed woodland of oaks and maples overshading a few lonely and decrepit hemlocks. In places, the Hemlock Trail is poorly defined and difficult to follow so keep alert. The Hemlock Trail makes a sharp switchback, then continues southward as Riverbottom Road on your trail guide. The wooded hillsides on either side of the trail offer nesting places for Worm-eating Warbler, Great Horned Owl, and Red-tailed and Broad-winged Hawks. Both hawks are most likely found first by their calls, and then spotted as they circle above the woodlands.

Watch for Old Pasture Trail which branches left. Take Old Pasture Trail which cuts through a small woods and then out across open fields along the trailside. The fields are a mix of blackberry and goldenrod, in which a few young cherry saplings are growing. The fields are especially good for sparrows in spring and fall. Even in mid-October a warm, sunny day can bring an assortment of sparrows, thrushes, waxwings, vireos, and other songbirds. Chipmunks chirp warnings as you walk the trail and snakes can be seen (and more often heard rustling through the leaves) as they hunt chipmunks, birds, and other prey.
Continue along Old Pasture Trail, which winds through an open woodland of beech, maples, and oaks that are guarded by the occasional "muscle-bound" hornbeam alongside the trail. Old stone walls winding through the woods give mute testimony to the time when "Old Pasture" meant something more than the woodland trail it denotes today.

Old Pasture Trail meets Clovis Trail, which continues through taller woodlands of oak, birch, and maple. Mainstays of the woods here and elsewhere at the center include the ubiquitous Blue Jay, Black-capped Chickadee, White-breasted Nuthatch, Tufted Titmouse, and Ruffed Grouse (occasionally). Below Indian Spring Pond, the Clovis Trail joins the Discovery Trail again. To return to the Nature Center go left at the trail junction. The right fork of Discovery Trail leads back to Mead Lake.

Hawk Watching at Quaker Ridge The hawk watch site along Quaker Ridge is just inside the front gate and to the left. Parking is to the right in the lot by the Ecology Workshop building. During the fall migration, from late-August into early November (weather permitting), the hawk watch site is staffed daily by Greenwich Audubon Society members and volunteers.

Hawk flights begin in late August with the appearence of the first few Broad-winged Hawks and American Kestrels. Counts build quickly in September, which is typically the peak migration month when thousands of hawks stream by overhead along this popular migration skyway. Mid-September features large numbers of Broad-wings (one year 30,000 were counted in a single day!) along with hundreds, and sometimes thousands, of Sharp-shinneds. Ospreys, American Kestrels, and Cooper's Hawks are also most commonly seen in September while Merlins, Northern Harriers, and Bald Eagles are occasional. In October, Turkey Vultures are especially common, along with continued high numbers of Sharp-shinned and Red-tailed Hawks. October is also the most likely month to spot Red-shouldered Hawk, and the rarer Peregrine Falcon, Golden Eagle (about 6 each year), Rough-legged Hawk, and Northern Goshawk. A Swainson's Hawk was an October surprise in 1991. The Red-tailed Hawk and Turkey Vulture movement continues into November, although sharply reduced in numbers. Except for an occasional straggler, other raptor species have pretty much completed their migrations through the area by then.

Audubon Fairchild Garden

When visiting the Audubon Center of Greenwich, a birding trip to the National Audubon Society's Fairchild Garden is also recommended. In late spring and summer especially, many birders consider this wild flower garden to be superior to the Audubon Center for birding variety. Fairchild Garden features 8 miles of trails through wooded hillsides, bottomland woods, meadows, and wet thickets.

To get to Fairchild Garden from the Audubon Center, go left (south) on Riversville Road for 0.4 miles and turn left onto North Porchuck Road for 0.5 miles. The entrance to Fairchild Garden is on the right. A pathway leads into the woods from the northwest corner of the parking lot. A trail map is displayed at a booth near the entrance or you can obtain one at the Audubon Center's bookstore. Fairchild Garden is open daily from dawn to dusk, so if you want to bird the gardens in the very early morning or late evening hours it is best to call

ahead and make arrangements.

A number of short trails such as the Rhododendron Trail, Alder Trail, and Dogwood Trail provide access to most of the habitats that comprise Fairchild Garden. Kentucky Warbler, a rare species threatened by forest fragmentation, nests along the western boundary of Fairchild Garden. The Kentucky Warbler typically builds its nest at the base of a shrub in dense undergrowth of wet woodlands. Listen for its song, a rapid 2-syllabled rolling *churry-churry-churry-churry*. With luck, you may spot a bird leaping up to pick insects off the undersides of leaves as it forages among the undergrowth. **Please respect this small breeding population. Don't use tapes or "pishing" to locate and annoy the birds. If you see a female performing the nest distraction display leave the area immediately!**

The wooded slopes provide nesting habitat for Worm-eating and Black-and-white Warblers, and American Redstart, as well as several woodpeckers including Red-bellied and Pileated. An early summer evening spent along the trails will almost invariably produce Eastern Wood-Pewee, Great Crested Flycatcher, Veery, Wood Thrush, Tufted Titmouse, Red-eyed Vireo, and Scarlet Tanager. A pair of Broad-winged Hawks usually nest in the woodland.

In the wet thickets and bottomland woods and wood edges, you can often find Eastern Phoebe, Gray Catbird, Carolina and House Wrens, White-eyed Vireo, Common Yellowthroat, and Eastern Towhee, all of which nest in the area.

The garden's shallow ponds may yield American Black Duck and Wood Duck. Ruby-throated Hummingbird and Blue-winged Warbler occur in the more open meadows. Formerly, Yellow-breasted Chat and Henslow's Sparrow nested in Fairchild Garden, but both species are now very rare in Connecticut.

Fairchild Garden provides exceptionally good birding during spring and fall migrations, when warblers and sparrows can be abundant. Look for the same spring and fall migrants that were listed for the Audubon Center. Rarer migrants that have been seen at Fairchild Garden include Yellow-throated and Mourning Warblers and Yellow-bellied Flycatcher.

50 *GREENWICH* *POINT* *PARK*

Greenwich

Located in southern Fairfield County close to the Connecticut and New York border, Greenwich Point Park, also known as Tod's Point, encompasses about 149 acres of coastal habitat. Jutting into Long Island Sound with its northern edge enclosing Greenwich Cove, Greenwich Point has proven excellent for a number of good birds through the years and boasts Wilson's Plover, Manx Shearwater, Gray Kingbird, and Burrowing Owl among its most famous rarities.

Birding habitat consists of sandy beaches, salt marsh, coastal ponds, and coastal deciduous woodland complemented with an admixture of ornamental trees and shrubs. Birding is especially productive during spring and fall. Winter offers the chance to pick up rarities. Summer is an "off" season for birding because of the high recreational use of the park's beaches and the restricted access for nonresidents.

Before the causeway was constructed, Greenwich Point Park was an island at high tide and thought to be the site where the original settlers resided in the early 1640's. Later, the point became a coastal estate which contained a private golf course. The town of Greenwich purchased the property in 1945 and converted it into a municipal park.

From April through November, Greenwich Point Park is open only to residents of Greenwich. During the rest of the year the park is open to all visitors during daylight hours. Birders may call the Greenwich Parks Department for information about the park.

DIRECTIONS

Take Exit 5 (Route 1, Riverside and Old Greenwich) off Interstate 95. Turn right at the traffic light at the end of the ramp, heading north on Route 1. At the first traffic light turn right onto Sound Beach Avenue (0.2 miles). Stay on Sound Beach Avenue for 1.8 miles, going through Old Greenwich to the junction with Shore Road. Bear right on Shore Road and continue 0.8 miles to the park entrance.

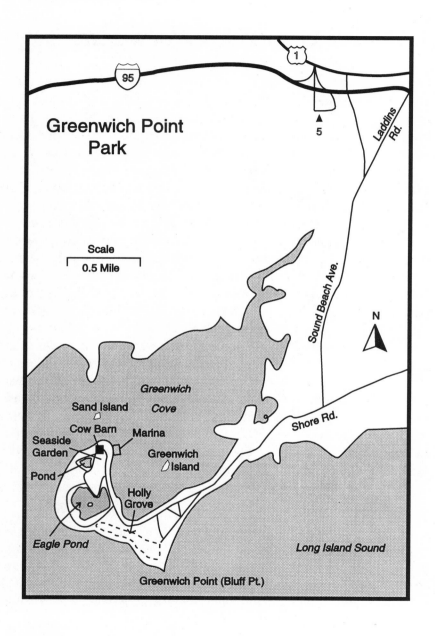

Greenwich Point
Park

Scale
0.5 Mile

Greenwich
Cove

Sand Island

Cow Barn   Marina

Seaside
Garden

Greenwich
Island

Pond

Holly
Grove

Eagle Pond

Greenwich Point (Bluff Pt.)

Long Island Sound

Shore Rd.

Sound Beach Ave.

Laddins Rd.

N

BIRDING

The park can be hiked in a few hours, or you can drive from one birding spot to another. Parking lots are just beyond the entrance and at a number of additional locations in the park. Check the beaches on either side of the causeway for gulls and shorebirds. The low, rocky island to the west is Greenwich Island which often harbors wintering Great Blue Herons. In fall, migrant waterfowl and shorebirds such as plovers, sandpipers, turnstones, and others occur along the shoreline. Rarer species reported along this stretch include Wilson's Plover, Cattle Egret, Tundra Swan, and King Eider. The sandy beach to the left (east) of the causeway has proven good for gulls. In winter, the gull flocks sometimes yield white winged species. Check the black-backed gulls carefully for Lesser Black-backed Gull which is a rare winter straggler.

A coastal hawk watch station at the nature center, just inside the park entrance, is staffed by the Greenwich Audubon Society and a few volunteers during the fall raptor migration in September and October. Good numbers of Ospreys, buteos, American Kestrels, and Sharp-shinned Hawks are tallied and the site has proven consistent for Merlins, Peregrine Falcons, Cooper's Hawks, and rarely, Bald Eagles.

After birding the beaches, continue along the park road following the inner shore to the parking area for Holly Grove on the left. Park and walk along the trails here which pass through the thickets of rose and other bramble topped by pines. In spring and fall migration, this area attracts warblers, vireos, and other songbirds. Rarities seen here include Blue Grosbeak, Orange-crowned Warbler, and Chuck-will's-widow. In fall and winter, the evergreens should be checked carefully for owls---Great Horned and Northern Saw-whet can be winter regulars and Long-eared and Barred Owls are always a possibility. In November, 1992, a Gray Kingbird spent several days in the vicinity. The bird feeders are often active in winter, and can feature Black-capped Chickadee, Blue Jay, Downy and Hairy Woodpeckers, Northern Cardinal,Tufted Titmouse, and American Tree, Song and White-throated Sparrows. Rarer birds that have been tallied at this feeder include Grasshopper Sparrow, Dickcissel, and Veery.

A walk through nearby thickets sometimes yields Hermit Thrush, American Robin, Gray Catbird, Brown Thrasher, Eastern Towhee, and, if you are really lucky, a Yellow-breasted Chat.

After birding the Holly Grove, return to your vehicle and drive slowly along the road to the next stop just past the Old Greenwich Yacht Club building by the marina. The low island to the northwest is known as Sand Island. Scan the sandbars and mud flats around the island for migrant shorebirds. During fall migration, these sandbars often attract large numbers of plovers, sandpipers, turnstones, and yellowlegs, along with a variety of terns and gulls. Past rarities recorded here include Black Tern, Little Gull, and American White Pelican. During low tide in winter, Ruddy Turnstone, Black-bellied Plover, and Dunlin can often be found on the island. In summer, Least Terns and a pair of American Oystercatchers usually nest on Sand Island, with the latter frequently lingering into fall.

The parking lot for Seaside Garden is on the left across from the marina. Also on the left is an old building known as Cow Barn which is flanked on its right by a small pond. During spring and fall migrations, the woods and thickets around Cow Barn and the small pond are considered to be the best spots at Greenwich Point for finding songbirds. Park in the lot and walk along the garden trail through the woods and down to the pond in back of the Cow Barn. In past years, this short loop has yielded Connecticut Warbler and Whip-poor-will among other interesting migrants. The pond may yield Bufflehead, American Black Duck and, occasionally, Red-breasted and Hooded Mergansers.

Continue along the park road which first parallels the shore and then bears left. In 0.1 to 0.2 miles, look for Eagle Pond on your left. From spring through fall, Eagle Pond is usually good for several species of waders (Great Blue and Green Herons, Black-crowned Night-Herons, and Great and Snowy Egrets), gulls, and waterfowl. The shallows around the small island near the center of the pond can be especially productive for these species. Scan the waterfowl carefully for rare or unusual ducks such as Lesser Scaup, Ruddy Duck, and Northern Pintail, which may share the pond with American Black Duck, Bufflehead, Hooded Merganser, Greater Scaup and Ring-necked Duck.

After birding Eagle Pond, continue slowly along the road around the pond. Where the road turns sharply left park and look for a trail that begins to the right of the road. The trail leads east along the top of a flood-control embankment past several brackish marshes on the left. Further along, the trail offers a good view of Long Island Sound which begins to the right of the road. The trail leads east along the top of a flood-control embankment past several brackish marshes on the left. Further along, the trail offers a good view of Long Island Sound which should be scoped for waterfowl and other waterbirds. In fall and winter, loons (Common and Red-throated), Horned Grebe, Brant, and scoters may occur, while Oldsquaw, Common Goldeneye, Greater Scaup, and Red-breasted Merganser can often be found in numbers. In fall (November) and spring (March/April), Northern Gannet are sometimes seen here. These offshore waters have also yielded such rarities as Red-necked Grebe (March/April), Manx Shearwater, Wilson's Storm-Petrel, Black Guillemot, and Black-legged Kittiwake.

Check the marshes carefully for long-legged waders, dabbling ducks, and rails. The scrubby vegetation bordering the marsh is often good for Yellow Warbler, Common Yellowthroat, and Red-winged Blackbird in summer and Palm Warbler during fall migration. Rarities that have occurred here in autumn include Western Kingbird, Sedge Wren, and Connecticut Warbler.

Continue along the trail to Greenwich Point (also called Bluff Point) which is located in the southeast corner of the park. This is an excellent spot to scope the sound for flocks of White-winged Scoter and other migrant waterfowl. Yellow Rail and Boat-tailed Grackle (both casual visitors) have occurred in the marshes around this area.

To return to the car, cut inland to the trail that borders the inner (northern) side of the marsh. The combination of fields, woodland edge, and marsh along this trail can sometimes yield a nice mix of migrants which includes sparrows. In fall (October-November), check for the regular Song, Swamp, Savannah, Chipping, and American Tree Sparrows. The less common, but regular Lincoln's, White-crowned and Saltmarsh Sharp-tailed Sparrows are also possible in the thickets and along the marsh edge.

51 *Southwest Shoreline Tour*

Stamford and Darien

Although densely populated and heavily urbanized, the coastal habitats from Stamford to Darien can attract a variety of waterbirds and landbirds. Nesting colonies of long-legged waders, gulls, terns, and shorebirds are found on many of the offshore islands near Norwalk and Westport.

The best time to bird the parks and other natural areas in Stamford and Darien is during spring and fall migrations. Spring is especially good for songbirds and shorebirds, while raptor movements along the coast add to the shorebird and songbird migrations in fall. Summer is typically a slow period for birders because most of the city parks have restricted access.

This birding tour begins at Cummings Park in Stamford and works eastward to Pear Tree Point Beach in Darien.

DIRECTIONS

We will begin the birding tour at Cummings Park in Stamford. To get to Cummings Park from Interstate 95 southbound take Exit 8 (Elm Street), turn left and follow Elm Street south. If northbound on Interstate 95 take Exit 8 (Atlantic Street), continue straight for 0.5 miles and turn right onto Elm Street. Continue on Elm Street for 0.4 miles and bear right onto Shippan Avenue. Follow Shippan Avenue 0.3 miles to the park entrance on the left. Inside the park, bear right on the park road to the parking lot which looks out over Westcott Cove.

BIRDING

Cummings Park

Cummings Park offers especially good birding in winter when offshore waters can hold a variety of waterbirds. From the parking lot, walk to the sandy beach and scan the offshore waters for loons, grebes, cormorants, and diving ducks. The fishing pier to the right (west) can also provide good views of the cove.

The marina often holds Canada Goose, Mute Swan, American Black

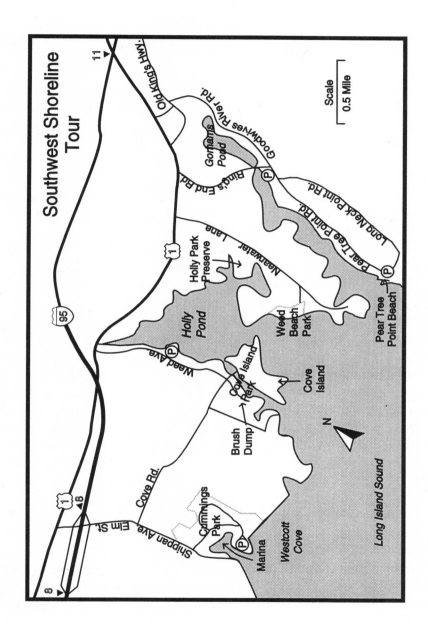

Southwest Shoreline Tour

Scale
0.5 Mile

Old King's Hwy.

11

Goodwives River Rd.

Gorhams Pond

Ring's End Rd.

Long Neck Point Rd.

Pear Tree Point Rd.

Nearwater Lane

Holly Park Preserve

95

1

Holly Pond

Weed Beach Park

Pear Tree Point Beach

Weed Ave.

Cove Island Park

Cove Island

Cove Island

Brush Dump

N

Cove Rd.

Shippan Ave.

Elm St.

Cummings Park

Marina

Westcott Cove

Long Island Sound

1

8

8

8

Duck and Mallard. The grassy areas in the park can be good for gulls and shorebirds, especially when rain pools are present and at high tides.

Cummings Park is also a good locale to compare the Fish Crow with the American Crow; both occur in the park. The American Crow is larger, but the two crows are best differentiated by their calls. The Fish Crow utters a short *ca* or *car,* very nasal and high pitched, while the American Crow sounds off with the louder, longer, and more familiar crow-like *caw* or *cahr.*

Cove Island Park

To get to Cove Island Park from Cummings Park, return to the intersection of Shippan Avenue and Elm Street (0.3 miles) and turn right onto Cove Road. Follow Cove Road for 1.1 miles and turn right into Cove Island Park. Access to this city park is restricted to Stamford residents from May 1 to October 30 but can be birded at other times of the year. In winter, however, the park often gets heavy use, especially on pleasant, sunny days that birders like, too.

To bird Cove Island Park, first check the brush dump and adjacent weedy fields behind the small brick building in the far right (southwest) corner of the parking lot. Enter the dump by the path just north of the building or through the gate. The brush dump and weedy fields can be great for migrant sparrows and also good for winter birding. In spring and fall, check for warblers, vireos, and sparrow flocks in the thick brush. Uncommon fall migrants to look for include Lincoln's, Vesper, and White-crowned Sparrows, and Dickcissel. Rarer fall migrants spotted in recent years include Sedge Wren, Yellow-breasted Chat, and Clay-colored Sparrow. In winter, the brush dump may yield Song, Field, and White-throated Sparrows, Northern Mockingbird, and Northern Cardinal. Fish Crow may be seen here and elsewhere in the park.

After birding the brush dump, walk or drive back to the parking area by the entrance. The footbridge just across from the parking lot leads to a small island. A hike around the island in fall and winter may produce Horned Lark, Snow Bunting, and Lapland Longspur in the open fields at the north end and a variety of songbirds and raptors in the trees and brush area at the south end of the island.

Holly Pond

This tidal estuary of the Noroton River is worth a stop in fall and winter to search for waterfowl, shorebirds, and gulls. To get to Holly Pond from Cove Island Park, exit the park and turn right onto Weed Avenue.

Drive 0.5 miles to the pulloff on the right which provides the safest place to bird Holly Pond. From fall into spring, scope the open waters of the cove for Gadwall, American Wigeon, Canvasback, Greater Scaup, Common Goldeneye, Bufflehead, and Hooded, and Red-breasted Mergansers. Check the Canada Goose flocks for Greater White-fronted Goose (very rare), and Snow Goose. Uncommon but regular waterbirds to look for include Northern Pintail, Lesser Scaup, Ruddy Duck, and American Coot. In fall and winter, check the concentrations of Great Black-backed, Ring-billed, and Herring Gulls for Bonaparte's (uncommon), and the rarer Little and Black-headed Gulls.

Holly Pond Preserve/Weed Beach Park

Owned by the Nature Conservancy, Holly Pond Preserve is a 2.5 acre sanctuary located on the eastern side of Holly Pond. To get to the preserve, continue along Weed Avenue and turn right onto East Main Street (Route 1) for 1.0 miles, then turn right onto Nearwater Lane. Follow Nearwater Lane for 0.5 miles and park by the roadside. Holly Pond Preserve (unmarked) is to the right of the road (west) and consists of small patches of open water surround by salt marsh. From the edge of the road, scan the water and marsh for ducks, long-legged waders, and shorebirds. The open water can hold American Wigeon, American Black Duck, and geese, especially from October through April.

To view the mouth of Holly Pond and Cove Harbor, continue south on Nearwater Lane for 0.3 miles to the Weed Beach Park entrance on the right (a private road is straight ahead). This town park also has restricted summer access, but can be birded during the "off" season from October through May. Check the shoreline for wading birds and shorebirds, the offshore waters for waterfowl, and the rocks for cormorants and Purple Sandpipers. An Eared Grebe was spotted near the mouth of Holly Pond in December 1989. In fall, the evergreens on the bluff behind the tennis courts can yield a mix of warblers, vireos, thrushes, sparrows, and occasionally, Long-eared or Northern Saw-whet Owls.

Gorhams Pond

This park in Darien can be an excellent location for winter waterfowl. To get to Gorhams Pond from Weed Beach Park, return to East Main Street (Route 1) and turn right. Turn right onto Ring's End Road (0.2 miles). Drive 0.5 miles, cross the bridge and turn right onto Goodwives River Road. Park in the pulloff on the right just a short distance beyond the bridge. You can walk north and south along the road to check out Gorhams Pond. In winter, the pond can hold Bufflehead, Hooded Merganser, scaup, other ducks, and gulls. The mudflats at the north end of the pond are often productive for egrets, herons, and shorebirds during the appropriate season. Yellow-crowned Night-Heron has nested nearby and can sometimes be spotted at the pond from May through September.

To get a good view of the mouth of the Darien River and Pratt Island, take Pear Tree Point Road south from the parking area and pull into Pear Tree Point Beach on the right (0.6 miles from the parking area). Check the offshore waters for species previously listed.

52 NORWALK HARBOR TOUR
Norwalk

Norwalk Harbor is a busy metropolitan area with an extensive waterfront development. And yet, within the maze of industrial, commercial, and residential development, Norwalk Harbor can still boast of several significant birding sites. Manresa Island is known for its variety of waders and shorebirds, while the Norwalk Islands at the mouth of the Norwalk Harbor historically supported one of the largest heron colonies in the Northeast.

DIRECTIONS

We will begin the Norwalk Harbor birding tour at Manresa Island which flanks the southwestern side of Norwalk Harbor. To get to Manresa Island from Interstate 95, take Exit 16 (East Norwalk) and follow East Avenue south. At 0.5 miles, turn right onto Van Zant Street (Route 136). At the stop sign (0.4 miles) turn left and continue on Route 136 by Veterans Park (on left). Cross the bridge and turn left at the traffic light (0.3 miles) heading south on Water Street (still Route 136). Turn right onto Burritt Avenue (0.5 miles) then left onto Woodward Avenue (0.1 miles). At 0.7 miles the road takes a sharp left to Longshore Avenue. To the right is the Norwalk Generating Station behind the chain-link fence. Park along the road just beyond the entrance to the generating station. **Do not trespass on the posted Northeast Utilities property**.

BIRDING
Manresa Island

To bird Manresa Island, walk along Longshore Avenue to the twin stone pillars which mark the entrance to Harborview, which is a private community. The salt marsh north of the road contains a variety of shorebirds and waterfowl during fall and spring, and long-legged waders from spring through summer.

Great Blue and Green Herons, Black-crowned Night-Heron, and Great and Snowy Egrets are usually the most common waders observed from spring into fall. Rarer species may include Tricolored and Little

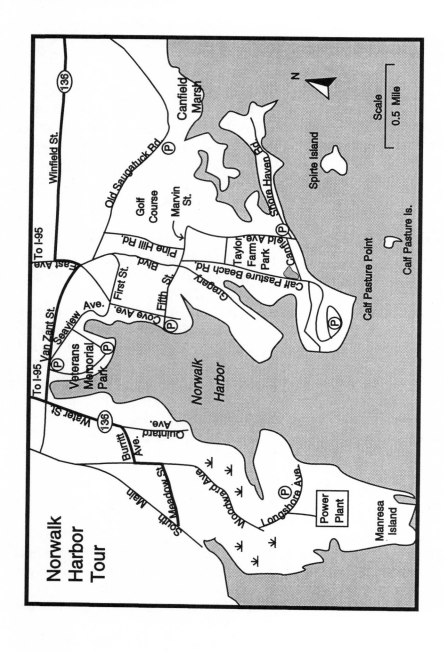

Blue Herons, Yellow-crowned Night-Heron, and Glossy Ibis. Scan the marsh edge for Clapper and King (rare) Rails, and Willet. The salt marsh should yield Saltmarsh Sharp-tailed and Seaside Sparrows. Fish Crows may forage along the marsh edge at any time of year.

During fall migration (mid-July into November), Short-billed Dowitcher, Ruddy Turnstone, various sandpipers, plovers, both yellowlegs, and Dunlin can turn up around the marsh. Rarer shorebirds include American Golden-Plover, Long-billed Dowitcher, American Oystercatcher, and Marbled and Hudsonian Godwits. Black Tern has been seen in August and September.

You need permission from Northeast Utilities to enter the marsh and scrubby growth south of the road just beyond the fence. From late fall into spring, the marsh and open area around the generating station property may harbor Short-eared Owl (rare) or Rough-legged (uncommon), Red-tailed, and Sharp-shinned Hawks, either foraging over the marsh or perching in the cedars and willows. The grassy areas around the marsh may also yield Ring-necked Pheasant.

Veteran's Park
To get to Veteran's Park, take Woodward Avenue back to Route 136 and follow Route 136 east. Cross the bridge over the Norwalk River, and turn right into Veteran's Park. This town-owned park is open from dawn to dusk.

Walk or drive to the south end of the park. At low tide the exposed mudflats below the sea wall can produce a good variety of birds, especially herons, shorebirds, and gulls. Look for the same species listed for Manresa Island. The ball fields in the park often attract an assortment of shorebirds during migration, especially at high tide or when rain pools are in the fields.

Some rare but regular species recorded in this park include American Golden-Plover, Hudsonian Godwit, Pectoral, Upland, Stilt, and Buff-breasted Sandpipers, and Black Skimmer. In 1985, the first documented state record of Sharp-tailed Sandpiper occurred here. The fields can be good for Laughing Gull in summer and early fall and other gulls throughout the year.

From September through October, hawks and other raptor species make a good showing at Veteran's Park. Red-tailed, Broad-winged, Sharp-shinned, and Cooper's Hawks are all regular while Peregrine

Falcon and Merlin are also possible. An evening visit to the park in late August and September may yield migrating Common Nighthawks.

Calf Pasture Beach

Located on the southeastern side of Norwalk Harbor, this city park is open to the public from dawn to dusk. To get to Calf Pasture Beach from Veteran's Park, exit the parking lot on Seaview Avenue. If the exit gate to Seaview Avenue is closed, exit the park the way you entered. Turn right and take the first right (about 50 yards) onto Seaview Avenue. Seaview Avenue curves right, then sharply left, and continues as First Street. Take the second right onto Cove Avenue (0.3 miles from the Seaview Avenue exit gate or 0.4 miles from the junction of Seaview Avenue and Route 136). Continue on Cove Avenue 0.2 miles and turn right onto Fifth Street. Fifth Street deadends by the east side of Norwalk Harbor. Check the harbor for waterfowl and the shoreline for waterbirds previously listed.

To continue, turn around and head east on Fifth Street to a rotary (0.2 miles). Just after the rotary bear right onto Beach Road (Calf Pasture Beach Road on city maps). Taylor Farm Park begins on the left, about 0.3 miles along Beach Road. Access to this city park, which is open from dawn to dusk, is through one of the gates along the road. In autumn, the fields may attract gulls and shorebirds, especially following rainy weather. Black-bellied Plover is common while American Golden-Plover is possible, but uncommon. Cattle Egret has been observed in spring and summer. Check the small park pond for waterfowl. In spring, a brief walk through the park woods can be productive for songbirds.

After birding Taylor Farm Park, continue on Beach Road another 0.2 miles to Calf Pasture Beach Park. During summer, non-residents must pay a nominal entry fee to this park. From October to May the park is open to all. Calf Pasture Beach provides an excellent view of the mouth of Norwalk Harbor and several of the Norwalk Islands. Across the harbor to the southwest is Manresa Island, which can be identified by its huge generating station building.

From fall through spring, the mudflats, sandbars, and beach around the park can be productive for waterfowl, long-legged waders, shorebirds, and gulls. Scope the offshore waters for Common and Red-throated Loons, Double-crested (summer) and Great (winter)

Cormorants, Brant (winter), Greater Scaup, Oldsquaw, scoters, Common Goldeneye, Bufflehead, Red-breasted Merganser, and Herring, Great Black-backed, and Ring-billed Gulls. In late summer and early fall, Black Skimmer can sometimes be seen resting on the low sandbars or in flight, skimming just above the water.

In summer, scope for American Oystercatchers on the sandbars and mudflats. Fish Crows are common throughout the year. During rainy periods, check the rain puddles and wet areas around the parking lot for gulls and sandpipers. Snowy Owl and Lapland Longspur are rare but possible visitors in winter.

Norwalk Islands

Scattered around the mouth of Norwalk Harbor are the Norwalk Islands, which include four major islands (Chimon, Sheffield, Cockenoe, and Shea), nine smaller islands and a number of sand bars rising just above the water. For many years the Norwalk Islands were famous for their nesting colonies of herons and egrets. The islands also served as important stop-over locales for hundreds of spring migrants.

For unknown reasons, the nesting colonies were abandoned in 1993, possibly because of competition with nesting cormorants (which still nest on some of the islands). Predation of heron eggs and young by gulls may also have contributed to the loss of these important breeding bird colonies, but the exact cause remains unknown. A few nesting populations relocated to Great Captain Island, located near Greenwich harbor, and Charles Island, located near the mouth of the Housatonic River in Milford. Whether herons will ever again return in numbers to breed on the Norwalk Islands remains questionable.

Most of the Norwalk Islands have been set aside as part of the Stewart B. McKinney National Wildlife Refuge. Access is restricted during the breeding season. Contact Refuge Manager, P. O. Box 1030, Westbrook, Connecticut 06498, or phone (203-399-2513) for information regarding visits to the islands.

Several of the Norwalk Islands can be identified from Calf Pasture Beach Park. **Sheffield Island** lies to the southwest, left of the power generating station on Manresa Island. Nesting colonies of Common Tern and pairs of American Oystercatcher still nest on the eastern end of Sheffield Island. Sheffied Island is the only island regularly visited. During the summer season, Sheffield Island Cruises offers a narrated 30 minute boat ride through Norwalk Harbor and past most of the Norwalk Islands to Sheffield Island. The tour boat departs from the Hope Dock in South Norwalk (next to the Norwalk Maritime Center). The boat docks on Sheffield Island and tourists can visit the historic lighthouse. For information about this boat trip, contact Sheffield Island Cruises, Norwalk Seaport Association, 132 Water Street, South Norwalk, CT, 06854, or call 1-800-220-9991.

Shea Island (Ram Island) is just east of Sheffield Island, and is actually connected to it by a long, narrow bar. Shea Island is owned by the city of Norwalk. The woods and thickets of Shea Island provided nest sites for Yellow-crowned Night-Heron and other waders in past years. The salt marsh and rocky beaches are still nesting spots for Clapper Rail, American Oystercatcher and other shorebirds, and gulls.

To the left (east) of Shea Island is **Chimon Island,** named for the Indian Chief Mamachimon. This 70-acre, heavily wooded island formerly supported the largest heron colony in Long Island Sound. Great, Snowy, and Cattle Egrets, Little Blue and Green Herons, Black-crowned and Yellow-crowned Night-Herons, and Glossy Ibis all nested in the dense woody growths of sumac, ailanthus and greenbrier. Herring and Great Black-backed Gulls still nest on the low, sandy beach at the south end of the island. Many species of passerines nest on the island or briefly take refuge in the thickets and scrubby growth during spring and fall migrations. The first documented state record of Painted Bunting was from Chimon Island in May, 1982.

The long, low island between Chimon Island and Calf Pasture Beach is **Betts Island.** Just to the southeast (left) of Betts Island (and partly hidden by it) is the smaller **Grassy Island** (Hay Island), about 14 acres in size and owned by the city of Norwalk. Several species of herons and egrets colonized Grassy Island when the nesting colonies of Chimon Island expanded to include other, nearby islands.

Still further to the east is Sprite Island, identified by the Sprite Island Yacht Club marina. Nearest to the shore is **Calf Pasture Island**, which is located to the left of the lighthouse and identified by an old A-frame house and trees bearing the large, clumsy stick nests of Double-crested Cormorants. The low island beyond Calf Pasture Island is **Cockenoe Island**. The sand dunes on Cockenoe Island support nesting Least Tern Colonies and Piping Plovers and a few pairs of American Oystercatchers.

Canfield Island Marsh

You can bird this marsh on the way back to Interstate 95. To get to Canfield Island Marsh, turn right at the park exit onto Canfield Avenue, heading east. At 0.2 miles turn right onto Shore Haven Road. Continue for 0.2 miles and park in the Knights of Columbus parking lot on the left. To bird the marsh, walk along the road to the bridge (about 250 yards east of the parking lot). Beyond the bridge the road is private and access is restricted.

The large salt marsh can provide good birding for the long-legged waders and shorebirds noted previously. After birding the marsh, backtrack on Shore Haven Road to the stop sign. Continue straight onto Canfield Avenue to Marvin Street (0.3 miles). Turn left onto Marvin Street and turn right at the stop sign (0.2 miles) and follow Pine Hill Road for 0.4 miles. Turn right onto Old Saugatuck Road, heading east for 0.5 miles and pull-off on the right, by the golf course. Check the fairways for gulls and shorebirds. Cattle Egrets were formerly reliable at this spot. The far edge of the golf course is bordered by Canfield Island Marsh.

To get back to Interstate 95, follow Old Saugatuck Road and turn right onto Saugatuck Avenue (Route 136), then follow signs back to Interstate 95.

53 SHERWOOD ISLAND STATE PARK

Westport

This 234-acre state park bordering Long Island Sound has long been a favorite of shoreline birders for the variety of birds that have been recorded (more than 275 species) and the rarities and exotics that have turned up over the years.

Sherwood Island was valued by the Pequot Indians for fishing and bird hunting. With the arrival of the early colonists, the island became the property of the Sherwoods, one of the first English families to settle in Fairfield around 1643. The lands owned by the Sherwood family eventually formed most of Connecticut's Sherwood Island State Park.

Sherwood Island State Park features coastal habitats including sandy beaches, tidal marshes, small coastal woodlands, fields, meadows, and lawns. The park is best birded from fall through spring when crowds are generally small. Birding specialties at the park include fall and spring migrants (especially shorebirds, gulls, terns, waterfowl, and passerines), wintering waterfowl, and waders in summer. Some of the rare and unusual species observed at the park include American White Pelican, Cattle Egret, Eurasian Wigeon, Black Vulture, Ruff, Red-headed Woodpecker, Northern Wheatear, and LeConte's Sparrow.

A bird checklist for Sherwood Island State Park is available from Robert Winkler, 7 Woodland Way, Weston, CT 06883. Enclose a large, SSAE envelope with your request. Copies of the checklist may also be available at the entrance to the Interpretive Nature Trail near the northeast side of the east parking lot.

DIRECTIONS

From Interstate 95 take Exit 18 (Sherwood Island State Park). Take the connector 0.3 miles to Sherwood Island State Park which is open daily from 8:00 am to sunset. A fee is charged on weekends from late April to Memorial Day and from Labor Day through September, and throughout the week from Memorial Day to Labor Day. During the rest of the year, entry is free.

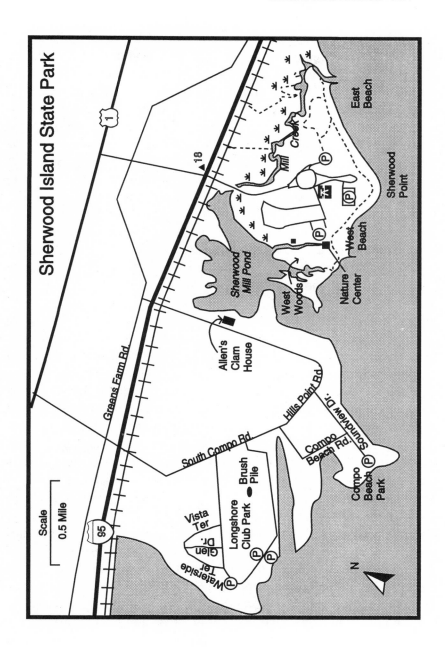

Sherwood Island State Park

BIRDING

Just after the Sherwood Island connector crosses over the railroad line, pull-off on the right to view Sherwood Mill Pond, which is a tidal pond visible to the right (west) of the connector. Scan the pond with a spotting scope for waders and waterfowl. American Wigeon, Green-winged Teal, Canvasback, Bufflehead, and Hooded and Red-breasted Mergansers are common migrants. Some linger into winter as long as the pond has open water. Other possible migrants at the mill pond may include Gadwall, Northern Pintail, and Blue-winged Teal. Eurasian Wigeon, Northern Shoveler, and Redhead are rarer visitors. In June, 1994, an American White Pelican was discovered at the mill pond.

After scoping the mill pond, continue on the connector to the park. Just inside the park, check the grassy area within the rotary for Buff-breasted Sandpiper (rare) in fall and flocks of Canada Geese for Snow Goose or the rarer Greater White-fronted Goose.

Sherwood Point. Park at the lot by the pavilion and walk out to Sherwood Point. The point provides a panoramic view of East Beach, West Beach, and the offshore waters of Long Island Sound. Wintering waterbirds on the sound may include Common and Red-throated Loons, Red-breasted Merganser, scoters, Bufflehead, Oldsquaw, and Common and Barrow's (rare) Goldeneyes. In spring, these offshore waters are popular staging areas for ducks moving northward. Herring, Great Black-backed, and Ring-billed Gulls occur from fall through spring and Laughing Gull from late spring to fall. Lesser Black-backed Gull is rare, but regular here. Listen for the nasal "*caw*" of Fish Crows which nest in trees near the pavilion.

West Woods and Sherwood Mill Pond. After birding the beaches and offshore waters, walk west along the park road to West Woods. On the way check the grassy area between the nature center and West Woods for shorebirds, especially plovers, and Wilson's Phalarope (rare). The thickets and wet areas along the park road are often good sparrow traps in fall. Song, Savannah, White-throated, and Field Sparrows are the more common species, but Lincoln's, Fox, White-crowned, and Vesper Sparrows are sometimes seen as well.

At West Woods, take the trail that leads through the mature oak and hickory trees. In spring (May) and fall, West Woods can be good for migrant warblers, thrushes, and vireos. Two rare fall migrants that have been found in these woods include Red-headed Woodpecker and Blue Grosbeak. The trail comes out on an overlook that provides a good view of the south side of the salt marsh and mill pond. Scan the marsh and mill pond for waterfowl and shorebirds (plovers, dowitchers, yellowlegs, and sandpipers in migration). In late spring and summer, listen and look for Clapper Rail, and Seaside and Saltmarsh Sharp-tailed Sparrows. After birding West Woods, backtrack to the nature center and walk north along the trail which is bordered by thickets, a small woodlot, and marsh. The thickets may hold Brown Thrasher and White-eyed Vireo in late spring and summer and a variety of sparrows in fall.

Continue to the observation platform which provides a great view of Sherwood Mill Pond and the salt marsh around it. From spring through fall, scan the mill pond for waterfowl and the salt marsh for Glossy Ibis and other long-legged waders.

The woodlot immediately north of the observation platform usually harbors nesting Warbling Vireo and Orchard Oriole among others. This woodlot can also be good for migrant songbirds. On the way back to the parking spot, scrutinize the ornamental trees and shrubs. In late fall and winter, the evergreens may yield nuthatches, kinglets, finches, and roosting owls including Great Horned and Northern Saw-whet (rare).

East Marsh and East Parking Lot. The east parking lot and adjacent fields often serve as resting sites for gulls and shorebirds during storms. This area can hold good numbers and a variety of shorebirds during fall migration. Plovers are often well represented; Black-bellied, Semipalmated, and American Golden-Plover (uncommon to rare) are good possibilities, along with the occasional Hudsonian Godwit or Wilson's Phalarope. Sandpipers may also be abundant; Semipalmated, Pectoral, and Least Sandpipers are likely while Western, Upland, White-rumped, Baird's, and Stilt Sandpipers are also distinctly possible, especially during a good shorebird movement in fall. Cattle Egret were formerly regular in the grassy areas, but this species is now very rare in the state. American Pipit is a regular migrant during October and November. In winter, check the fields for Snow Bunting, Horned Lark, and occasionally, Lapland Longspur.

If you have time, take a short hike along the Interpretive Nature Trail.

This 0.5 mile-long trail starts at the edge of the East Parking Lot and loops around along the edge of the East Marsh and Mill Creek before returning by way of the East Beach. Along the trail, several vantage points offer good views of the salt marsh and mudflats along Mill Creek. Long-legged waders (spring to fall) and migrant shorebirds highlight a hike along the trail. Clapper Rail and Marsh Wren are uncommon migrants and locally rare nesters on the marsh, while Willow Flycatchers breed in the shrub thickets bordering the tidal creek. The return loop by East Beach affords another chance to scan for waterbirds on Long Island Sound.

During migration, Eastern Meadowlark and Common Snipe may occur in the grassy fields bordering the model airplane field by the parking lot. A LeConte's Sparrow (rare) was observed in this general area in 1991.

The open space around East Beach is a hawk watch site in fall. September and October provide the best variety and numbers of migrating raptors. American Kestrel and Sharp-shinned Hawk can usually be spotted while Bald and Golden (very rare) Eagles are sometimes seen during migration. A few Northern Harriers are regularly seen during migration and some may linger into winter. Rough-legged Hawk is also an occasional winter visitor to the area. In late August and early September, Common Nighthawks move through at dusk, often in impressive numbers.

Longshore Club Park

After birding Sherwood Island State Park check out this town park fronting the Saugatuck River in Westport. To get to Longshore Club Park from Sherwood Island State Park, drive north on the connector and turn left at the second traffic light (0.7 miles) onto Greens Farms Road. Go west on Greens Farms Road 1.6 miles and turn left at the traffic light onto South Compo Road. Head south for 0.6 miles to the entrance of Longshore Club Park on the right. Turn right onto the park road (Julian Brodie Road) and continue, bearing right at the fork (0.3 miles), and continue another 0.3 miles to the parking lot by the club house.

To bird the coastal woodland north of the parking lot walk up Waterside Terrace to Vista Terrace and Glen Road. In May, the woods along these roads can produce an extraordinary variety of flycatchers, kinglets, thrushes, vireos, and warblers. In fall, bird the woods and edge for sparrows.   Rare migrants to look for include Yellow-bellied Flycatcher, Gray-cheeked Thrush, and Kentucky, Hooded, Connecticut (fall), and Mourning Warblers.

After birding the woods, scout along the Saugatuck River and Hendrick's Point which can be accessed by several short trails that begin on the west side of the parking lot near Hendrick's Point. Scan the river for swans, geese, and ducks. In the past, the parking lot at Hendrick's Point has been a good hawk watch site in fall, especially for Osprey, buteos, and accipiters with several "thousand count" days.

After birding the Saugatuck River, continue along the one-way park road to the parking lots (on either side of the road) near the marina on the right (0.3 miles).   Park and walk down the road about 200 yards to view Gray's Creek salt marsh and mudflats on the right.   Gray's Creek often attracts large wintering concentrations of American Black Ducks. During the proper season, most of the waterfowl, waders, rails, shorebirds, and gulls noted previously can be turned up in this marsh.

The brush dump has proven to be another good birding spot at Longshore Club Park.   To get to the brush dump, continue walking along the one-way road and turn left on the service road just before the exit to South Compo Road. The scrubby growth around the dump and by the small pond is known for fall finches and sparrows. Song, Savannah, Field, American Tree, White-throated, White-crowned, Vesper, and Lincoln's Sparrows are all possible during a good sparrow push.   Blue Grosbeak, Dickcissel, and Lark and Grasshopper Sparrows are rarer specialties at this site.

Compo Beach

To get to Compo Beach from Longshore Club Park, take a right onto South Compo Road and go right at the rotary (0.1 miles) onto Compo Beach Road.   Continue for 0.5 miles to the entrance of Compo Beach on the right. Non-residents must pay a hefty parking fee from May through October. At other times entry is free.

From fall through spring, the ball fields and parking lot may attract gulls, Horned Larks, and Snow Buntings.   In winter, check the rocky West Beach for shorebirds, particularly Purple Sandpipers (rare). Scope the offshore waters for sea ducks, loons, grebes, and cormorants. Cockenoe Island (one of the Norwalk Islands) is visible to the right along with other low hummocks. In winter, scan the islands with a scope for the occasional Snowy Owl.

Sherwood Mill Pond

To get another view of Sherwood Mill Pond, turn right at the Compo Beach exit onto Compo Beach Road, which shortly becomes Soundview Drive. At the stop sign, turn right onto Hillspoint Road (0.3 miles). After 0.6 miles, turn right into the parking lot behind Allen's Clam and Lobster House. The western edge of Sherwood Mill Pond fronts the gravel parking lot. In summer, Great and Snowy Egrets, Black-crowned Night-Heron, and Great Blue, Green, and Little Blue (uncommon) Herons are fairly regular along with Common and Least Terns. In fall, the marsh can hold a variety of shorebirds, waterfowl, and gulls.

Winter is good for waterfowl and gulls as long as the pond remains ice-free. A Sandhill Crane wintered in this part of the mill pond in 1983-84.

54 *Connecticut Audubon Society Sanctuaries*
Fairfield

Fairfield is home to two important Connecticut Audubon Society (CAS) Sanctuaries, the Roy and Margot Larsen Sanctuary located on Burr Street in a wooded suburban part of Fairfield, and the Birdcraft Sanctuary located near downtown Fairfield, adjacent to Interstate 95. Both sanctuaries preserve enclaves of natural habitat amidst urban and suburban sprawl and consequently act as wildlife magnets in an otherwise suburban environment. The two sanctuaries harbor migrating songbirds in spring and fall and the Larsen Sanctuary also has a good assortment of breeding birds.

DIRECTIONS

To get to the Roy and Margot Larsen Sanctuary from Interstate 95 take Exit 21 (Mill Plain Road). Follow Mill Plain Road north for 1.8 miles. Just beyond the stop sign Mill Plain Road becomes Burr Street. Follow Burr Street 2.3 miles to the Roy and Margot Larsen Sanctuary on the left (marked by a sign, Connecticut Audubon Society).

BIRDING

Roy and Margot Larsen Sanctuary

Best birded for spring and summer nesting species, this pleasant sanctuary features some 7 miles of easy hiking trails that provide access to most of the sanctuary's 152 natural acres. The trails traverse a variety of mostly wooded habitats comprised of submature and mature hardwood stands interspersed with occasional ponds and wetlands. Habitat highlights include a pin oak swamp, azalea shrub swamp, and wet woodlands.

Open from 9:00 am to 4:30 pm Tuesday through Saturday, Sunday from 12:00 pm to 4:30 pm (fall and spring only), the sanctuary has an environmental center building with a bookstore, library, and wildlife exhibits. There is a nominal fee for non-CAS members. An animal education compound behind the environmental center features wildlife display pens with injured raptors kept for educational purposes. Bald

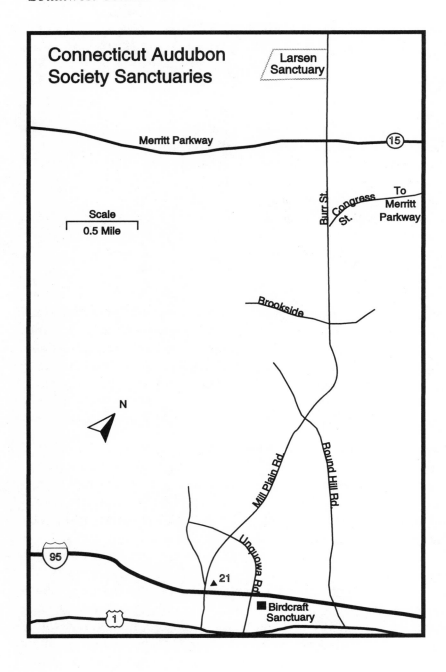

Eagle, Broad-winged and Red-tailed Hawks, Peregrine Falcon, and Great Horned, Eastern Screech, and Barred Owls are sometimes present.

Old Farm Trail to Wildlife Pond.   Old Farm Trail offers a nice sampling of the birding habitats that are available within the sanctuary. Old Farm Trail begins just north of the parking lot opposite the bookstore. Both House and Carolina Wrens are sometimes heard and seen near the trail entrance. Old Farm Trail goes through open woods and over a footbridge to Garden Marsh, marked by a sign on the left. Check Garden Marsh for Wood Ducks, which occasionally nest in the wood duck boxes, and Green Herons which regularly nest nearby and forage in the shallow water. Continue around the edge of Garden Marsh, then through an open field flanked by hemlock and spruces and past where Azalea Trail enters from the left. About 60 yards beyond the junction with Azalea Trail take the Wildlife Pond/Deer Meadow Trail on the right.   Watch along the trail for Barred Owl, which is occasionally seen here in late afternoons. The trail works through wet, open woodlands with strategically located boardwalks to get beyond the wettest spots.

From May through July, the woods here and elsewhere throughout the sanctuary will generally yield an assortment of nesting songbirds including Great Crested Flycatcher, White-breasted Nuthatch, Tufted Titmouse, Black-capped Chickadee, Veery, Red-eyed Vireo, Scarlet Tanager, and Rose-breasted Grosbeak.

Wildlife Pond is nesting home to a small Red-winged Blackbird colony, occasionally vocal American toads, and several species of salamanders. Check the edge and wetlands behind the pond for Great Blue and Green Herons. Common Yellowthroat, Baltimore Oriole, and Song Sparrow are regular nesting species. During migration, White-throated Sparrow, warblers, and flycatchers may be found here.

Trillium Trail to Dirty Swamp Pond.   After birding Wildlife Pond, work around the shoulder of the pond and bear left on Trillium Trail, which cuts through Pin Oak Swamp. Trillium Trail ends at Country Lane. In May, breeding Ovenbirds and Wood Thrushes can be quite vocal here. Turn left and follow Country Lane for 140 yards, then turn left again and head down Chipmunk Run for about 40 yards to where

Muskrat Hollow Trail begins on the right. Muskrat Hollow Trail crosses a gasline cut with bluebird nest boxes, then continues through wet woodlands of red maple and American beech, bordering a small brook before coming out at Dirty Swamp Pond. Northern and Louisiana Waterthrushes can be found along here in spring and fall migration.

Dirty Swamp Pond consists of several acres of open water, scrubby wetlands, and a small, tree-covered island. The pond is home to green frogs and American bullfrogs. Tree Swallows nest in the boxes around the pond. Check along the edge and open water for Wood Duck, American Black Duck, Mallard, and Green Heron. The scrubby wetlands surrounding most of the pond often hold Eastern Phoebe, Eastern Kingbird, Gray Catbird, Common Yellowthroat, and American Goldfinch. The dead trees toward the back of the pond can yield Northern Flicker and Red-shouldered Hawk.

After birding Dirty Swamp Pond, take Dirty Swamp Trail through a mature hardwood of oaks and American beech, which is home to Wild Turkey and Pileated Woodpecker, a regular nester whose deep drumming can often be heard. Dirty Swamp Trail returns to junction again with Chipmunk Run. Turn right and follow Chipmunk Run back to Streamside Trail which leads back to the sanctuary entrance.

Birdcraft Sanctuary
To get to the Birdcraft Sanctuary from the Roy and Margot Larsen Sanctuary, backtrack down Burr Street to Mill Plain Road. Continue on Mill Plain Road and turn left on Unquowa Road. Follow Unquowa Road for 0.6 miles to the Birdcraft Sanctuary which is on the left, just after you pass underneath Interstate 95. Alternately, to get to the Birdcraft Sanctuary from Interstate 95 take Exit 21 and follow Mill Plain Road north for 0.4 miles and turn right onto Unquowa Road at the stop sign. Proceed on Unquowa Road as above.

Only six acres in size, the Birdcraft Sanctuary claims a place in history. In 1914, it was the first privately-owned bird sanctuary ever established in the United States. The buildings include a museum that features dioramas of Connecticut's seasonal bird life, a honeybee observation hive, and displays of the Frederick T. Bedford collection of African Animals. The Birdcraft Sanctuary grounds have been birdscaped to promote maximum habitat diversity for attracting birds and butterflies and offers a short loop-trail (0.5 miles) around a pond and wetland.

More than 120 species of birds have been recorded in this tiny sanctuary. The best birding is in spring and fall when a variety of flycatchers, thrushes, vireos, warblers, and sparrows seek refuge during migration. The sanctuary features an active bird-banding program during migration periods (April-May) and (August into November). If your visit is properly timed, you may be rewarded with close views of captured birds.

55 Fairfield to Bridgeport Shoreline Tour

Fairfield and Bridgeport

Like most of the southwest Connecticut shoreline, the Fairfield and Bridgeport areas are also heavily developed. What little remains of the natural shoreline habitats has been much modified and sandwiched between industrial, commercial, and residential development. In this birding tour we offer several good birding sites in the Fairfield and Bridgeport areas. Like all shoreline tours, the birding possibilities on this tour can range from excellent to downright poor depending on weather conditions, seasonal bird movements, and human activity. Generally, winter birding can be interesting for waterbirds and gulls while shorebirds can often be turned up during spring and fall migrations.

DIRECTIONS

Begin this birding tour at Pine Creek Preserve in Fairfield. To get to Pine Creek from Interstate 95 take Exit 21 (Mill Plain Road) and head south onto Mill Plain Road (0.2 miles) to Route 1 (Post Road). Turn right onto Route 1 and then left at the traffic light onto South Pine Creek Road (0.2 miles). Drive 1.1 miles and turn left onto Old Dam Road and then continue 0.3 miles to the parking lot on the left between the baseball fields. The entrance to the Pine Creek preserve is in the back of the parking lot and is marked by a sign.

BIRDING

Fairfield
Pine Creek

Most of this 220-acre sanctuary consists of a former landfill and a restored salt marsh. An old access road leads across a dike and then uphill to the top of the former landfill. Another trail branches to the right and follows the dike around the salt marsh to the southeast. Take the trail up to the top of the former landfill. The scrubby growth of sumac and *Ailanthus* gives way to goldenrod fields on either side of the

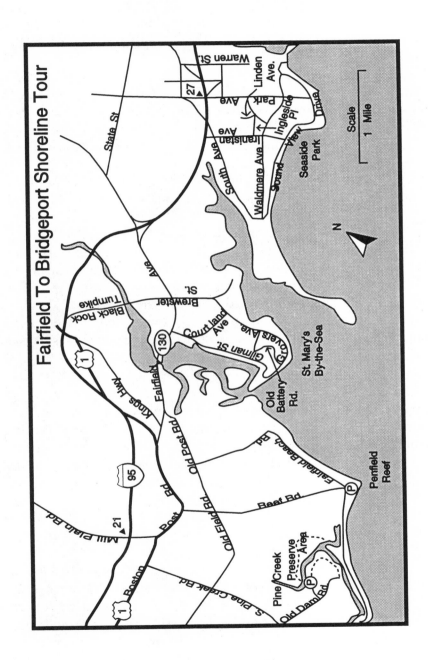

Fairfield To Bridgeport Shoreline Tour

road which can hold a good assortment of sparrows during the fall sparrow push. The top of the landfill provides a great view of the Pine Creek salt marsh below.

In fall, the salt marsh is interesting for raptors that drift by overhead, occasionally pausing to forage low over the marsh. Peregrine Falcon, Merlin, Northern Harrier, and Osprey are all possible during a day's birding, and Short-eared Owl can sometimes be glimpsed in twilight hours. The scrubby trees along the dike have harbored Long-eared Owls in winter.

Check the weedy growth along the marsh edge for flocks of finches and migrant sparrows including American Tree, Song, Savannah, Swamp, Fox (uncommon), and Field. Rarities such as Grasshopper Sparrow sometimes appear so study the sparrows carefully.

The salt marsh and the narrow mudflats along Pine Creek may yield migrant shorebirds; Ruddy Turnstone, Black-bellied and Semipalmated Plovers and Short-billed Dowitcher are common while American Golden-Plover and Buff-breasted Sandpiper are occasionally spotted. Breeding species in the Pine Creek salt marsh and adjacent fields include Ring-necked Pheasant, Clapper Rail, and sometimes Seaside and Saltmarsh Sharp-tailed Sparrows.

Penfield Reef

This long, rocky bar is exposed only at low tide but the reef has a "reputation" among birders for attracting good birds. To get to Penfield Reef from Pine Creek, return to South Pine Creek Road, turn right and continue to Old Field Road (0.6 miles). Turn right onto Old Field Road and continue 0.7 miles to Reef Road. Turn right onto Reef Road and follow it 0.9 miles to the end where it junctions with Fairfield Beach Road. Park in the parking lot just ahead and slightly to the right if there is room. Alternately, park in one of the legal spaces along Reef Road.

Walk to the beach via an access way marked "Penfield Reef Public Right of Way" which is on the right (west side) of the parking lot. A sidewalk leads to the stone jetty and out to the reef. The reef can be good for shorebirds in spring and fall and gulls in winter. Autumn shorebird concentrations can be impressive. Plovers, sandpipers, yellowlegs, dowitchers, Dunlin, Red Knot, and turnstones can turn up on any good day, while Caspian and Roseate Terns are some of the rarer migrants to look for.

In winter, the gull flocks may yield an occasional Glaucous or Iceland Gull, which are uncommon but regular visitors to the reef. The offshore waters around the reef are usually good for wintering bay and sea ducks including scoters, Common Goldeneye, mergansers, scaup, and Bufflehead. Rarities have included Harlequin Duck, Common Eider, and Black Scoter. Visible across the bay to the east is Ash Creek estuary with its extensive salt marsh to the north. This is the next stop on the birding tour.

Bridgeport
Ash Creek
To get to Ash Creek, follow Reef Road north to Route 1 (1.1 miles) and turn right, heading north. Bear right on Route 130 east (0.9 miles) and then right onto Courtland Avenue (0.8 miles) and follow it to a stop sign (0.1 miles). Turn right onto Gilman Street, which follows the east side of Ash Creek and the tidal marsh estuary.

Park and study the estuary and salt marsh. In summer, long-legged waders are usually in evidence (Yellow-crowned Night-Heron nested here in 1991) along with an assortment of more common waterfowl. Mute Swan and American Black Duck nest in the marsh. From late July into October, the mudflats along the upper marsh can hold a variety of shorebirds including plovers, sandpipers, dowitchers, and yellowlegs. Less common birds that have occurred include Hudsonian Godwit, Wilson's Phalarope, and Black-headed Gull.

Saint Mary's-by-the-Sea
As you continue driving along the east side of Ash Creek, Gilman Street becomes Grovers Avenue, at the sharp left curve. The area along the seawall is called Saint Mary's-by-the-Sea. Park along the road. The offshore waters can be good for loons, grebes, ducks, geese (including Brant), and gulls.

After birding the offshore waters in front of the seawall, continue on Grovers Avenue. Look for Old Battery Road on the left, guarded by short lengths of white fence on either side of the road. Old Battery Road leads to Battery Park Drive and a former Monk Parakeet colony which dispersed when the tree in which the colony nested blew over in a storm. The former colony was active for many years and consisted of more than 100 birds that built several large stick nests. In 1992, a pair of Great Horned Owls appropriated the top of one of the nests and successfully raised one young in the middle of suburbia---feeding on neighborhood squirrels and rats from the nearby salt marsh. Monk Parakeets are still in the area, and a slow drive along neighborhood streets may reveal a couple of the green chatterboxes (the parakeets).

To get back to Interstate 95 from Saint Mary's-by-the-Sea, return to Grover's Avenue and turn left (0.6 miles) onto Brewster Street. At the traffic light (0.3 miles) turn right onto Fairfield Avenue which junctions with Interstate 95 in 0.8 miles. The entrance ramp for Interstate 95 northbound is on the right, just before the highway.

Seaside Park
This is the last stop on the tour. Seaside Park is located adjacent to the University of Bridgeport campus. To get to Seaside Park from Interstate 95 northbound, take Exit 27 (Lafayette Boulevard, downtown) and drive to the traffic light at the end of the ramp. Go straight one block and turn left onto Warren Street. Take an immediate left and stay to the right (if you don't merge right you will either get back on the interstate southbound or be forced to turn left and return to where you started from). Drive two blocks (0.2 miles) and turn left onto Park Avenue. Follow Park Avenue for 0.6 miles to the large arch at the entrance to Seaside Park. Drive through the archway and turn left or right onto Sound View Drive, which parallels the shoreline and offers good views of Long Island Sound to the south and Bridgeport Harbor to the east, as well as the lawns and ponds of Seaside Park.

From Memorial Day to Labor Day an entrance fee is charged. The park is best birded during the off-season, but a wet August can produce rain pools on the lawns and ball fields that attract a nice assortment of shorebirds. For example, during August 1992 (an unusually rainy month) many uncommon shorebirds were spotted in the rain pools including Pectoral Sandpiper, Whimbrel, and Marbled Godwit. Regulars include Greater and Lesser Yellowlegs, Least and Semipalmated Sandpipers, and Short-billed Dowitcher.

From fall through spring, Seaside Park can be good for waterfowl, gulls, and a variety of shorebirds. Scan the shoreline and Long Island

Sound from various vantage points around the park for waterfowl. American Wigeon congregate in winter and the flocks sometimes yield an Eurasian Wigeon. White-winged gulls and Snowy Owls are also possible winter visitors.

A colony of Monk Parakeets is located nearby on the University of Bridgeport campus. To get to this colony from the junction of Park Avenue and Waldermere Avenue (in front of the arch) follow Waldermere Avenue west for 0.3 miles, turn right onto Iranistan Avenue for one short block and then turn right again onto Ingleside Place. Ingleside Place is one block long, terminating on Linden Avenue. The parakeet colony is located immediately to the right, at the corner of Ingleside and Linden. Listen for the chatter of the adults and look for the bulky stick nests in the row of tall white pines by the road. This completes your shoreline birding tour.

56 GREAT MEADOWS MARSH
AND LORDSHIP AREA
Stratford

Great Meadows Marsh scores high among environmentalists and birders because it is the largest unditched salt marsh in Connecticut. The expanses of open salt marsh habitats and sandy beach provide one of the more significant coastal marsh complexes in southern New England for migrating, wintering, and breeding shorebirds and waterfowl. Over 270 species of birds have been observed at Great Meadows Marsh and along its barrier sand spit, which is called Long Beach. The site also supports one of the most productive Piping Plover and Least Tern breeding colonies along the Connecticut coast and serves as a staging and stopover area for many species of herons, shorebirds, and raptors.

The marsh is also of crucial economic importance to Long Island Sound fisheries. Between the marsh and Long Beach is a saltwater slough known as Lewis Gut which supports an oyster seed bed used by over 200 shell fishermen. The tidal flats and offshore waters are important breeding and feeding sites for western Long Island Sound's finfish populations.

DIRECTIONS
Northbound on Interstate 95 take Exit 30 (Route 113, Lordship Boulevard). At the end of the ramp continue straight on Lordship Boulevard for 0.2 miles to the second traffic light. If travelling southbound on Interstate 95 take Exit 30 (Surf Avenue) and turn left onto Surf Avenue. Follow Surf Avenue 0.1 miles and turn left onto Lordship Boulevard (Route 113).

BIRDING
Sikorsky Airport
Follow Route 113 North (but you are actually heading south), bear right at the Y junction (0.8 miles) and continue 0.5 miles to Airport Road on the left. Between the junction and the airport, Route 113 bisects an impressive salt marsh, but unfortunately no pull-offs exist to view the marsh. (Stopping along this road is not recommended because it is

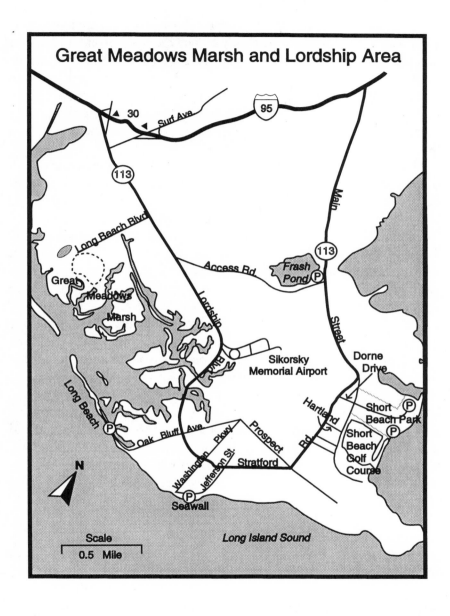

Great Meadows Marsh and Lordship Area

▲ 30 Surf Ave

95

113

Long Beach Blvd

Access Rd

Frash Pond

113

Great Meadows Marsh

Lordship

Main

Street

Sikorsky Memorial Airport

Dorne Drive

Blvd

Long Beach

Hartland

Short Beach Park

Oak Bluff Ave

Prospect

Short Beach Golf Course

Washington Pkwy

Jefferson St.

Stratford

Rd

N

Seawall

Scale

0.5 Mile

Long Island Sound

narrow and heavily traveled). Airport Road makes a short counter-clockwise loop by the terminal building and returns to Route 113. After driving by the terminal building, you can usually park briefly along the road if you remain near the car. However, this is a "no-parking" area and security may come along and prompt you to move. After completing the loop, you can also park off the road to the right of the stop sign, near the fence. The best place for parking at the airport is in the fee area located in the center of the loop.

The airport lawns attract a good assortment of shorebirds during fall migration. Species consistency found include Killdeer and Black-bellied Plover. When rain pools are present the Pectoral Sandpiper sometimes forage in the pools. Upland Sandpiper occurs regularly in August, while Buff-breasted and Baird's Sandpipers are sporadic during August and September. Horned Lark can usually be found throughout much of the year and a few individuals breed here. In winter, check the Horned Lark flocks for the occasional Lapland Longspur. This area yielded a Chestnut-collared Longspur in July, 1994.

Scan the marsh to the south of Route 113 and west of the airport for a variety of long-legged waders and rails in summer and shorebirds during spring and fall migration. Common waders are Great Blue Heron, and Snowy and Great Egrets. Black-crowned Night-Heron also is common, but nocturnal, and is best observed during twilight hours. Uncommon species may include Glossy Ibis, Little Blue Heron, and Yellow-crowned Night-Heron. Northern Harrier occurs year-round and may breed nearby. Some marsh nesting species include Clapper Rail, Marsh Wren, and Saltmarsh Sharp-tailed and Seaside Sparrows. In winter, survey the marsh for the Rough-legged Hawk and Snowy and Short-eared Owls which are uncommon to rare.

Long Beach
Exit the airport and turn left on Route 113 to the stop sign (0.7 miles) and turn right onto Oak Bluff Avenue. Follow Oak Bluff Avenue 0.3 miles to the entrance of Long Beach Park. Long Beach is a long, narrow sand spit owned by the town of Stratford. In summer, the park is extensively used by beach-goers and parking is restricted to town residents. Birding is best during the remainder of the year when parking restrictions are not enforced.

Scan the marsh and the offshore waters of Long Island Sound from the western end of the parking lot. During migration, check the inland bay for dabbling and diving ducks (American Black Duck, Green-winged Teal, Gadwall, American Wigeon, and Bufflehead); shorebirds (Killdeer, Black-bellied and Semipalmated Plovers, yellowlegs and peeps among others); and Common and Forster's Terns.

From fall through spring, the offshore waters can yield Common and Red-throated Loons, Horned and occasionally Red-necked Grebes, Greater Scaup, Common Goldeneye, Oldsquaw, and scoters. Winter shorebirds along the sandy beach usually include Sanderling, Dunlin, Purple Sandpiper (occasional), and a few Black-bellied Plovers. Gulls are represented by Ring-billed, Herring, and Great Black-backed throughout the year, Laughing Gull in summer and early fall, and Bonaparte's Gull during migration (normally offshore) and sometimes in winter. Glaucous and Iceland Gulls have occurred sporadically during winter months.

A winter walk along the beach may produce Savannah Sparrow (Ipswich race), Short-eared Owl, and flocks of Horned Larks and Snow Buntings. In summer, Piping Plovers and Least Terns nest on the upper beach.

Lordship Seawall

The seawall at Lordship offers another good location to scope the offshore waters for a variety of gulls, cormorants, and waterfowl. To reach the Lordship Seawall, return via Oak Bluff Avenue to the Route 113 intersection (0.3 miles), turn right, and follow Stratford Road to Washington Parkway (0.2 miles). Turn right and continue along Washington Parkway 0.3 miles until it ends at the seawall. Bear left at the seawall on Beach Drive and park.

From the seawall, scope the offshore waters for loons, grebes, waterfowl, and gulls from fall through spring. Carefully check the Great Black-backed Gulls for the similar, but smaller Lesser Black-backed Gull, which has been a regular winter visitor to the beach along the eastern end of the seawall since 1992. Northern Gannets have put in several appearances since November 1985, and are most likely in November and again from March through April.

Edward S. Yeoman Park Complex (Short Beach Park)

To access Short Beach Park from the stop sign at the eastern end of the Lordship Seawall continue straight on Jefferson Street to the second stop sign (0.2 miles). Turn right onto Stratford Street and continue 0.4 miles to the intersection with Route 113 at the traffic light. Drive straight across the intersection (the road jogs slightly left) and follow Stratford Street/Route 113 for 0.5 miles and turn right at Short Beach Road, which leads straight into the park.

The Edward S. Yeomans Park is owned and maintained by the city of Stratford. From Memorial Day to Labor Day, nonresidents must pay an entrance fee to visit the park. Follow the park road to the parking area by the shore. The road borders a former landfill on the left that can harbor sparrows from fall to spring. Continue past the tennis and paddleboard courts, turn left, and drive to the parking area at the north end of the park.

The tidal inlet just beyond the parking lot is Marine Basin. This little inlet frequently yields migrant waterbirds and waterfowl. Check the basin for herons, egrets, Pied-billed Grebe, ducks, and gulls in the appropriate season. A short walk to the beach offers a good view of the mouth of the Housatonic River and its sandbars and mudflats. Winter waterbirds along the river may include Great Cormorant, Greater Scaup, Common Goldeneye, and Red-breasted Merganser. In fall, the thickets and trees along the beach can yield Palm and Yellow-rumped Warblers, a variety of sparrows, and in some years, the rarer Western Kingbird.

Frash Pond

This little pond can provide good birding for waders, waterbirds, and waterfowl during migration and waterfowl and gulls in winter if it doesn't freeze over. To reach Frash Pond from Short Beach Park, turn right and follow Short Beach Road to Route 113 (0.2 miles). Continue on Route 113 for 0.7 miles to Access Road on the left. Turn onto Access Road and park behind the plaza on the right, near Dunkin Donuts. You can also park in the pull-off on the right just after the plaza. Frash Pond is the open water just behind the plaza and along the north side of Access Road.

From spring through fall, Frash Pond can yield a variety of waterfowl including Mute Swan, Mallard, Gadwall, American Wigeon, Bufflehead, Greater Scaup, Canvasback, Hooded Merganser, and Green-winged Teal. Check the Green-winged Teal closely for the Eurasian subspecies which generally shows up at the pond every three or four years. Less common migrants may include Pied-billed Grebe, Northern Pintail, Northern Shoveler, Lesser Scaup, and Blue-winged Teal. Some rarer species that occasionally appear during migration are American Bittern and Common Moorhen. Throughout much of the year, Herring, Ring-billed, and Great Black-backed Gulls are present. Check the gulls for Glaucous or Iceland Gulls in winter and Laughing Gull in summer and early fall.

Great Meadows Marsh and Warehouse Pond

To reach Great Meadows Marsh and the pond from Frash Pond, follow Access Road west for 1.2 miles (in 0.8 miles Access Road becomes Lordship Boulevard) and turn left onto Long Beach Boulevard. Follow Long Beach Boulevard 0.4 miles to the gate. Park at the end of the road or in the parking lot on the right.

This whole area has been extensively modified by filling, draining, and mowing and the marsh has suffered substantially. Access to the marsh has also changed several times during recent years and more changes are likely to occur, especially since some of Great Meadows Marsh has been purchased for the Stewart P. McKinney Wildlife Refuge. Currently, the U.S. Fish and Wildlife Service will not allow access to this marsh. We anticipate that birders will be allowed limited access in the future; so we are providing the following directions to the marsh.

The Stratford Development Company owns the property between the end of Long Beach Boulevard and Great Meadows Marsh refuge so you should obtain permission to walk across their land. If you arrive on a week day (and sometimes Saturday) during normal working hours, stop at the small trailer and ask for permission to bird the area. If you plan to bird the marsh on a weekend request permission in advance. To obtain current information regarding access to the refuge part of the marsh, contact the Stewart P. McKinney National Wildlife Refuge, P. O. Box 1030, Westbrook, CT 06498, or call 203-399-2513.

To bird the area, walk around the gate and across the semi-trailer driving schoolyard, staying to the left. After crossing the open area, you will notice a dirt road continuing from the left (southeast) corner of the yard toward the marsh. The dirt road skirts a small pond on the right which is frequently overgrown by marsh vegetation. Look for a small path to the pond made by previous birders. In spring and summer, check the pond for Least Bittern and Pied-billed Grebe, which nest intermittently from year to year. Green Herons are common. Summer waterfowl include American Black Duck, Gadwall, and occasionally, Blue-winged Teal. During migration, these species may be augmented by Green-winged Teal and other species.

Migrant shorebirds at the pond often include Semipalmated, Least, and Spotted Sandpipers, Lesser and Greater Yellowlegs, Killdeer, and Short-billed Dowitcher. King and Virginia Rails and Common Moorhen have also been recorded during migration.

After birding the pond, continue along the dirt road to view the part of Great Meadows Marsh which overlooks Lewis' Gut. In May of 1990, 1991, and 1996, Black Rail was heard singing here in the early evening hours. This area is also noted for the first state nesting record of Boat-tailed Grackles, which were found in 1995.

Follow the road along the marsh edge to the open field which was once used for flying model airplanes. Typical spring and summer species that nest in the marsh include Clapper Rail, a few pairs of Willet, Marsh Wren, and Saltmarsh Sharp-tailed and Seaside Sparrows. The sparrows can be difficult to find so be patient. Herons and egrets are also regular in summer. Migrants to the marsh include an assortment of shorebirds, hawks, Peregrine Falcon (uncommon), Merlin (uncommon), and swallows (frequently large concentrations in August and early September).

To return to the parking area, follow the path/dirt road through the left side of the field back to the driving schoolyard along a former railroad spur. In late summer and fall, this stretch of path can produce a variety of sparrows (Song, Savannah, Swamp, and Field are most common, but White-crowned should be expected). The pathway is sometimes overgrown with marsh grasses and can be difficult to follow. If so, just return the way you came.

57 MILFORD POINT

Milford

One of the best shoreline birding sites in Connecticut is Milford Point, where the Housatonic River empties into Long Island Sound. The salt marshes, mudflats, and sandbars at Milford Point provide an important staging and stopover area for migrant shorebirds and waterfowl, which pause to rest and feed before continuing their migration. A summer highlight is the nesting colony of Least Terns and pairs of Piping Plovers which are safely enclosed behind a protective fence along the upper sandy beach. In winter, birders dare strong, often bitterly cold winds and snow drifts to scout this site for wintering waterfowl and the chance to spot a rarity or two. Milford Point is also one of the more reliable sites in Connecticut to find wintering Snowy and Short-eared Owls.

Birding specialties at Milford Point include migrant shorebirds, terns, and waterfowl, and wintering waterfowl, and owls. Some of the interesting species that have been recorded at Milford Point include Black Skimmer, American Oystercatcher, Wilson's Phalarope, American Golden-Plover, Royal, Black and Roseate Terns, and King Eider. Noteworthy accidentals that have been recorded at the point include American Avocet, Gyrfalcon, Thick-billed Murre, Curlew Sandpiper, Sandwich Tern, and White-winged Dove.

DIRECTIONS

Take Interstate 95 to Exit 34 (Route 1, Milford). The exit ramp is about 0.2 miles long and connects with Route 1. Turn right onto Route 1 for 0.5 miles and turn left onto Naugatuck Avenue. Follow Naugatuck Avenue 0.6 miles and turn right onto Milford Point Road. Follow Milford Point Road 2.2 miles to Seaview Avenue. Turn right onto Seaview Avenue and continue 0.3 miles to a fork. The right fork leads to the parking lot for the Connecticut Audubon Center at Milford Point. **Do not take the left fork which is a private road.**

BIRDING

Milford Point offers three birding areas. The parking lot is part of the 8-acre Connecticut Audubon Coastal Center (formerly known as the

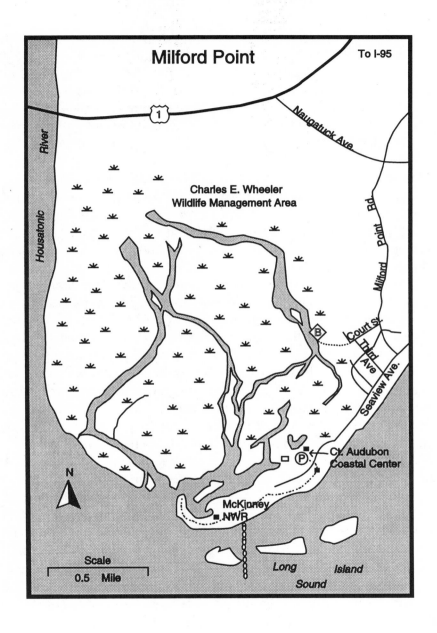

Milford Point

Smith-Hubbell Wildlife Sanctuary). The 22-acre Milford Point abuts the coastal center on the west. Milford Point is actually a part of the Stewart B. McKinney Wildlife Refuge which includes more than 700 acres of salt marsh and islands in Connecticut. Just north of Milford Point is the state-owned Charles E. Wheeler Wildlife Management Area (WMA) called Nells Island, which is an 865-acre expanse of tidal salt marsh that borders the Housatonic River. The eastern half of the Charles E. Wheeler WMA can be birded from the boat launch at Court Street.

Milford Point---Connecticut Audubon Coastal Center
Milford Point is open from dawn to dusk, seven days a week. The large, two story building next to the parking lot is the Connecticut Audubon Coastal Center at Milford Point. It is open daily from Tuesday through Saturday, between the hours of 10:00 am to 4:00 pm. The center is run by the Connecticut Audubon Society and provides ecological displays and research facilities for visiting ornithologists.

Begin birding at the observation platform which fronts the parking lot to the north and provides a good overview of the Charles E. Wheeler WMA. From spring through fall, the extensive tidal salt marsh, inlets, and pools offer great possibilities for scoping waders, waterfowl, and, at low tide, Short-billed Dowitcher. Watch for Clapper Rail, and Marsh Wren among the reeds. Check the nesting platforms in the salt marsh for Osprey. Even better views of the Charles E. Wheeler salt marsh can be obtained from the Coastal Center's second story balcony on the west side of the building, and the three-story observation tower.

After birding the salt marsh take the trail leading to the beach which begins in front of the building and continues south towards Long Island Sound. Before walking the trail, stop and check the trailside box. Inside is a birding logbook in which birders record the species they observed while at Milford Point. Check dates and times for hints on what species to look for and carefully replace the notebook. The trail to the beach crosses a private road which leads to the houses and upper beach further along to the right (west); both are private property and should not be trespassed by birders. Beyond the road, a boardwalk leads through a small stand of beach plum and dune grass to an observation platform that provides an excellent view of the sandy beach, mudflats, and offshore sandbars. To the right, the sandy beach curves out toward Milford Point.

At low tide, the open water in front of the observation platform is hedged by narrow sandbars that are partly connected by extensive mudflats. At high tide only the long, narrow sandbars are visible. The best time to look for shorebirds is the two hours before high tide when most of the birds congregate on the remaining exposed bars and flats.

Begin birding by scanning the entire area from the elevated platform. Stay away from the water's edge to avoid disturbing shorebirds on the nearby beach and mudflats. At the peak of fall migration the numbers and variety of shorebirds can be impressive. Peeps and plovers rest and forage in the mudflats. The most common migrants are Black-bellied and Semipalmated Plovers, Sanderling, Ruddy Turnstone, Short-billed Dowitcher, Greater and Lesser Yellowlegs, Willet, and Least and Semipalmated Sandpipers. Additional species that may turn up in fall include Red Knot, American Oystercatcher, American Golden-Plover, and Western, White-rumped and Pectoral Sandpipers. Rarer species that occasionally appear include the Stilt and Buff-breasted Sandpipers, Wilson's Phalarope, Long-billed Dowitcher, and Hudsonian and Marbled Godwits.

The upper sandy beach to the right of the platform is fenced by the U.S Fish and Wildlife Service to protect a nesting colony of Least Terns and pairs of Piping Plovers. Midsummer birders can watch the behavioral antics of the young terns as they greet the adults returning with food.

The observation platform provides a good view of how shorebirds forage in different parts of the mudflats at low tide. Note how the Ruddy Turnstones dart about along the newly exposed mudflats, turning over rocks to expose invertebrate prey hidden beneath. American Oystercatchers prowl the dark blue shellfish patches in the shallows to extract mussels from their shells. The Short-billed Dowitcher uses its long bill to probe deeply into the mud (in a sewing machine motion) for marine worms while the Dunlin probes for insects and crustaceans hidden just below the mud surface. Further up on shore, Least Sandpipers search the drier mud for small invertebrates while Red Knots forage through the wet sand and mud. Avoiding the crowds, Semipalmated Plovers search for invertebrates on the mud surface not yet disturbed by other shorebirds. Sanderlings dart back and forth along the water's edge to probe the briefly exposed sand for crustaceans. Further out, Greater Yellowlegs swing their bills back and forth just beneath the water surface to catch small fishes.

This area is almost always good for gulls. Herring, Great Black-backed, and Ring-billed Gulls are regulars throughout the year. Laughing Gulls are fairly common in summer, while Bonaparte's Gulls occur in fall and again from late winter into spring. Common Terns are regular in summer. By mid-August, terns start concentrating into large flocks which normally yield stragglers such as Caspian, Royal, Black, Forster's, and Roseate.

By late fall, most of the shorebirds are gone but the shallow offshore waters hold a variety of waterfowl. Look for Red-breasted Merganser, American Black Duck, Common Goldeneye, Bufflehead, and the occasional Oldsquaw. Brant, scoters, Horned Grebe, and Common and King Eiders (both eiders are rare) are always possible as well.

Milford Point--Stuart B. McKinney National Wildlife Refuge.
Milford Point is a 22-acre barrier peninsula comprised of sandy beaches and dredge-fill that lies west and south of the Connecticut Audubon Coastal Center. The long, low point partially shelters the Charles E. Wheeler WMA salt marsh to the north and east. To get to the point, walk west along the beach from the observation deck, staying below the high-tide line and keeping well away from the beach houses to the right. Along the way, the sandbars and breakwaters can be checked for cormorants, shorebirds and gulls, American Oystercatcher, and Black Skimmer. A pair of American Oystercatchers nested on one of these offshore sandbars in 1994 and 1995.

A fence marks the boundary of the Stuart B. McKinney National Wildlife Refuge, which was established to protect terns and plovers that nest at the point from May to July. Milford Point is closed during the nesting season but is open for birding during the rest of the year. **Note: the outer point may be closed throughout the year in the future.**

Use the observation platform by the fence to scope the marsh to the north and the point to the west. From April through September, the marsh is the best place to spot waders, some of which nest on offshore islands, but feed at Milford Point and other coastal marshes. Great Blue Heron, Great and Snowy Egrets, and Black-crowned and Yellow-crowned (uncommon) Night-Herons may be present. Waterfowl that nest and feed in the marsh are Mallard, American Black Duck, Gadwall, Mute Swan, and Canada Goose. From late July to September, check the

egrets for white plumaged immature Little Blue Heron. During fall and spring migration, an occasional Glossy Ibis and other shorebirds feed on the exposed mudflats. Migrant waterfowl to scope for include several dabbling ducks such as Green-winged and Blue-winged (uncommon) Teals, Gadwall, Northern Pintail, American Wigeon, and Northern Shoveler (uncommon).

Continue birding out to the point (if access is not restricted). At mid-to-high tide, the migrant flocks of sandpipers and plovers can number in the thousands and put on quite a show when they are startled up. Check the flocks of Semipalmated Plover and Semipalmated Sandpiper for less common species such as Western and White-rumped Sandpipers and Red Knot. Between August and October, Hudsonian and Marbled Godwits are sometimes spotted.

At the point, check the river, buoys, and pilings for waterfowl, gulls, terns, and cormorants. Loons, Red-breasted Merganser, Greater Scaup, and American Black Duck are likely seen from fall to spring. Wintering shorebirds at the point may include Dunlin, Sanderling, an occasional Black-bellied Plover, and Purple Sandpiper---the last is most likely seen out on the rocks and breakwater. Northern Harrier is sometimes spotted hunting over the marsh.

Fall and winter is also the time to check for two rarer owls; Short-eared Owls are sometimes spotted at dawn and dusk, hunting low over the marsh while Snowy Owls may rest on the offshore sandbars or perch on pilings or dunes along the point.

The scrubby growth along the way to the point may yield migrant sparrows, warblers, and occasional rarities such as Yellow-breasted Chat, Western Kingbird, or Henslow's Sparrow. Horned Lark nest on the point and small flocks are common throughout the year. In winter, Snow Bunting is regular, but sporadic, and Savannah Sparrow (Ipswich race) can usually be flushed from the dune grass.

Charles E. Wheeler Wildlife Management Area
After birding the point, return to the parking lot. To view the northeastern part of the Charles E. Wheeler WMA, backtrack along Seaview Avenue and turn left onto Milford Point Road. About 0.1 miles along Milford Point Road there is a Purple Martin nest box on the left (by the dead-end street) but the area around the nest box is becoming overgrown and the birds may soon abandon the nesting site. Monk

Parakeet has nested in the larger white pine to the right. Continue on Milford Point Road for another 0.1 miles and turn left onto Third Avenue. Continue one block and turn left onto Court Street. Drive one block and park near the corner where the road makes a sharp right. The Charles E. Wheeler WMA is straight ahead, and can be accessed by the dirt road beyond the bar-gate which leads to the boat launch.

The eastern side of the Charles E. Wheeler WMA encompasses an oak and maple woodland honeycombed with woodbine, honeysuckle, and poison ivy. The scattered cedars were once the fall and winter roosting sites for Long-eared Owl and, occasionally, Northern Saw-whet Owl, but are now being choked out by bittersweet. Wood edges are carpeted with bramble and greenbriar thickets while many of the trees are draped with Oriental bittersweet.

The woods and thickets are accessed by paths and are good for migrating landbirds. Spring warblers may include Palm, Tennessee, Northern Parula, Magnolia, Canada, and American Redstart. Other spring migrants to look for are Eastern Towhee, Northern Flicker, Great Crested Flycatcher, Ruby-crowned and Golden-crowned Kinglets, and Red-eyed and Solitary Vireos. In fall, the Yellow-rumped Warbler and White-throated Sparrow can be numerous. Orchard Oriole, Swainson's Thrush, White-crowned Sparrow, and Connecticut Warbler (a rare fall migrant) are some of the less common migrants to check for. Merlin, Sharp-shinned, and Cooper's Hawks are among the raptors that can be tallied during migration.

In spring and summer, a variety of songbirds nest in the woods and thickets. The woods to the right of the boat launch have harbored roosting Black-crowned Night-Herons in past years.

The boat launch provides a good view of the Charles E. Wheeler salt marsh which comprises most of the waterfowl management area. Scope the marsh for herons, shorebirds, and waterfowl. In spring this is a good spot to watch the prenuptial behavioral antics of waterfowl. The knotweed thickets along the edge of the marsh can yield migrant sparrows and finches, while the trees and shrubs that border the boat launch can be a haven for spring migrants listed above.

In summer, watch for waders feeding in the marsh. On quiet summer evenings listen for Clapper Rail calling and Marsh Wren singing in the marsh.

58 GULF POND
Milford

Gulf Pond is a small estuary formed near the outlet of the Indian River on Long Island Sound. This estuary is a haven for waterfowl during migration and winter. Herons, egrets, shorebirds, and gulls can also be tallied at Gulf Pond. A causeway bisects Gulf Pond, forming an upper and lower pond. The lower pond discharges into Milford Harbor which can be scanned from the town beach on Gulf Street.

Birding at Gulf Pond is best from August through April; while summer (August and September) and spring (April and May) are most productive for shorebirds and long-legged waders and the remainder of the year is good for waterfowl, loons, grebes, and cormorants.

DIRECTIONS

Northbound on Interstate 95 take Exit 40 (Old Gate Lane, Woodmont Rd) and turn right at the end of the exit ramp onto Old Gate Lane. If southbound on Interstate 95, take Exit 40 (Woodmont Road), turn left at the bottom of the exit ramp, go under the interstate and turn right onto Old Gate Lane. Follow Old Gate Lane 1.1 miles (0.8 miles from northbound exit ramp) to New Haven Avenue (Route 162) just beyond the railroad overpass. Turn right and continue for 0.6 miles on New Haven Avenue. Turn left onto Buckingham Avenue and proceed to the causeway (0.4 miles) that bisects Gulf Pond.

BIRDING

Causeway. Park along the causeway in a safe place. This road is heavily traveled so be careful when getting in and out of the car and crossing the road. Do not stand in the road. The causeway offers a good view of Gulf Pond which is on both sides of the road. Most migrant waterfowl appear at Gulf Pond about mid-October and many species linger through the winter.

Both the upper and lower ponds can be good for dabbling ducks and, during mid-to-high tide, some diving ducks as well. Common waterfowl that can usually be spotted from the causeway include American Black Duck, Gadwall, Northern Pintail, Green-winged Teal (check the teal carefully because the Eurasian subspecies has occurred

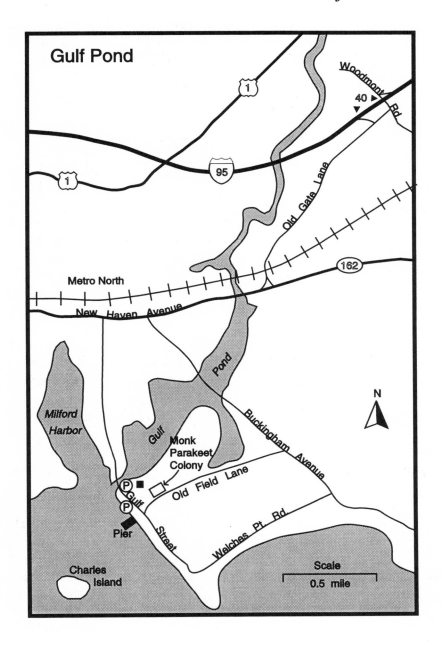

Gulf Pond

Woodmont Rd

1

40

95

Old Gate Lane

1

162

Metro North

New Haven Avenue

Pond

Milford
Harbor

Gulf

Buckingham Avenue

Monk
Parakeet
Colony

P

Old Field Lane

P

Gulf Street

Pier

Welches Pt. Rd.

N

Charles
Island

Scale

0.5 mile

irregularly at Gulf Pond), American Wigeon, Ring-necked Duck, Canvasback, Bufflehead, and Red-breasted Merganser. Species that are usually observed annually, but in small numbers are Blue-winged Teal, Wood Duck, Hooded Merganser, and Ruddy Duck. Rarer waterfowl observed here have included Redhead, Northern Shoveler, and Eurasian Wigeon.

Scan the mudflats around the ponds for shorebirds during the fall and spring migrations. Killdeer, Black-bellied Plover, Greater and Lesser Yellowlegs, and Least Sandpiper are likely species at Gulf Pond during migration, while Dunlin and Sanderling (normally found on the beach near the mouth of the harbor) may overwinter.

Breeding species found along the edges of the marsh are Clapper Rail and Saltmarsh Sharp-tailed Sparrow. Great and Snowy Egrets are common from late April until early October. Both of these egrets nest on Charles Island but use the marsh around Gulf Pond to forage and rest. Great Blue Herons can usually be spotted year-round, although numbers are reduced during winter.

Lower Pond and Long Island Sound. To explore the south end of the Gulf Pond (lower pond) and Long Island Sound near the mouth of Milford Harbor, continue on Buckingham Avenue 0.3 miles and turn right at the traffic light onto Old Field Lane. Follow Old Field Lane until it ends at Gulf Street (0.7 miles). At Gulf Street turn right and park in the town parking lot on the left side of the road. From here you can access the sandy beach or fishing pier to scout out Long Island Sound. Alternately, park on the right side of the road to view the lower end of Gulf Pond from the observation platform.

During September and October, the observation platform can be a productive spot for hawk watching. Raptor species that are regularly seen include Sharp-shinned Hawk, American Kestrel (may overwinter but during recent years numbers have been greatly reduced in the state), Broad-winged Hawk, Red-tailed Hawk (overwinter), Northern Harrier, and Osprey. Merlin or Peregrine Falcon are less common, but a few are spotted each year as they work their way southward.

The sandy beach and fishing pier across the road offer views of Long Island Sound near the mouth of Milford Harbor. Common and Red-throated Loons, Horned Grebe, Double-crested Cormorant (common in fall and spring, uncommon during winter), and Great Cormorant are fairly regular species in fall and winter (October through April). Some of the diving ducks further offshore may include Greater Scaup, Common Goldeneye, Oldsquaw, scoters (mainly White-winged and Surf, rarely Black), and Red-breasted Merganser. A few rarities such as Red-necked and Eared Grebes and the Thick-billed Murre have also been reported at this locale.

Herring, Ring-billed and Great Black-backed Gulls are often present along the beach, parking lot, or resting on the offshore waters throughout the year, while Laughing Gull is a summer and early fall visitor and Bonaparte's Gull shows up in fall and spring (rarer in winter). Glaucous and Iceland Gulls have been seen and the rarer Lesser Black-backed Gull (an annual winter visitor along the coast) is always possible.

The wooded island southwest of the fishing pier is Charles Island which hosts a heron colony from May through July. The colony consists mainly of Snowy and Great Egrets and Black-crowned Night-Herons. A few pair of Glossy Ibis may also nest on the island.

A colony of Monk Parakeets is located about 0.1 miles from the parking lot near the end of Old Field Lane. To see the colony, walk back up Old Field Lane about 100 yards and look for their large stick nests in the white pine just before the first house on the left.

59 LAUREL RESERVOIR
Stamford

Located near the New York border in north Stamford, Laurel Reservoir is a staple birding locale for birders in the southwest corner of the state. Surrounded by deciduous woodland and conifer stands, Laurel Reservoir provides a secluded retreat for waterfowl and waterbirds migrating in spring and fall. Even during winter (when the water remains ice free) and summer the reservoir hosts a good variety of species. By making a clockwise loop around the reservoir a number of vantage points allow good views (although some are obstructed) of the reservoir and its small islands.

DIRECTIONS

From the Merritt Parkway (Route 15) take Exit 35 (Route 137, High Ridge Road, Stamford) and follow Route 137 north 6.5 miles to Trinity Pass Road (just beyond the blinking caution light) on the right. Continue on Trinity Pass Road to Ponus Ridge Road (1.1 miles), turn right and follow Ponus Ridge Road south.

BIRDING

By following Ponus Ridge Road to Reservoir Lane (1.2 miles), turning right and right again onto Laurel Road (0.4 miles), you can loop the reservoir. Along Ponus Ridge and Laurel Roads there are a few good locations to pull-off and scope the reservoir.

During migration, waterbirds and waterfowl can be plentiful. Check the reservoir for Pied-billed Grebe, Double-crested Cormorant, American Black Duck, American Wigeon, Bufflehead, Ring-necked Duck, Wood Duck, and Common and Hooded Mergansers. Ruddy Duck and American Coot are consistently found during fall migration; both species are uncommon in the state. Less common species that appear from time to time include Blue-winged Teal, Northern Pintail, and Lesser Scaup (the latter also occurred during the 1995 summer bird count).

Scope the shoreline and islands for Great Blue and Green Herons, and gulls. Even in summer, the reservoir can be a productive birding site; Turkey Vulture and Osprey are regularly observed roosting on the larger island, while Double-crested Cormorant, Mute Swan, and several other species of waterfowl foray in the water. During mid-summer an assortment of herons and egrets can be viewed following post-breeding dispersal from local offshore breeding islands. Pine Warblers nest in the scattered pine stands around the reservoir.

Central Coastal

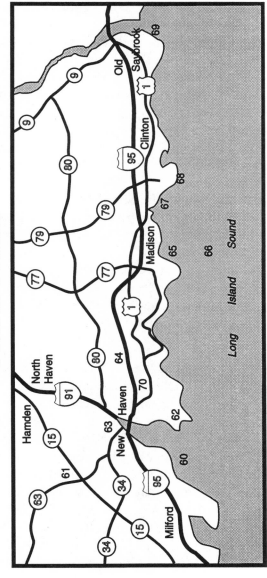

60. Greater New Haven Harbor
61. West Rock Ridge State Park
62. Lighthouse Point Park
63. East Rock Park

64. Branford Supply Ponds
65. Guilford Sluice
66. Falkner Island
67. Middle Beach

68. Hammonasset Beach State Park
69. Lower Connecticut River Tour
70. Furnace Pond

-377-

60 NEW HAVEN HARBOR TOUR
Milford, West Haven, and New Haven

Greater New Haven Harbor includes some of the most outstanding shoreline birding sites in the state. Its estuarine and coastal environments attract an exceptionally wide diversity of waterfowl and other avian species. During a peak migratory period a birding expedition to the Greater New Haven Harbor may produce over 120 species. This area also has a reputation for attracting rarities and many of the "first" state bird records have been documented by birding enthusiasts along the shores of this harbor.

In this birding tour, we concentrate on eight major stops that afford especially good birding, starting at Merwin Point in Milford and ending at Nathan Hale Park in New Haven.

Fall and spring generally provide the best birding, but winter can also be productive. The shorebird migration between July and September at Long Wharf and Sandy Point can be especially rewarding and challenging.

As elsewhere along the coast, tidal conditions are an important factor. Low tide or incoming tide conditions is generally the best time to bird for shorebirds. High tide brings waterfowl closer to the shore.

DIRECTIONS

The first stop on this birding tour is Merwin Point in Milford. To get to Merwin Point, take Exit 40 (Old Gate Lane, Woodmont Road) on Interstate 95 northbound and turn left at the traffic light at the end of the exit ramp. Drive past the Mayflower Truck stop and turn right at the traffic light onto Woodmont Road (0.3 miles). On Interstate 95 southbound take Exit 40 (Woodmont Road) and turn left at the end of the exit ramp onto Woodmont Road. Follow Woodmont Road 0.6 miles and continue straight on Anderson Avenue when Woodmont Road turns right. Drive 0.8 miles on Anderson Avenue and turn right onto Merwin Avenue which leads to New Haven Avenue (0.4 miles). Continue across New Haven Avenue and take the first left onto Chapel Street (0.1 miles). Drive two blocks and turn right at the stop sign onto Kings Highway (0.1 miles). Take King's Highway to Beach Avenue on the left (0.1 miles) and park near the rocky shore which is Merwin Point.

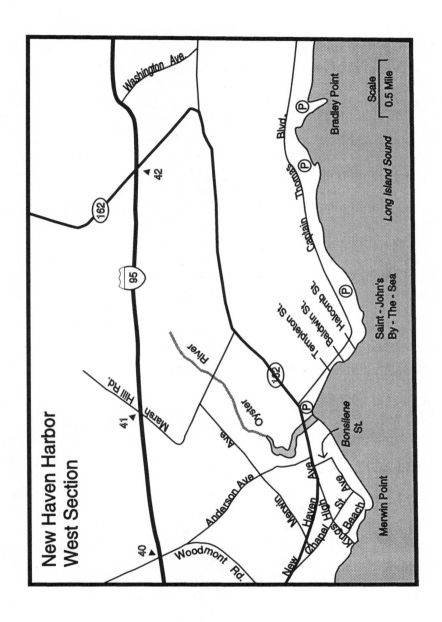

New Haven Harbor
West Section

Birding
Merwin Point

This rock promontory located in the Woodmont part of Milford is most productive from October through April. Scan the offshore waters for Common and Red-throated Loons, Red-necked (uncommon to rare) and Horned Grebes, Great (winter) and Double-crested (mainly spring and fall) Cormorants, American Black Duck, American Wigeon, Oldsquaw, Bufflehead, White-winged and Surf Scoters, Red-breasted Merganser, and other waterfowl. In winter, large rafts of Greater Scaup frequently occur on the offshore waters. Check the rafts for Lesser Scaup. Many gull species forage and roost in the area. Scan the coast for Bonaparte's Gull in winter and spring and Black-headed Gull in spring (usually March-April). The rock outcropping is a fairly consistent place to observe the foraging behavior of Purple Sandpipers from November-April. Both Common and King Eiders have been spotted at Merwin Point. In November-December and again in March-April scan the offshore waters for Northern Gannet, a species which now occurs regularly during migration. Before leaving Merwin Point, check the taller trees that line the nearby streets for Monk Parakeet which has taken up residence in the area.

Oyster River

From Merwin Point proceed along Beach Avenue which winds along the shoreline. At 0.8 miles just past the small park on the left (which also is a convenient stopping point for scoping the offshore waters), the road turns left and becomes Bonsilene Street. Continue two short blocks, turn right onto New Haven Avenue (0.1 miles). Drive 0.4 miles east to Oyster River and park in the sandy lot on the right.

This small cove is at the confluence of Oyster River with New Haven Harbor. The cove can concentrate large flocks of gulls and numbers of waterfowl and shorebirds. Study the gull flocks for rarities. From November through March, white-winged gulls (Glaucous and Iceland) are uncommon but regular visitors, and Lesser Black-backed Gulls are becoming more regular along the shoreline. Bonaparte's Gull is seen in small numbers throughout the winter. In March and April this Bonaparte's may congregate in large flocks of several thousand individuals. The rarer "European" gulls frequently appear so be on the lookout for the Little and Black-headed Gulls. To differentiate adult Bonaparte's Gulls from Black-headed Gulls (which is really a misnomer since the Black-headed Gull has a dark brown hood) we offer a tip: the Black-headed Gull is frequently the first to obtain the adult breeding plumage (hood). However, once most of the Bonaparte's attain breeding plumage, good luck! Oyster River was the site of Connecticut's first state record of Ross' Gull which lingered about a month (March-April) in 1983. Gadwall, American Wigeon, and other waterfowl are often seen at this stop.

Saint John's-By-The-Sea

From Oyster River, continue on Ocean Avenue for 1.0 miles to the next stop at Saint John's by-the-sea. Along the way, you can take a quick detour down one of the dead-end streets (Holcomb Street, Baldwin Street, or Templeton Street) on the right to get another view of Oyster River and the harbor. Saint John's by-the-sea is a church on the inland (left) side of the street. Park in the lot on the right (sea side) across from the church. This part of the harbor is good for loons, grebes, and waterfowl during winter. Scan the harbor and shoreline for American Black Duck, Common Goldeneye, Red-breasted Merganser, and American Wigeon. Check the wigeon flocks for Eurasian Wigeon which has been found here each winter for the past eight years or so. Although fairly regular at this stop, Eurasian Wigeon may also occur anywhere between Oyster River and Bradley Point, which is the next stop on the tour.

Bradley Point

To get to Bradley Point, continue east on Ocean Avenue and park in one of the lots on the right (1.0 or 1.2 miles). Scope the sandy beach, mudflats, pools, and rocks for gulls (large flocks frequently stay in the puddles and pools). You can also walk to Bradley Point and scope the rocks near the shore. Herring, Ring-billed and Great Black-backed Gulls are common for most of the year. Bonaparte's Gull is regular but numbers are generally smaller than at Oyster River. Lesser Black-backed and Black-headed Gulls are observed more frequently from December to April, although both species are still fairly rare. Shorebirds typically found in the pools include Lesser and Greater

Yellowlegs, Killdeer, Black-bellied Plover, and Least, Semipalmated, and Pectoral Sandpipers. In August, the pools should be checked for Wilson's Phalarope. Hudsonian Godwit has occurred in November and December.

Sandy Point

Also known as the West Haven sand spit, Sandy Point can be reached by continuing along Ocean Avenue, which becomes Captain Thomas Boulevard at the next traffic light. At the stop sign (0.9 miles from the second parking lot at Bradley Point), turn right onto Washington Street and then take a quick left onto Beach Street. Go 0.6 miles to a parking lot on the right (across from Captain's Galley Restaurant). In summer there is a parking fee, but you can park in the lot across the road or on Second Avenue which is just around the corner.

Sandy Point is a long sand peninsula that bends northward into New Haven Harbor. This stretch of beach and dune grass can be exceptional during the late summer and autumn (August-September) tern and shorebird migration. To bird Sandy Point, walk out to the end of the point and back, a round trip of about 1.0 miles. Watch the tide to avoid getting stranded out on the point by high tide. Typical shorebirds to look for during the fall migration include Ruddy Turnstone, Black-bellied and Semipalmated Plovers, Dunlin, Short-billed Dowitcher, Red Knot, Least, Semipalmated, and Western Sandpipers, Willet, and Sanderling. Occasionally American Golden-Plover, Buff-Breasted Sandpiper, and Wilson's Phalarope make a brief appearance. A variety of herons and egrets may also frequent the point, including Great Blue and Green Herons, and Snowy and Great Egrets. Little Blue and Tri-colored Herons are sometimes spotted. Least and Common Terns and a few pairs of Piping Plovers nest at Sandy Point behind the protective fence. In July, 1996, a pair of Black Skimmers also nested here.

From mid-to-late August, large flocks of terns sometimes numbering a thousand or more individuals may be seen. Common and Least Terns are the staple components of these flocks, but Forster's, Roseate, Black, and Caspian Terns are occasionally intermixed. An Arctic Tern (rare) was found and photographed at Sandy Point in August, 1994.

Loons, grebes, and waterfowl become more frequent in November and many stay through the winter. In November, 1978, a Western

Grebe showed up and stayed to overwinter. The winter flocks of Snow
Bunting and Horned Lark should be checked for Lapland Longspur.
One November, an immature Lark Sparrow was found in these flocks.

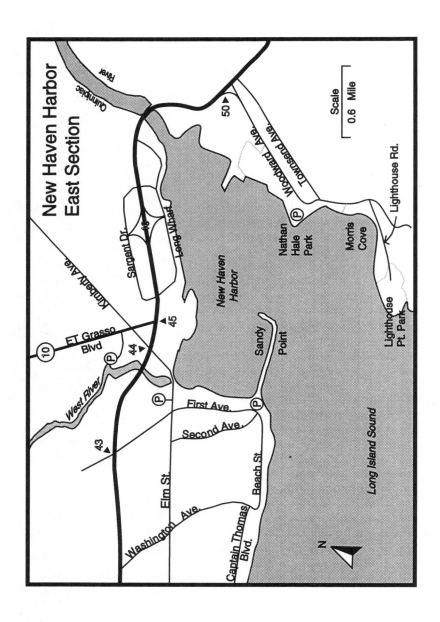

New Haven Harbor
East Section

Quinnipiac River

50 ▲

Scale
0.6 Mile

Townsend Ave.

Woodward Ave.

Lighthouse Rd.

Sargent Dr.

Long Wharf

46

Kimberly Ave.

45 ◄

Nathan
Hale
Park

Morris
Cove

New Haven
Harbor

FT Grasso
Blvd

10

44 ▲

Lighthouse
Pt. Park

West River

P

Sandy
Point

P

First Ave.
P

43 ▲

Second Ave.

Long Island Sound

Elm St.

Beach St.

Washington Ave.

Captain Thomas
Blvd.

N

West Haven Boat Launch
The town boat launch is located on the right, 0.3 miles up the road from the parking lot for Sandy Point and just north of the West Haven Wastewater Treatment Plant. The boat launch area affords another view of New Haven Harbor. In winter, note the large concentration of Mute Swans which, on rare occasions, may hold a Tundra Swan. The boat launch area is also an ideal spot to view the winter flocks of Greater Scaup. Occasionally stragglers such as Lesser Scaup or Redhead are associated with these groups.

West River
Return to Beach Street (which becomes First Avenue) and continue north. Follow First Avenue to the second traffic light and turn right onto Elm Street (0.8 miles). At the first traffic light turn left (0.1 miles) and continue to the Coast Guard Station at the end of road. Park and scope the West River and harbor for gulls and waterfowl. In late fall and winter, Canvasback, Common Goldeneye, Bufflehead, American Black Duck, American Wigeon, and Greater Scaup are common. Check the reedgrass along the river's edge for the less common Green-wing Teal and Northern Pintail. Rarely, Barrow's Goldeneye, Lesser Scaup, and Redhead are observed.

To view more of West River, return to Elm Street, turn left and continue over the bridge (Elm Street becomes Kimberly Avenue after you cross the bridge) to the traffic light (0.5 miles). Turn left onto Ella Grasso Boulevard (Route 10) and take the first left (0.1 miles) to the New Haven Regional Fire Training Academy. This short road ends at a cul-de-sac. Scope West River from the lawn on the north side of the training center. In winter, this stretch of river sometimes yields the waterfowl listed above. The salt marsh and grassy hillsides of the former landfill are good hunting grounds for a variety of wintering raptors such as Red-tailed and Rough-legged (uncommon) Hawk, American Kestrel, Northern Harrier (uncommon), and more rarely, Snowy Owl.

Long Wharf
Return to Ella Grasso Boulevard, turn right and follow the signs to the northbound ramp for Interstate 95 North (0.3 miles). Take Interstate 95 to Exit 46 (Long Wharf). At the end of the exit ramp turn left and park

in the lot fronting New Haven Harbor. The tidal mudflats at Long Wharf attract large numbers and a good variety of shorebirds and waterbirds in fall and spring. A number of vagrants and rarities have been recorded at this site---Spotted Redshank, Burrowing Owl, Gyrfalcon, Marbled Godwit, and American Avocet.

In fall, the variety of shorebirds can be impressive. Typical fall shorebirds at Long Wharf are Semipalmated and Black-bellied Plovers, Killdeer, Ruddy Turnstone, Greater and Lesser Yellowlegs, Red Knot, Dunlin, Short-billed Dowitcher, Least and Semipalmated Sandpipers, and Sanderling. Less common fall shorebirds may include Willet, Spotted, Pectoral, Western, and White-rumped Sandpipers, American Golden-Plover, and Wilson's Phalarope (early August).

Gulls are common in much of the year. Black-headed and Little (mainly March and April) Gulls are some of the rarer possibilities. Terns can be observed from May through September, with a few (mainly Forster's) lingering to late October. Black, Royal, and Caspian Terns infrequently appear in August and September, along with an occasional Black Skimmer.

Nathan Hale Park/Morris Cove Seawall

From Long Wharf take Interstate 95 north to Exit 50 (Woodward Avenue, Lighthouse Point). Turn right at the end of the ramp onto Woodward Avenue which leads to Nathan Hale Park (1.4 miles). Park in the lot on the right just as the road turns left.

Scan the eastern side of New Haven Harbor. In winter, this area can be good for loons, waterfowl (mainly diving ducks), and gulls. An albino Ring-billed Gull spent a couple of winters in the Nathan Hale Park area. Typical fall and winter birds are Common and Red-throated Loons, Horned Grebe, Double-crested and Great (late fall and winter) Cormorants, Oldsquaw, Greater Scaup, Common Goldeneye, and Red-breasted Merganser.

The Morris Cove Seawall offers another view of the east side of New Haven Harbor. To get to Morris Cove, turn right when exiting the parking lot, drive to Townsend Avenue (0.1 miles) and turn right. Continue for 0.2 miles to the seawall along the right. The sheltered waters of Morris Cove can hold the same species of waterfowl and gulls previously listed for Nathan Hale Park.

61 WEST ROCK RIDGE STATE PARK, KONOLD'S POND, AND LAKE WINTERGREEN

New Haven, Hamden, Woodbridge, and Bethany

For hundreds of years the Quinnipiac Indians hunted deer and turkey on West Rock Ridge and fished the nearby streams. In winter, they used the eastern side of the ridge as shelter from the cold northwest winds. The ridge changed hands in 1638 when Theophilus Eaton purchased 130 square miles of ridge and land from Chief Montowese of the Mettabeseck tribe. The settlers called the ridge Providence Hill because it provided them with a God-sent shelter from winter storms. New Haven gradually acquired over 600 acres of roadside ridgetop which were transferred to the state in October, 1982, to establish West Rock Ridge State Park.

West Rock Ridge State Park is actually the southernmost terminus of a long line of trap rock ridges that run northward through Massachusetts and into Vermont. The portion known as West Rock Ridge gradually rises to 500 feet in elevation before abruptly ending in the spectacular orange basalt cliffs that overlook New Haven. Cliffs line a portion of the steep, west flank of the ridge, beneath which Konold's Pond, Lake Dawson, and Lake Watrous sit amidst deciduous woodland and conifer stands. To the east, West Rock Ridge slopes gradually to West Rock Nature Center in New Haven and Lake Wintergreen in Hamden.

Over 225 bird species have been recorded along the ridge and nearby Konold's Pond and Lake Wintergreen, including 30 species of warblers. The ridge is home to a variety of woodland nesting species in late spring and summer and an important stopover for migrant songbirds in spring. In fall, the overlook at the southern terminus is a good spot to watch migrating raptors as they parallel the ridge southward.

Lake Wintergreen can be good for waterbirds and adjacent woodland species. The fields around Lake Wintergreen are considered to be one of the best spots to watch the aerial courtship antics of American Woodcock in spring. Konold's Pond has a reputation for attracting an outstanding assortment of migrant waterbirds and wintering gulls.

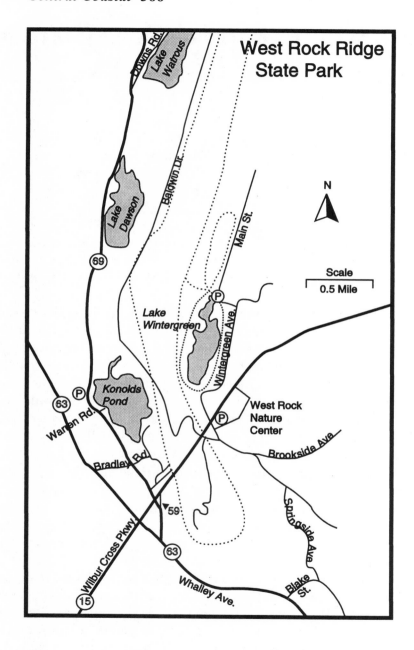

West Rock Ridge
State Park

DIRECTIONS

The only tunnel on the Wilbur Cross Parkway (Route 15) runs beneath West Rock Ridge. To get to the entrance to West Rock Ridge State Park, take Exit 59 (New Haven, Route 69) on the Wilbur Cross Parkway. Turn right and follow Route 69 south 0.3 miles to the junction of Route 63 and Route 69 (Whalley Avenue), turn left and follow Whalley Avenue to Blake Street (1.0 miles). Go left on Blake Street for 0.3 miles, left on Springside Avenue for 1.2 miles and left on Wintergreen Avenue for 0.3 miles. The park entrance is to the left. If the gate is barricaded you can park in the West Rock Nature Center, which is located 0.1 miles further up Wintergreen Avenue on the right. Hide valuables and lock the car. From here you can walk across the street and hike the park roadway (Baldwin Drive) up the hill to the overlook.

BIRDING

West Rock Ridge State Park

During spring migration, the wooded hillsides that line Baldwin Drive can hold a variety of warblers, especially Yellow-rumped Warbler (otherwise known as butterbutt), vireos, and thrushes. In late spring and summer, the woods may harbor nesting Veery, Wood Thrush and a variety of warblers such as Hooded, Worm-eating, and American Redstart and a variety of other common woodland breeding species.

Baldwin Drive terminates at the southern end of West Rock Ridge where there is a spectacular overlook and a pavilion for shelter. The overlook can be great for fall hawk watching, providing a nearly eye-level view of migrant accipiters, buteos, Ospreys, and the occasional Bald Eagle. The cliff-face below the pavilion was used as a roosting site by a Gyrfalcon that spent the 1987-88 winter. It feasted on starlings and pigeons at the nearby New Haven Landfill.

After birding the overlook, you can hike or drive northward along Baldwin Drive which continues northward for several miles along the crest of the ridge through a dry, oak-hickory forest. Here and elsewhere in the park it is possible to spot permanent residents such as Wild Turkey, Ruffed Grouse, Blue Jay, and American Crow. The talus slopes and rock jumbles in the more secluded sectors may hold Turkey

Vulture nests while Red-tailed Hawk, Great Horned Owl, and Pileated Woodpecker nest in the more heavily wooded areas.

Lake Wintergreen

To get to Lake Wintergreen from the West Rock Nature Center parking lot, turn right when exiting the lot and continue on Wintergreen Avenue for 1.1 miles, then turn left onto Main Street. At 0.1 miles, Main Street takes a sharp right but continue straight ahead into the parking lot, marked by a sign "West Rock Ridge State Park, Lake Wintergreen Area, open 8:00 am to sunset." Park in the lot, lock your car and hide your valuables.

Quietly walk down the trail to the bridge over the brook that empties into Lake Wintergreen a short distance on the left (south) of the trail. In mid-April evenings, American Woodcock perform their aerial courtship displays in the grassy areas near the brook to the north and south. In summer, check the brook to the north for Green Heron and Wood Duck. A path leading north from the bridge parallels the brook. The blend of wet thickets and line of spruces along this path can yield an assortment of migrants in late April and early May, including Palm, Yellow-rumped, Black-throated Green, and Wilson's (uncommon) Warblers. The nearby woods and thickets are usually good for Brown Thrasher, Gray Catbird, Yellow Warbler, Common Yellowthroat, Common Grackle, Eastern Towhee, and Baltimore Oriole. At dusk in late spring and summer, Whip-poor-will call from the hillsides. There is also a spring record (May) of Chuck-wills-widow at Lake Wintergreen.

Beyond the bridge, take the trail on the left which loops all the way around Lake Wintergreen, to end back near the parking lot. This trail is about 2 miles in length. The trail first works through wooded slopes on the right and a red maple swamp on the left. Further along it curves around the southern part of the lake through a white pine stand which is good for Pine Warblers in summer. Take advantage of the various overlooks along the trail to frequently scan the lake for swallows in spring and waterbirds throughout the year. From spring through fall, long-legged waders such as Great Egret and Great Blue Heron are possible anywhere along the lake.

Konold's Pond.

This broad but shallow pond has long been a favorite site for New Haven birders in search of waterfowl and wetland species. Konold's Pond owes much of its "popularity" to migrant and wintering birds because it is a convenient stopover for birds migrating south along the ridge. Its proximity to the coastline also catches shoreline migrants looking for an "oasis" in an otherwise major metropolitan area. Konold's Pond is particularly good from fall through spring when waterfowl can be abundant---rarities are possible throughout the year.

To get to Konold's Pond take Exit 59 (New Haven, Route 69) from the Wilbur Cross Parkway (Route 15) in New Haven and head north on Route 69 for 0.4 miles, then turn right (east) onto Bradley Road and left at the "T" junction. Continue 0.1 miles to the pond on the left. From here you can get a clear view of most of the southern portion of the pond. To view the western side of Konold's Pond, return to Route 69, turn right and drive 0.4 miles to Warren Road on the right, and park in the cul-de-sac. For a view of the north end of the pond, return to Route 69, turn right and continue north 0.2 miles to a dirt pull-off on the left. Cross the road and scan the pond through openings between the trees. **Be careful when crossing Route 69.**

Konold's Pond offers good birding from fall through spring. Waterfowl and waterbirds can frequently be abundant. Scan the open waters of the pond for Pied-billed Grebe, Snow Goose (uncommon), Gadwall, Blue-winged and Green-winged Teals, Northern Pintail, American Wigeon, Eurasian Wigeon (rare), Ring-necked Duck, Redhead (rare), Lesser Scaup (uncommon to rare), Bufflehead, and Common and Hooded Mergansers (which can be common from late March to early April). Check the Mute Swans for the very rare, but occasional, Tundra Swan which sometimes can be found in their company.

In winter, large concentrations of gulls congregate in this area, resting on the open water or on the ice when the pond freezes over. Be on the lookout for the white-winged varieties (Iceland and Glaucous) and Lesser Black-backed Gulls intermixed with the Herring, Ring-billed, and Great Black-backed Gulls. In winter, Bald Eagles occasionally hunt waterfowl on the pond and can be spotted soaring overhead or roosting in the tall trees along the northern and eastern shoreline.

During late March and April, two good birds to find in the marshy area and wet edge are American Snipe and Rusty Blackbird. Black Tern (rare) has been seen in mid-May. Konold's Pond is also considered to be one of the best sites in the south-central area of the state to view the spring swallow migration: Tree Swallows arrive in late March, followed shortly by Northern Rough-winged and Barn (mid-April), and by Cliff and Bank Swallows in late April or early May. Other early May arrivals may include Spotted and Solitary Sandpipers which can be observed in the marshy areas and low vegetation along the shoreline. Both sandpipers are regular throughout the month. In late spring, flocks of up to 100 or so Wood Duck may be seen at the northern end of the pond.

Summer nesting waterfowl at Konold's Pond include Mute Swan, American Black Duck, Mallard, and Wood Duck. Common Moorhen is irregularly observed and may breed. If present, their raucous call can generally be heard during early morning from May through July. Great Blue Heron frequent the weedy pond edge---during migration (mainly April) as many as a dozen or more may be seen at one time. The woods and edge habitat can be good for edge species such as Eastern Kingbird, Eastern Phoebe, Warbling Vireo, and Baltimore Oriole.

Lake Watrous

After birding Konold's Pond, continue north on Route 69 past Lake Dawson on the right. Turn right onto Down's Road (2.3 miles) and drive to the pull-offs on the left side of the road (0.4 and 0.7 miles). From either pull-off you can walk along the road to bird the reservoir and adjacent wooded hillside to the east. Do not trespass on the property owned by the water company around Lake Watrous.

The reservoir is especially good for swallows and waterfowl during migration, although the variety and numbers of both are generally smaller than at Konold's Pond. Flocks of diving ducks (mainly Ring-necked Duck and Common Merganser) are regularly observed. Sea ducks (Oldsquaw, White-winged Scoter and Common Goldeneye) are sporadically seen, normally as lone individuals. Wild Turkey frequent the woodlands and fields around the lake while the white pines at the north end of the reservoir for Pine Warblers in spring and summer.

62 *L*IGHTHOUSE *P*OINT *P*ARK
New Haven

Although small in size, Lighthouse Point Park is one of the most important birding sites in the state. Its 84 acres of gently sloping terrain juts southward into Long Island Sound, serving as a natural funnel for songbirds migrating along the Atlantic Flyway. The park is also famous as one of the most important hawkwatch sites in New England. Winter birding features offshore rafts of ducks, while gulls and crows patrol the sandy beaches, mudflats, and tide pools.

Lighthouse Point Park is named for the lighthouse at the end of the peninsula. A lighthouse has stood on this site since 1804. Over the years, birders have recorded more than 200 species at Lighthouse Point Park. Migratory songbirds, shorebirds, hawks, and waterfowl lead the list of specialties regularly seen. A variety of shorebirds makes brief stopovers in spring and fall. Unusual raptors, such as Peregrine Falcon, Bald Eagle, and an occasional Long-eared Owl are likely in the fall. Other rarities have included Barrow's Goldeneye, King Eider, Buff-breasted Sandpiper, Red-headed Woodpecker, Western Kingbird, Boreal Chickadee, and Boat-tailed Grackle. The first state record of Tropical Kingbird was established here in November, 1990.

DIRECTIONS

Northbound on Interstate 95 take Exit 50 (Woodward Avenue, Lighthouse Point). Turn right onto Townsend Avenue (0.1 miles) at the second traffic light. Continue south on Townsend Avenue for 2.2 miles to Lighthouse Road. Turn right onto Lighthouse Road which leads to the park entrance (0.6 miles). Travelers heading south on Interstate 95 should take Exit 51 (Route 1, Frontage Road, Lighthouse Point) which merges with Frontage Road (Route 1) paralleling the interstate for 0.8 miles. Turn left at the traffic light onto Townsend Avenue and continue as described above. From May into September a nominal admission fee is charged at the park entrance. The park road is a one-way, counterclock-wise loop with two spur roads, one providing access to the boat launch and the other to the hawk watch area and the sandy beach that lies along the park's southern boundary.

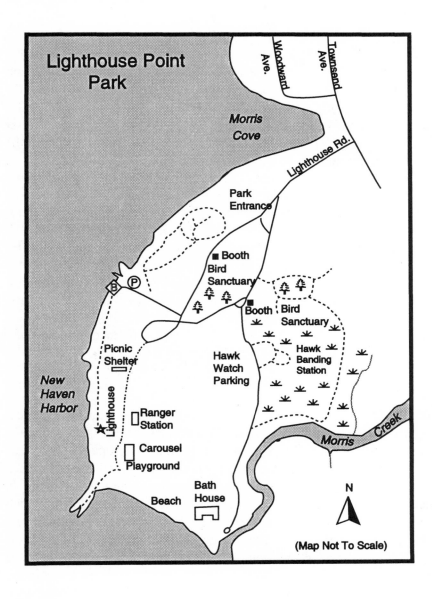

Lighthouse Point
Park

Morris
Cove

Woodward Ave.

Townsend Ave.

Lighthouse Rd.

Park
Entrance

■ Booth
Bird
Sanctuary

■ Booth Bird
Sanctuary

Hawk
Banding
Station

Picnic
Shelter

Hawk
Watch
Parking

New
Haven
Harbor

Lighthouse

☆ Lighthouse

Ranger
Station

Carousel
Playground

Bath
House

Beach

Morris Creek

N

(Map Not To Scale)

BIRDING

The park can be profitably birded in two or three hours at almost any season of the year. To begin, enter the park and follow the main road to one of the parking lots near the boat launch on the right. From here, all of the park's birding habitats are visible. The oak, maple, and hickory woodlots that border the northern end of the park have been designated as a bird sanctuary to help protect migrant songbirds. Most of the rest of the park is landscaped, consisting of gently sloping expanses of lawns, parking lots, and recreational fields ornamented with scattered pines, junipers, and deciduous growth. Morris Creek, with its fringe of salt marsh and reedgrass, forms the eastern border of the park. The shoreline features a variety of habitats along its brief length: small stretches of sandy beach, rocky and gravelly beaches, tide pools, and bedrock outcrops all provide an abundance and variety of food, which attracts shorebirds and waterfowl.

The most important birding event at Lighthouse Point Park is the fall migration of songbirds, shorebirds, and raptors. Shorebird migration begins in late July and continues through October, with a few species lingering longer. Most shorebird appearances are brief and the increased recreational activity in the summer months drives them away quickly. September and October are best for shorebirds, especially during morning hours after Labor Day when human disturbance is minimal. Species to look for include Sanderling, Dunlin, and Ruddy Turnstone along the beaches and rocky shorelines; Black-bellied Plover, Killdeer, and the rarer American Golden-Plover, and Upland and Buff-breasted Sandpipers can frequently be spotted resting or foraging on lawns and ballfields. Greater and Lesser Yellowlegs, Willet, and Semipalmated, Least, and Pectoral Sandpipers are often near the marsh edge and mudflats along Morris Creek.

Lighthouse Point Park is an important staging area for songbirds during the fall migration, which runs from August into November. During this time birders should check the woods, lawns, thickets, and marshes, which can be alive with thousands of birds of dozens of species, all resting and refueling before continuing the southward journey. The best time to catch the songbird migration is during the early morning hours. The Blue Jay migration can be especially spectacular, with thousands of jays swarming in the air at one time.

Flocks of Tree Swallows and blackbirds can number in the hundreds. Other migrant species to watch for include Northern Rough-winged, Barn, and Bank Swallows, Purple Martin, Cedar Waxwing, Northern Flicker, Chimney Swift, and American Goldfinch. Thousands of Bobolinks move through the park in September. Flocks of winter finches, mainly Purple Finch, Pine Siskin, and Evening Grosbeak add color and excitement to fall birding. Overhead, flocks of Canada and Snow (mainly in October) Geese make their noisy way south.

To appreciate the variety and abundance of migrating songbirds, explore the woodland trails. The most productive trail begins near the park exit. Take the trailhead (unmarked but easy to find) on the east (right) side of the road. The path leads to a loop-trail through the woodland. About halfway around the loop a spur trail winds southeast and out along an elevated walkway above a reedgrass marsh on both sides. Some of the migrants that pause in the woods near the trail include Yellow-bellied Sapsucker, Ruby-crowned and Golden-crowned Kinglets, Red-eyed Vireo, cuckoos, flycatchers, thrushes, warblers, and grosbeaks. The trail becomes more rugged as it continues south through the last of the reedgrass community to Morris Creek. An alternative is to return to the park road and walk a short distance south to where the trailhead comes out. You can enter here and hike along Morris Creek.

Either alternative offers a view of the tidal marsh and the creek. The reeds and grasses along this stretch can hold Common Yellowthroat, Yellow and Palm Warblers, and Saltmarsh Sharp-trailed and Swamp Sparrows. Peek through the reeds to spot marsh waders such as Great Blue and Green Herons, Snowy Egret, and with luck, American Bittern. Other elusive inhabitants of the marsh grasses and sedges include Common Snipe, Virginia and Clapper Rails, and an occasional Sora. Sparrows can always be found in the thickets and grassy areas and along the marsh border throughout October and into early November. Chipping, Song, Savannah, Lincoln's (uncommon),White-crowned, White-throated, Vesper (uncommon), American Tree, and occasionally, Seaside Sparrows are fairly reliable. Clay-colored and Grasshopper Sparrows have also been recorded. Some other rarities spotted here are Blue Grosbeak, Lark Sparrow, and Boat-tailed Grackle. Dickcissel has also been observed consistently in September and October.

The thickets of willow, sumac, and knotweed along the park road and across from the hawkwatch station may harbor Ruby-throated Hummingbird, Gray Catbird, chickadees, wrens, and thrushes. These thickets may be the spots to find the real migration rarities: Connecticut, Kentucky, and Mourning Warblers. Always check the chickadee flocks carefully for Boreal Chickadee, a rarity found occasionally from mid-October through November.

The trail network at the park's northwest corner offers additional birding opportunities. Several short trails traverse the woodland, shrub thicket, and grassy environment. A longer trail leads from the park entrance along the shoreline, past the boat launch, and then down to the lighthouse. An assortment of flycatchers, thrushes, warblers, and sparrows can be tallied along the trail. The large white pines may harbor Black-crowned Night-Heron or Great Horned Owl. In November, 1990, a Tropical Kingbird was first reported from this section of the park.

Two other species that usually put in an appearance at Lighthouse Point Park each year are Red-headed Woodpecker (September-October) and Western Kingbird (mid-October into November). Both species have been regularly spotted in the large solitary shade trees along the western and southern sections of the park.

In winter, bird the rocky beach and offshore waters of New Haven Harbor around the boat launch. From here you can walk the entire length of the shoreline in about 30 minutes. The common beach scavengers include the gulls and crows (American and Fish). Gulls expected throughout the year are the usual Great Black-backed, Herring, and Ring-billed. In summer and early fall, these species may be augmented by Laughing Gulls; in winter, check for Bonaparte's and the rarer Black-headed, Little, Glaucous, Iceland, and Lesser Black-backed Gulls.

The pier near the boat launch offers a good vantage point to spot waterfowl. Rafts of American Black Duck, Greater Scaup, American Wigeon, Canada Goose, Mute Swan, and Common Goldeneye can be found in the harbor. Scout the rafts carefully for the less common Oldsquaw, White-winged and Surf Scoters, Lesser Scaup, and Gadwall.

Rarer waterfowl recorded at the park include Common and King Eiders, Eurasian Wigeon, Redhead, and Barrow's Goldeneye. Small numbers of Red-throated and Common Loons, Horned Grebe, and Great

Cormorant are also regularly seen during fall and winter. The Red-necked Grebe is more of a rarity, but is occasionally observed during migration. Snow Buntings usually arrive in early November and are sporadic throughout the winter along the beach or around the gravel lots. Occasionally you may find a Lapland Longspur in a bunting flock. Horned Larks occur in the same habitat during much of the year.

Upland winter species include permanent residents (Hairy, Downy, and Red-bellied Woodpeckers, Black-capped Chickadee, Tufted Titmouse, White-breasted Nuthatch, Carolina Wren, Northern Mockingbird, Northern Cardinal, and House Finch), and winter visitors (Winter Wren, Golden-crowned Kinglet, Dark-eyed Junco, and American Tree and White-throated Sparrows).

Spring birding at Lighthouse Point Park is best in late April and May during the songbird migration. While it is not as extravagant in numbers and variety as fall migration, a two- or three-hour early morning stroll through the park can turn up an excellent assortment of songbirds. Again, the best way to catch the migrant action is to take the looping trails that wind through the northeast woods and along the northwest border. Warblers are the featured attractions along these trails. Common Yellowthroat and Yellow Warbler are abundant in the tangle and shrub vegetation. Overhead, the songsters are already practicing their melodies. On a good day, more than a dozen warblers can be heard along the trails, including American Redstart, Ovenbird, and Magnolia, Black-throated Blue, Black-throated Green, Blue-winged, Chestnut-sided, Black-and-white, Northern Parula, and Canada Warblers, and occasionally, Wilson's and Hooded Warblers.

Hawk Watching and Owl Hunting. In addition to its other birding attractions, Lighthouse Point Park has one of the most active hawk-watching stations in all of New England. The best hawk watching area is at the parking lot in the center of the park between the lawn and the marsh. The lot is bordered to the northeast by deciduous woods and to the east by thickets and reedgrass. This site provides a clear view of raptors approaching from the east and flying overhead, or slipping along the coastline or just above the woods.

In season, which extends from late August into November, the station is manned every day. On some days (mainly weekends) a hawk-banding station is also active. Hundreds of birders may gather on weekends to watch the parade of hawks. They are rarely disappointed. From dawn to dusk, hawks of a dozen species fly by in a steady stream, sometimes only one or two at a time and at other times in kettles of several hundred soaring overhead. In recent years, between 20,000 and 30,000 hawks have been counted during the fall migration. Sharp-shinned Hawks are most often seen--more than 10,000 were counted in 1993--but American Kestrel, Broad-winged Hawk, and Osprey are also frequently tallied. Given good hawk flight weather (best conditions are the clear days following passage of a recent cold front with falling temperatures and moderate north or northwest winds), a one or two-day visit will provide most of New England's diurnal birds of prey; fifteen diurnal raptor species were recorded in 1991. The list of migrating raptors likely to be seen includes the species described above plus Turkey Vulture, Northern Harrier, all the accipiters, Red-tailed, and Red-shouldered Hawks, and falcons including Merlin, and Peregrine Falcon. Rarer species may include Bald Eagle (about ten to twenty a year in September and October), Golden Eagle (a few per year, mainly in October), and Rough-legged Hawk (about five to six a year, mainly in November).

From mid-October on, hawk flights are slow. During the occasional lull in hawk watching activity, check the woodlands, thickets, and marsh edge tangles along the short loop-trail just northeast of the parking lot for Long-eared and Northern Saw-whet Owls, both of which sometimes roost in the tangles and scrubby evergreen for the day before renewing their southward migration at night. Great Horned Owls often overwinter, while Barred Owl is recorded annually during postbreeding dispersal. Snowy Owl has been seen along the beach during November and December, and from November through the winter you may see a Short-eared Owl hunting the marshes and fields. Eastern Screech-Owl is a permanent resident and can sometimes be spotted in the northern woodlots of the park sunning in a tree cavity.

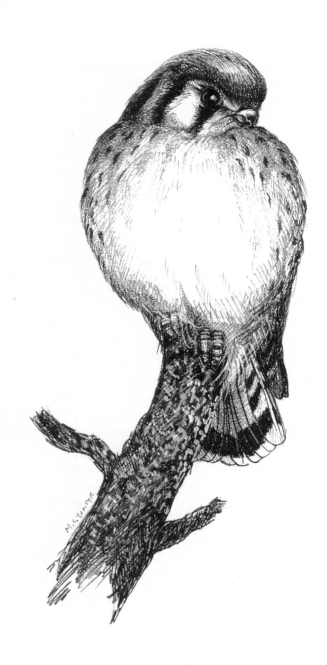

63 East Rock Park

New Haven and Hamden

This 450-acre park set amidst urban New Haven is famous for the spring migration of warblers and vireos that use the park's natural habitats as a stopover area for resting and feeding before moving northward. East Rock Park is dominated by the 300-foot high orange-brown traprock ridge that dates from the age of dinosaurs of 170 million years ago. The traprock sits on an even older layer of red sandstone from the early Mesozoic. The western half of the park straddles the Mill River which empties into New Haven Harbor a short distance further south. The park is owned and managed by the New Haven Parks and Recreation Department.

The New Haven Bird Club has published a list of over 200 species that have been seen at East Rock Park, but the spring influx of songbirds is the main birding attraction. A good spring birding day at East Rock Park can yield an assortment of warblers, vireos, thrushes, flycatchers, and sparrows. The spring warbler movement begins in early April with the arrival of Pine and Palm Warblers, peaks in mid-May, then declines rapidly. During this period, almost every species of eastern warbler puts in an appearance at the park.

Some notable warbler rarities seen at the park include Prothonotary, Hermit, Yellow-throated, and Connecticut. The autumn migration of warblers produces some fairly regular species, but the fall sparrow push can prove even more challenging. Birders also use the parking lot by the hilltop monument as a hawk watch site in September and October.

DIRECTIONS

East Rock Park's traprock ridge topped by a Civil War monument is clearly visible from Interstate 91. Take Exit 6 (Route 5, Willow Street, Blatchely Avenue) from Interstate 91. At the end of the exit ramp turn right onto Willow Street heading west 0.8 miles to Whitney Avenue at the traffic light (at the "T"). Turn right onto Whitney Avenue and continue for 0.7 miles to the parking lot for Eli Whitney Museum on the right. The covered bridge behind the museum leads into East Rock Park.

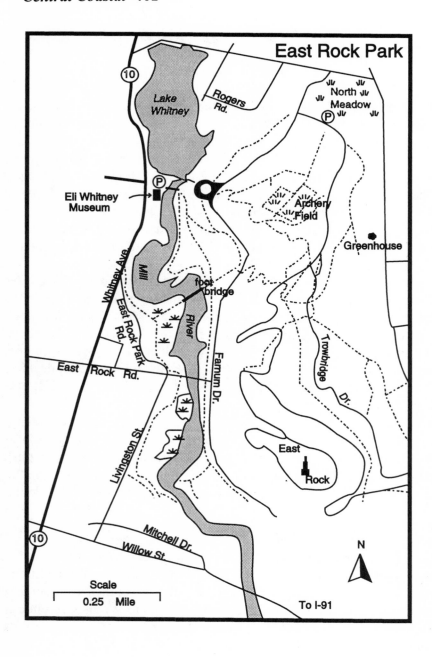

East Rock Park

BIRDING

Begin birding at the covered bridge. Swallows, flycatchers, and the occasional gull are all likely along this stretch of the Mill River, but the most exciting possibility is a Prothonotary Warbler which has put in an appearance in the first week of May or so every year for several years now. Search for the Prothonotary in the vegetation along the water's edge south of the bridge. On late summer evenings, Black-crowned Night-Heron and Chimney Swifts may be seen overhead. The night-heron hunts fish along the river and in the shallows of Lake Whitney just to the north of the dam. A 1.5 mile loop-trail through East Rock Park begins on the other side (the east side) of the covered bridge. A few feet beyond the covered bridge the trail branches. The right branch (of the loop) works southward and along the east side of Mill River while the left branch continues straight ahead through a small field and into a woodland. Take the left branch and continue straight through the floodplain forest of maples, oaks, and beeches which, in spring, can be good for thrushes, warblers, and vireos. In May, the trees along this trail can hold Tennessee, Nashville, Cape May, Canada, Black-throated Green, Blackburnian, Black-and-white, and Blackpoll Warblers, and American Redstart.

If you want to see spring warblers and vireos at tree-top level, take the white trail which branches to the left, about 180 yards east of the covered bridge. The trail ascends a steep hill and then forks. Bear left and the trail comes out on an overlook by a loop off of Farnum Drive. The overlook affords a good vantage point to watch warblers.

After birding from the overlook, return to the main trail which continues south through an oak-beech woodland. The swamp to the right of the trail is often good for Northern Waterthrush during migration. In spring and summer, the steep, wooded hillsides on the left harbor nesting White-breasted Nuthatch, Black-capped Chickadee, Tufted Titmouse, Red-bellied, Downy, and Hairy Woodpeckers, Blue Jay, Great Crested Flycatcher, Worm-eating, Black-and-white and Hooded (in the understory on upper slopes) Warblers, Ovenbird, and Red-eyed Vireo. Red-tailed Hawk and Great Horned Owl sometimes nest among the more heavily wooded hillsides while American Kestrel and Eastern Screech Owl take up residence in cavities among the trees and snags by the river.

After a short distance the trail emerges from the woodlands and follows alongside the river. Swamp Sparrow is a regular breeder in the shrubby marsh vegetation along the river's edge while Eastern Towhee nest beneath the mountain laurel thickets.

The trail ends at East Rock Road. Turn right and cross the bridge over the Mill River. From the bridge vantage point, scan the river and river edge for waterfowl and other waterbirds. In spring, Eastern Phoebe may nest in the bridge girders. Just beyond the bridge the trail continues on the right, working through a small woodlot which includes an impressive undergrowth of rhododendron. Check the thickets along the trail for House Wren and Common Yellowthroat. The trees along this stretch of trail can hold all of the warblers listed previously.

Lined by mature hardwoods and conifers, the trail gradually descends to a marshy area that borders the west bank of the river. Rarer warblers that have turned up along this trail (as well as elsewhere in the park) include Golden-winged, Cerulean, Yellow-throated, and Kentucky.

About 100 yards further along the trail branches; take the right branch which passes through moist thickets of willows, rose, and bittersweet to a narrow footbridge across the Mill River. For most of the year, the thickets can be good for Carolina Wren, Northern Cardinal, Northern Mockingbird, and Song Sparrow. From spring through fall, look for Gray Catbird, Brown Thrasher, and Yellow Warbler. Mourning Warbler is a rare migrant from late May into early June. Check among the taller trees along the marsh edge for Blue-winged and Chestnut-sided Warblers.

Stop on the bridge to check the river's edge and cattail marsh for migrant Solitary and Spotted Sandpipers, Green and Great Blue Herons, and the rarer Least and American Bitterns. From spring through summer, swallows and swifts forage over the water while Eastern Kingbird forays out of the taller trees to catch an occasional insect. The bridge is also a good spot to listen for, and perhaps glimpse, birds that nest in the trees along the river including Yellow-throated and Warbling Vireos, Rose-breasted Grosbeak, Scarlet Tanager, Baltimore Oriole, and Common Grackle. Red-winged Blackbirds sally about their territories in the small cattail marsh and Belted Kingfisher announces its presence with a throaty rattle.

Just across the bridge the trail branches again. Take the left trail which continues along the east side of the river back to the covered bridge by the museum parking lot. The swampy backwaters to the right of the trail often hold Mallard, American Black Duck, and Wood Duck.

The thickets and woody growth along the trail can be very active. Migrant kinglets, Blue-gray Gnatcatcher, Yellow-rumped Warbler, and American Redstart and other species previously mentioned are possible.

Trowbridge Drive. To get to Trowbridge Drive from the museum parking lot, turn left and head south on Whitney Avenue for 0.4 miles to East Rock Road (at the traffic light). Turn left onto East Rock Road and continue 0.2 miles to the "T" junction just beyond the bridge over the Mill River. Turn left onto Farnum Drive and drive up the windy road for 0.8 miles to the park road on the right, and park in the lot.

From the parking lot walk up the park road to Trowbridge Drive (about 0.3 miles) which branches to the left behind the rotary. Vehicle access to Trowbridge Drive is blocked by a stone barricade but you can hike it. **Note: do not park by the entrance to Trowbridge Drive as you may be ticketed or towed.** The road crosses over a stone bridge (about 100 feet along) with laurel thickets beneath on either side. Hooded and Kentucky Warblers have occurred in this area. This is also a good spot to find migratory cuckoos in May.

The road continues through a hillside hemlock forest, now much in decay because of woolly adelgid infestation. For years this hemlock stand supported a small nesting population of Fish Crow. Now the stark landscape of diseased trees and dead snags serve instead as a vivid reminder of the impact brought about by the inadvertent introduction of biological pests from other countries.

The denser standing remnants of hemlock and deciduous growth are good for spring warblers, vireos, and thrushes so look and listen for the warblers listed for other parts of the park. Since the hill slopes you don't have to strain your neck so much to see the warblers and other songbirds along the roadway. In spring, the woodland and roadway can produce migrant Hermit, Swainson's, and the rarer Gray-cheeked Thrushes. Summer nesting thrushes include Wood and Veery. Check along the small brooks for Louisiana Waterthrush. The most famous bird seen along this road is undoubtedly a male Hermit Warbler---the only state sighting which occurred in 1977.

Further down Trowbridge Road, the woodland opens up to a dryer slope good for nesting Worm-eating Warbler. Higher up the slopes in the open thicket-deciduous areas, Indigo Bunting and Prairie Warbler are regular breeders.

Monument Overlook. To get to the monument overlook---the best known landmark in New Haven---follow the park road (past Trowbridge Drive) which winds up the western slope of East Rock ridge. Several parking lots are available at the top. In fall, the overlook can be used as a hawk watch site allowing good views of hawks migrating southward along the ridge and above the Mill and Quinnipiac Rivers.

64 BRANFORD SUPPLY PONDS
Branford

Acquired by the town in 1969, the Branford Supply Ponds are comprised of approximately 359 acres of varied habitat. A single pond was formed at the turn of the century by the damming of Pisgah Brook, but with the construction of Chestnut Street the original pond has been divided into the East and West Ponds connected by a culvert. Historically, the pond was used as a water supply and in the early 1900's as a source of ice. The foundation of the ice house still remains on the south shore of the East Pond.

The park is crisscrossed with numerous trails and wood roads that access the various habitats and provide good birding opportunties. In recent years this has proven to be a good site for spring migration with such rarities as Prothonatary and Yellow-throated Warblers occasionally occuring. A Summer Tanager showed up in spring one year.

The mixed habitats provide breeding areas for an assortment of species including Red-shouldered Hawk, Barred Owl, Pileated Woodpecker, Willow Flycatcher, Pine Warbler, and a host of others. It is best to bird this location in early morning, because later in the day the trails are clogged with hikers and mountain bikers.

DIRECTIONS
From Interstate 95 take Exit 54 (Branford, Cedar Street) and follow Cedar Street south 0.2 miles to Route 1. Turn left and continue on Route 1 north to Chestnut Street (0.7 miles), turn left and follow Chestnut Street past the park entrance sign (with legend "Welcome to Branford Supply Ponds") to the main parking lot just beyond West Pond on the left (0.6 miles from Route 1).

BIRDING
A number of trails crisscross the park and access the varied habitat. A short, but productive loop around West Pond should produce an assortment of species during spring and summer. From the parking lot, take the trail which flanks the right side of West Pond for 100 yards, then bear left onto the white trail which continues along the pond's edge. The trail winds through wet thickets and mixed deciduous-coniferous

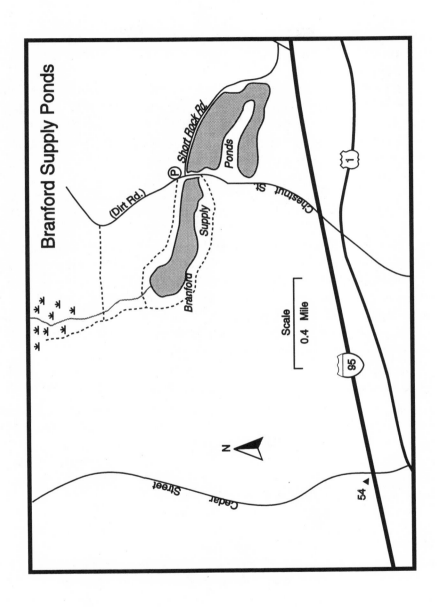

Branford Supply Ponds

woodlands which from mid-April into mid-May should harbor an array of migrants including Ruby-crowned and Golden-crowned Kinglets, and Palm and Yellow-rumped Warblers. Pine Warbler, Scarlet Tanager, Rose-breasted Grosbeak, and Baltimore Oriole are regular migrants and breeding species.

Scope the pond from time to time for migrant Pied-billed Grebe, Great Blue Heron, Ring-necked Duck, and swallows. Nesting waterfowl include Mute Swan, Mallard, and Wood Duck (the latter may be deep in the emergent vegetation after early morning). At the junction of the white trail and red trail, bear left, and walk over the foot-bridge. Check the streamside vegetation for nesting Gray Catbird and Common Yellowthroat. Blue-gray Gnatcatcher, and Warbling and Yellow-throated Vireos may be nesting in the mature trees lining the stream or pond.

After crossing the bridge, a left will continue the pond-loop, but you may elect to turn right and explore the large shrub swamp and powerline right-of-way a little further to the north. The shrub swamp is quite extensive covering numerous acres. Here you should find nesting Red-winged Blackbird, Common Grackle, Yellow Warbler, and possibly a migrant Virginia Rail. Blue-winged Warbler and Indigo Bunting are summer residents along the powerline right-of-way.

In March and April, check the swamp for migrant Rusty Blackbird. In May, Willow Flycatcher, Northern Waterthrush, and Wilson's Warbler are also possibilities. Scan the hillside for raptors including Turkey Vulture, Red-tailed, Red-shouldered and Broad-winged Hawks which all nest within the park or nearby.

Return to the trail and continue the loop. The trail winds through scrubby thickets and red maple bottomland before ending at a field near the road. The thickets and woodland along this walk can yield an assortment of migrants during spring and also hosts many nesting species. Breeding species to expect include Carolina Wren, Veery, Wood Thrush, Brown Thrasher (uncommon), Chestnut-sided Warbler, Scarlet Tanager, Northern Cardinal, and Rose-breasted Grosbeak.

The East Pond offers similar birding opportunities. East Pond can be birded from the road on the north or from trails that work from Chestnut Street down through the woods to the pond. In fall and winter, the sheltered cove by the dam at East Pond can yield waterfowl.

65 GUILFORD SLUICE
Guilford

Guilford Sluice is comprised of 147 acres of the state-owned East River Wildlife Management Area and a smaller parcel of town-owned property. Habitat in this location consists of open salt marsh with tidal creeks and a number of "wooded hummocks". Birding is best during the spring and fall waterfowl and shorebird migration. Summer birding can produce an array of interesting breeding species unique to the salt marsh community.

Rarities that have shown up at Guilford Sluice include Ruff, Upland, and Baird's Sandpipers, King Rail, Long-eared Owl, Mountain Bluebird, and Loggerhead and Northern Shrikes.

Guilford Sluice is a wildlife management area and therefore duck hunting is common from about mid-October into January, except for Sundays. When hiking the area during the hunting season wear bright colors and be alert for hunters. Alternately, bird Guilford Sluice on Sunday only.

DIRECTIONS

On Interstate 95 take Exit 59 (Goose Lane). Go south on Goose Lane straight across Route 1 to the stop sign on Route 146 (0.1 miles). Turn right and follow Route 146 for 0.6 miles, turn left onto South Union Street and continue 0.5 miles, bear left onto Saw Pit Road and drive to the barrier before the railroad tracks (0.1 miles). Park near the barrier, but do not block the driveway on the right at the end of the road.

BIRDING

From Saw Pit Road scope the marsh to the east (north of the railroad tracks). You can view the marsh from Saw Pit Road or hike along the train tracks for a short distance, about 100 feet (**be extremely careful -- this is a busy Amtrack line and the trains travel through this area rapidly**). During spring, scan the marsh for dabbling ducks including American Black Duck, Green-winged and Blue-winged (uncommon) Teals, and the occasional Gadwall. Herons (Great Blue and Green) and egrets (Great and Snowy) are regular visitors from April through

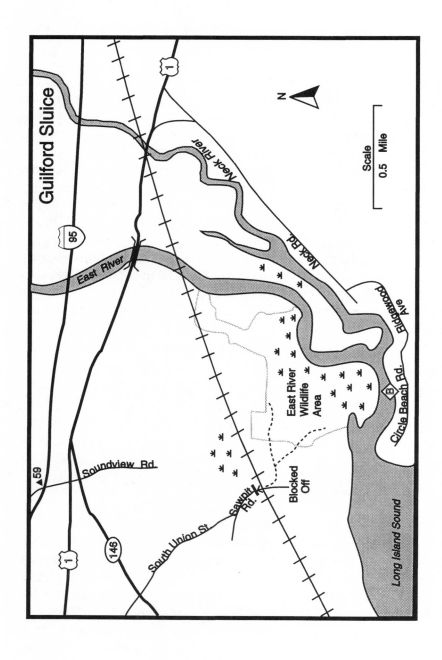

October or so. Shorebirds frequently observed in the marsh and along the edge include Killdeer, Least Sandpiper, and Greater and Lesser Yellowlegs. Check closely for the easily overlooked Common Snipe and Pectoral Sandpiper.

Cross the railroad track and view the salt marsh to the south. This area should harbor species similar to those found north of the railroad tracks. In addition to the common species, the salt pannes of the high marsh has produced Ruff a number of times (no recent records); most occurrences are from late March into May. Other shorebirds that periodically show up are Stilt and Upland Sandpipers and Whimbrel. Follow the dirt road between the tracks and the salt marsh to the bridge.

Cross the bridge and take the path that veers off to the right. This path flanks a wooded island lined by red cedar, rose, and other thicket shrubs. During fall migration the woodland-marsh interface can harbor many migrant wrens, thrushes, Cedar Waxwings, warblers (mainly Palm and Yellow-rumped), and sparrows. Migrant sparrows regularly found include Savannah, Song, Chipping, Field, White-throated, Fox, Swamp, and White-crowned. The food and shelter provided by the thickets usually accounts for various semi-hardy species overwintering such as American Robin, Hermit Thrush, Gray Catbird, Brown Thrasher, Golden-crowned Kinglet, Yellow-rumped Warbler, and Eastern Towhee. In fact, during the winter of 1994-1995, the state's first documented record of a Mountain Bluebird (female) occurred in this area.

In winter, scan the marsh for Northern Harrier, Red-tailed Hawk, and the rarer Rough-legged Hawk and Short-eared Owl. Seaside and Saltmarsh Sharp-tailed Sparrows, Marsh Wren, and Clapper Rail breed in the salt marsh and along the mosquito ditches, whereas Eastern Meadowlark nest in the drier areas of the upper marsh.

Return to the dirt road and follow it through a wooded island. This and the other protected coastal woodlots often harbor nesting Red-bellied and Downy Woodpeckers, House Wren, Tufted Titmouse, Wood Thrush, Veery, White-eyed Vireo, Northern Cardinal, and Eastern Towhee.

Continue along the road which emerges from the woods and skirts along a field edge then turns right and ascends a dike. The dike is actually a retention pool for dredge spoils and a recent addition to this locale. The elevated dike offers a good view of the field and marsh to the east. The marsh at the field's edge harbored migrant Least Bittern in the past, but since the habitat has been modified future occurrences remain uncertain. When scanning south from the impoundment, a small round "pothole" called Hoehn Pond is visible in the marsh. This small man-made pond was dug by the Youth Conservation Corp and attracts migrant dabbling ducks and shorebirds in season. The mudflat and retention pool created by the spoil within the dike may provide a new staging area for shorebirds during high tide cycles.

In winter the wooded hammocks frequently conceal a few species of owls. Check the conifers for Great Horned Owl, a common winter resident, and Long-eared Owl, uncommon, but generally appearing for at least short periods each winter. Northern Saw-whet Owl is occasionally observed during fall migration (mainly November) and in winter.

East River Boat Launch. To view the marsh from its southern boundary along the East River, return to Route 146 and turn right. Follow Route 146 for 0.8 miles straight through the stop sign (a left puts you back onto Goose Lane and back to Interstate 95) to Route 1. Turn right and continue on Route 1 for 1.9 miles, turn right at Neck Road (follow the boat launch signs) and right again at the stop sign (200 feet). Continue along Neck Road for 1.2 miles, turn left onto Ridgewood Avenue at the sharp turn. Follow Ridgewood Avenue (which becomes Circle Beach Road) for 0.7 miles and turn right into the boat launch access road.

The boat launch road turn is just before Ridgewood Road deadends. If a gate blocks the access road, open it, drive through and close it again. The boat launch area offers a good view of East River and the salt marsh. Species composition in this area is similar to the other location.

In late spring and summer, a walk along the access road and riverbank may produce Saltmarsh Sharp-tailed and Seaside Sparrows. At low tide the river and exposed mudflats attract migrant shorebirds, especially Short-billed Dowitcher and both species of yellowlegs. Common and Least Terns forage along the tidal river. If you hike back to Ridgewood Road and continue west to the end of the road, a walk along the beach may yield Roseate Tern fishing in the offshore waters.

66 FALKNER ISLAND
Guilford

This 5- acre island in Long Island Sound located just three miles off of the Guilford coast has been known for its nesting colonies of terns since Adrian Block surveyed the island in the early 1600's. The Indians, who may have harvested the eggs and chicks of the nesting terns called the island Massancummock, meaning "the place of fishing hawks," or, in our parlance, Ospreys. Less well known is that the island is also a good spot for spring songbird migrants and the occasional rarity, straying in following a storm or just plain wandering. Falkner Island also boasts the second oldest lighthouse along the Connecticut coastline.

A part of the Stewart B. McKinney National Wildlife Refuge system, Falkner Island is cooperatively managed by the U.S. Fish and Wildlife Service, the State DEP, and The Nature Conservancy. For many years birders tracked the status of the nesting tern colony. The grassy upland and rocky shore habitats supported thousands of nesting pairs of Common Tern and the endangered Roseate Tern. Beginning in 1978, the Falkner Island Tern Project was started. Each year the island hosts a number of volunteers under the direction of Dr. Jeffrey Spendelow, director of the project, who monitor the breeding season through the summer and depart in fall with the last of the birds.

DIRECTIONS
The island and its magnificent lighthouse are visible just off the coast of Guilford. Getting to the island presents something of a problem, however. Since the island supports both breeding colonies and breeding colony researchers, visitors are not permitted unless you volunteer your services. However, the Connecticut Audubon Society has an open-house or rather open-island one day each year when visitors may be boated over from the mainland to observe---from a safe and supervised distance---the nesting facilities that have been prepared and the birds that take advantage of them. Contact the Stewart P. McKinney National Wildlife Refuge, P. O. Box 1030, Westbrook, CT 06498, phone 203-399-2513; or the Connecticut Audubon Society at 2325 Burr Street, Fairfield, CT 06430, phone 203-259-6305, for more information about visits to Falkner Island.

BIRDING

Falkner Island is best known for its nesting colonies of terns. Each year several hundred Roseate Terns (a federally and state endangered species) arrive from their wintering grounds in the waters off Trinidad and northern South America from Columbia to eastern Brazil. The Roseates claim nesting sites amidst a specially prepared habitat of half sunken tires, cobble, and shell beach. They share the island with several thousand nesting Common Terns and even a pair of American Oystercatchers. The oystercatchers attempted to nest in 1991 and succeeded in raising chicks in 1993. The two tern species divide the island nesting sites and offshore island fishing sites; Roseate Terns tend to hunt sand lance and anchovy in the deeper and clearer waters while the Common Terns most often fish the shallower, inshore waters towards Guilford. Other unusual nestings documented at Falkner Island in recent years include a Roseate-Common Tern nesting pair in 1993.

Protecting the tern colony at Falkner Island and enhancing their nesting habitat on the island continues to pay dividends. The tern colonies represent the largest nesting populations along the Connecticut coast and also provide a unique opportunity for ornithologists to continue to monitor and study these important species.

Spring migrants at Falkner Island include dozens of songbird species. Migration peaks run from the first week in May through the first week in June. Largest numbers of White-throated, Swamp and Savannah Sparrows, Eastern Towhee, and Ruby-crowned Kinglet are tallied in the first two weeks in May, then taper off quickly. The middle weeks of May include Common Yellowthroats, which remain strong into June, along with Gray Catbird, Yellow Warbler, and Magnolia Warbler. A less common May migrant is Lincoln's Sparrow. The island has also proven a fairly consistent site for Mourning Warbler, a later migrant that generally appears in late May or early June.

Falkner Island occasionally catches interesting vagrants or accidental species. The first documented record of the Bridled Tern was observed at Falkner Island on June 27, and again on the 13th, 14th, and 16th of August, 1992. Other unusual species that have been reported over the years include Northern Gannet, Magnificent Frigatebird, Long-billed Curlew, and Sooty Tern.

67 MIDDLE BEACH

Madison

The Middle Beach section of the Madison shoreline is a good birding area for migrating and wintering waterbirds and waterfowl. A 2-mile stretch of road that parallels the shoreline provides excellent views of Long Island Sound, Tuxis Island, and Gull Rock. This route offers several vantage points (including the East and West Wharfs) that are ideal for studying the assorted birdlife.

DIRECTIONS

From Interstate 95 take Exit 62 (Hammonasset State Park) and follow the Hammonasset Connector 1.3 miles south to Route 1. Turn right onto Route 1 (south) and proceed 0.6 miles to the first left at a blinking light. Turn left onto Liberty Street and continue 0.4 miles before turning left onto Waterbury Avenue. Drive along Waterbury Avenue 0.9 miles to the second stop sign (Waterbury Avenue becomes Seaview Avenue after taking a sharp right corner and eventually turns into Middle Beach Road). At the stop sign, turn left into the East Wharf parking lot. During winter, the parking lot gate is closed at 3:00 pm.

BIRDING

East Wharf. You can view Long Island Sound from the beach or the wharf, whichever you prefer. Either spot offers a fine view of the area. From October through winter, check the offshore waters for Common and Red-throated Loons, Double-crested Cormorant (common in fall, but scarce in winter), Great Cormorant (regular in winter), and Horned Grebe. Usually a variety of diving ducks can be spotted from this area. Species here can include Red-breasted Merganser, Common Goldeneye, Oldsquaw, and Surf and White-winged Scoter. This site has been somewhat dependable for finding Black Scoter, a species that is normally difficult to locate elsewhere in the state. Gulls are regular throughout most of the year and terns in the summer.

Tuxis Island. From the East Wharf parking lot, return to Middle Beach Road, turn left and continue for 0.4 miles to a small parking area (suitable for four cars) on the left directly across from Tuxis Road.

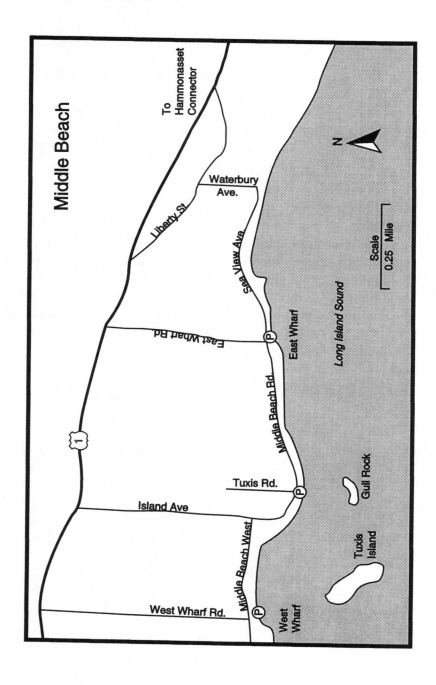

Park here and scope the offshore island and rocky outcropping. Tuxis Island is the land mass with the flag pole to the right of the parking area and Gull Rock is offshore slightly left of the parking area. Check Gull Rock for roosting cormorants, ducks, and gulls. Purple Sandpiper (uncommon but regular) often roost on Gull Rock during winter as do Common Tern in summer. Tuxis Island has an active Common Tern nesting colony and, intermittently, Roseate Tern also nests on the island.

American Oystercatcher occur in the area from early spring through fall. Other shorebirds also use the rock and island for foraging and roosting.

West Wharf. Continue west along Middle Beach Road from the parking area and turn left at Middle Beach West (0.2 miles), follow this road 0.3 miles to the West Wharf Road, turn left and drive straight down to the West Wharf parking lot (0.1 miles). Like the other sites, this area can be good for waterbirds, waterfowl, and gulls. The western shoreline of Tuxis Island can be viewed from the wharf. From late fall through early spring, check the normal contingent of gulls (Herring, Ring-billed, and Great Black-backed) carefully for Bonaparte's Gull, which is normally observed foraging a distance offshore, and the rarer Iceland Gull which is usually intermixed with the other gulls.

68 HAMMONASSET BEACH STATE PARK
Madison

The narrow strip of land between the river and the sound was known to the Indians as Athammonasset, meaning "the place where we dig holes in the ground." The Indians grew corn, beans, and squash in the fertile ground, using seaweed and fish for fertilizer. Early records document the land transfer to the first colonists, when "Uncas the Mohegan" conveyed the land between Tuxis Pond and the river to Mr. Fenwick of Guilford. The colonists fished Hammonasset waters for shad and hunted Heath Hen in the salt marshes. Later, Willard's Island became an orchard. In 1898, the Winchester Repeating Arms Company purchased the land to test their "Lee Straight Pull Rifle" and other new weapons. During World War I, the army test-fired ammunition on the beaches and among the sand dunes. Following the war, Hammonasset became a state park which opened to the public on July 18, 1920. Today, Hammonasset is the state's most popular shoreline park, annually attracting 1.5 million visitors.

For birders, this 919-acre state park is one of Connecticut's premier shoreline birding hot spots. Its diverse coastal habitats of tidal creeks and coves, salt marshes, ocean beach, rocky shores, and coastal hardwoods combine to attract a remarkable variety of waterfowl, shorebirds, waterbirds, raptors, and migrant songbirds. Birders claim that about 240 species can be seen each year with diligent birding. Hammonasset is also known as the place to find the unexpected---every day brings the possibility of a rare species.

Hammonasset offers good birding throughout the year, but spring, summer (August/September), and fall are the best months. Summer can be a hassle as the beaches are usually clogged with bathers who invariably spill over into the better birding locales. During peak migration periods (late April through May in spring, August into early November in fall), plan to spend at least half a day at the park.

The long list of rare species includes American White Pelican, King Eider, Swainson's Hawk, Upland, Baird's, and Curlew Sandpipers, White-faced Ibis, Mew Gull, Western Kingbird, Northern Wheatear, Clay-colored and Henslow's Sparrows, and Chestnut-collared Longspur.

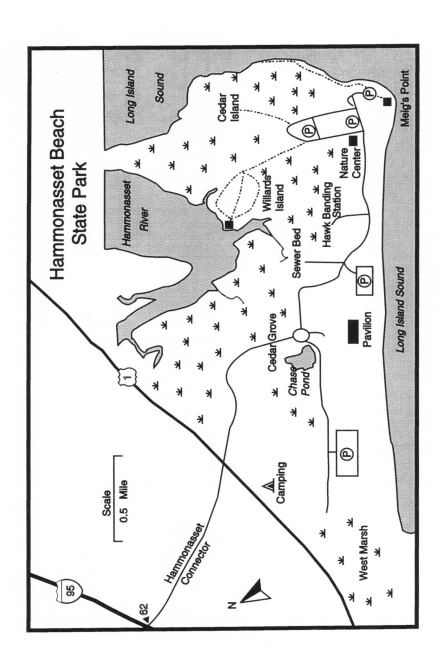

DIRECTIONS

Take Interstate 95 to Exit 62 (Hammonasset State Park). At the end of the exit ramp turn south on the connector (signs for Hammonasset State Park are at the end of the northbound and southbound exit ramps). The Hammonasset Beach State Park connector is a "straight shot" to the park, crossing Route 1 (at 1.3 miles) a short distance before the park entrance. The park is open from 8:00 am to sunset. There is a vehicle entry fee from Memorial Day to Labor Day and on weekends from late April to Memorial Day and from Labor Day to the end of September.

BIRDING

To bird Hammonasset, begin at the Meigs Point Nature Center near the east end of the park and work through the separate birding spots described below.

Meig's Point Nature Center. To get to the Nature Center take the main park road 0.6 miles to the rotary, turn left and follow the signs to East Beach and Meig's Point. The parking lot for the Nature Center is on the left, 1.1 miles beyond the rotary. Park in the lot near the building.

Start by checking the log book, which is kept on a small stand by the porch. Maintained by the Menunkatuck Audubon Society, the log book lists interesting and unusual birds that have recently been seen in the park. It is updated each day. The Nature Center has an active bird feeding station which attracts a variety of songbirds. In summer, the Purple Martin nest box in the nearby field houses a dozen or so nesting pairs. Sparrows frequent the brushy edges of the fields, especially the Song Sparrow in summer. In fall (October and November), the lawn and brush may yield the uncommon Vesper and White-crowned Sparrows or perhaps the rarer Grasshopper and Clay-colored Sparrows.

Check the grassy fields and gravel parking area around the Nature Center for open habitat species. Horned Lark generally occur from fall through spring. Snow Buntings arrive in November and occur sporadically through April. Scope the Horned Lark and Snow Bunting flocks carefully for the rarer Lapland Longspur. Look for Eastern Meadowlark on the grassland or adjacent salt marshes; they are most often seen during migration but a few usually overwinter. Migrant shorebirds that rest or forage in the grassy fields and parking lot may include Killdeer, Pectoral, Buff-breasted (rare) and Upland (rare) Sandpipers, Black-bellied Plover, American Golden-Plover (rare to uncommon), and Dunlin.

The parking lot also affords a good vantage point for watching migrating raptors as they work their way south over the fields and salt marshes. American Kestrel, Osprey, Sharp-shinned, Cooper's, and Broad-winged Hawks are fairly common migrants, but the rarer Peregrine Falcon and Merlin are regular, and the Gyrfalcon has been reported. From late fall into spring, Northern Harrier and Short-eared Owl sometimes hunt just over the salt marshes. Both Red-tailed and Rough-legged (uncommon) Hawks are winter visitors which most often are spotted perched in the taller trees or soaring overhead.

The salt marsh which borders the parking lot on the right (east) has yielded both the Short-billed and Long-billed (rare) Dowitchers, Glossy Ibis, Greater and Lesser Yellowlegs, Stilt Sandpiper, and Willet. In May 1995, the first state record for White-faced Ibis occurred in this salt marsh.

Willard's Island. To get to Willard's Island from the Nature Center parking lot, follow the gravel road back to the picnic area (identified by the pavilion) and park. To the left of the picnic area is an old barricaded road marked by a sign "Willard's Island Nature Trail." If available, pick up a copy of the Willard's Island Trail Guide, which is usually kept in the box by the sign.

Willard's Island is a cedar-clad peninsula in a sea of salt marsh. Once an orchard, Willard's Island is ecologically reverting to coastal woodland and now consists mostly of a mixed growth of red cedars, scrubby oaks, and apple and cherry trees covered with woodbine (which turns a gorgeous scarlet in fall), honeysuckle, and greenbriar. The grassy areas and shrub thickets of bayberry, wild rose, and blackberry provide ample food and shelter for birds. In both spring and fall, Willard's Island can be a birder's paradise during favorable migration weather (recent passage of a cold front in winter and a warm front in spring). Migrant raptors, warblers, and sparrows are the island's birding specialities.

Begin birding along the cedar-lined roadway leading to the island which can hold an assortment of warblers, blackbirds, and sparrows. Common spring and summer residents along the road include Gray Catbird, Northern Mockingbird, Common Yellowthroat, Yellow Warbler, Baltimore Oriole, Scarlet Tanager, Common Grackle, Song Sparrow, and House Finch. Swallows work the adjacent salt marsh on either side of the road. Purple Martin, Barn, and Tree Swallows are common while Northern Rough-winged, Cliff, and Bank Swallows are possible migrants, especially in early May.

At the island, take either the left or right road which loops around the island's outer perimeter and start birding for finches, warblers, vireos, thrushes and other songbirds. Work your way to the northern end of the island, which acts as a welcome landfall for birds migrating south over the river and salt marsh. A middle road also provides access to the interior of the small island as well.

In fall, Willard's Island is a natural migrant trap for sparrows and other songbirds. Common fall sparrows include the Dark-eyed Junco, White-throated, Song, Swamp, Savannah, and Chipping, while Lincoln's and White-crowned Sparrows are the more consistent uncommon species. Other field and thicket species to look for are the Carolina and Winter Wrens, Brown Thrasher, and Eastern Towhee. Unusual migrants that turn up on Willard's Island include the Yellow-breasted Chat, Swainson's and Gray-cheeked Thrushes, and Connecticut and Mourning Warblers. The fall warbler movement is well represented with Yellow-rumped, Black-and-white, Nashville, Northern Parula, Blackpoll, and Yellow Warblers among the most common.

Spring migration can rival the fall season. Solitary, White-eyed and Red-eyed Vireos, all of the thrushes including Gray-cheeked, most of the warblers including Black-throated Green, Canada, Mourning (rare) and Wilson's are likely in May.

The observation platform at the northwest end of Willard's Island provides a good view of the tidal creeks and coves, the salt marsh, and the Hammonasset River. To get to the observation platform, follow the path through the thickets where the perimeter road begins looping back.

In fall, a quiet approach may yield sight of a Merlin, American Kestrel, or perhaps a Peregrine Falcon sitting in the trees along the edge, just waiting to pick off a tired songbird migrating in over the open marsh. From the observation platform scan the salt marsh for long-legged waders such as Great Blue and Green Herons, Great and Snowy

Egrets, and Glossy Ibis. Look closely for the more secretive and elusive American Bittern (migrant) and Black-crowned Night-Heron. They feed on mummichugs, Atlantic silversides, and winter flounder that summer in the nearby tidal creek. Check the ditches for nesting Seaside and Saltmarsh Sharp-tailed Sparrows. Listen and look for rails- --Sora (locally rare), Virginia, King (rare), Clapper (breeding) and Yellow (very rare) have all been found here during migration. This is also one of the more consistent places to spot Short-eared Owls (rare to uncommon) and Northern Harriers quarrying back and forth just above the marsh in fall and winter. The mudflats along the Hammonasset River provide good feeding grounds for migrant Black-bellied and Semipalmated Plovers, Greater and Lesser Yellowlegs, Willet, and Least, Semipalmated and Western Sandpipers. Check the river for ducks, Brant and Snow Goose (uncommon, most often seen during April and October movements).

From fall through early spring, the red cedars may harbor an occasional Long-eared or Northern Saw-whet Owl. Great Horned and Barred Owls are also possible fall and winter visitors to the island and can sometimes be spotted roosting in the taller conifers.

Cedar Island. From the parking lot, the trail to Cedar Island begins behind the picnic area pavilion in the far right corner of the grassy field near the outhouses.

The trail works through a narrow strip of coastal hardwoods before terminating in an elevated walkway which offers good views over the open salt marsh. Along the trail, check the trees and understory for the same warblers and other songbirds listed for Willard's Island. A few lonely red cedars at the very end of the trail remind us that this is Cedar Island. The view from the elevated walkway encompasses the Hammonasset River straight ahead, beyond the sandy beach, with Willard's Island to the left and Back Beach and Meig's Point to the right.

In spring and summer, check the grassy mosquito ditches for Seaside and Saltmarsh Sharp-tailed Sparrows. Clapper Rail and Willet nest in the interior marsh while Piping Plover and Least Tern evacuate their nesting scrapes on the outer beach.

Meig's Point. From the picnic area parking lot, Meig's Point can be seen as a small hill (actually a glacial moraine) to the southwest. To get to Meig's Point, return to the main park road, turn left and drive 0.2 miles to the parking lot for Meig's Point located at the base of the hill.

Walk south to the sandy beach and check the breakwater, built in 1955 from stones quarried in northern New England. When fishermen are absent (which isn't often), Double-crested Cormorants often roost on the rocks, along with an assortment of gulls. In autumn, plovers and sandpipers are good possibilities along the beach, especially Sanderling, Semipalmated Sandpiper, Semipalmated and Black-bellied Plovers, and Dunlin. American Oystercatcher is an uncommon spring and fall migrant.

After birding the beach, return to Meig's Point and take one of the paths through the thickets of bayberry and shiny sumac to the observation platform overlooking the rocky point and Long Island Sound. The overlook is a favorite spot for artists, nature lovers, and birders, all busy pursuing their respective hobbies. This is a great spot to scope loons, cormorants, grebes (Red-necked Grebe is rare from November-April), ducks, and pelagic rarities such as kittiwakes and gannets. On any day, a number of gull species can be tallied searching for food among the rocks, including all of the usual shoreline gulls--- Herring, Great Black-backed, and Ring-billed are the expected species throughout most of the year. Laughing Gull can be common in summer and fall and Bonaparte's Gull is likely during migration and sometimes in winter. Least and Common Terns are regularly observed from May to September. Less common terns to check for include Forster's, Roseate, Royal, and Caspian. The Meig's Point overlook is also the place to spot rarities such as Red Phalarope, Black-legged Kittiwake, and Northern Gannet (best time is in November to early December and March into April) which are sometimes blown in by offshore storms and strong easterly winds, especially in fall and early winter.

To the east, the path along Meig's Point drops back off the hilltop to gravelly Back Beach which can be good for shorebirds and gulls, especially at low tide. Throughout most of the year, the offshore rocks hold Double-crested Cormorant (uncommon in winter) while Great Cormorant is regular in winter. The shrubby fringe of marsh elder and groundsel-tree is often good for Northern Mockingbird, Common Grackle, and a variety of sparrows. Much of Back Beach is an important nesting habitat for shorebirds and access is prohibited so birders have to scope the beach from higher ground offered by Meig's Point. Summer also is a good time to watch Osprey which usually appropriate one of the nesting platforms out in the middle of the salt marsh.

Hawk Banding Station. After birding Meigs Point, return to the car and head west on the main park road, back toward the rotary. The first right beyond the Nature Center (0.5 miles) leads to the hawk banding station which is usually active from September to November during good weather.

Sewer Bed Road. Still on the main park road, the next right beyond the hawk banding station (0.2 miles) leads to the Sewer Bed. Vehicle traffic is prohibited, so park in the East Beach parking lot on the left and hike down the service road. The ditches and roadway are good for sparrows, especially in fall when Field, Song, Swamp, and Savannah are likely and Saltmarsh Sharp-tailed Sparrows are possible. Less common fall sparrows in the roadside brushy areas include the Vesper, White-crowned, Henslow's (rare), and Lincoln's. Fall rarities seen here include the Blue Grosbeak and Western Kingbird which have been spotted on the fence posts surrounding the sewer bed.

In summer, the water-filled ditches and pools may hold egrets and herons. Eastern Phoebe, House Wren, Yellow Warbler, and Common Yellowthroat are nesting species. The salt marshes on either side of the roadway are good habitat for Clapper Rails and American Bittern (mainly October and April) among the reeds.

Chase Pool. To get to this small pond, also known as Swan Pond, continue west on the main park road to the rotary. At the rotary, follow the signs toward West Beach. Chase Pond is visible on the right, 0.1 miles past the rotary. Park in the field on the right, just beyond the pond or in the lot to the left (the entrance to this parking lot is on the left, 0.2 miles beyond the rotary.

Chase Pool can be surprisingly productive, considering its small size. Mute Swans nest at the pond along with Canada Goose, American Black Duck, and Mallard. Willow Flycatchers nest in the shrubs north of the pond while Purple Martins occupy the nearby martin nest box.

Regular migrants that occasionally turn up at the pond include American Wigeon, Bufflehead, Blue-winged (uncommon) and Green-winged Teals, and Greater Scaup. Pied-billed Grebe, Lesser Scaup (rare), Ruddy Duck, Northern Pintail, Wood Duck, and American Coot may also turn up in fall and spring.

Check the water's edge and reedgrass for Common Moorhen, American Bittern, Solitary (usually in May), Spotted and Pectoral Sandpipers, Greater and Lesser Yellowlegs, and Common Snipe. Some of the pond's notable list of rarities include Tundra Swan and Eurasian Wigeon.

The stand of red cedars between the pond and the entrance road is always worth checking for signs of Barn (very rare), Barred, Great Horned, Long-eared, Eastern Screech, and Northern Saw-whet Owls--- all have been spotted here from time to time, usually between October and April. During migration the red cedars offer concealment for kinglets, warblers, vireos, thrushes, and finches. Rarities found in the groves include Western Kingbird and Red-headed Woodpecker.

Picnic Areas, Lawns, and Parking Lots. The grassy lawns, gravel parking lots, and picnic areas that line both sides of the road west of Chase Pool should always be checked for birds, especially from fall through spring before the summer crowds drive the birds away. They are most productive during and following periods of wet weather when the shallow pools of water attract a host of gulls and shorebirds feeding on the earthworms and other invertebrates. Shorebirds can sometimes be plentiful in the pools; Killdeer, Greater and Lesser Yellowlegs, Black-bellied Plovers and Semipalmated, Least and Pectoral Sandpipers are the species most commonly seen, but also check for the rarer American Golden-Plover, Baird's, Buff-breasted, Western, Stilt, and White-rumped Sandpipers, Hudsonian Godwit, Wilson's Phalarope, and Common Snipe. Herring, Ring-billed, Great Black-backed and Laughing (summer and fall) Gulls also congregate at the parking lots and lawns.

In winter, the flocks of gulls should be checked for Lesser Black-backed, Iceland, and Mew (a single record) Gulls. The grassy areas are good for flocks of Horned Lark and Savannah Sparrow foraging in the grass. Again, check the lark flocks for Lapland Longspur. Winter may also bring large flocks of Snow Bunting to this area. In good finch years, the scattered Austrian pines can yield surprising numbers of Red and White-winged Crossbills and sometimes a few warblers such as Palm, and Yellow-rumped.

West Marsh. To get to West Marsh, continue west on the park road until it ends in a gravel parking lot 0.6 miles from the rotary. Park and walk to the tidal inlet surrounded by marsh. Known as West Marsh, this area is good for herons and egrets from spring to fall. Herons and egrets are consistent while Whimbrel is an occasional migrant. Belted Kingfisher may be seen throughout the year.

In fall and winter, take the trail down to the beach, which is deserted now except for the solitary fisherman or nature-lover. A short hike westward can produce all of the usual gulls and offshore loons, mergansers, and rafts of ducks. Species usually seen include Horned Grebe, Common and Red-throated Loons, Red-breasted Merganser, White-winged and Surf Scoters, and more rarely, Black Scoter, and sometimes rafts of Greater Scaup.

Horse Pond

A visit to Horse Pond can be quite productive, especially during the fall and spring migration. To get to Horse Pond, follow the Hammonasset Connector north to Interstate 95. Do not get on the interstate---instead, continue north along the road for 1.1 miles and turn left onto Old Duck Hole Road. At 0.2 miles along Old Duck Hole Road, bear left at the Y. The pond is on the right.

Horse Pond is a small, shallow pond with an amazingly good record for late summer and fall migrants. Uncommon birds such as Solitary and Stilt Sandpipers seem to turn up here with surprising frequency, often in the company of Killdeer, Semipalmated Plover, Least and Semipalmated Sandpipers, and Greater and Lesser Yellowlegs. Ducks also can be quite common in fall and spring depending on the pond's water level. Look for American Black Duck, American Wigeon, and Green-winged Teal. Uncommon migrants include Blue-winged Teal, Northern Pintail, and Northern Shoveler. Rarities that have turned up at Horse Pond include Little Blue Herons, seen in August, 1993, and September, 1994.

NEARBY ATTRACTION

The Audubon Shop

Hammonasset Beach State Park is just a few minutes from the Audubon Shop in Madison. Located at 871 Boston Post Road (Route 1) in downtown Madison, the Audubon Shop is the oldest nature store in Connecticut. The Audubon Shop maintains a complete supply of birding books, binoculars, and other birding supplies. The Audubon Shop also keep a current list of rare and unusual birds spotted at Hammonasset. To get to the Audubon Shop from Hammonasset Beach State Park, turn left on Route 1, heading south for 1.6 miles. The shop is on the right.

69 LOWER CONNECTICUT RIVER TOUR
Old Saybrook, Essex, Lyme, and Old Lyme

Originating in northern New England, the Connecticut River forms the largest riverine system in the state. This majestic river helped shape and carve the state's central lowlands as it meandered southward to Long Island Sound. South of Middletown, the Connecticut River scoured a channel through the rolling hills and deposited this sediment load at the river's confluence with Long Island Sound to form a magnificent delta consisting of Great Island and several other biologically productive habitats. The delta area attracts abundant wildlife including significant concentrations of birds and fish. Atlantic salmon, shad, striped bass, flounder, and the annual run of bluebacks all contribute to making the lower Connecticut River an important wildlife resource.

Bird diversity and abundance along the lower Connecticut River includes many migrant species that pause to rest and refuel (including some 10,000 waterfowl each year). Other species use the estuary as staging and feeding areas during winter months and as a breeding habitat in summer. Several coastal and upland habitats at or near the mouth of the Connecticut River enhance local birding opportunities.

The lower Connecticut River has a number of exceptional birding locations in Essex, Lyme, Old Lyme, and Old Saybrook that consistently produce interesting and unusual species for birders. The best birding sites occur on the the east and west banks along the river, as well as along the coastline, and include South Cove, Saybrook Point, and several less well known but potentially productive birding sites.

Specialties of the tour include waterfowl, gulls, terns, raptors, and shorebirds.

DIRECTIONS

Begin the tour at North Cove in Old Saybrook. Directions to other locations will be from this site. To reach North Cove take Exit 67 (Route 154, Old Saybrook) from Interstate 95 northbound and follow Route 154 south through the center of Old Saybrook to North Cove Road (2.0 miles). Traveling southbound on Interstate 95 take Exit 68 (Route 1, Old Saybrook) which merges with Route 1. At the yield sign

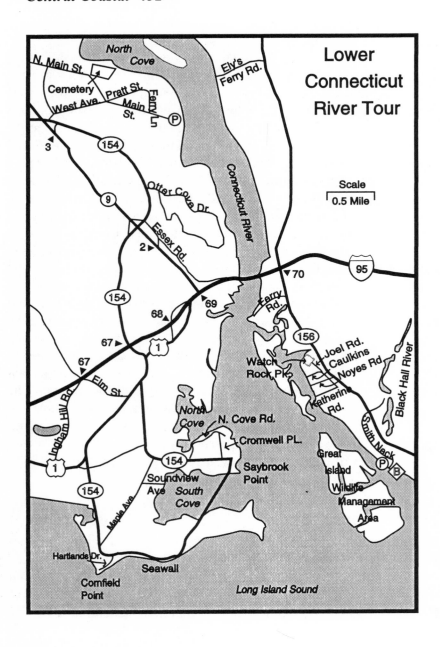

Lower
Connecticut
River Tour

Scale
0.5 Mile

North Cove

N. Main St.

Ely's Ferry Rd.

Cemetery

Pratt St.

West Ave.

Main St.

Ferry Ln.

P

154

3

9

Otter Cove Dr.

Essex Rd.

Connecticut River

2

95

70

154

Ferry Rd.

69

68

156

67

67

1

Elm St.

Joel Rd.

Caulkins

Noyes Rd.

Watch Rock Pk.

Black Hall River

Ingham Hill Rd.

Katherine Rd.

Smith Neck

North Cove

N. Cove Rd.

Cromwell PL.

Great Island

P

B

1

154

154

Saybrook Point

Soundview Ave

South Cove

Wildlife Management Area

Maple Ave.

Hartlands Dr.

Seawall

Cornfield Point

Long Island Sound

bear right and follow Route 1 south to the intersection with Route 154 (0.7 miles), turn left and follow Route 154 south to North Cove Road (1.9 miles). Turn left onto North Cove Road and drive 0.4 miles to a boat launch and cove overlook area on the left. Park and scan the water and marsh below.

BIRDING

North Cove, Old Saybrook

The boat launch offers a panoramic view of North Cove and the surrounding estuary. From November through April, scout the cove for American Black Duck, Green-winged Teal, American Wigeon, Common Goldeneye, Bufflehead, and Red-breasted and Common Mergansers. Check the waterfowl closely for Barrow's Goldeneye; this species occurs sporadically in January or February.

During spring (April/May) and late summer (August/September), North Cove can be productive for shorebirds such as Killdeer, Black-bellied Plover, Greater and Lesser Yellowlegs, Short-billed Dowitcher, and Semipalmated Sandpiper, all of which forage and rest on the mudflats at low tide. From April through October, long-legged waders (Great Blue Heron, Snowy Egret, Black-crowned Night-Heron and the occasional Great Egret) are expected. Osprey return in April to nest and can usually be observed throughout the summer.

Saybrook Point, Old Saybrook

To get to Saybrook Point from North Cove continue along North Cove Road, turn right onto Cromwell Place (0.4 miles) which returns to Route 154 (0.3 miles). Turn left onto Route 154 and continue to the stop sign (0.1 miles). At the stop sign Route 154 makes a sharp right turn that passes over a causeway. Parking is available in the small town park to the left or straight ahead in one of the lots at Saybrook Point.

From Saybrook Point, scan the Connecticut River and the west bank of Great Island. This area can be good for cormorants, waterfowl, gulls, and terns during the appropriate season. Late fall through spring is the best period to bird Saybrook Point. Double-crested Cormorant is common in fall and spring but retreat to warmer climates during winter at just about the time that Great Cormorant returns as a winter resident.

Species found regularly include Common and Red-throated Loons,

Horned Grebe, American Black Duck, Canvasback, Greater Scaup, Common Goldeneye, Bufflehead, Oldsquaw, and Red-breasted Merganser. In summer, Common Tern patrol the river in search of small fish to feed their young in nearby nesting colonies.

Bald Eagles are uncommon from January into March. The waters around Saybrook Point can also be rewarding after northeastern storms or hurricanes; some of the rarities recorded here include Red-necked Grebe, Caspian Tern, Northern Gannet, and Black-legged Kittiwake.

South Cove, Old Saybrook

From Saybrook Point, return to Route 154 and follow the road across the causeway. The causeway splits South Cove to the west from the mouth of the Connecticut River. Unfortunately no pull-offs or parking areas exist on the causeway, so park on the road north or south of the causeway and walk back to a good vantage point.

South Cove is a protected inlet that provides shelter and good foraging for birds throughout the year. During inclement weather the inlet offers protection from rough seas and high winds. Waterfowl are common occupants of the cove, especially from October through April. Scan the open water for divers such as Ring-necked Duck, Canvasback, Lesser Scaup (occasional), Common Goldeneye, Bufflehead, and Hooded Merganser. The mudflats and shallow water areas should yield Mute Swan, American Black Duck, Green-winged Teal, American Wigeon, Northern Pintail, and the rarer Northern Shoveler. A small flock of Ruddy Duck usually occur on an annual basis during the month of November. Snow Goose has also occurred during this period.

In winter and early spring, check the gull flocks for European stragglers. Black-headed and Little Gulls occur with consistency and are most common from mid-March through early April as they congregate with the similar Bonaparte's Gull. Iceland and Glaucous Gulls also appear irregularly throughout winter and generally intermix with the flocks of Herring, Ring-billed and Great Black-backed Gulls.

In spring (late April through May) and fall (August through October), the mudflats and shallows can produce a variety of shorebirds including Killdeer, Black-bellied Plover, Greater and Lesser Yellowlegs, Semipalmated and Least Sandpipers, and Short-billed Dowitcher. The

hardy Dunlin usually overwinter and can frequently be found probing the cold, hardened mud in search of invertebrates during this season.

In summer and early fall, Least, Common, Forster's, and rarely, Roseate Terns hunt along the cove or perch on the nearby pilings. Clapper Rail are regular and may be seen foraging along the edge of the marsh especially at low tide.

South Cove can also be birded effectively from another location at the northwest corner of this area. To access this site, refer to the directions immediately following the next location (Cornfield Point/Seawall).

Cornfield Point/Seawall, Old Saybrook

To get to the Seawall and Cornfield Point from the south end of the causeway at South Cove, continue south along Route 154 about 1.7 miles and turn left onto Hartland Drive (this road is identified by two stone pillars and a sign announcing "Castle Inn"). Follow Hartland Drive 0.3 miles through several stop signs until it ends at the majestic stone Castle Inn at Cornfield Point. Between South Cove and Cornfield Point the road merges with the shoreline and parallels a seawall. In this area the road is well above the water and offers an outstanding view of Long Island Sound below. Although "No Parking" signs are posted along the roadway, during the off season (fall through early spring) you can normally park briefly along the roadside or side streets without being prompted to move along by the police. At Cornfield Point you can park in the large lot and scan the sound from the high point near Castle Inn.

This locale can produce grebes (Horned is the most common species, but Red-necked is seen almost annually, and even Eared has occurred in March 1991), Red-throated and Common Loons, cormorants, scoters (White-winged and Surf, rarely Black), Oldsquaws, and other seaducks. In winter, check the rocky outcrops and jetties for Purple Sandpiper and the beach for Sanderling and Dunlin.

Ingham Hill Road Pond, Old Saybrook

On the way to Ingham Hill Road Pond you can stop and check out the northwest corner of South Cove. From the inn at Cornfield Point return to Route 154, turn left and follow Route 154 to the stop sign (0.1 miles). Turn right onto Maple Avenue and continue 1.1 miles, turn right onto Soundview Avenue for 0.3 miles to the sharp right corner at the cove. Check for the same waterbirds listed previously for the cove. To reach Ingham Hill Road, return to the junction of Maple Avenue and Route 154 and continue west 2.0 miles to Route 1. Turn left on Route 1 and take an immediate right (just before McDonald's) at Ingham Hill Road. Follow Ingham Hill Road 0.3 miles to a small pond on the left. This is private property so bird from the roadway.

Being near the Oyster River and close to the shore, this small pond has attracted a few surprises over the years. This pond can be especially productive for shorebirds and waterfowl during fall and spring migration. In fall, American Coot and Ruddy Duck are regular. The pond usually harbors species of dabbling ducks including Blue-winged (uncommon) and Green-winged Teals, American Black Duck, American Wigeon, and occasionally a Northern Shoveler. In fall, check for shorebirds along the water's edge. Most shorebirds are common species (Lesser and Greater Yellowlegs, Spotted Sandpiper, and Killdeer) but Stilt Sandpiper has occurred a few times in the fall. Herons, egrets, and gulls also occur during the appropriate seasons.

To continue to the next site (or Interstate 95 northbound) follow Ingham Hill Road north to the stop sign at the junction of Elm Street. The entrance ramp for northbound I-95 is directly across the street.

Otter Cove, Old Saybrook

To get to Otter Cove from Interstate 95 take Exit 69 (Route 9, Essex, Hartford) onto Route 9 north and exit at Exit 2. Turn left onto Essex Road and bear right onto Route 154 north (Middlesex Turnpike) at the intersection. Follow Route 154 north 0.4 miles to Otter Cove Drive on the right (this right is directly before the Saybrook Oil Company). Otter Cove Drive is announced by an oval, wooden sign with the inscription "District of Otter Cove". Continue along this twisting and winding road about 1.1 miles until the road bears right 90 degrees and bisects a small brook and marshlands which border the Connecticut River. Park along the roadside and survey the wetland habitat.

Otter Cove is conveniently small and can be birded in a short time. This birding area has received limited coverage in the past but with greater exposure it has the potential for producing a variety of species. Unusual species recorded during the winter of 1991-92 included Virginia Rail, Sora, and a remarkable Least Bittern. Bald Eagle is infrequently observed during winter foraging along the nearby Connecticut River.

Town Dock and North Cove, Essex

From Interstate 95 take Exit 69 (Route 9, Essex, Hartford) and follow Route 9 north to Exit 3. Turn left onto Route 154 and take the first right (0.1 miles) onto West Avenue. Follow West Avenue (bearing right at the Y) 0.8 miles until you reach the rotary in the center of town. Stay to the right at the rotary and take Main Street (which is a one-way road along this section) 0.4 miles until it ends at the Connecticut River. Drive between the two stone pillars on the left and park at the Connecticut River Museum parking lot. Walk to the wharf and scan the river, North Cove, and the nearby marsh.

This area is famous for "eagle watching". On any given weekend during winter there are normally a handful of birders scouting the river and Nott Island on the river's eastern bank for Bald Eagles. Bald Eagles are regular along this stretch of river and are frequently observed hunting along the river, soaring over the river valley, or roosting in the barren deciduous trees on Nott Island. Check the eagles carefully, because Golden Eagle has occurred! One obliging immature Golden Eagle spent an entire winter at this locale in 1989-90, much to the delight of birders. Other winter raptors may include the Rough-legged (uncommon) and Red-tailed Hawks (the latter is a permanent resident).

Waterfowl are usually conspicuous and can include Mute and Tundra (rare) Swans, American Black Duck, American Wigeon, Common Goldeneye, Bufflehead, and Red-breasted and Common Mergansers. Occasionally a Common Raven is spotted on the ice flows or thermalling above the river valley.

For a better viewpoint of North Cove, follow Main Street back to Ferry Lane and turn right (actually you have to turn right onto Ferry Lane because Main Street is a one-way road from the rotary to this point) and take an immediate left onto Pratt Street. Follow Pratt Street to North Main Street (0.3 miles), turn right and travel 0.2 miles to Riverside Cemetery on the right. Drive to the rear of the cemetery and park overlooking North Cove.

North Cove is a sheltered inlet of the Connecticut River. Check the cove for all of the same species of waterfowl listed above as well as dabbling ducks including Green-winged Teal and Gadwall which feed along the cattail and reedgrass edges.

Ely's Ferry Road, Lyme

To get to Ely's Ferry Road from Interstate 95 northbound take Exit 70 (Routes 1 and 156, Old Lyme) immediately after crossing the Baldwin Bridge. Turn left at the bottom of the ramp and proceed west on Route 156 for 3.4 miles and turn left onto Ely's Ferry Road. Southbound travelers on Interstate 95 take Exit 70 (Old Lyme). From the bottom of the ramp continue straight and drive 0.8 miles to the intersection of Route 156, turn right and follow Route 156 west to Ely's Ferry Road (3.3 miles) on the left.

Ely's Ferry Road deadends at the Connecticut River (1.9 miles).

Enroute to the river, the road passes by fields and an extensive marsh owned by The Nature Conservancy. In winter, Bald Eagle and a variety of waterfowl can usually be spotted from the small parking lot at the end of the road. The marsh habitat can also be good for rails, bitterns, and other marsh dwellers during migration and the breeding season. On the way to the river, check the fields for breeding Eastern Bluebird and Eastern Meadowlark.

DEP Marine Headquarters, Old Lyme
To reach this area from Interstate 95 northbound take Exit 70 (Routes 1 and 156, Old Lyme) immediately after crossing the Baldwin Bridge. Turn right at the bottom of the ramp and proceed east on Route 156. Southbound travelers on Interstate 95 take Exit 70 (Old Lyme). From the bottom of the ramp continue straight and drive 0.8 miles to the intersection of Route 156, turn left, drive under the highway and proceed as follows: Follow Route 156 east for 0.4 miles and turn right at Ferry Road which continues to the river.

Located near the mouth of the Connecticut River, the DEP Marine Headquarters has picnic tables and can be ideal for a brief rest stop while birding the Lower Connecticut River complex. Check the river for grebes, cormorants, diving ducks, and gulls from late fall through spring. In winter, Bald Eagle is occasionally sighted.

Watch Rock Park, Old Lyme
To get to the next stop on this tour, Watch Rock Park, from the DEP Marine Headquarters, return to Route 156 and turn right. On the way, stop and scan the marsh at the Lieutenant River Bridge (less than 0.1 miles). To continue to Watch Rock Park, follow Route 156 east another 0.9 miles and turn right onto Noyes Road. Take an immediate right and then 100 yards further turn right again onto Joel Road. Proceed 0.1 miles to the parking area at Watch Rock Park.

The extensive salt marsh to the north of Great Island can be viewed from Watch Rock Park which is a small promontory immediately south of Route 156. Watch Rock Park is a town owned park that abuts the salt marsh. A loop-trail about 0.6 miles in length wanders through deciduous woodland interspersed with red cedar and bittersweet nightshade thickets. To reach the overlook that gives a good view of the marsh, follow the path located in the southwest corner of the parking lot through the woodland.

Watch Rock is a good locale to study migrating shorebirds. Due to its strategic location toward the north end of the marsh, the mudflats here are the last to be inundated by the rising tide. Therefore, shorebirds tend to filter in from other areas of the marsh and concentrate on the exposed mudflats during the incoming tide. The area can produce waterfowl in spring and fall and usually raptors in winter. In addition, the woodland hosts a small compliment of breeding species and occasionally a small movement of migrating passerines. A thorough search of the spruce grove or red cedar may produce Great Horned or Long-eared Owls during winter.

The marsh can also be checked from the end of Katherine Road, which can be accessed as you return to Route 156. Instead of turning left back onto Route 156 (at Noyes Road), continue straight and follow Katherine Road 0.2 miles until it deadends at the marsh.

Black Hall River, Old Lyme
From Watch Rock Park return to Route 156, turn right and proceed 1.2 miles. Park immediately past the bridge after crossing the Black Hall River.

Note: Enroute to Black Hall River you will drive by Smiths Neck Road which leads to Great Island Wildlife Management Area, a birding site covered in a separate chapter.

Black Hall River can be scanned from the roadside or the bridge. South of the bridge, the river converges with the Great Island marsh ecosystem and forms its southeastern boundary just north of Griswold Point.

The river and marsh are most productive for waterfowl and gulls and are best birded from late fall through spring. Waterfowl normally found include Mute Swan, American Black Duck, Green-winged Teal, Canvasback (occasional), scaup (Greater are regular but Lesser are possible), Bufflehead, and Hooded, Common, and Red-breasted Mergansers. Also check for herons and egrets. Osprey nest in the area and can be spotted during the same period.

70 FURNACE POND

Branford

Located between Route 1 and Interstate 95 in Branford, Furnace Pond is actually a southern spur of Lake Saltonstall. The eastern end of the pond is edged by a lush growth of emergent vegetation which attracts many wetland species. During spring and fall migrations, Furnace Pond can yield an interesting variety of waterbirds and waterfowl.

DIRECTIONS.

From Interstate 95 northbound take Exit 53 (Routes 1, 143 and 146, Short Beach) and follow the long exit ramp to Route 1. Turn right and continue along Route 1 south for 1.3 miles. Take a right turn onto Jackson Drive (marked by a sign, Lake Saltonstall). Bear left and park on Holsey Road. Southbound travelers take Exit 52 (Route 100, East Haven) turn left at the end of the ramp, drive over the bridge and turn right (0.2 miles) at Kimberly Avenue. Follow Kimberly Avenue 0.2 miles, turn right and take another quick right onto Route 1 north. Continue along Route 1 for 1.2 miles, turn left and park along Holsey Road.

BIRDING

A nice mix of waterbirds and waterfowl are regular during spring and fall migration. Dabbling ducks (American Black Duck, Gadwall, American Wigeon, Green-winged, and the less common Blue-winged Teals, Wood Duck, and an occasional Northern Shoveler or Northern Pintail) are regular visitors to the pond. Check the wigeon closely for Eurasian Wigeon which has been a regular straggler to Furnace Pond, especially in fall. Diving ducks may be represented by Ring-necked Duck, Bufflehead, and Hooded and Common Mergansers. Other migrants to the pond include Great Blue and Green Herons, Pied-billed Grebe, and Double-crested Cormorant.

Southeastern Coastal

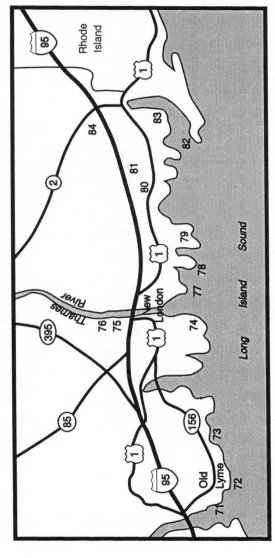

71. Great Island Wildlife Management Area
72. Griswold Point Preserve
73. Rocky Neck State Park
74. Harkness Memorial State Park
75. Connecticut College Arboretum
76. Smith Cove
77. Eastern Point
78. Bluff Point Coastal Reserve
79. Haley Farm State Park
80. Mystic River
81. Denison Pequotsepos Nature Center
82. Stonington Point
83. Bam Island Wildlife Management Area
84. Assekonk Swamp Wildlife Management Area

71 GREAT ISLAND
WILDLIFE MANAGEMENT AREA
Old Lyme

This wildlife management area represents one of the finest salt marshes remaining in Connecticut. Great Island is difficult to bird because much of the surrounding property is private and the marsh is difficult to access and traverse. Most of the Great Island salt marsh can be birded from Smiths Neck Road or Griswold Point Preserve or by canoe.

In summer, the waters around Great Island are heavily used for recreational purposes, especially boating. In fall (mainly October to January) hunters invade the marsh. Be careful if canoeing during summer----try and stay in the less traveled small creeks and drainage swales where the recreational boaters do not travel. During hunting season wear brightly colored clothing when birding the marsh proper.

Great Island hosts a variety of waterfowl, shorebirds, gulls, terns, and rails. Birding is best during spring and fall migrations, but summer and winter can also provide noteworthy species.

DIRECTIONS

To reach the Great Island WMA take Interstate 95 northbound to Exit 70 (Route 1 and Route 156, Old Lyme), turn right at the bottom of the ramp and proceed east on Route 156. Southbound travelers on Interstate 95 take Exit 70 (Old Lyme). From the bottom of the ramp continue straight and drive 0.8 miles to the intersection of Route 156, turn left, drive under the highway and proceed as follows: To access Smiths Neck follow Route 156 east for 1.7 miles and turn right at Smiths Neck Road. Follow Smiths Neck Road 0.8 miles to the state-owned boat launch and marsh viewing area.

BIRDING

Most of Great Island and the extensive tidal marsh between Smiths Neck and Griswold Point can be viewed from the newly constructed observation platform adjacent to the boat launch at the end of Smith Neck Road. In early April, Osprey arrive and start setting up nesting territories; platforms in the marsh have been erected to entice this

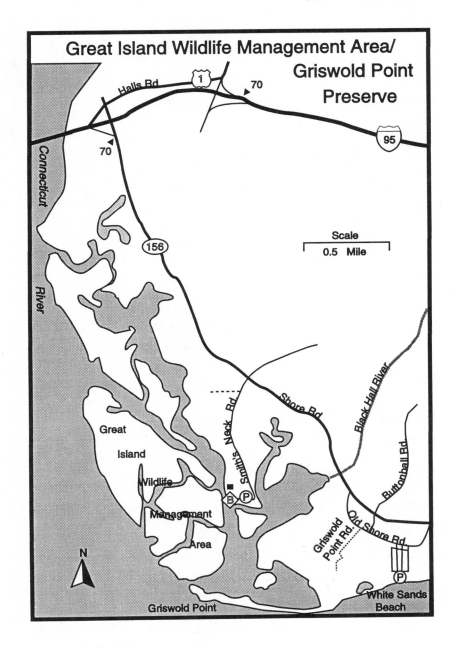

Great Island Wildlife Management Area/
Griswold Point
Preserve

species to nest and have been successful. Great Blue Heron, Great Egret, and Snowy Egret all arrive during this period. Great Blue generally leads the vanguard (a few may even overwinter) followed shortly thereafter by the latter two species. Bitterns (American and Least) are both rare and elusive species that occur as migrants from late April through May.

Species to scout for from May through September include Green Heron, Black-crowned and occasionally, Yellow-crowned Night-Herons, Glossy Ibis, American Black Duck, Clapper, King (rare) and Virginia Rails, Marsh Wren, and Saltmarsh Sharp-tailed and Seaside Sparrows. Some uncommon or rare long-legged waders to look for include Tricolored and Little Blue Herons. The threatened Least Tern nests within protected areas at Griswold Point Preserve, but are regularly seen foraging along the canals and inlets in the marsh. Roseate Terns nest on nearby islands and occasionally can be sighted foraging along the periphery of Great Island. From August into early September, terns stage in the area prior to migration. Although the flock size is not as impressive as the Milford Point concentration, it nonetheless contains an attractive variety of species; most individuals are Common and Least, but Forster's and Roseate occur in limited numbers. Also, during this period, a Black Tern or two will usually make an annual appearance.

The shorebird migration during August and September can be quite impressive and can approach Milford Point in the abundance and number of species encountered. Common species regularly found include Killdeer, Ruddy Turnstone, Semipalmated and Black-bellied Plovers, Greater and Lesser Yellowlegs, Red Knot, Least, Semipalmated and Spotted Sandpipers, Short-billed Dowitcher, Dunlin, and Sanderling. Limited numbers of American Oystercatcher, American Golden-Plover, Whimbrel, Solitary, Pectoral, White-rumped, Stilt, and Western Sandpipers, and Willet also are annual. Some rarer species that have occurred and should be anticipated include Baird's Sandpiper, Long-billed Dowitcher, Marbled and Hudsonian Godwits, and Wilson's Phalarope.

With good weather conditions from mid-to-late August, tremendous concentrations of swallows are possible in the marsh and along its edge. These species demonstrate impressive aerial skills in pursuit of one of

the marsh's most abundant food sources---the countless mosquitos.
All of the swallows that normally occur in the state (Bank, Barn, Tree, Northern Rough-winged, Cliff and Purple Martin) can usually be found during this time period. Check the telephone lines along Smiths Neck Road for roosting birds which can be lined "shoulder-to- shoulder" for hundreds of feet. Northern Bobwhite can occasionally be heard calling along this road and in the field and marsh east of the boat ramp parking lot; they are most vocal from April through July but may call anytime throughout the year. Northern Bobwhite is an uncommon permanent resident east of the Connecticut River but rare west of the river.

Waterfowl are always conspicuous components of this salt marsh system. Species that nest in the marsh include Mute Swan, American Black Duck, and Gadwall. A variety of waterfowl also stop over at the island during migration and some overwinter. The best area to observe waterfowl in the marsh and on Long Island Sound is from Griswold Point, but the observation platform also offers good viewing opportunities. From October through March, you should be able to locate Green-winged Teal, American Wigeon, Greater Scaup, Common Goldeneye, Bufflehead, Canvasback, and Common and Red-breasted Mergansers from the observation platform and other vantage points.

A variety of raptors can also be spotted at Great Island. In winter, check the sky, trees, and dead snags for Red-tailed and Rough-legged Hawks. Northern Harrier and American Kestrel can also be regular winter visitors. Bald Eagle is occasionally sighted and Golden Eagle rarely. Snowy and Short-eared Owls are erratic, but usually occur every year, even if only for a brief period. During fall and spring migration, Merlin and Peregrine Falcon are sometimes spotted hunting the shorebird flocks.

Historically, the mouth of the Connecticut River supported an Osprey colony that numbered some 200 breeding pairs. In the 20-year period between 1950 and 1970, the colony all but disappeared, primarily because of DDT contamination of adults and eggs. The colony has made a slow recovery to date, and from late March through summer Osprey can be fairly common. More than 20 pairs use the nesting platforms placed at intervals throughout the marsh.

72 GRISWOLD POINT PRESERVE
Old Lyme

Griswold Point is another of the premier shoreline birding areas in eastern Connecticut. Owned by The Nature Conservancy, Griswold Point Preserve is a narrow 0.7- mile-long, sparsely vegetated sand spit that extends west into the extensive salt marsh formed at the mouth of the Connecticut River. From the point, Great Island with it's associated estuarine habitat, the Connecticut River and the water of Long Island Sound can be birded. Griswold Point Preserve is an excellent location for viewing shorebirds during spring (May) and fall (late July through September) migrations, and terns which congregate into large flocks in August and early September. Waterfowl are also numerous from fall through spring.

Some interesting birds that have been seen at Griswold Point Preserve include Northern Gannet, Tricolored Heron, Common Eider, Barrow's Goldeneye, Golden Eagle, American Avocet, Royal and Caspian Terns, Thick-billed Murre, and Short-eared and Snowy Owls.

DIRECTIONS

The map for Griswold Point Preserve is included in the map for Great Island Wildlife Management Area found on page 445. From Interstate 95 northbound take Exit 70 (Route 1, Route 156, Old Lyme) and turn right onto Route 156 heading east. Southbound travelers on Interstate 95 take Exit 70 (Old Lyme), at the bottom of the exit ramp continue straight for 0.8 miles, turn left onto Route 156 east and continue under the interstate to the junction with the northbound exit ramp. Follow Route 156 for 2.7 miles, turn right onto Old Shore Road immediately after passing over the Black Hall River Bridge. Continue along Old Shore Road 0.4 miles, turn right onto Hartford Road (not marked but recognized by two stone pillars on each corner and a sign "White Sands Beach") and follow this road 0.3 miles to the parking area for White Sands Beach. White Sands Beach is town-owned property that allows resident parking only from Memorial Day through Labor Day. Parking is not restricted at other times. Walk the beach below the high tide mark west to Griswold Point Preserve (to the right as you view the sound).

BIRDING

Summer is not the best time to bird the point due to heavy recreational usage. However, in summer, the point hosts two important breeding species, Piping Plover and Least Tern. Both species are protected in Connecticut due to their threatened status. Following breeding from late July into September, numerous terns are present and frequently congregate in large concentrations, prior to and during migration. Scout the tern flock carefully for Least, Common, Forster's, and the rarer Roseate (which nest in nearby locales). Also check for the occasional Royal and Caspian Terns as well as the interesting and unusual Black Skimmer.

Shorebird migration occurs from late July through early October but peaks in August. All species regular in Connecticut can also be seen at Griswold Point. Common species to tally up include Killdeer, Ruddy Turnstone, Semipalmated and Black-bellied Plovers, Greater and Lesser Yellowlegs, Dunlin, Least, Semipalmated and Spotted Sandpipers, Sanderling, Short-billed Dowitcher, and Willet. Shorebirds which occur in more limited numbers are Pectoral, White-rumped and Western Sandpipers, Red Knot, Long-billed Dowitcher (rare), and American Oystercatcher. Griswold Point Preserve also boasts an American Avocet which was sighted in early November! Long-legged waders are present throughout summer and into early fall. Great Blue Heron and Great and Snowy Egrets are normally seen, while Little Blue and Tricolored Herons are irregular. The latter herons are usually observed following post-breeding dispersal in late July.

Fall is an exciting time to bird Griswold Point Preserve, especially for waterfowl. Sea ducks can often be found on the open waters of Long Island Sound while dabbling and bay ducks are common in the marsh and river north and west of the point, respectively. Waterfowl are most abundant from October into December, but many species remain throughout the winter. Scan the sound for Greater Scaup, the occasional Lesser Scaup, Common Goldeneye, Barrow's Goldeneye (rare), Oldsquaw, scoters (Surf and White-winged are regular, Black is rare), and Red-breasted Merganser. Common Eider (usually a female or first-year male) has occurred sparingly over the years, so be on the lookout for this species from November to March. Along the river and marsh channels you should observe Brant (uncommon), Mallard,

American Black Duck, Gadwall, Green-winged and Blue-winged (uncommon) Teals, Northern Shoveler (uncommon), Northern Pintail, Canvasback, Bufflehead, and Common Merganser.

In autumn, check for migrating raptors and songbirds. During September and October, Sharp-shinned Hawk, Northern Harrier, Osprey, and American Kestrel are common, while Merlin and Peregrine Falcon are also recorded annually. In November, Snow Bunting show up at this locale and are fairly common until December, after that the birds are erratic throughout the winter. Another interesting species to check for from November until spring is the Ipswich race of the Savannah Sparrow---look for this pale, inconspicuous subspecies darting through the sparse dune grass in front of you. American Pipit occur in small flocks during October and can be observed foraging in the dead vegetation along the high tide line.

Late fall and winter has produced Northern Gannet (mainly in November and early December, following periods of strong, northeastern winds), Thick-billed Murre (January record), and white-winged gulls (Glaucous and Iceland). Snowy Owl is an irregular late fall or winter visitor. From November through April, Short-eared Owls and Rough-legged Hawks are occasionally seen.

73 ROCKY NECK STATE PARK
East Lyme

This 708-acre shoreline state park is bounded on the west by the tidally influenced Four Mile River and a salt marsh on the east. Rocky Neck was historically known as a place of abundant fish and wildlife. The park boasts a long, crescent shaped sandy beach that is a haven for sunbathers during summer months. Other attractions include a seasonal campground (169 sites), a gigantic stone pavilion overlooking Long Island Sound (built during the depression era with native materials and primarily by hand labor), and an extensive salt marsh stretching nearly a mile in length. There is an entrance fee if you visit the park between Memorial Day and Labor Day and weekends in May and September.

Rocky Neck State Park has a variety of habitats which attracts an assortment of birds throughout the year. Fall and spring are the best birding seasons, notably for herons, egrets, shorebirds, and waterfowl. The upland and marsh habitats have a fine compliment of breeding birds, but during this period the park is often packed with the beach crowd. About 5 miles of trails are available for nature exploration. The red trail traverses about 3 miles of the park's upland habitat. An active Osprey nest situated near the main parking lot rewards the quiet observer with an intimate view of the nesting behavior of this species.

DIRECTIONS

Take Exit 72 (Rocky Neck State Park) from Interstate 95 and follow the Rocky Neck Connector to Route 156, turn left and travel 0.2 miles to the park entrance on the right. After passing the entrance booth turn left and follow the park road 1.2 miles (beyond the Bride Brook Bridge) to a dirt parking area on the right.

To enter the park via trails from Route 156, take a right onto Route 156 at the end of the connector and an immediate left (0.1 miles) onto an abandoned portion of the former state road (blocked by a guard rail). Park and follow the signs which identify the trailheads to the Bride Brook Trail and Blue Trail. Two additional access points are located along Route 156: at 0.3 miles from the end of the connector diagonally across from a restaurant (small parking area on left next to a metal barrier gate); and at 0.6 miles (metal barrier gate on the left immediately before Four Mile River and Old Lyme town line).

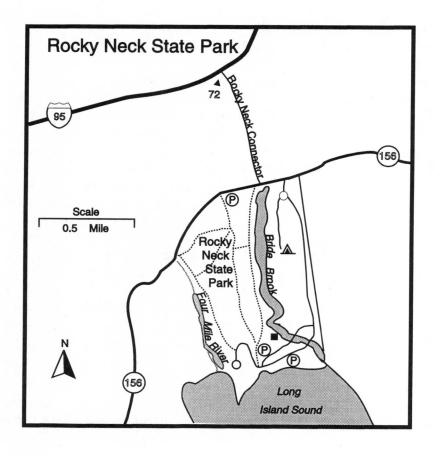

Rocky Neck State Park

BIRDING

Walk to the observation platform overlooking the marsh near the northeast corner of the parking lot. An informative visual display greets the visitor and provides interesting facts regarding the ecology of the salt marsh. The observation platform and the handicapped fishing bridge (located 200 yards east) are two excellent places to view the variety and abundance of marsh wildlife. During August and September scan the salt marsh carefully for shorebirds foraging along the *Spartina* lined creek, the exposed mudflats, and marsh pools. Species that can be frequently observed are Killdeer, Black-bellied Plover, Greater and Lesser Yellowlegs, Pectoral, Least, and Semipalmated Sandpipers, and Short-billed Dowitcher. With the onset of autumn, shorebirds are replaced by waterfowl which use the marsh for resting and foraging. Dabbling and diving duck to look for include Mallard, American Black Duck, Gadwall, Green-winged and Blue-winged Teals, Northern Pintail (uncommon), Wood Duck, American Wigeon, and Hooded Merganser. This is a reliable site to find Northern Shoveler, an uncommon-to-rare species in the state.

From March through September, the marsh host a number of herons and egrets. Regular species include Great and Snowy Egrets, Black-crowned Night-Heron, and Green and Great Blue Herons. Glossy Ibis stop by from time to time and an immature White Ibis once spent about two months (November and December) here in 1979. A park feature that impresses most visitors is the Osprey nest located near the observation platform. Nesting behavior of the species can be studied at close range. Ospreys return to Rocky Neck in late March, set up nest, and depart for warmer climates in September or October.

To scout the marsh from a different viewpoint, walk to the northwest corner of the parking lot and follow the red trail (next to the outhouse) through the marsh to the upland beyond. After a short distance the trail splits; follow the right fork onto the white trail (Bride Brook Trail). You can make a loop (about 1.5 miles) by hiking the trail to a cutoff (on the left) and returning by the red trail. The white trail skirts the salt marsh and river and passes through thickets of greenbriar. Along the way there are numerous openings to bird the river. The edge and salt marsh habitat can be good for passerines during spring and fall migration and a variety of breeding species such as Clapper Rail,

Eastern Kingbird, Carolina Wren, White-eyed Vireo, Yellow Warbler, Common Yellowthroat, Gray Catbird, Saltmarsh Sharp-tailed Sparrow, and Eastern Towhee.

If you make the loop, the red trail returns to the parking lot by traversing an oak hardwoods with a dense shrub understory of laurel. Woodland breeding species may include various woodpeckers, Great Crested Flycatcher, Eastern Wood-Pewee, Wood Thrush, Veery, Yellow-throated and Red-eyed Vireos, Black-and-white Warbler, American Redstart, Ovenbird, Scarlet Tanager, and Northern Cardinal.

From late November throughout winter, check the gravel/dirt parking lots for flocks of Snow Bunting and Horned Lark. Both species occur on an annual basis but are erratic. On the western side of the bathhouse is a tunnel leading to the beach. Although the beach and adjacent waters are usually fairly slow birding, a quick scan doesn't take very long. Check the off shore water for cormorants, Horned Grebes, Common and Red-throated Loons, and diving ducks from October through April. Sanderlings may also be found in winter.

If you have time hike the trail along the western edge of the park, which passes through woodland habitat similar to the red trail but is occasionally interspersed with small fields. This trail eventually connects back to the red trail previously discussed. Breeding species found along this route are similar in composition to those species described above.

74 HARKNESS MEMORIAL STATE PARK
Waterford

This estate-turned-state park is situated on a small peninsula that extends into Long Island Sound, about five miles southwest of New London. While much of the park is landscaped for picnic and associated recreational activities there are also a variety of small but profitable coastal birding habitats such as open salt water, a narrow sand and gravel barrier beach, a tidal inlet, and small salt marsh. The manicured grounds include magnificent shade and ornamental trees, an enormous expanse of lawn, and formal gardens. The former mansion is now used as office space for park personnel. Picnic and bathroom facilities are available in the park. During the summer months a nominal fee is charged for admission to the park.

Harkness Memorial is good for migrating shorebirds and waterfowl especially in fall and can hold some interesting offshore winter species. The open shoreline vista also provides a good area to spot migrant raptors in fall and Purple Sandpiper in winter. From late May through June, the state park can be a good area to spot Roseate Terns foraging along the shoreline (terns nest on Great Gull Island). A number of rarer gulls have been reported including Iceland, Lesser Black-backed, Black-headed, and Black-legged Kittiwake. An American White Pelican was observed in October, 1992!

DIRECTIONS

From interstate 95 take Exit 75 (Route 1, Waterford); northbound travelers need only to turn right onto Route 1 north. For southbound travelers on the interstate the Exit 75 (Route 1, Waterford) exit ramp merges with Route 1 south---therefore, as soon as you merge with Route 1, bear left at the turn-around and head north on Route 1 for 4.2 miles (3.9 miles from the northbound exit ramp). Turn right at the traffic light onto Avery Lane and continue to Route 213 at 0.3 miles. Continue straight onto Route 213 for 3.1 miles to the park entrance on the right. Follow the entrance road to the parking lot on the right.

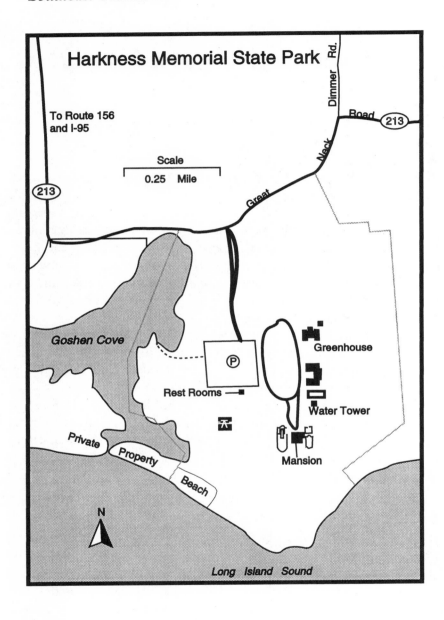

Harkness Memorial State Park

To Route 156
and I-95

Scale

0.25 Mile

Dimmer Rd.

Road (213)

Neck

Great

(213)

Goshen Cove

(P)

Greenhouse

Rest Rooms ■

Water Tower

Private

Property

Beach

Mansion

N

Long Island Sound

BIRDING

From spring through fall, a good place to start birding is the tidal inlet and salt marsh that borders the park on the west. From the parking lot scan the inlet for Double-crested Cormorant, Great and Snowy Egrets, Great Blue and Green Herons, and a variety of gulls. Check the nesting platform for Osprey. Waterfowl that may occur during migration include Bufflehead, Northern Pintail, Green-winged Teal, American Wigeon, and Hooded Merganser.

Near the parking lot a trail leads through the tall grass field (near the last picnic table) of little bluestem and orchard grass down to the sand flat along the inlet. Check along the trail for American Tree and White-throated Sparrows in winter. In summer, both Common and Least Terns are often seen either on the water or along the sand flat. In spring, late summer, and fall a variety of shorebirds--Greater and Lesser Yellowlegs, Black-bellied, Semipalmated and Piping (rare) Plovers, and Spotted, Semipalmated and Least Sandpipers make the short hike to the sandy flat worthwhile. The rattling call of the Belted Kingfisher can be head on almost any birding trip.

After birding the salt marsh retrace your path back to the picnic area. From here work south through the picnic area and down to the shore. In spring and fall, search the ornamental trees and shrubs for migrant warblers and vireos. The rose thickets and grassy fields can be good for sparrows including Field, Savannah, White-crowned (uncommon), Lincoln's (uncommon), Song, and Clay-colored (rare). A boardwalk leads through the reedgrass to the beach where Dunlin and Sanderling occur from fall through spring.

The lawns can often be good for Eastern Meadowlark (spring and fall), American Pipit (usually October), Horned Lark (fall), Snow Bunting (erratic from November through April), and sometimes migrant geese. Check the rocky shoreline east of the beach for plovers, Ruddy Turnstone, and sandpipers.

Scope the offshore water for migrant and wintering sea ducks including all three scoters, King (rare) and Common (rare but annual in recent years) Eiders, and Red-breasted Merganser. Other wintering waterbirds may include Red-necked (rare) and Horned Grebes, Great Cormorant, and Red-throated and Common Loons. In winter, the rocky areas along the beach and offshore may yield Purple Sandpiper, a regular winter visitor.   Winter is also the best time to turn up the rarer gulls, Iceland, Lesser Black-backed, and Black-headed have all been spotted here, usually in the company of the common species. Be sure to take a few minutes and scan the horizon and off-shore waters for Northern Gannet, a species which is becoming more regular in Long Island Sound in recent years, especially from November to early December and from March into April.

75 CONNECTICUT COLLEGE ARBORETUM
New London and Waterford

The Connecticut College Arboretum provides good to excellent birding throughout the year. Winter birding is highlighted by the waterfowl concentrations along the Thames River. The spring and fall seasons feature noteworthy movements of warblers and other songbirds. The Arboretum's varied habitats---grasslands, maintained fields, thickets, open woodlands, hemlock ravines, and tidal wetlands--- support an impressive variety of nesting species in late spring and early summer.

The Connecticut College Arboretum is a 435-acre preserve of fields, thickets, woodlands, and wetlands set in the middle of urban and suburban sprawl. Consisting of natural and managed habitats, the Arboretum exemplifies the value of urban open space in attracting a wide variety of wildlife. Over 200 birds have been observed, including a number of important nesting and migrant species. The Arboretum also features native and ornamental trees and shrubs planted in selected family groupings which may be of interest to students of natural history.

Owned by Connecticut College, the Arboretum was established in 1931. The main part of the Arboretum is just west of the campus and consists of the Arboretum Native Tree and Shrub Collection, the Bolleswood Natural Area, and the Science Center of Eastern Connecticut. Arboretum property to the east of the campus includes the Avery Tract, Matthies Tract, and the Mamacoke Island Natural Area. Another good birding area, the Thames River, flanks the eastern side of the Arboretum. Access to most of the Arboretum habitats is provided by roadways and a system of well maintained trails.

Birders may obtain a copy of *Birds of the Connecticut College Arboretum,* by Robert Askins, which may be purchased at the Connecticut College bookstore (The College Center) and at the Arboretum office located in the Olin Science Center.

Noteworthy birds that regularly occur at the Connecticut College Arboretum include Little Blue Heron, Black-crowned Night-Heron, Redhead, Lesser Scaup, Orchard Oriole, and Worm-eating and Hooded Warblers. Rare and accidental species at the arboretum have included the Eurasian Wigeon, Tufted and Harlequin Ducks, Chuck-wills-widow, Philadelphia Vireo, Yellow-throated Warbler, Summer Tanager, and Blue Grosbeak.

DIRECTIONS

The Connecticut College Arboretum is located just over a mile north of Interstate 95 in New London. If traveling on Interstate 95 southbound, take Exit 83 (New London and Frontage Road) and turn right onto the Briggs Street and Coast Guard Academy exit. Turn left at the traffic light at the end of the ramp. Drive 0.4 miles and turn left at the traffic light onto Williams Street and continue for 0.6 miles. The entrance to the arboretum is on the left, flanked by an iron fence. The Connecticut College campus is on the right. If northbound on Interstate 95 take Exit 83 (Route 32 North, Norwich) and turn left onto Williams Street at the traffic light at the end of the ramp. Continue straight for 1.2 miles to the arboretum entrance on the left, as above.

BIRDING

Different sections of the Connecticut College Arboretum yield different seasonal birding opportunities. In spring, the Bolleswood Natural Area is good for migrants. In late spring and summer it is home to a variety of woodland nesting species. In fall, the burn fields and scrub growth of the Avery Tract and Matthies Tract can be good migrant traps. In winter, the Mamacoke Island Natural Area and Thames River are often super for waterbirds.

Arboretum Native Tree and Shrub Area/Bolleswood Natural Area. The entrance to the Arboretum Native Tree and Shrub Area is on Williams Street as indicated in the directions above. Obtain a copy of *A Self-Guided Tour of the Connecticut College Arboretum* which is usually available (free) near the arboretum entrance.

Near the entrance, take the left trail which winds downhill through beech trees bordered on the left by hawthorn, plum, and shadbush shrubs. At the bottom of the hill bear left. The arboretum pond is on your right. In spring, the trees and shrubs along the trail and bordering the pond can be very good for warblers and other passerines; a warm front may bring 20 or more species of warblers on a good birding day. Palm and Pine Warblers start to appear in mid-April. From late April through May, look for Blackburnian, Black-throated Green, Blackpoll, Canada, Magnolia, Northern Parula, and Yellow-rumped Warblers.

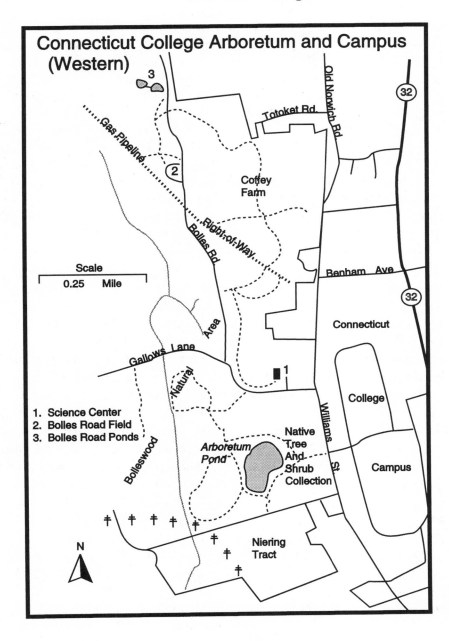

Connecticut College Arboretum and Campus (Western)

3

(2)

32

Totoket Rd.

Old Norwich Rd.

Gas Pipeline

Coffey Farm

Right-of-Way

Bolles Rd.

Scale
0.25   Mile

Benham   Ave

32

Area

Connecticut

Gallows   Lane

Natural

1

Williams

College

St.

1. Science Center
2. Bolles Road Field
3. Bolles Road Ponds

Native
Tree
And
Shrub
Collection

Campus

Arboretum
Pond

Bolleswood

Niering
Tract

N

Other spring migrants by the pond may include the Rose-breasted Grosbeak, Ruby-crowned and Golden-crowned Kinglets, and Ruby-throated Hummingbird. Two rarer species reported from this area include the Yellow-throated and Kentucky Warblers.

Bird the arboretum pond from available vantage points. The pond is ringed by plantings of trees and shrubs. Much of the northern half is covered by scattered pickerelweed and water-lily spreading into the deeper waters. Spring migrants on the pond include Wood Duck (which also nest), Solitary Sandpiper, and Tree, Barn, and Northern Rough-winged Swallows foraging just over the water. Red-winged Blackbirds claim territories in the cattails. Eastern Phoebe, Eastern Kingbird, and Baltimore Orioles nest in the trees around the pond.

The park-like habitat of trees and shrubs of the arboretum support a variety of forest edge and open woodland nesting species such as the House Finch, Carolina and House Wrens, American Redstart (infrequent), Cedar Waxwing, Northern Mockingbird, Gray Catbird, Yellow Warbler, Common Yellowthroat, White-eyed Vireo, and Song Sparrow. A Summer Tanager (rare) was spotted at the pond on May 17, 1989.

In fall, check the shrubs for Fox (uncommon), Swamp, Chipping, and White-throated Sparrows. In winter, Dark-eyed Junco, and Field and American Tree Sparrows frequent the more open areas.

Continue on the trail around the pond. Take the Bog Loop Trail on the left which winds around a bog and through a hemlock-hardwoods woodland ravine before rejoining the main trail. Great Crested Flycatcher, Eastern Wood Pewee, Ovenbird, Black-and-white Warbler, Red-eyed Vireo, Wood Thrush, Veery, and Scarlet Tanager are some of the forest breeding species that may occur along the trail in late spring and summer. Downy, Hairy, and Red-bellied Woodpeckers are permanent residents in these woods.

Barred Owls nest along the ravine while Louisiana Waterthrushes sing along the stream banks. In fall and winter, the deciduous and mixed woodlands can be good for mixed foraging flocks of Tufted Titmouse, Black-capped Chickadee, White-breasted Nuthatch, Golden-crowned Kinglet, and Brown Creeper. Some less common winter birds include Red-breasted Nuthatch, Yellow-breasted Sapsucker, and Hermit Thrush.

The Bog Trail rejoins the main trail by the arboretum collection of nut trees, mostly hickories and hybrid chestnuts. The main trail branches again; take the left branch, which loops through the Bolleswood Natural Area woodland of oak and hemlock forest.   Long-term studies of breeding bird populations in these woods have revealed sharp changes: several formerly common nesting species such as the Black-throated Green and Canada Warblers, and American Redstart, have been replaced by suburban species like the Black-capped Chickadee, Tufted Titmouse, House Finch, and Northern Cardinal.

Some uncommon species that may occur along this trail include the Acadian Flycatcher and Pileated Woodpecker. The trail loops back and joins the main trail, which continues around the pond and back up the hill to Williams Street.   Check the open woodlands along this trail for Black-billed and Yellow-billed Cuckoos, Rose-breasted Grosbeak, and Mourning Dove.

Bolles Road/Coffey Farm Trail.   At the arboretum entrance, take a left and walk north to Gallows Lane (the first road on the left). Walk up Gallows Lane about 0.3 miles to an arboretum trail on the right, behind a metal bar-way.   The trailside woods are excellent for spring migrants (late April-May), especially for warblers. Spring and summer nesting species include Hooded, Worm-eating, and Black-and-white Warblers, and Ovenbirds. On quiet summer evenings listen for Whip-poor-will.

Near the gas pipeline the woods give way to shrubby fields which can be good for Blue-winged, Chestnut-sided, Prairie, and Yellow Warblers, White-eyed Vireo, Field and Song Sparrows, Northern Mockingbird, Common Grackle, and an occasional Brown Thrasher. In fall, the fields can be birded for mixed warbler and vireo flocks in September, and sparrows in October. Check the vireos carefully for the rarer Philadelphia Vireo.

At the Bolles Road Ponds take the Coffey Farm Trail, which begins on the left, just south of the ponds. The Coffey Farm Trail passes through mature hemlocks, open woodlands, and grassy fields of little bluestem and scattered red cedars before ending at Gallows Lane. Along the trail watch for Ruffed Grouse at the trail edge or a Northern Bobwhite near the pipeline. Both Great Horned Owl and Broad-winged Hawk nest in this area of the arboretum.

Eastern Arboretum: the Avery Tract/Matthies Tract.   Return to

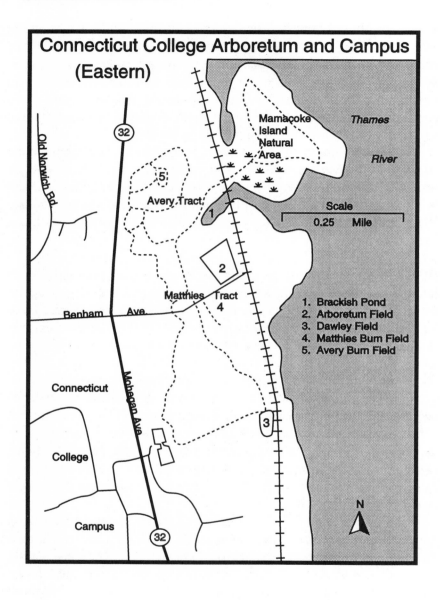

Connecticut College Arboretum and Campus (Eastern)

Old Norwich Rd.

32

Mamaçoke Island Natural Area

Thames

River

5

Avery Tract

1

Scale
0.25   Mile

2

Matthies Tract
4

Benham   Ave.

1. Brackish Pond
2. Arboretum Field
3. Dawley Field
4. Matthies Burn Field
5. Avery Burn Field

Connecticut

Mohegan Ave.

3

College

N

Campus

32

your car and head north on Williams Street. Take the first right (about 0.3 miles) onto Benham Avenue. Continue on Benham Avenue for 0.5 miles (crossing Route 32/Mohegan Avenue) to the arboretum field on the left (north) side of the road, at the bottom of the hill. **Be careful crossing Route 32, which is a busy highway.** This field is bordered by red cedars and scrubby woods. Park and bird the field and woodland edge, both of which can be good for songbirds and sparrows during spring and fall migration. In March, the fields and burn areas along Matthies Tract feature the courtship flights of American Woodcock males. From late April through June, Cedar Waxwing, Blue-winged Warbler, White-eyed Vireo, and Orchard Oriole breed in the scrubby woods while Prairie Warbler and Field and Chipping Sparrows may nest in the nearby thickets.

After birding the field, walk up the road to the arboretum trails (on both sides). Take the trail on the right (north side of the road) which leads to the Avery Tract and the Mamacoke Island Natural Area. The trail first works through an open white pine stand with a dense shrub layer of azaelea, arrowwood, and greenbrier. In fall, this combination of open woodland and understory growth can be good for warblers and sparrows, so take plenty of time to scout out all of the trailside birding opportunities. About 210 yards along, the trail passes over a small brook that is surrounded by thickets. In winter, the ice-free waters of this little brook can be a magnet for American Woodcock, Hermit Thrush, Winter Wren, Northern Cardinal, and White-throated Sparrow.

About 350 yards from the road the trail branches. The left branch loops up the hill to the Avery Tract and can be good for spring and summer nesting birds. The right trail leads to Mamacoke Island Natural Area.

Mamacoke Island Natural Area/Thames River. The trail enters a small open woodland of beech and birch. The brackish pond on the right is an inlet of South Cove which in season may harbor Pied-billed Grebe, Hooded Merganser, and Belted Kingfisher.

The trail to Mamacoke Island crosses the Central Vermont Railroad tracks **(observe caution as this is an active train line)** and continues through a narrow salt marsh forming the neck of Mamacoke Island. The marsh is bordered to the left (north) by North Cove and to the right by South Cove, both small inlets of the Thames Rivers. In summer, herons and egrets hunt along the reedy edges of the coves. Snowy and Great Egrets, and Great Blue, Little Blue, and Green Herons may occur from spring through fall. Black-crowned Night-Heron is most often seen during the twilight hours in spring and summer. Osprey frequent the open waters of the cove and the Thames River beyond.

In winter, South Cove usually supports large concentrations of waterfowl, including flocks of Greater Scaup, Hooded, Red-breasted and Common Mergansers, and Gadwall. Mute Swan, Canada Goose, American Black Duck, and Mallard are also usually present.

The trail branches at the island. Take the right branch, which loops around the perimeter of Mamacoke Island Natural Area. The scrubby oak woodland that covers most of Mamacoke Island Natural Area can be good for spring and fall migrants. The trail provides some good views of the coves and sheltered inlets along the Thames River. In most winters, rafts of hundreds of Canvasbacks may occur. Check the rafts for Redhead (rare, but occurs annually), Bufflehead, Ring-necked Duck, and Common Goldeneye. Scan the river for Common and Red-throated Loons, and an occasional sea duck. Rarer waterfowl that have been spotted along the river include Tufted Duck and Harlequin Duck (an immature male spent the winter of 1989 here).

Bird the woods and undergrowth along the trail for American Tree and Song Sparrows, Downy Woodpecker, Dark-eyed Junco, and Eastern Towhee.

Other Birding Trails. The trail on the south side of Benham Avenue works through Matthies Burn Field and down to the lower arboretum and Dawley Field. The brushy area along the trail and especially around the railroad tracks by the lower fields can provide excellent birding during a sparrow push in fall, generally from October into early November. Sparrow flocks may include Song, Field, Chipping, White-throated, White-crowned, Savannah, and Fox Sparrows.

76 Smith Cove, Thames River
Waterford

Smith Cove is a small inlet along the Thames River in Waterford, almost directly opposite the submarine base. In winter, the cove and adjacent river harbor impressive concentrations of waterfowl. The Smith Cove area is still one of the best sites in the state to observe Redhead.

DIRECTIONS

From Interstate 95 northbound take Exit 83 (Route 32 North, Norwich) and turn left onto Williams Street. Continue 0.5 miles and turn right onto Route 32 north (at the traffic light at the top of the hill). Drive 2.4 miles (past the Coast Guard Academy on your right and Connecticut College on the left) to Scotch Cap Road. At the traffic light, turn right, and follow Scotch Cap Road 0.3 miles to its deadend at the railroad tracks. Southbound travelers on Interstate 95, take Exit 84N (Route 32, Norwich), the first exit after the Gold Star Memorial Bridge, which merges with Route 32. Follow Route 32 about 2.2miles to Scotch Cap Road (at traffic light), turn right and proceed as described above.

BIRDING

From the parking area walk across the railroad tracks and turn right, heading south, with the Thames River on your left. **This is an active railroad line, so observe caution when walking along the tracks.** Follow the tracks south for 200 yards to the small inlet on the right. This sheltered inlet is known as Smith Cove. A good place to scan the cove and river is just before the railroad bridge which crosses over the inlet.

From October through April, the cove and the river can produce a variety of waterbirds, waterfowl, and gulls. Check the inlet and river for Red-throated and Common Loons, Great and Double-crested Cormorants (regular during winter along the river, generally rare elsewhere in Connecticut during this season), Great Blue Heron, American Black Duck, American Wigeon, Canvasback, Ring-necked Duck, Common Goldeneye, Greater Scaup, and Bufflehead.

All three merganser species (Hooded, Common, and Red-breasted)

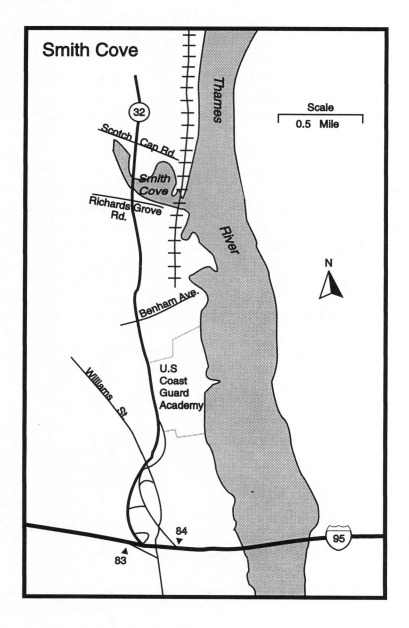

occur here, making this a good spot to compare the subtle plumage differences of the females. Smith Cove is also one of the best locations in the state to find wintering Redheads; normally a few individuals are spotted among the rafts of Canvasback or Greater Scaup. Uncommon species occurring somewhat regularly include Lesser Scaup and Ruddy Duck. The cove is also noted for the large wintering concentrations of Mute Swan (100-200 individuals).

Gulls frequently forage along the inlet. Herring, Ring-billed, and Great Black-backed Gulls are the most common species. During winter, check for Glaucous and Iceland Gulls. Also, Red-tailed Hawk and an occasional Bald Eagle drift by overhead to harass waterfowl along the river.

After birding Smith Cove, you can also check the waterfowl concentrations in South Cove if time permits. To get to South Cove, go south on Route 32 and turn left on Benham Avenue. Refer to the **Connecticut College Arboretum** birding site in this book for more information about this birding area on the Thames River.

77 EASTERN POINT
Groton

Eastern Point is a rocky protrusion located at the mouth of the Thames River in Groton. The point juts westerly from the mainland and offers an ideal vantage point for viewing the Thames River, Fisher's Island Sound, and Long Island Sound. A small town park is situated on the point. Eastern Point provides good winter birding for loons, grebes, cormorants, waterfowl, and gulls. Purple Sandpiper is a regular winter visitor at this location. Nearby Avery Point can also be a worthwhile stop at this birding locale.

DIRECTIONS

From Interstate 95 take Exit 87 (Route 349, Clarence B. Sharp Highway) which becomes the Clarence B. Sharp Highway (Route 349). Follow this road about 1.5 miles to a traffic light, and then bear right continuing along Route 349 for 0.5 miles until you reach the intersection of Eastern Point Road. Turn left onto Eastern Point Road and travel 1.8 miles to Beach Pond Road. Turn right and follow Beach Pond Road a short distance (0.2 miles) and drive straight into the park (identified by the small entrance booth) as the road bears sharply right and becomes Shore Avenue.

BIRDING

This small park is most productive from October through April. In summer, a fee is required to access the point. In this season the park and river can be busy with recreational users, curtailing birding activities.

Check the rocky coastline during the prime season for geese (Canada Goose and Brant), dabbling ducks (Mallard, American Black, Gadwall, and American Wigeon), and shorebirds (American Oystercatcher and Ruddy Turnstone both occur during late fall and early spring). Study the wigeon flocks closely for Eurasian Wigeon, a species reported from here during a number of winters. Look for Purple Sandpiper along the rocky outcrops foraging in the rock weed at, or just above, the waterline. Purple Sandpiper is best found during receding to low tide.

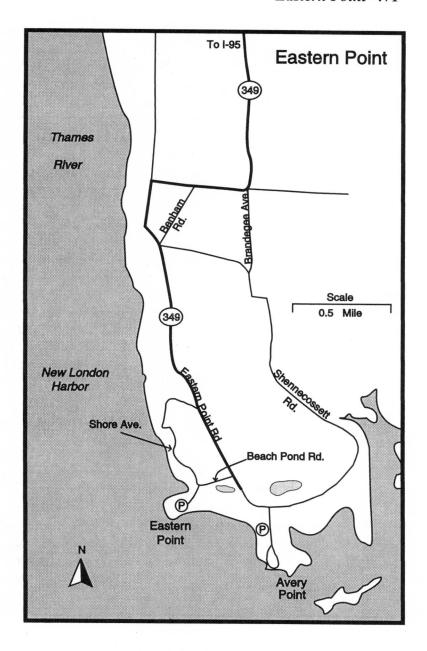

Eastern Point

Scan the river and off shore water for Great (winter) and Double-crested (common fall and spring, rare during winter) Cormorants, Horned and Red-necked (rare) Grebes, Greater Scaup, Oldsquaw, scoters (Black is rare), Common Goldeneye, Bufflehead, and Red-breasted Merganser. Gulls are a common avian component of the area, especially Herring, Ring-billed, and Great Black-backed. Bonaparte's Gull is regularly sighted throughout winter, and increase somewhat in number during March and April. Be on the lookout for the occasional European straggler such as Iceland, Glaucous, Lesser Black-backed, Little, and Black-headed Gulls; all have been reported from Eastern Point or the surrounding area. Northern Gannet has been recorded various times in the past decade, mainly from November to December and from March into April.

When leaving the point explore the rocky coastline, inlets, and protected bays just north of the park along Shore Avenue. These areas usually harbor dabbling ducks and sometimes other species. As you backtrack to Eastern Point Road stop at Beach Pond located at the junction of Eastern Point and Beach Pond Roads. Beach Pond is fringed with reedgrass and typically contains the same species of dabbling ducks as observed elsewhere near the point. Occasionally Great Blue Heron or Black-crowned Night-Heron are nestled in the vegetation.

Avery Point

Before leaving the area bird Avery Point which is just east (0.1 miles) of Beach Pond on Eastern Point Road. Parking at the college is restricted except for weekends, but even then it is still at a premium. It is best to park off-campus and walk the short distance to Avery Point.

Avery Point also offers an exceptional view of the mouth of the Thames River and the offshore waters. In July, 1995, an unprecedented concentration (up to 45 individuals) of Wilson's Storm Petrels spent almost three weeks feeding at the mouth of the Thames River between Eastern and Avery Points. Was this just a one-time phenomena, or an annual occurrence which had previously been overlooked?

The small pond across from the campus entrance frequently sports a few dabbling ducks as well as an occasional Hooded Merganser. Check the shoreline for Wood Duck during late fall and early spring.

78 BLUFF POINT COASTAL RESERVE
Groton

Located in Groton, this 806-acre coastal reserve is best known for producing impressive fall migrations of warblers and other songbirds, but its varied coastal habitats can attract an assortment of birds throughout much of the year. Bluff Point was first established as a state park and later designated as a coastal reserve by the Connecticut legislature in 1975. Its status as a coastal reserve preserves the unique wildlife, geological features, and scenic qualities of the area.

Bluff Point is a peninsula that juts southward into Fisher's Island Sound. The peninsula is bordered on the east by Mumford Cove, on the west by the Poquonock River, and to the south by Fisher's Island Sound. The northern boundary of the coastal reserve is formed by the mainline Amtrack railroad running from Boston to New York.

Some unique geological features of the reserve include the rocky promontory known as Bluff Point at the reserve's southern terminus and a narrow, mile-long sand spit that extends westward from the peninsula out into the confluence of the Poquonock River and Fisher's Island Sound.

Bluff Point Coastal Reserve offers an interesting mix of coastal habitats including open water, a 100-acre tidal marsh, beach, mudflat, river, field and thicket, and coastal woodland. A well-maintained network of trails provide access to all of the major habitats that occur within the coastal reserve. A 3.5-mile loop-trail to the point and back offers varied birding opportunities in most of the park's habitats. A straight walk to the point and return by the same route is about 2.0 miles. A spur trail that begins near the headland provides access to the sand spit and good views of the salt marsh.

Bluff Point Coastal Reserve is open to birders and others throughout the year. There is no entrance fee at the coastal reserve. Picnic benches and pit toilets are located adjacent to the parking area. Additional toilets are located near the headland just before the spur trail to the sand spit.

Bluff Point also offers saltwater fishing, shellfishing, hiking, and biking opportunities throughout much of the year. In winter, cross-country skiing is a popular pastime.

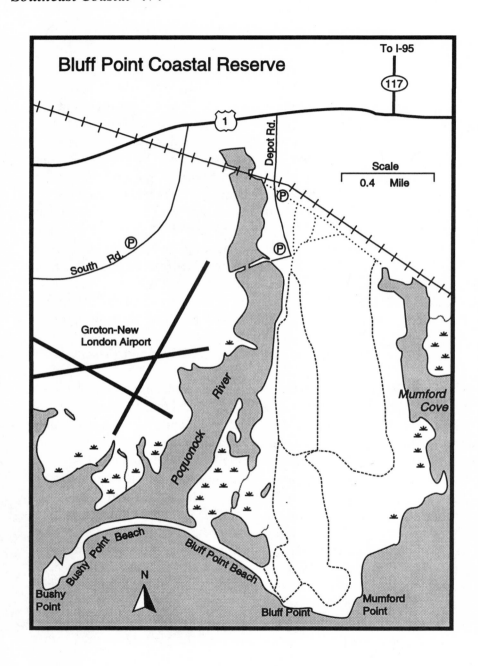

Bluff Point Coastal Reserve

To I-95

117

1

Depot Rd.

Scale

0.4   Mile

P

South   Rd.   P

P

Groton-New
London Airport

River

Poquonock

Mumford
Cove

Bushy Point Beach

Bluff Point Beach

N

Bushy
Point

Bluff Point

Mumford
Point

DIRECTIONS

From Interstate 95 take Exit 88 (Route 117) and follow Route 117 south for 1.0 miles. Turn right onto Route 1, go 0.3 miles and turn left at the first traffic light onto Depot Road (adjacent to the Groton Town Hall). Continue for 0.3 miles on Depot Road and go under the railroad overpass. Just beyond the trestle, the road becomes dirt. Continue on the dirt road for another 0.3 miles to the gravel parking area. To bird the the northwest corner of Bluff Point Coastal Reserve, park on the left just beyond the railroad overpass, but don't block the barrier gate.

BIRDING

Birding at the Bluff Point Coastal Reserve can be superb or very slow depending on the time of year, tides, and weather. Late summer and fall usually provide the best birding, especially following the passage of a cold front which often creates a burst of migrant songbirds and other upland species.

Northwest Corner. From August through September, the northwest corner of Bluff Point is undoubtedly the best spot to view migrants. Often after a cold front passes, hundreds of migrants funnel down to the headland of Bluff Point Coastal Reserve, then retreat through the northwest corner of the reserve before resuming their southward migration. The influx of migrants can produce fast and furious birding activity during the first hours of day-break after a cool, clear night. For example, in September, 1994, a big day birding team, counted 70 species, including 19 species of warblers while virtually standing in one spot in this part of the reserve.

To bird the Northwest Corner, walk around the bar-way and explore the grassy patches, small stands of trees, and scrubby growth in the area just to the south of the railroad tracks. On a good morning the area can be teeming with flycatchers, vireos, warblers, tanagers, and other passerines. On some peak days in September and October, you may spot 20 species or more of warblers including Golden-winged, Tennessee, Cape May, Orange-crowned (rare), Bay-breasted, Mourning (rare), and Wilson's as well as the more common species. Philadelphia Vireo, a migrant in the state, is annual in mid-September along with the more numerous Red-eyed and Solitary Vireos.   Sparrow migration peaks from mid-to-late October when good numbers of White-throated, Song, Swamp, and Savannah Sparrows pass through. Uncommon or rare species that may also occur at this time include Dickcissel, Blue Grosbeak, and White-crowned, Lincoln's, Fox and Clay-colored Sparrows.

Loop Trail. To bird the rest of Bluff Point Coastal Reserve, hike the dirt road that begins just beyond (south) the bulletin board by the barrier gate at the southeast corner of the main parking lot. This dirt road parallels the Poquonock River on the right. Check the river, mudflats, and salt marsh for shorebirds, waders, and waterfowl.

In spring, summer, and early fall some shorebirds to look for include Killdeer, Semipalmated and Black-bellied Plovers, Ruddy Turnstone, Greater and Lesser Yellowlegs, Spotted, Least, and Semipalmated Sandpipers, and occasionally other species. Waders such as Snowy and Great Egrets, Great Blue and Green Herons, and Black-crowned Night-Heron are often present in the shallows along the river. However, the nocturnal night-heron is usually seen in the twilight hours of dawn and dusk. Clapper Rail, an uncommon breeder in the salt marsh, is normally heard rather than observed. Osprey nest in the area from April into August and can usually be spotted as they forage along the river.

During the nesting season, the tangles of bittersweet, cat-brier, rose, and poison ivy that border the trail to the point can harbor many elusive species. Check these trailside habitats for Carolina Wren, House Wren, Gray Catbird, Brown Thrasher, Common Yellowthroat, White-eyed Vireo, Northern Cardinal, Eastern Towhee, and other skulkers. During fall migration, Mourning (September) and Orange-crowned Warblers (most records from late September and October) are rare, but regular. Yellow-breasted Chat is a rare annual visitor which is often recorded in September.

In late spring and summer, the fields and wetter areas further along the trail may produce Eastern Kingbird, Willow Flycatcher, Northern Mockingbird, and Chipping and Field Sparrows. Northern Bobwhite is a resident that can be quite vocal from April through July.

The upland woods of oak and aspen just beyond the trailside tangles hosts the usual variety of deciduous woodland birds. Breeding species often spotted are Red-bellied Woodpecker, Eastern Wood-Pewee, Eastern Phoebe, Tufted Titmouse, Wood Thrush, Veery, Red-eyed Vireo, various warblers (Blue-winged, Chestnut-sided, Black-and-white, and Ovenbird), Rose-breasted Grosbeak, and Baltimore Oriole. Both cuckoos (Yellow-billed and Black-billed) occur but populations are irregular and closely associated with gypsy moth infestations; in many years the birds are scarce or absent.

Fall migration can fill the woodland and thickets with an assortment of flycatchers (Great Crested, Empidonaxes, and the rarer Olive-sided), vireos (Yellow-throated, Solitary, Warbling, and the rarer Philadelphia), and warblers (Northern Parula, Yellow, Magnolia, Yellow-rumped, Blackpoll, American Redstart, and Canada).

Sand Spit. Just before the headland, a trail diverges on the right to the sand spit. The sand spit offers a pebble beach to explore on the seaward side and provides a good view of the marsh and mudflats along the bayside.

> **Note: Please refrain from walking on the dune grass and associated vegetation when exploring the sand spit, this vegetation is fragile and easily destroyed. Crosswalks have been spaced along the spit to facilitate the passage of visitors from the seaward side to the bayside (or vice versa) of the spit. The Connecticut Department of Environmental Protection has initiated a Dune Grass Restoration Project along the spit and request that visitors adhere to the posted "keep off" policy.**

During August and September, the mussel beds and mudflats that are exposed at mid-and-low tides attract shorebirds. Species to search for include all shorebirds identified previously and Sanderling (along the beach), Dunlin, Short-billed Dowitcher, and the rarer American Golden-Plover, Buff-breasted Sandpiper, and Hudsonian Godwit. Recently the post-breeding dispersal of American Oystercatcher has resulted in the sighting of impressive number foraging on the mussel beds. A total of 42 Oystercatchers were observed on September 6, 1992! The endangered Piping Plover has nested on the spit in the past, but not since 1986; hopefully the species will return to nest in the future. Terns (Common, Least which formerly nested, and the rarer Roseate) are casual throughout the summer and are joined by Forster's in early fall. Small flocks of American Pipits are generally spotted during October. In winter, the Ipswich race of the Savannah Sparrow is sometimes observed scurrying through the dune vegetation. Snowy Owl perched on a post or sand dune is always a winter possibility.

Check the promontory for an unobstructed view of Fisher's Island Sound and the waterbirds, waterfowl, and gulls which are associated with this ecosystem. During October through April, various species of grebes (Horned and the rarer Red-necked), cormorants (Double-crested are common most of the year but displaced in abundance by Great during winter), waterfowl (American Black Duck, Greater Scaup, Common Goldeneye, Bufflehead, Oldsquaw, White-winged and Surf Scoters, and Red-breasted Merganser), and gulls (Ring-billed, Herring, Great Black-backed, Bonaparte's, and the occasional Glaucous or Iceland) may be found.

In November and December, strong northeastern or eastern winds have blown in rare pelagic visitors such as the Northern Gannet and Black-legged Kittiwake.

Continue along the loop-trail from the headland back to the parking lot. Again, the woodlands, fields, and shrub thickets host many of the passerines previously listed. At the first Y a left leads back to the main trail (about half-way between the headland and the parking lot). If you bear right you will shortly come to a second Y, the left trail returns to a point near the parking lot and the right path will bring you along the eastern part of the peninsula to Munford's Cove and eventually the former railroad bed at the north end of the park. During August and September, a variety of wild fruit trees and shrubs are available to attract birds and hungry birders; be on the lookout for wild grape, wild black and choke cherries, black raspberry, and apple. If the birding is slow at least you can have an inexpensive lunch!

Groton - New London Airport
A birding trip to the nearby Groton-New London Airport can also be worthwhile when visiting Bluff Point Coastal Reserve. Located on the

west side of the Poquonock River, the habitats around the airport frequently yield open grassland species.

To get to the airport from Bluff Point, return to Route 1, turn left and drive 0.3 miles to South Road. Turn left (sign posted for Groton-New London Airport) and follow South Road 0.6 miles. Park at the pull-off on the right, by the runway.

The lawns and grassy fields around the airport often contain a variety of "grassland shorebirds," especially during the fall migration from August through October. Killdeer and Black-bellied Plover are usually common while Upland and Buff-breasted Sandpipers and American Golden-Plover are rarer, but regularly occur. A flock of 12 or more Buff-breasted Sandpipers was present at the airport in September 1995.

In winter, the airport environs often host flocks of Horned Lark and Snow Bunting (more regular in November and early December, sporadic thereafter). Check the flocks carefully for the occasional Lapland Longspur. Snowy Owl and Rough-legged Hawk irregularly overwinter in the area.

79 HALEY FARM STATE PARK
Groton

Acquired by the state in 1970, this small coastal park of 198 acres was a coastal farm for nearly three centuries. Today, Haley Farm is managed for recreation and features hiking, jogging, cross-country skiing, and biking trails. Much of Haley Farm consists of coastal habitats that are rapidly diminishing in Connecticut---weedy fields, thickets, and scrubby woodlands, all of which attract an interesting array of birds for much of the year. Nesting species of interest include American Kestrel, Carolina Wren, Brown Thrasher, Eastern Bluebird, White-eyed Vireo, and Orchard Oriole. In recent years, Yellow-breasted Chat has nested. The thickets and scrub growth can be good for vireos, thrushes, and sparrows during spring and fall migration. During migration, a smattering of waterbirds and shorebirds can be viewed in Palmer Cove.

DIRECTIONS
From Interstate 95 take Exit 88 and follow Route 117 south 1.0 miles to Route 1. Turn left and travel north on Route 1 for 0.9 miles, turn right onto Route 215 and follow it to Brook Street (0.6 miles). Turn right onto Brook Street and travel 0.4 miles to Haley Farm Lane, turn right and continue 0.1 miles to the parking lot on the right.

BIRDING
The best way to explore the park is to take the loop-trail (about 1.2 miles in length) that starts at the parking lot and allows access to most of the good birding habitats. A few other short trails wind through the field in the northwestern section of the park. If time allows, you may also elect to hike the bike trail that bisects the park and continues along to Groton.

   The parking lot is abutted by grassy fields to the north and west where there are a few scattered deciduous trees and foundations of old buildings. Nest boxes in the fields and along the brushy edge attract Tree Swallow, House Wren, and Eastern Bluebird. Check the sugar maples and other shade trees scattered around the parking area and field for the uncommon Orchard Oriole, a species that has nested within the

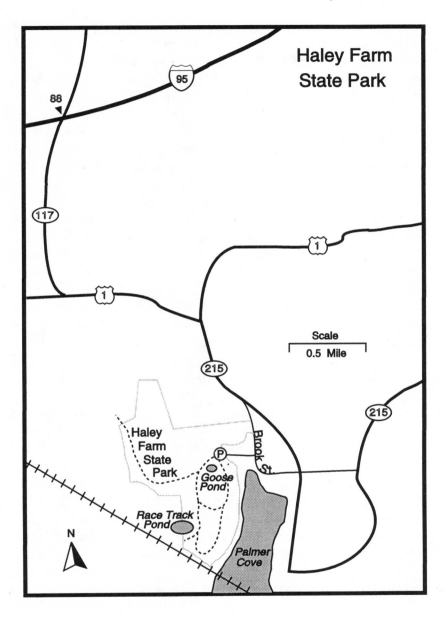

park in the last few years. Other species likely nesting nearby include Northern Flicker, Eastern Kingbird, Eastern Phoebe (nests in the old foundations), Barn Swallow, House Finch, American Goldfinch, Common Grackle, Brown-headed Cowbird, Northern Mockingbird, Common Yellowthroat, and Chipping Sparrow.

Take the gravel bike path which passes between fields bordered by a massive stone wall on the right and Goose Pond on the left. Check the weedy field for Eastern Meadowlark (during migration and winter) and Bobolink (breeding). The American Kestrel is also possible---it nests nearby. Goose Pond is worth a quick check also for waterfowl, waders, and shorebirds. About 200 yards along the path, a narrow trail veers left. Take the left trail, which passes through rose and sumac thickets loaded with bittersweet and greenbrier. A scrubby growth of oaks, maples, and red cedar line the back of the thickets. This combination of fields, thickets, and scrubs can be excellent for birds. Typical nesting species along this part of the trail should include Carolina Wren, Gray Catbird, Brown Thrasher, White-eyed Vireo, Blue-winged, Chestnut-sided, Yellow and Prairie Warblers, Field Sparrow, Eastern Towhee, Northern Cardinal, and rarely, Yellow-breasted Chat.
Northern Bobwhite is an uncommon resident within the park and frequently forages along the thicket and field interface. The fields and thickets are also productive during migration, when the thickets can hold an array of thrushes, kinglets, vireos, warblers, and sparrows. In August and September, these fields can yield an attractive assortment of butterflies which visit the panoply of butterfly weed, goldenrod, and pye-weed flowers.

A few hundred feet further along, the trail turns left and Palmer Cove is visible in the distance. The trail passes near an active Osprey nest which affords an opportunity to study this magnificent bird at close range. Avoid spending too much time near the nest, however. Scan Palmer Cove for gulls, herons, egrets, Double-crested Cormorant, Mute Swan, and swallows (occasionally Purple Martin is observed as well as Northern Rough-winged) from late spring through summer. During fall and spring migration a smattering of waterbirds, waterfowl, and shorebirds are possible in the Cove.

The fall (October into November) sparrow movement can be very good in the thicket and edge habitats along the trail and in the fields. Search for Savannah, Saltmarsh Sharp-tailed (mainly in tidal marsh habitat along Palmer Cove), Chipping, Field, Song, White-throated, Swamp, American Tree (November through winter), and Dark-eyed Junco. Less common but regularly occurring sparrows include White-crowned, Vesper, Lincoln's, and Fox.

The trail loops back to the parking lot passing the little pond and cattail marsh on the left and a house on the right. If you haven't yet spotted an Orchard Oriole, check out the ornamental trees in this yard where it has nested in the past.

In winter, the park usually contains a handful of permanent residents. In fall and winter, search beneath the scattered red cedars for pellets and whitewash of Long-eared Owl or Northern Saw-whet Owl. Both species occur sporadically from year to year.

80 Mystic River

Stonington

The Mystic River north of Mystic Seaport in Stonington offers birders and wildlife photographers an opportunity to observe and photograph waterfowl at close range. A 7-mile loop route around the river by Mystic Seaport can produce cormorants, wading birds, waterfowl, gulls and occasionally, a few raptors. Primary viewing areas along the loop are on River Road which parallels the river's west bank.

The best time to bird Mystic River is from mid-October through April when waterfowl are plentiful. During summer the whole area is inundated by tourists which dramatically reduce opportunities to view and study wildlife.

The Mystic River area also boasts two noteworthy attractions; Mystic Seaport and the Mystic Marinelife Aquarium. The seaport is the nation's largest maritime museum and consists of 17 acres of riverfront property that features sailing ships, historic buildings, and exhibits. The Mystic Marinelife Aquarium contains over 6,000 sea animals and plants grouped into 48 exhibits. Other features include demonstrations with whales, dolphins, sea lions, and a Penguin Pavilion.

DIRECTIONS

From Interstate 95 take Exit 90 (Route 27, Mystic Aquarium/Mystic Seaport) and follow Route 27 south to Route 1 (1.9 miles from southbound exit, 1.7 miles from northbound exit). Turn right onto Route 1 and follow the winding road over the Mystic River Bridge. Take the second right after the bridge onto Pearl Street (0.6 miles). Travel 0.3 miles and take the second left onto Grove Street. Follow Grove Street 0.2 miles to the stop sign, then continue straight onto River Road. River Road parallels the Mystic River for more than 2 miles, passing beneath the interstate and eventually terminating at Route 27.

BIRDING

As you travel along River Road, stop frequently at convenient pull-offs to scope the river. Along this stretch, the Mystic River is close to Fisher's Island Sound, so the ebb and flow of tides can rapidly alter the depth and flow of the river. This, in turn, can change the location and

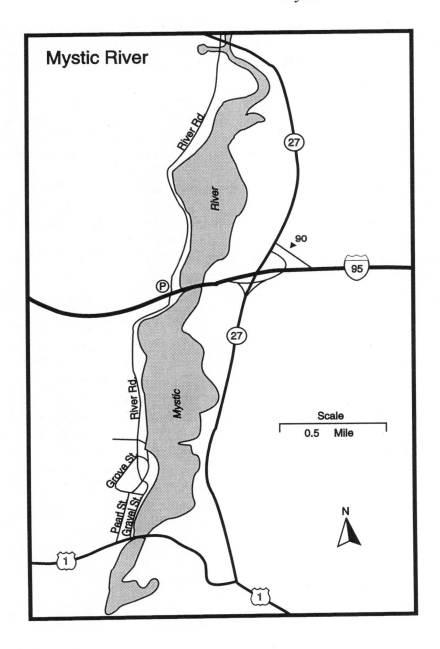

Mystic River

complexion of waterfowl resting and feeding on the river and adjacent wetland and bankside habitats.

At vantage points from the roadway check the river for cormorants (Double-crested is common during fall and spring, rare in winter, Great Cormorant is fairly common from October through April), Mute Swan, Canada Goose, Green-winged Teal, American Black Duck, American Wigeon, Greater and, occasionally, Lesser Scaups, Bufflehead, Red-breasted Merganser, and Common Goldeneye. Survey the goldeneye carefully for Barrow's---a species that irregularly occurs.

When the river freezes upstream, many species of ducks congregate in the vicinity of the interstate overpass (about 1.0 miles north on River Road). During most winters, this is also a good location to view and photograph concentrations of Hooded Merganser and Canvasback. Gulls can be numerous here, especially Herring, Ring-billed, and Greater Black-backed Gulls, but occasionally you can also spot a Bonaparte's or white-winged variety.

North of Interstate 95, the Mystic River is designated as a Scenic Wildlife Drive. In late spring and early summer, this section can harbor nesting pairs of Osprey and Mute Swan. The ospreys actually return to this site in late March and soon begin rebuilding their nests which are located on the platforms placed out in the marsh. Mute Swan is a permanent resident that also nests around the periphery of the river. The salt marsh along this stretch of the Mystic River often contains Great and Snowy Egrets from April into October, and Great Blue Heron occurs throughout the year, although it may be scarce in some winters.

At the junction of River Road and Route 27 turn right and drive 0.2 miles and park immediately after the gas station. This location provides a good view of the marsh and upper river. To return to Interstate 95 continue south on Route 27 for another 1.1 miles.

81 Denison Pequotsepos Nature Center
Mystic

This small nature center located near Mystic Seaport has a variety of attractions, activities, and trails to interest the birder and nature enthusiast. The nature center's wildlife sanctuary offers over 125 acres of varied habitat crisscrossed by seven miles of trail. Five or six loop-trails transverse the terrain consisting of four small ponds, open field, lowland wooded swamp, and deciduous woodland comprised predominately of oak and maple.

A total of 169 species of birds has been tallied from the grounds of the sanctuary and at least 66 species have nested. Throughout the seasons, Denison Pequotsepos Nature Center can yield a noteworthy assortment of birds. Spring migration can be particularly rewarding, bringing a good assortment of passerines, while the diverse habitat hosts a variety of breeding species from May through July. In winter, the feeding station attracts an array of permanent residents, winter visitors, and procrastinating birds.

The nature center also has a Trailside Interpretive Museum containing exhibits depicting the habitat and local wildlife native to Connecticut and live displays of animals in their natural surroundings. An aviary with Great Horned and Barred Owls is always a big hit with visitors. The museum is open from 9:00 am to 4:00 pm. During these hours a nominal entrance fee is required to visit the nature center.

DIRECTIONS
From Interstate 95 take Exit 90 (Route 27, Mystic Aquarium/Mystic Seaport) and follow Route 27 south 0.1 miles, turn left onto Coogan Boulevard and continue along this road until it ends at Jerry Browne Road (0.7 miles). Turn right and follow Jerry Browne Road 0.3 miles, bear right onto Pequotsepos Road (just before the large water tower) and drive 0.5 miles to the nature center parking lot on the left.

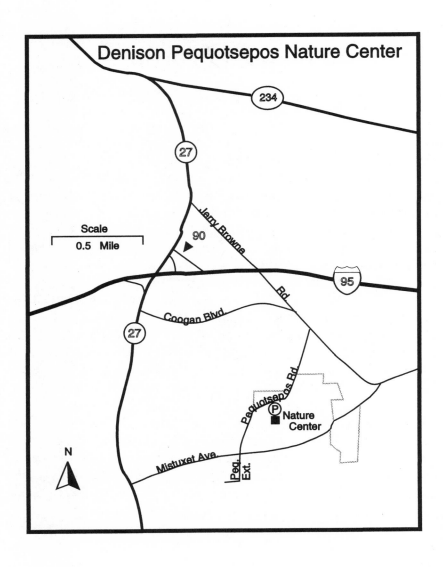

Denison Pequotsepos Nature Center

234

27

Jerry Browne

90

Scale

0.5 Mile

95

Bd.

Coogan Blvd.

27

Pequotsepos Rd.

Ⓟ **Nature Center**

N

Mistuxet Ave.

Peq. Ext.

BIRDING

If you arrive during normal operating hours visit the museum and inquire about the presence of any unusual species. You can also get a map of the trail system which will assist your exploration of the area. The feeding station at the museum is always worth a quick check during any season. Typical species include most of the permanent residents such as Mourning Dove, Hairy, Downy, and Red-bellied Woodpeckers, Blue Jay, Black-capped Chickadee, Tufted Titmouse, White-breasted Nuthatch, Carolina Wren, Northern Cardinal, House Finch, American Goldfinch, and Song Sparrow. During winter the feeder can yield all the resident species plus Red-breasted Nuthatch, Purple Finch, White-throated and Fox Sparrows, and Eastern Towhee among others.

A hike through the woodland trails from May through July can produce a fine variety of deciduous woodland species such as Ruffed Grouse, Great Crested Flycatcher, Eastern Phoebe, Eastern Wood-Pewee, House Wren, Wood Thrush, Veery, Yellow-throated and Red-eyed Vireos, Black-and-white and Hooded (uncommon) Warblers, Ovenbird, American Redstart, Scarlet Tanager, Rose-breasted Grosbeak, and Baltimore Oriole. The trails that transverse the field, thicket, and woodland edge (mainly southwest of the visitor center) are fairly reliable for Northern Flicker, Least Flycatcher, Northern Mockingbird, Gray Catbird, Brown Thrasher, White-eyed Vireo, Blue-winged, Yellow, Chestnut-sided and Prairie Warblers, Common Yellowthroat, and Chipping and Field Sparrows.

A small colony of Purple Martin occupy the nest box in the meadow behind the duck pond (southwest of the nature center). Eastern Bluebird and Tree Swallow also take advantage of nest boxes placed around the periphery of this field. A quiet approach to the duck pond enroute to the field may reward the birder with Green Heron, Wood Duck, or Belted Kingfisher, all which nest or use the sanctuary for resting or foraging.

82 STONINGTON POINT

Stonington

Located just to the south of Stonington village, Stonington Point is a narrow peninsula which juts out into Fisher's Island Sound. The point offers a panoramic view of Fisher's Island (part of New York state) to the southwest, and Westerly, Rhode Island, to the southeast. Immediately west of the point is Stonington Harbor which supports Connecticut's busiest commercial fishing fleet.

Stonington Point can be a productive birding area year-round, but is best birded from late summer through early spring when tourists, visitors, and recreational users are at a minimum. Species to look for in this location include waders, waterbirds, waterfowl, gulls, and terns. A small squadron of Brown Pelicans put in a brief appearance at the point in late July, 1992.

The Old Lighthouse that guards the point, now a museum, was the first government lighthouse in Connecticut. A variety of 19th century portraits, whaling and fishing gear, swords, and Stonington made-firearms and stoneware are on display at the museum.

DIRECTIONS

From Interstate 95 take Exit 91 (Route 234, No. Main Street, Stonington Borough) and follow Route 234 west for about 0.4 miles. Turn left and follow North Main Street 2.3 miles (through the Route 1 junction at 1.6 miles) to Trumbull Avenue. Turn left onto Trumbull Avenue and take an immediate right onto Alpha Avenue. Continue on Alpha Avenue, which becomes Water Street, for approximately 1.0 miles, through the center of town to Stonington Point.

BIRDING

Enroute to Stonington Point you may want to stop and scope out Quonaduck Cove on the west side (right) of North Main Street after crossing Route 1. This area can yield shorebirds (Killdeer, Black-bellied and Semipalmated Plovers, Greater and Lesser Yellowlegs, Semipalmated and Least Sandpipers, and Short-billed Dowitcher, among others) during migration and waders (Great Blue Heron, Snowy and Great Egrets, and Black-crowned Night-Herons from about April

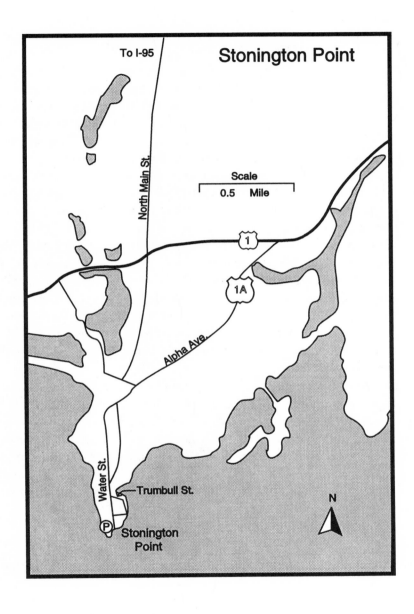

To I-95

Stonington Point

North Main St.

Scale

0.5   Mile

1

1A

Alpha Ave.

Water St.

Trumbull St.

P Stonington
Point

N

through October, and sometimes later.

The point itself is a very small area mostly taken up by a gravel parking lot. This locale can be birded quickly or you may want to set up camp for awhile and periodically scan the open water, breakwater, and offshore rocks for species moving into or through the area. From October through April, scan the coastline and offshore water for Red-throated and Common Loons, Horned and Red-necked (rare) Grebes, Great (winter) and Double-crested (common throughout most of year, rare in winter) Cormorants, Great Blue Heron, Mute Swan, American Black Duck, American Wigeon, Greater Scaup, scoters (Black Scoter is rare), Common Goldeneye, Bufflehead, and Red-breasted Merganser. Study the goldeneye flocks carefully because Barrow's Goldeneye has occurred a few times, usually in February or March.

Stonington Point is an ideal site to watch for pelagic species during fall migration from late October into December. Here, as elsewhere along the Connecticut coast, the best time to search for pelagic species is during or following a period of northeast winds. A nice feature about the point is that you can bird almost the entire area directly from the car which can prove highly beneficial while waiting for storm-tossed rarities to blow in. An incredible incursion of over 300 Northern Gannet occurred here on November 15, 1991.

Scan the area for gulls (Herring, Ring-billed, and Great Black-backed occur throughout the year) and terns (May through September). Winter gulls include the species noted above, plus Bonaparte's and the occasional white-winged variety (Iceland and Glaucous). During summer Laughing Gull occurs. Common and Least Terns can be observed in summer. Both species nest nearby. With luck, you may find a Royal or Caspian Tern which occasionally forage along the coastline.

83 Barn Island
Wildlife Management Area
Stonington

Located in the extreme southeastern corner of the state, this 707-acre coastal wildlife management area lies in a protected enclave sheltered by headlands. Habitats at Barn Island include open salt water, large expanses of tidal marshes, waterfowl impoundments, and coastal scrub woodlands and thickets. The waterfowl impoundments at Barn Island have been reopened to tidal flow and are returning to marsh habitat.

Barn Island is good during spring and fall migrations. Summer can be good for wetland and coastal scrub species while winter may produce such raptors as Rough-legged Hawk, Northern Harrier, and Bald Eagle. Coastal wetland birds are a specialty and spring and fall songbird migrations can also be good. Barn Island also has a reputation for drawing noteworthy species including Tricolored Heron, White Ibis, Hudsonian Godwit, Long-billed Dowitcher, Wilson's Phalarope, Stilt, and Curlew Sandpipers, Yellow Rail, and Scissor-tailed Flycatcher.

Barn Island can be a popular hunting locale during fall so birders should take suitable precautions such as wearing bright clothing and staying along the trails.

DIRECTIONS

Take Interstate 95 to Exit 91 (Route 234, North Main Street, Stonington). Follow Route 234 west for 0.4 miles and turn left onto North Main Street. At 1.5 miles turn left onto Route 1 for 1.7 miles and turn right on Greenhaven Road. Take an immediate right onto Palmer Neck Road and drive to the end by the boat launch (1.7 miles).

BIRDING

Check out the expanse of open water in front of the boat launch area and the salt marsh to the left. Afterwards, hike or drive back along the roadway about 0.1 miles, to the trailheads on either side of the road. The trail to the left (west) of the road goes to Wequetequock Cove. The trail on the right works eastward through the complex of Barn Island

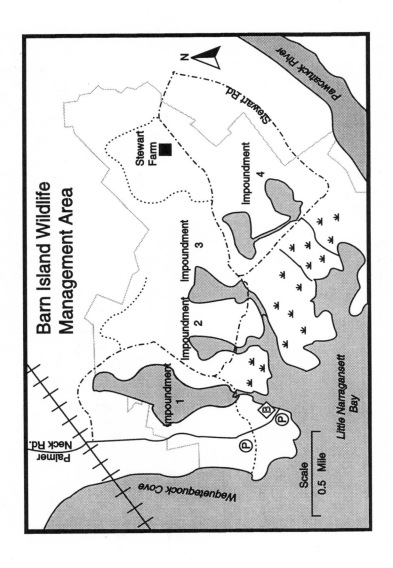

Barn Island Wildlife Management Area

marshes and impoundments and out to Stewart Farm. About two miles long, this offers an abundance of salt marsh habitats ranging from mudflats to tidal and brackish salt marshes, cattail marshes, and open water; all of which grade into more upland grassy fields, brushy borders, thickets, and scrubby woodlands. You can also bird the side trails which head into more mature deciduous woodlands on either side of the road.

Little Narragansett Bay Salt Marsh. Begin birding by the boat launch, which provides a good view of the bay directly ahead and the salt marsh to the left. From October through April, a variety of waterbirds---waterfowl, loons, cormorants, and gulls may be spotted in the bay including Common and Red-throated Loons, Common Goldeneye, American Black Duck, Red-breasted Merganser, and Herring, Great Black-backed, and Ring-billed Gulls. In spring and summer, the salt marsh to the left can be viewed from the observation platform. The salt marsh may yield many of the waders including Great and Snowy Egrets, Great Blue, Green, Tricolored (uncommon), and Little Blue Herons, and Glossy Ibis.

Wequetequock Cove. The trail to Wequetequock Cove begins on the left, just north of the boat launch. The trail winds through thickets and scrub woods before emerging at the shore of Wequetequock Cove. The tangle of vine and scrubby trees provide breeding habitat for several species including Common Yellowthroat, Yellow, Chestnut-sided and Prairie Warblers, Brown Thrasher, Gray Catbird, Song Sparrow, and Eastern Towhee. At the overlook check for swallows---Purple Martin, Tree, and Bank Swallows nest nearby. Barn and Tree Swallows can be especially abundant during migration.

The shoreline is used by gulls and shorebirds which can be plentiful at times. The regular gulls are augmented by Laughing Gull in summer.

Most of the species of shorebirds that regularly occur in Connecticut can be recorded here in the course of a year, including American Oystercatcher, Ruddy Turnstone, Black-bellied and Semipalmated Plovers, Semipalmated Sandpiper, and other species of peeps.

The sheltered waters of the cove can usually yield Mute Swan (sometimes in large numbers), Canada Goose throughout most of the year, and Brant in fall and spring. From spring to fall, you should find Double-crested Cormorant. In winter, check for Great Cormorant. Other possible wintering waterbirds include Horned Grebe, Greater Scaup, Bufflehead, and occasionally, Ruddy Duck. The long sandbar in the middle distance off to the south affords nesting for large colonies of Herring and Great Black-backed Gulls. Recently, Black Skimmer and American Oystercatcher have attempted nesting there. Common and Least Terns work the waterways throughout much of the summer and are joined by Forster's Tern in fall.

Tidal Salt Marshes---Impoundments. After birding the cove, backtrack to the road and take the trailhead on the other side to the tidal marshes and impoundments that comprise most of Barn Island. The trail winds through a scrubby growth of oaks and black cherry woodland which can be good for migrant warblers and vireos in spring, and nesting White-eyed Vireo, Black-billed Cuckoo, Whip-poor-will, and Carolina Wren. As you exit the woods a *Spartina* marsh is on the right and the first impoundment---a large cattail marsh and open water area--- is on the left.

Check the vegetation along the edge of the water for herons fishing in the shallows and bitterns hiding in the reeds. This area was famous for the Least Bittern but a salt marsh restoration project has made the species an unlikely breeder now at Barn Island. More likely species that might turn up include Great Blue, Green, Tricolored (uncommon) and Little Blue Herons, and Great and Snowy Egrets. Glossy Ibis is a possible breeder here. During migration all of these species may be seen as well as American Bittern and Cattle Egret. Marsh Wren and Seaside Sparrow can be heard throughout the spring and early summer as they defend nearby nesting territories. The latter species can be found very near the trail at this spot.

The salt marsh to the right is good for shorebirds, especially during migration and at high tide. Semipalmated Plover, Sanderling, Dunlin, Greater and Lesser Yellowlegs, Killdeer, Semipalmated and Least Sandpipers, Whimbrel (uncommon to rare), and Short-billed Dowitcher feed and rest here. Another occasional fall visitor is the Ruff. In summer, Willet and Spotted Sandpipers nest nearby in the marsh. From fall through spring, the Northern Harrier can usually be seen hunting just over the marsh. Both Rough-legged Hawk and Short-eared Owl occur in some years. Check the branches of the scrubby trees along the marsh edge for American Kestrel in summer and fall and the Belted Kingfisher throughout the year.

The trail continues east, skirting the low salt marsh to the right and passing through another scrubby woodland to the second impoundment. This small woodland is often good for Black-capped Chickadee and White-eyed Vireo. Listen for Fish Crow and Eastern Phoebe in summer. In fall and winter, the scattered conifers have held roosting Great Horned, Northern Saw-whet, Long-eared, and Barred Owls. Cottontails, squirrels, and meadow mice provide an abundant prey supply for these owls and also Red-tailed Hawk, which are seen year-round.

The second impoundment is a narrow strip of salt marsh and can be a quiet area but the third impoundment is often excellent. Approach the third impoundment quietly as birds may be quite close to the trail. Shorebirds and waders can be numerous here. During spring migration White-rumped Sandpiper is consistent in late May. Unusual possible migrants include Hudsonian Godwit, Wilson's Phalarope (June but best in August), Stilt, Western, and Baird's Sandpipers (all in fall), and Long-billed Dowitcher (late September and October). The mosquito ditches are likely spots for herons and egrets. Little Blue Heron occurs regularly in spring and early fall. Check the Snowy Egrets for Little Blue Heron; the immature Little Blue has dull olive legs and a gray bill with a black tip. A Scissor-tailed Flycatcher was spotted near the third impoundment in June, 1993.

The taller saltwater cord grass along the mosquito ditches are nesting habitat for Swamp Sparrow and particularly Seaside and Saltmarsh Sharp-tailed Sparrows. These marsh sparrows can be numerous here but are elusive in the tall grasses. Watch for them to perch and sing. You can distinguish the buzzy Sharp-tail's *tuptup-sheeeeee* song from that of the equally buzzy *cutcut zhe-eeeeee* song of the Seaside by the pronounced *zhe* in the middle, to which the Seaside adds an occasional Red-winged Blackbird-like *schaak*. The ditches are occasionally worked by Black Skimmer in spring.

The nesting platforms in the marsh were put up for Ospreys. In early spring, use a spotting scope to study the female on the nest. As the season progresses, the young are more conspicuous as they sit on the edge of the platform, awaiting the arrival of the adults with fish food. After fledgling, the young will continue to hang around the nest site until fall migration.

During migration, watch for rails, especially Virginia and Sora, furtively creeping along the ditches and mudflats. Clapper (has nested) and King Rails were formerly found here but are now rare or absent. Least Terns regularly hunt the impoundments in summer.

The trail through the third impoundment can be a good hawk watch area during September and October after the passage of a cold front. On especially good days, hundreds of raptors can be tallied including Turkey Vulture, Osprey, Northern Harrier, all three accipiters, Red-shouldered and Red-tailed Hawks, American Kestrel, Merlin, Peregrine Falcon, and occasionally, Bald Eagle.

The trail continues to skirt the marsh before reentering the woods, winding by an old gravel bank now overgrown with brushy vegetation. In a short distance, the trail forks. The left trail leads to farm fields and a conifer stand. Check the conifers for wintering owls and the fields for Eastern Bluebird throughout the year. Sparrows seen around the fields in fall and winter have included American Tree, Chipping, Field, Vesper (rare), Savannah, Song, White-throated, and White-crowned. The right trail at the fork continues through the marsh to the fourth impoundment.

The fourth impoundment begins about 100 yards after the fork. In late spring and summer, check along the trail for nesting Willow Flycatcher, Yellow Warbler, and Red-winged Blackbird. The marsh and open water are good for shorebirds and waders. Green Heron is often here while Black-crowned and Yellow-crowned (rare) Night-Herons are sometimes encountered. Willet nest in the marsh and take flight when disturbed, sounding their *whee-wee-wee* alarm calls. Least Bittern formerly nested and may occasionally be encountered along the marsh edge.

A tidal channel flows beneath the trail near the eastern end of the impoundment. The mud flat to the north can be excellent for shorebirds. A scope is essential to view the more distant birds. Black-bellied and Semipalmated Plovers, Greater and Lesser Yellowlegs, Semipalmated and Least Sandpipers, and Short-billed Dowitcher are common migrants that can be spotted on the mudflats. Less common but regular migrants include Solitary, Western, White-rumped, and Pectoral Sandpipers, and Common Snipe. In fall, Whimbrel regularly occur in small numbers on the marsh. Caspian Tern is occasionally observed near the fourth impoundment during summer.

The wetter areas of the fourth impoundment offer good waterfowl habitat during migration. Look for Blue-winged and Green-winged Teals, Gadwall, and other dabbling ducks. Glossy Ibis are often seen in spring, sometimes dozens at a time. Outstanding rarities seen at the fourth impoundment include White Ibis (in 1970) and Yellow Rail. The grassy fields are a favorite habitat for migrant Eastern Meadowlark. In the brushy woods listen for Brown Thrasher, White-breasted Nuthatch, White-eyed Vireo, and Black-and-white Warbler.

Stewart Farm. If you continue to hike along the trail it eventually comes out to the state-owned Stewart Farm. The fields, thickets, and woods around the farm are always good for nesting Gray Catbird, Red-eyed Vireo, Common Yellowthroat, Yellow Warbler, American Redstart, Scarlet Tanager, and Baltimore Oriole. Other species seen between the fourth impoundment and the farm may include Northern Bobwhite, Ring-necked Pheasant, American Woodcock, and Rose-breasted Grosbeak. The American Woodcock is best observed at dusk, from late March into June, performing its aerial courtship. Eastern Phoebe nest in the building foundations around the farm property.

84 Assekonk Swamp Wildlife Management Area

North Stonington

This wildlife management area is comprised of wetland, deciduous woodland, and reverting field habitats. More than half of its 694 acres consist of wetlands which offer good waterbird opportunities from spring through late October. From late October into February, the area is extensively used for hunting, and consequently, is poor for birding.

Assekonk Swamp WMA has received limited coverage as a birding site, but can produce a variety of avian fauna with diligent birding. Access by canoe may be the best way to explore the swamp, since it places you in the midst of this unique area. Among the more interesting species found at Assekonk Swamp are herons, American Bittern, Sora, Common Moorhen, and Virginia Rail. In 1987, the state's first documented record of Fulvous Whistling Duck occurred here.

DIRECTIONS

Traveling on Interstate 95 northbound take Exit 92 (Routes 2 and 49, No. Stonington and Pawcatuck), turn left and follow Route 2 west for 2.8 miles. Southbound on Interstate 95 take Exit 92 (Routes 2 and 49, Pawcatuck and No. Stonington), and continue straight at the end of the ramp for 0.8 miles to Route 2. Turn right onto Route 2 (west) and drive 2.6 miles. Just past the North Stonington Fire Station, park on the left side of the road before the school or in the school parking lot. Walk along the left side of the field which parallels the swamp. If you intend to canoe, walk along the left side of the field about 200 feet from the road to where a narrow path leads to the river directly above the dam. This is an ideal launch point for the canoe.

BIRDING

The swamp can host an assortment of wetland dwelling species. During the breeding season (May through July), scan the shoreline, emergent vegetation, and open water for Great Blue and Green Herons, Mute

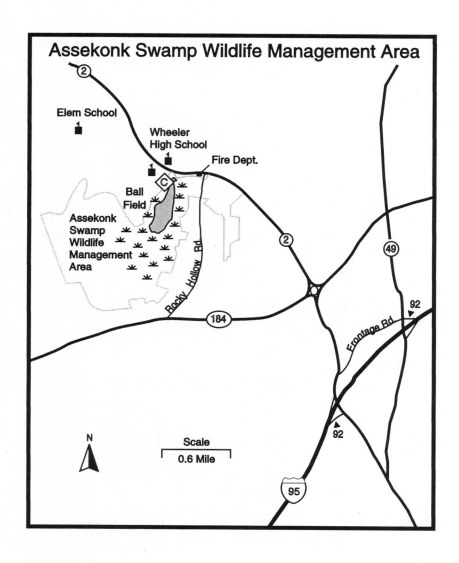

Assekonk Swamp Wildlife Management Area

Elem School

Wheeler
High School

Fire Dept.

Ball
Field

Assekonk
Swamp
Wildlife
Management
Area

Rocky Hollow Rd.

184

2

49

92

Frontage Rd.

92

95

N

Scale
0.6 Mile

Swan, Canada Goose, Mallard, Killdeer, and Spotted Sandpiper. The trees and shrubs along the edge of the swamp may yield Red-shouldered Hawk (uncommon) and Willow Flycatcher. Belted Kingfisher can usually be spotted, while Tree Swallows perform aerobatics over the swamp. Marsh Wren and Swamp Sparrow are likely among the cattails and wetland shrubs. A few secretive members of the rail family heard much more frequently than seen include Common Moorhen, Sora, and Virginia Rail. Wood Duck breed in most of the nest boxes placed throughout the swamp and after breeding the population swells to well over 100 individuals.

A variety of woodland and edge species nest in the surrounding upland habitat that fringes the swamp. A hike within the woods should produce Black-billed Cuckoo (irregular), Red-bellied Woodpecker, Northern Flicker, Eastern Phoebe, Eastern Kingbird, Great Crested and Least Flycatchers, Carolina Wren, Veery, Wood Thrush, Gray Catbird, Cedar Waxwing, Warbling Vireo, and several nesting warblers such as Blue-winged, Yellow, Common Yellowthroat, Black-and-white, and Ovenbird. Common Grackle, Northern Cardinal, Barred Owl, and Red-shouldered Hawk all nest in the immediate vicinity of the swamp. The warning whistle of the Red-shouldered Hawk may denote an active nest.

During spring, (April/May) and fall (August until hunting season) migrations, the open water may harbor Pied-billed Grebe, cormorants (both Double-crested and Great occur sporadically), American Bittern (uncommon), Glossy Ibis, dabbling ducks (Blue-winged and Green-winged Teals, and American Black Duck), Ring-necked Duck, the occasional Hooded Merganser, and Solitary Sandpiper. Osprey is somewhat regular from April through September.

Assekonk Swamp WMA is a locale that has received little attention from the birding community. This site has great potential and with increased coverage should reveal an array of interesting species. The extensive wetland habitat could, quite possibly, harbor nesting Least Bittern. Maybe with luck, you might stumble upon something as terrific as the three Fulvous Whistling Ducks that spent more than a week at the swamp in May, 1987!

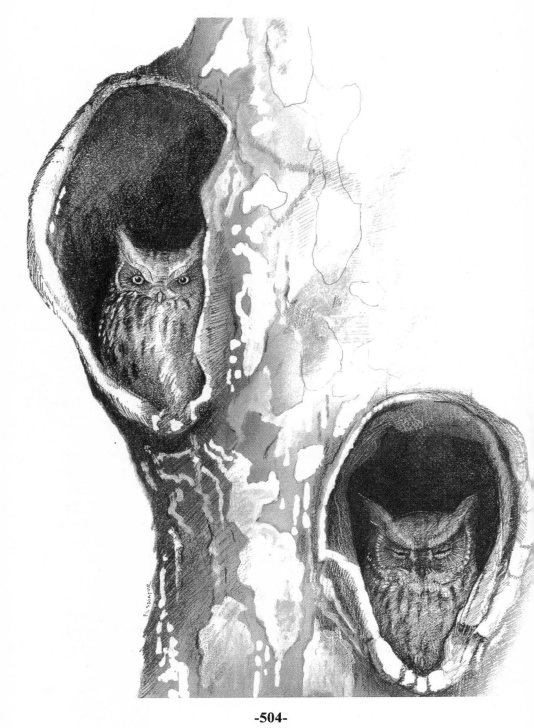

IV ANNOTATED SPECIES LIST

This list includes almost 400 species of birds that have been recorded in Connecticut and accepted by the Connecticut Rare Records Committee. Accidental and casual rarities with few records are listed at the end of this list. Species names and sequences follow the A.O.U. *Checklist of the Birds of North America* (6th ed. 1983 and supplements).

For each species we have noted its common and scientific names, status within the state, most likely dates of occurrence, relative abundance during the normal times it is found in the state, and several birding sites where it may be seen in Connecticut in season.

Information on species status was obtained from the Connecticut Ornithological Association's *Field Checklist Birds of Connecticut* (COA, 1994), the *Atlas of Breeding Birds of Connecticut* (Bevier, 1994), and *Connecticut Birds* (Zeranski and Baptist, 1990). Information regarding approximate times of occurrence was obtained from *Connecticut Birds* which we have modified based on our field notes. The abundance of birds is presented on a scale ranging from abundant, common, fairly common, uncommon, rare, very rare, casual, and accidental. For most species we have indicated several birding sites where the species has been seen during the appropriate season. To find a particular species, read the site description for more exact information about where and when the species may likely be seen. Consult the index for additional sites where the species may occur. The abbreviations used for sites include CR = coastal reserve, NC = nature center, SF = state forest, SP = state park, WMA = wildlife management area. An * denotes rare species for which a report to the Connecticut Rare Records Committee is appropriate.

Red-throated Loon *Gavia stellata* Uncommon to fairly common migrant in small numbers in coastal waters, rare on inland lakes. Mainly March-April, mid-October into December. Bluff Point CR, Greater New Haven Harbor, Greenwich Point Park, Hammonasset Beach SP, Milford Point.

Common Loon *Gavia immer* Uncommon to fairly common migrant, October into December, March to May; on inland lakes and along coastal surf, inlets, coves, and bays. Uncommon in winter. Bantam Lake, Greenwich Point Park, Merwin Point, Nepaug Reservoir.

Pied-billed Grebe *Podilymbus podiceps* Uncommon migrant, early April to late May, August to November; ponds, brackish marshes, bogs, and estuaries; rare nesting species. Great Meadows Marsh, Konold's Pond, Roy Swamp WMA, Smith Cove, Station 43.

Horned Grebe *Podiceps auritus* Common to fairly common coastal migrant and winter visitor, rare inland; from late October through April. Bluff Point CR, Cornfield Point, Greater New Haven Harbor, Middle Beach, Milford Point.

Red-necked Grebe *Podiceps grisegena* Rare to uncommon migrant and winter visitor, November to April but abundance varies greatly from year to year. Mainly found along coast, occasionally on inland lakes and ponds. Eastern Point, Greenwich Point Park, Griswold Point, Merwin Point, Sherwood Island SP.

Eared Grebe* *Podiceps nigricollis* Casual migrant (several August-September records) and winter visitor in quiet waters along coast and on inland ponds. Few records and no regular locations.

Northern Gannet *Morus bassanus* Formerly very rare and accidental coastal migrant, November and December, March and April; more numerous in past decade. Bluff Point CR, Greenwich Point Park, Hammonasset Beach SP, Merwin Point, Stonington Point.

Great Cormorant *Phalacrocorax carbo* Uncommon to fairly common migrant and winter visitor, September through May. Coastal areas along jetties, docks, pilings, buoys, breakwaters, sandbars. Rare inland, usually only during migration. Eastern Point, Greenwich Point Park, Middle Beach, Milford Point, Saybrook Point.

Double-crested Cormorant *Phalacrocorax auritus* Common to abundant migrant along coast, fairly common on inland lakes and along larger rivers; migrant April to late May and September through October. Uncommon in winter but numbers increasing. Breeds on offshore islands. Bluff Point CR, Cornfield Point, Greater New Haven Harbor, Milford Point, Mystic River, Norwalk Harbor.

American Bittern *Botaurus lentiginosus* Rare migrant, April and May, September into November, mostly in tidal and inland marshes; very rare in winter. A very rare nesting species in inland marshes. Cromwell Meadows, Durham Meadows, Great Island WMA, Hammonasset Beach SP, Roy Swamp WMA.

Least Bittern *Ixobrychus exilis* Rare migrant and nesting species,

May through September, coastal tidal marshes and ponds, inland marshes. Durham Meadows, Great Meadows Marsh, Mohawk SF, Roy Swamp WMA, Station 43.

Great Blue Heron *Ardea herodias*   Common to fairly common migrant; uncommon nesting species; rare to uncommon in winter. Coastal marshes, rivers, inland lakes, ponds, and marshes. Barn Island WMA, Great Island WMA, Konold's Pond, Milford Point, Natchaug SF, Sherwood Island SP.

Great Egret *Ardea alba* Uncommon to fairly common migrant and summer resident from April-November; nests on offshore islands. Found mainly in coastal marshes, less commonly in inland marshes, lakes, ponds, and along rivers. Barn Island WMA, Griswold Point, Milford Point, Norwalk Islands, Rocky Neck SP.

Snowy Egret *Egretta thula* Same as Great Egret. Coastal marshes and tidal ponds, inland lakes, and ponds. Barn Island WMA, Bluff Point CR, Great Island WMA, Great Meadows Marsh.

Little Blue Heron *Egretta caerulea* Uncommon summer visitor (May-September) in coastal marshes, bays, brackish water habitats; rare inland. Barn Island WMA, Connecticut College Arboretum, Manresa, Milford Point, Norwalk Islands.

Tricolored Heron *Egretta tricolor*   Rare along coast from May through September. Formerly a rare nesting species at Norwalk Islands, but no recent breeding records. Barn Island WMA, Great Meadows Marsh, Manresa, Milford Point.

Cattle Egret *Bubulcus ibis* Rare migrant along coast, occasionally inland from April to November. Numbers are declining. Formerly nested on Norwalk Islands. Barn Island WMA, Hammonasset Beach SP, Sherwood Island SP.

Green Heron *Butorides virescens* Uncommon to fairly common migrant and nesting species along coastal and inland marshes, ponds and wooded swamps, April through October. Assekonk Swamp WMA, Durham Meadows, Great Meadows Marsh, Station 43.

Black-crowned Night-Heron *Nycticorax nycticorax* Uncommon to fairly common migrant and summer resident, March-October, a few overwinter. Present in tidal marshes, mosquito ditches, and pools along coast, larger rivers (postbreeding dispersal), and swamps. Uncommon nesting species along coast and offshore islands. Barn Island WMA, Great Island WMA, Great Meadows Marsh, Manresa, Milford Point.

Yellow-crowned Night-Heron *Nyctanassa violacea* Rare to uncommon summer resident in brackish water habitats, primarily along western Connecticut coastline; rare nesting species. Ash Creek, Manresa, Milford Point.

Glossy Ibis *Plegadis falcinellus* Uncommon coastal migrant and summer resident, late April to mid-September in coastal marshes. Barn Island WMA, Great Island WMA, Great Meadows Marsh, Hammonasset Beach SP, Manresa.

Tundra Swan *Cygnus columbianus* Casual migrant, late October through December, March and April; primarily found along coastline in quiet bays and backwaters, occasionally inland lakes and ponds. Has occurred at Konold's Pond, Greater New Haven Harbor, Greenwich Point Park, South Cove in Old Saybrook.

Mute Swan *Cygnus olor* Common to abundant permanent resident; increasing rapidly. Winters in bays, estuaries, tidewater areas along the coast; nests lakes, ponds, tidal marshes. Large wintering concentrations at Smith Cove, South Cove in Old Saybrook, West Haven Boat Dock adjacent to Sandy Point.

Greater White-fronted Goose* *Anser albifrons* Rare migrant and winter visitor occurring with flocks of Canada Geese.

Snow Goose *Chen caerulescens*   Regular migrant from March to May, October into December; rare in winter. Found in coastal marshes, bays, inlets, lakes and ponds. Frequently seen overhead during migration. Greenwich Point Park, Harkness Memorial SP, Lighthouse Point Park, Southbury Training School, Station 43.

Brant *Branta bernicla* Uncommon to locally common migrant from March to May, mid-October through November along coast; rare inland during migration; uncommon winter visitor along coast. Eastern Point, Greenwich Point Park, Griswold Point, Saint Mary's-by-the-Sea.

Canada Goose *Branta canadensis* Common permanent resident, numbers augmented in winter by migratory population; found along coast, estuaries, inland lakes and ponds, open areas.

Wood Duck *Aix sponsa* Fairly common migrant, March to May, late September-November, occasionally overwinters. Fairly common nesting species, in freshwater marshes and swamps, vegetated edges of lakes, and ponds. Assekonk Swamp WMA, Miles Wildlife Sanctuary, Osbornedale SP, Station 43, White Memorial Foundation.

Green-winged Teal *Anas crecca* Uncommon to common migrant, mid-March to early May, August into December, uncommon winter visitor present in fresh water marshes, ponds and lakes, tidal and estuarine marshes. Milford Point, Sherwood Mill Pond, Station 43.

American Black Duck *Anas rubripes* Common to locally abundant migrant and wintering species, uncommon nesting species in coastal and inland waters, ponds, lakes, marshes. Found at most coastal locations fall through spring.

Mallard *Anas platyrhynchos* Common year-round resident in fresh water lakes, ponds, marshes, rivers, and coastal marshes. Easy to spot on almost any body of fresh or brackish water.

Northern Pintail *Anas acuta* Uncommon but regular migrant from March through April, September-November; rare in winter. Found in coastal marshes, estuaries, bays, inlets, ponds, and lakes. Bantam Lake, Gulf Pond, Holly Pond, Sherwood Mill Pond, Smith Cove.

Blue-winged Teal *Anas discors* Uncommon migrant from late March to mid-May, mid-August through October; rare in winter; in coastal marshes, inland waterways, lakes, ponds, streams. Rare nesting species in larger inland and coastal marshes. Durham Meadows, Konold's Pond, Sherwood Mill Pond, Station 43, White Memorial Foundation.

Northern Shoveler *Anas clypeata* Rare but regular migrant from mid-March to late May, September to mid-November in coastal marshes, estuaries, inland marshes, lakes, and ponds. Bantam Lake, Griswold Point, Konold's Pond, Milford Point.

Gadwall *Anas strepera* Uncommon to locally common migrant and wintering species along coast from mid-August to mid-May; rare nesting species. Eastern Point, Frash Pond, Holly Pond, Oyster River, Sherwood Mill Pond, Smith Cove.

Eurasian Wigeon *Anas penelope* Rare but regular migrant and winter visitor with most records at coastal locations. Look for this typically among flocks of American Wigeon. Aspetuck Reservoir, Furnace Pond, Greater New Haven Harbor (Oyster River to Bradley Point).

American Wigeon *Anas americana* Common to fairly common during migration from March to May, September through December; uncommon but regular in winter in fresh and tidal marshes along the coast, inland on rivers, lakes, and ponds. Aspetuck Reservoir, Frash Pond, Eastern Point, Oyster River, Sherwood Mill Pond.

Canvasback *Aythya valisineria* Uncommon to locally common migrant and winter visitor from late October to late April; present on tidal marshes, inlets along coast, rarer inland on lakes and reservoirs. Gulf Pond, Frash Pond, Holly Pond, Sherwood Mill Pond, Smith Cove.

Redhead *Aythya americana*   Rare to very rare, but regular coastal migrant and winter visitor in tidal marshes, inlets; very rare inland on lakes and ponds. Greater New Haven Harbor, Holly Pond, Smith Cove (best location), South Cove in Old Saybrook.

Ring-necked Duck *Aythya collaris* Uncommon to common migrant from March to mid-April, October to December on inland lakes and ponds, rivers. Bantam Lake, Great Pond SF, Greenwich Point Park, Konold's Pond, Mansfield Hollow SP, River Road in Southbury.

Greater Scaup *Aythya marila* Locally common migrant and winter visitor along coast from October-April; rare inland on lakes and ponds. May occur along coast in rafts of several hundred to several thousand individuals. Eastern Point, Greater New Haven, Penfield Reef, Seaside Park, South Cove in Old Saybrook.

Lesser Scaup *Aythya affinis* Rare to uncommon migrant from March to mid-April, late October to December; rarer in winter and summer. More apt to be found inland than Greater Scaup. A few individuals usually associated with Greater Scaup rafts. Bantam Lake, Frash Pond, Sherwood Mill Pond, Smith Cove, South Cove in Old Saybrook.

Common Eider *Somateria mollissima* Very rare winter visitor but occasional sightings from late October to April along coast. Harkness Memorial SP, Merwin Point, Milford Point, Sherwood Island SP.

King Eider * *Somateria spectablis* Rare to very rare in winter on Long Island Sound. Hammonasset Beach SP, Harkness Memorial SP, Lighthouse Point Park, Milford Point, Sherwood Island SP.

Harlequin Duck* *Histrionicus histrionicus* Very rare in winter offshore along rocky coast. No regular site, but has been seen near Eastern Point, Merwin Point, Norwalk Islands, Penfield Reef.

Oldsquaw *Clangula hyemalis* Uncommon to common migrant and winter visitor from October to April along coast, inlets, bays; generally more numerous along western coast. Very rare inland. Great Meadows Marsh, Milford Point, Saybrook Point, Sherwood Island SP.

Black Scoter *Melanitta nigra* Rare but regular migrant and winter visitor, October into May along coast. Look for this species in offshore scoter flocks. Greenwich Point Park, Hammonasset Beach SP, Harkness Memorial SP, Middle Beach.

Surf Scoter *Melanitta perspicillata* Uncommon to locally common migrant and winter visitor, October into May along coast; very rare inland on lakes, rivers. Greenwich Point Park, Griswold Point, Hammonasset Beach SP, Harkness Memorial SP, Middle Beach.

White-winged Scoter *Melanitta fusca* Uncommon to locally common migrant and winter visitor along coast, October into May; very rare inland on lakes and rivers. Cornfield Point, Greenwich Point Park, Harkness Memorial SP, Merwin Point, Seaside Park.

Common Goldeneye *Bucephala clangula* Uncommon to common migrant and winter visitor, November to April on coastal bays, inlets, larger inland lakes and rivers. Connecticut River in Enfield, Greater New Haven Harbor, Saybrook Point, Stonington Point.

Barrow's Goldeneye* *Bucephala islandica* Rare from December through March along coastal inlets, estuaries and larger rivers. In recent years fairly reliable in January and February on the Connecticut River in Enfield; occasionally at Griswold Point, Sherwood Island SP.

Bufflehead *Bucephala albeola* Uncommon to common migrant and winter visitor, mid-October to May on fresh and salt water habitats; along coast, inlets, bays, open marshes, lakes, ponds, and rivers. Frash Pond, Mystic River, Smith Cove, South Cove in Old Saybrook.

Hooded Merganser *Lophodytes cucullatus* Uncommon to fairly common on inland lakes, ponds, and rivers from mid-October to December, mid-March through April; uncommon in winter along coastal inlets, estuaries, and bays. Rare nesting species in wooded swamps. Bantam Lake, Blackhall River, Konald's Pond, Sherwood Mill Pond, Miles Wildlife Sanctuary, Mystic River.

Common Merganser *Mergus merganser* Common migrant and winter visitor from November through April on lakes, ponds, rivers, estuaries, and rarely, along shore. Rare nesting species. Connecticut River in Essex, Connecticut River in Enfield, Great Pond, River Road in Southbury, Stevenson's Dam.

Red-breasted Merganser *Mergus serrator* Common migrant and winter visitor found in small numbers along coast, inlets and bays and rarely, inland on larger rivers and lakes. Eastern Point, Great Pond, Gulf Pond, Norwalk Harbor, Saybrook Point.

Ruddy Duck *Oxyura jamaicensis* Uncommon to locally common migrant, October to December and March to April in fresh and salt water habitats; rare winter visitor. Bantam Lake, Laurel Reservoir, Sherwood Mill Pond, Smith Cove, South Cove.

Black Vulture *Coragyps atratus*   Rare but increasingly observed along the Housatonic River Valley in the Northwest Highlands. Usually seen in winter and spring near the New Milford Landfill, Sunny Valley Farm, River Road in Kent.

Turkey Vulture *Cathartes aura*   Uncommon to locally common migrant and summer resident, normally seen soaring above woods, farms, open areas throughout state. Seen at hawk watch stations during fall migration from September to November. Spring migration late February into April. Lighthouse Point Park, River Road in Kent.

Osprey *Pandion haliaetus* Uncommon to fairly common migrant from September through October, less common from late March to May. Found at lakes, ponds, rivers, and along the coast. Common nesting species along the coast, primarily east of Hammonasset Beach State Park, Barn Island WMA, Great Island WMA, Harkness Memorial SP, Lighthouse Point Park, Quaker Ridge.

Bald Eagle *Haliaeetus leucocephalus*   Rare to locally uncommon winter visitor. Winter concentrations along the Connecticut and Housatonic Rivers. Very rare nesting species at Barkhamsted Reservoir. Barkhamsted Reservoir, Connecticut River in Enfield and Essex, Lighthouse Point Park, Miles Wildlife Sanctuary, River Road in Southbury, Stevenson's Dam.

Northern Harrier *Circus cyaneus*   Uncommon to locally common migrant and winter visitor, September into May; uncommon winter resident mainly in coastal marshes. May nest in Great Meadows Marsh area. Usually seen foraging over tidal marshes along shore, larger freshwater marshes, or croplands. Barn Island WMA, Great Island WMA, Great Meadows Marsh, Hammonasset Beach SP, Milford Point.

Sharp-shinned Hawk *Accipiter striatus*   Fairly common to common fall migrant from September   into   November,   uncommon   spring migrant April and May; rare in winter; small and local nesting population. Greenwich Point Park, Lighthouse Point Park, Quaker Ridge, and other coastal locations.

Cooper's Hawk *Accipiter cooperii* Rare to uncommon throughout the year. More commonly observed during fall migration. Uncommon nester.   Lighthouse Point Park, Mount Riga, Quaker Ridge, Sunny Valley Farm, White Memorial   Foundation.

Northern Goshawk *Accipiter gentilis* Rare nesting species in deciduous and mixed woodlands; rare to uncommon migrant from late

October into November. Lighthouse Point Park, Quaker Ridge, Steep Rock Reservation, White Memorial Foundation.

Red-shouldered Hawk *Buteo lineatus* Uncommon to fairly common migrant, late March through May and mid-October through November. Uncommon nesting species inland, especially in swamps; rare winter resident. Great Pond, Lighthouse Point Park, Nehantic SF, Quaker Ridge, White Memorial Foundation.

Broad-winged Hawk *Buteo platypterus* Uncommon nesting species in deciduous and mixed woodlands in less settled regions. Uncommon to very common migrant along ridges and hills from early September into October, and April to mid-May. Collis P. Huntingdon SP, Lighthouse Point Park, Miles Wildlife Sanctuary, Mohawk SF, Quaker Ridge, White Memorial Foundation.

Red-tailed Hawk *Buteo jamaicensis* Common throughout the year along edge and open habitat, and farmlands throughout state; nest in woodlands. Lighthouse Point Park, Naugatuck SF, Pachaug SF.

Rough-legged Hawk *Buteo lagopus* Rare and irregular migrant and winter visitor, late October into April. Look for this hawk perched or soaring above coastal marshes, inland marshes, cropland, floodplains near rivers. Connecticut River in Essex, Great Island WMA, Great Meadows Marsh, Hammonasset Beach SP, Lighthouse Point Park.

Golden Eagle *Aquila chrysaetos* Rare during migration and in winter, but small numbers usually seen on hawk watches from October into December, less likely from March into April. Barkhamsted Reservoir, Connecticut River in Essex, Lighthouse Point Park, River Road in Southbury, Quaker Ridge, Under Mountain Road.

American Kestrel *Falco sparverius* Uncommon nesting species throughout the state in fields, farmland, and edge habitat; population declining. Uncommon to common during migration, especially along coast from September through October, and April and May; rare to uncommon in winter. Hammonasset Beach SP, Lighthouse Point Park, Northwest Highlands Tour, Station 43, Storrs at Horse Barn Hill.

Merlin *Falco columbarius* Rare to uncommon migrant, primarily along coast from September to mid-November; occasionally during winter along coast. Greenwich Point Park, Hammonasset Beach SP, Lighthouse Point Park.

Peregrine Falcon *Falco peregrinus* Rare but regular coastal migrant from September into November, March to early May; irregular in winter and summer. Greenwich Point Park, Hammonasset Beach SP, Lighthouse Point Park, Milford Point, Quaker Ridge.

Gyrfalcon* *Falco rusticolus* Accidental migrant and casual winter visitor along coast. Check Rare Bird Alert tapes for reports of this species. Wintered twice in Greater New Haven Harbor area.

Ring-necked Pheasant *Phasianus colchicus* Uncommon introduced species; resident in farmlands, dry marshes, fields, meadows, brushy edges. Barn Island WMA, Cromwell Meadows WMA, Manresa, Pine Creek, West Rock Ridge SP.

Ruffed Grouse *Bonasa umbellus* Uncommon to fairly common resident of deciduous and mixed woodlands throughout state, especially in more remote locales. Population cyclic. Mohawk SF, Naugatuck SF, Natchaug SF, Nehantic SF, Roaring Brook NC.

Wild Turkey *Meleagris gallopavo* Uncommon to locally common permanent resident now throughout much of state in meadows and woodland mosaics, brushy edges. Collis P. Huntington SP, Northwest Highlands Tour, Roaring Brook NC, Under Mountain Road.

Northern Bobwhite *Colinus virginianus* Rare to uncommon permanent resident, more frequent east of the Connecticut River. Found in open and brushy areas, woodland edge, dryer areas of coastal marshes. Barn Island WMA, Bluff Point CR, Great Island WMA.

Black Rail* *Laterallus jamaicensis* Very rare, scattered reports from May to October at a few coastal and inland marshes; no recent breeding records. Listen for calls of this rail in twilight hours of dusk and dawn at marsh edges. Cromwell Meadows WMA, Great Meadows Marsh, Great Island WMA.

Clapper Rail *Rallus longirostris* Uncommon to fairly common nesting species in coastal salt and brackish marshes, April to November all along shoreline. Rare during winter in coastal marshes. Great Island WMA, Great Meadows Marsh, Hammonasset Beach SP, Milford Point.

King Rail *Rallus elegans* Rare migrant and breeding species in larger inland and coastal marshes from April through October. Durham Meadows, Manresa, Station 43.

Virginia Rail *Rallus limicola* Uncommon to fairly common in inland and coastal marshes as migrant and nesting species; rare in winter. Cromwell Meadows WMA, Durham Meadows, Station 43, White Memorial Foundation.

Sora *Porzana carolina* Uncommon migrant and nesting species from April through October; very rare in winter; nests in fresh water marshes. Durham Meadows, Miles Wildlife Sanctuary, Station 43, White Memorial Foundation.

Common Moorhen *Gallinula chloropus* Rare to locally uncommon migrant and nesting species, found in coastal brackish marshes, larger inland marshes, and ponds at widely scattered localities. Assekonk Swamp WMA, Konold's Pond, Northeast Audubon Center, Roy Swamp WMA, Station 43, White Memorial Foundation.

American Coot *Fulica americana* Uncommon migrant and rare wintering species on inland lakes and ponds, coastal tidal marshes from March to mid-April, October into December. Bantam Lake, Batterson Park Pond, Bishops Pond, Konold's Pond, Laurel Reservoir.

Sandhill Crane* *Grus canadensis* Casual migrant from September to late October in open habitats. A few records from scattered locations.

Black-bellied Plover *Pluvialis squatarola* Common to locally abundant migrant, April into May, late July into November along coast, on sandbars, beaches, and mudflats. Uncommon along coast in winter. Barn Island WMA, Greenwich Point Park, Griswold Point, Milford Point, Sherwood Island SP.

American Golden-Plover *Pluvialis dominicus* Rare to uncommon migrant from late August into November along coast on mudflats, sandbars, flooded fields, dry marshes; rarer inland on plowed fields and airport fields. Bluff Point CR, Hammonasset Beach SP, Harkness Memorial SP, Milford Point, Sandy Point.

Semipalmated Plover *Charadrius semipalmatus* Common to abundant migrant from early May to June, late July into October on mudflats, beaches, and sandbars. Barn Island WMA, Griswold Point, Milford Point, South Cove.

Piping Plover *Charadrius melodus* Rare to locally uncommon coastal migrant and breeding species, mid-March to September. Nests at scattered locales along coast in summer. Griswold Point, Long Beach, Milford Point, Sandy Point.

Killdeer *Charadrius vociferus* Uncommon to common migrant and nesting species, March to mid-November, variable in winter. Found along coast on mudflats, sandy and gravel beaches, parking lots, inland on open fields, gravel lots, farm fields. Nests on open areas with gravel substrate. Bradley International Airport, Bluff Point CR, Hammonasset Beach SP, Milford Point, Station 43.

American Oystercatcher *Haematopus palliatus* Rare but population increasing; observed from April to October in small numbers along coast on mudflats, rocky beaches, salt marshes, and mussel beds; nests on offshore islands. Bluff Point CR, Eastern Point, Falkner Island.

Greater Yellowlegs *Tringa melanoleuca* Common migrant along coast, uncommon inland from early April to June, July to November; a few remain through winter. Found along shores of lakes, ponds, wetlands, coastal flats, estuaries, pools along coast. Barn Island WMA, Milford Point, Sherwood Island SP, South Cove.

Lesser Yellowlegs *Tringa flavipes* Fairly common coastal migrant, uncommon inland; from mid-July to late October, smaller numbers in April and May; found in same locations as Greater Yellowlegs.

Solitary Sandpiper *Tringa solitaria* Uncommon spring migrant from late April through May, rarer from late July through September; seen along edges of ponds, lakes, streams, and, rarely, coastal wetlands. Durham Meadows, East Rock Park, Mansfield Hollow SP, Station 43.

Willet *Catoptrophorus semipalmatus* Locally uncommon coastal migrant and nesting species from late April into October; along coast in tidal marshes, sandy beaches, and mudflats. Barn Island WMA, Hammonasset Beach SP, Milford Point, Sandy Point.

Spotted Sandpiper *Actitis macularia* Common migrant from late April into June, August to early October, a few linger into November and December, lakes and ponds, shores, tidal marshes, and mudflats; locally uncommon nesting species. Barn Island WMA, East Rock Park, Griswold Point, River Road in Kent, Station 43.

Upland Sandpiper *Bartramia longicauda* Rare to locally uncommon migrant, May, August-September, on open fields, grassy areas throughout state. Nests at Bradley International Airport, May into July. Bluff Point CR--Groton-New London Airport, Great Meadows Marsh, Sherwood Island SP, Veterans Park.

Whimbrel *Numenius phaeopus* Uncommon migrant mid-July to mid-September, very rare late April into early June; found along coastal wetlands, mudflats, salt marshes. Barn Island WMA, Great Island WMA, Hammonasset Beach SP, Sherwood Island SP.

Hudsonian Godwit *Limosa haemastica* Rare coastal migrant from late August into November, mainly coastal on fresh and salt water pools, lawns and ball fields. Barn Island WMA, Griswold Point, Milford Point, Long Wharf, Sandy Point.

Marbled Godwit *Limosa fedoa* Rare coastal migrant from August through September; same habitat and locations as Hudsonian Godwit.

Ruddy Turnstone *Arenaria interpres* Fairly common migrant along coastal beaches, mudflats, sandbars and islands, May to June, usually more common in late July to mid-October; uncommon in winter. Griswold Point Preserve, Harkness Memorial SP, Milford Point.

Red Knot *Calidris canutus* Uncommon coastal migrant late April to early June, uncommon to locally common in small to large flocks from late July to November; seen on sandbars, beaches, tidal flats. Griswold Point Preserve, Milford Point, Sandy Point.

Sanderling *Calidris alba* Common migrant, uncommon winter visitor to mudflats and sandy beaches along coast. Great Meadows Marsh, Greenwich Point Park, Griswold Point Preserve, Milford Point.

Semipalmated Sandpiper *Calidris pusilla* Common migrant during May to June, mid-July to early October, on coastal mudflats, estuaries, inland ponds, lakes, and rivers. Barn Island WMA, Griswold Point Preserve, Milford Point, Sandy Point.

Western Sandpiper *Calidris mauri* Generally uncommon migrant from late July to mid-October, usually seen on coastal mudflats, sandy beaches. Barn Island WMA, Bluff Point CR, Milford Point.

Least Sandpiper *Calidris minutilla* Uncommon to common coastal migrant from May to early June, July to October on mudflats of tidal marshes and inland wetlands. Bluff Point CR, Griswold Point Preserve, Hammonasset Beach SP, Milford Point, Sherwood Island SP.

White-rumped Sandpiper *Calidris fuscicollis* Rare to uncommon coastal migrant from mid-May to early June, mid-August through October on tidal marshes, beaches, and sandbars; occasionally found on inland mudflats, edges of lakes and ponds. Barn Island WMA, Griswold Point Preserve, Hammonasset Beach SP, Milford Point.

Baird's Sandpiper *Calidris bairdii* Rare coastal migrant August to October, on shortgrass wetlands, coastal lawns with rain pools, tidal mudflats. Bluff Point CR, Great Meadows Marsh, Griswold Point Preserve, Hammonasset Beach SP, Windham Airport.

Pectoral Sandpiper *Calidris melanotos* Uncommon coastal and inland migrant from mid-April into May, August-November; regularly found in coastal and inland marshes, wet fields, airports. Groton-New London Airport, Great Meadows Marsh, Guilford Sluice, Hammonasset Beach SP, Station 43, Veteran's Park.

Purple Sandpiper *Calidris maritima* Uncommon coastal migrant and winter visitor, found along rocky coastline, breakwaters, and jetties, November to May. Eastern Point, Harkness Memorial SP, Merwin Point, Middle Beach.

Dunlin *Calidris alpina* Fairly common coastal migrant mid-September to early December, late March to late May; uncommon to locally common in winter on coastal mudflats, sandbars, and edges of tidal marshes. Bluff Point CR, Greater New Haven Harbor, Griswold Point Preserve, Milford Point.

Stilt Sandpiper *Calidris himantopus* Rare but regular migrant, late July to October, very rare in May; mudflats, brackish and coastal marshes, and coastal pools. Barn Island WMA, Great Meadows Marsh, Hammonasset Beach SP, Milford Point.

Buff-breasted Sandpiper *Tryngites subruficollis* Rare but regular migrant, late August into October, both inland and coastal open habitats such as plowed fields, croplands, airports, and sometimes mudflats and beaches. Bluff Point CR, Great Meadows Marsh, Hammonasset Beach SP, Veteran's Park

Short-billed Dowitcher *Limnodromus griseus* Fairly common to locally abundant migrant, July to late September, uncommon from late April into June on coastal mudflats and tidal marshes. Barn Island WMA, Great Island WMA, Hammonasset Beach SP, Milford Point.

Long-billed Dowitcher *Limnodromus scolopaceus* Rare coastal migrant in May and late August to November; found in same habitats as the Short-billed Dowitcher. Barn Island WMA, Great Island WMA, Hammonasset Beach SP, Milford Point.

Common Snipe *Gallinago gallinago* Uncommon but regular migrant, mid-March to May, early August to November; rare in winter. Seen at inland and coastal marshes, wet meadows, often near seeps or adjacent to wetlands. Cromwell Meadows WMA, Durham Meadows, Lighthouse Point Park, Station 43.

American Woodcock *Scolopax minor* Uncommon migrant and nesting species from March to early November; rare in winter. Found in inland and coastal marshes, wet fields. Connecticut College Arboretum, Great Meadows Marsh, Miles Wildlife Sanctuary, Station 43, White Memorial Foundation.

Wilson's Phalarope *Phalaropus tricolor* Rare but regular coastal migrant from August to early September, casual in spring; in fresh and tidal pools, quiet inlets. Barn Island WMA, Griswold Point Preserve, Hammonasset Beach SP, Milford Point, Sherwood Island SP.

Laughing Gull *Larus atricilla* Uncommon to common coastal migrant and summer visitor, April to November, on coastal beaches, sandbars, and mudflats. Griswold Point Preserve, Long Wharf, Manresa, Milford Point, Sherwood Island SP.

Little Gull* *Larus minutus* Rare but regular migrant and casual winter visitor, October to November and mid-March to April. Regular in Bonaparte's Gull flocks, mid-March to mid-April. Oyster River, South Cove in Old Saybrook.

Black-headed Gull *Larus ridibundus* Rare but regular migrant and winter visitor from late October through mid-April along coast and open waters of Long Island Sound. Found in same locations as Little Gull.

Bonaparte's Gull *Larus philadelphia* Fairly common coastal migrant and winter visitor from October to mid-May; abundant at estuaries during peak migration days in late March and early April. Griswold Point Preserve, Holly Pond, Long Wharf, Oyster River, South Cove.

Ring-billed Gull *Larus delawarensis* Common to abundant coastal migrant and winter visitor from late August to May. Uncommon in summer. Can be found year-round along inland waterways, landfills, farm fields, coastal beaches, sandbars, and mudflats. Long Wharf, Milford Point, Saybrook Point, Sherwood Island SP, Stevenson's Dam, Sunny Valley Farm.

Herring Gull *Larus argentatus* Common to abundant year-round in coastal and inland locations, sandbars, mudflats, rivers, ponds, lakes, impoundments, landfills, farm fields. Can be found at most coastal locations, inland landfills, waste areas, ball fields.

Iceland Gull *Larus glaucoides* Rare to uncommon but a regular winter visitor, November through April; along coastal sandbars and mudflats, inland along rivers, impoundments, and landfills. Bradley Point, Holly Pond, New Milford Tour, Oyster River, Stevenson's Dam.

Lesser Black-backed Gull *Larus fuscus* Rare but increasingly regular winter visitor from September through April; found along the coast and inland on lakes, rivers, and landfills. Great Meadows Marsh, New Milford Tour, Greater New Haven Harbor, Sherwood Island SP.

Glaucous Gull *Larus hyperboreus* Rare but regular winter visitor from November through April, same habitats as Iceland Gull. Connecticut River in Enfield, Lower Connecticut River, New Haven

Harbor, New Milford Tour, Stevenson's Dam.

Great Black-backed Gull *Larus marinus* Common at coastal locations, uncommon inland; present offshore, sandy beaches, mudflats, parking lots, farm fields, lakes, ponds, larger rivers. Breeds on sandy offshore islands. Barn Island WMA, Middle Beach, Milford Point, New Haven Harbor, Stevenson's Dam.

Black-legged Kittiwake* *Rissa tridactyla* Casual and irregular migrant and winter visitor from October into April; occurs mainly offshore during strong easterly winds. Try Bluff Point CR, Griswold Point Preserve, Hammonasset Beach SP, Harkness Memorial SP.

Caspian Tern *Sterna caspia* Rare coastal migrant and summer visitor, mid-May to early October, at scattered coastal locations, sandbars, and beaches. Milford Point, Sandy Point, Griswold Point, Hammonasset Beach SP.

Royal Tern *Sterna maxima* Rare summer visitor, June to October, along coastal beaches and sandbars. Griswold Point Preserve, Hammonasset Beach SP, Milford Point, Sandy Point.

Roseate Tern *Sterna dougallii* Rare spring migrant along coast in May. Local nesting species, May through September on offshore islands. Nests on Falkner Island, occasionally other small offshore islands. Often seen at post-breeding dispersal sites from mid-August to mid-September at Griswold Point Preserve, Milford Point, Sandy Point.

Common Tern *Sterna hirundo* Common coastal migrant and breeder found from late April to October; abundant on peak migration days in September. Occurs on beaches, inlets, bays, tidal marshes, sandbars. Barn Island WMA, Bluff Point CR, Griswold Point Preserve, Milford Point, Sandy Point.

Forster's Tern *Sterna forsteri* Uncommon coastal visitor, August and September, but occasional through November; rare in April-May. Found in fresh, brackish, and salt water marshes along coast. Griswold Point Preserve, Milford Point, Sandy Point, South Cove.

Least Tern *Sterna antillarum* Uncommon to locally common coastal migrant and breeder from May to September; found in tidal marshes, sandbars, inlets. Several protected breeding colonies on sandy beaches along coast. Griswold Point Preserve, Milford Point, Sandy Point.

Black Tern *Childonias niger* Rare but regular migrant, mainly coastal but occasional on inland lakes and ponds, August to late September, less numerous in May and early June. Barn Island WMA,

Griswold Point Preserve, Milford Point, Sandy Point.

Black Skimmer *Rynchops niger* Rare but regular summer visitor from mid-May into October along coast, on sandbars, low islands, sandy seashores. Greenwich Point Park, Griswold Point Preserve, Manresa, Milford Point, Sandy Point.

Rock Dove *Columba livia* Introduced resident throughout the state; common to abundant, usually near human habitation.

Mourning Dove *Zenaida macroura* Common breeding species and migrant throughout state, abundant during peak migration days in March and October, fairly common wintering species. Easy to find.

Monk Parakeet *Myiopsitta monachus* Permanent resident in limited but expanding locales, spreading from a colony at Bridgeport. Look for large stick nests and noisy foraging individuals of this species along the southwest coast at Milford Point, Seaside Park, St. Mary's-By-the-Sea.

Black-billed Cuckoo *Coccyzus erythropthalmus* Irregular to fairly common migrant and nesting species from May to October in dense woodlands, edge, frequently near water. Population fluctuates. Bluff Point CR, Durham Meadows, East Rock Park, Mohawk SF, Quinebaug River WMA, White Memorial Foundation.

Yellow-billed Cuckoo *Coccyzus americanus* Rare to uncommon migrant and breeding species, May to September, in deciduous woodlands and brushy woodland edges. Bluff Point CR, East Rock Park, Lighthouse Point Park, Quinebaug River WMA, Valley Road.

Barn Owl *Tyto alba* Rare nesting species. A few nesting records each year at widely scattered locales, near the coast and in the vicinity of Middletown. The DEP has implemented a nest box program which may attract breeding pairs to the major coastal parks and wildlife management areas. No regular sites known, but can sometimes be observed at Great Meadows Marsh on summer evenings.

Eastern Screech Owl *Otus asio* Fairly common permanent resident in central and western part of the state, uncommon elsewhere in deciduous and mixed woodlands, farmlands, suburban and urban open space where suitable nesting and roosting trees are available. Nests from late March into June. Listen for the evening songs of this species at Connecticut River in Enfield, East Rock Park, Naugatuck SF, River Road in Southbury, Station 43.

Great Horned Owl *Bubo virginianus* Uncommon but widespread permanent resident throughout state, more common in remote deciduous, mixed and conifer woodlands in state forests and game lands. Hammonasset Beach SP, Mansfield Hollow SP, Miles Wildlife Sanctuary, Sperry Park, West Rock Ridge State Park.

Snowy Owl *Nyctea scandiaca* Rare winter visitor, early November into April, mostly along coast, occasionally inland. Look for this species along coast on sandbars, beaches, and offshore islands at Bluff Point CR, Great Meadows Marsh, Hammonasset Beach SP, Milford Point.

Barred Owl *Strix varia* Uncommon permanent resident throughout state in mixed and conifer woodlands, hemlock ravines, and water company plantations. Connecticut College Arboretum, Great Pond SF, Mohawk SF, Naugatuck SF, Pachaug SF, White Memorial Foundation.

Long-eared Owl *Asio otus* Rare to uncommon migrant and winter visitor, mid-October to early April; very rare nesting species. Pellets and whitewash help locate this owl at winter roost sites, normally along the coast in conifers, pines, spruces, or cedars. Barn Island WMA, Guilford Sluice, Hammonasset Beach SP, Lighthouse Point Park.

Short-eared Owl *Asio flammeus* Rare migrant and winter visitor, from late September into late April or early May; mostly seen over tidal marshes, open areas along coast, larger marshes inland. Great Island WMA, Great Meadows Marsh, Hammonasset Beach SP, Milford Point.

Northern Saw-whet Owl *Aegolius acadicus* Rare to uncommon migrant and winter visitor; occasional local wintering concentrations of several birds; November through March in conifer stands, especially red cedar stands along waterways and coast. Very rare and secretive nesting species in deciduous and mixed woodlands. Hammonasset Beach SP, Mohawk SF, Quinnipiac River SP, Sperry Park.

Common Nighthawk *Chordeiles minor* Common migrant from mid-August through September, uncommon in May; usually observed hawking insects during evening hours. Uncommon to rare nesting species on gravel roofs. Look for this species at twilight over cities and landfills. Great Meadows Marsh, Manresa.

Chuck-will's-widow* *Caprimulgus carolinensis* Rare migrant, May to June along coast. Listen for this species at dawn and dusk.

Whip-poor-will *Caprimulgus vociferus* Uncommon nesting species. Listen for this species at dawn and dusk along woodland edges, frequently near water. Barn Island WMA, Naugatuck SF, Miles Wildlife Sanctuary, Pachaug SF.

Chimney Swift *Chaetura pelagica* Common migrant, May into June and late August into October. Uncommon but locally common nesting species in chimneys throughout state. Look for this species hawking insects over towns, cities, rivers. East Rock Park, Northwest Highlands Tour, River Road in Kent.

Ruby-throated Hummingbird *Archilochus colubris* Uncommon migrant and uncommon to rare nesting species throughout state, May through September. Seen in open woodlands, especially adjacent to wetlands. Mohawk SF, Miles Wildlife Sanctuary, River Road in Kent, River Road in Southbury, Station 43.

Belted Kingfisher *Ceryle alcyon* Fairly common nesting species throughout state in burrows along rivers, lakes and ponds, coastal inlets and estuaries. Less frequent in winter along coast, occasionally inland if open water is available. Barn Island WMA, Connecticut River in Enfield, River Road in Kent, River Road in Southbury.

Red-headed Woodpecker *Melanerpes erythrocephalus* A rare migrant from September-October, irregular nesting species; rarer winter visitor from November-April. Open woods, beaver swamps. Best location during migration is Lighthouse Point Park.

Red-bellied Woodpecker *Melanerpes carolinus* Uncommon to fairly common permanent resident throughout state in deciduous woodlands, river valleys, and floodplains. Bluff Point WMA, Cromwell Meadows WMA, East Rock Park, Hartman Park, Osbornedale SP.

Yellow-bellied Sapsucker *Sphyrapicus varius* Rare to locally uncommon nesting species, rare to uncommon migrant April-May and September-November. Breeds in deciduous and mixed woodlands, especially in the Northwest Highlands. Found in coastal woodlands during migration and occasionally in winter. Lighthouse Point Park, Miles Wildlife Sanctuary, Mohawk SF, White Memorial Foundation.

Downy Woodpecker *Picoides pubescens* Common resident in deciduous and mixed woodlands throughout state and at suet feeders in winter. Found throughout state in appropriate habitat.

Hairy Woodpecker *Picoides villosus* Uncommon resident in deciduous woodlands throughout state, frequently at feeders in winter. Denison-Pequotsepos NC, East Rock Park, Flanders Nature Center, Natchaug SF, Naugatuck SF, Roaring Brook NC.

Northern Flicker *Colaptes auratus* Common migrant and breeder throughout state from March through October in open woodlands, fields, farmlands, urban open space. Uncommon to rare in winter in same habitats. Cromwell Meadows WMA, Mohawk SF, Station 43.

Pileated Woodpecker *Dryocopus pileatus* Uncommon permanent resident in deciduous and mixed woodlands throughout state. Less common in the Eastern Hills. Devil's Hopyard SP, Flanders Nature Center, Mohawk SF, Pachaug SF, White Memorial Foundation.

Olive-sided Flycatcher *Contopus borealis* Uncommon spring and fall migrant, mid-May to mid-June, late July into September. Usually seen in treetops. Miles Wildlife Sanctuary, Naugatuck SF, Station 43, White Memorial Foundation.

Eastern Wood-Pewee *Contopus virens* Fairly common migrant and breeder; found from mid-May into October in deciduous woods throughout Connecticut. Bigelow Hollow SP, Mohawk SF, Northwest Park, Osbornedale SP, River Road in Kent.

Yellow-bellied Flycatcher *Empidonax flaviventris* Rare to uncommon migrant, late May into June, August to mid-September. Usually seen in open conifer or mixed woodlands. Bluff Point CR, Boston Hollow, Flanders NC, River Road in Kent, White Memorial Foundation.

Acadian Flycatcher *Empidonax virescens* Uncommon nesting species and migrant, mid-May to September. Normally near streams, wet areas in open woodlands, woodland edges, and thickets. Bigelow Hollow SP, Devil's Hopyard SP, River Road in Kent, Valley Road.

Alder Flycatcher *Empidonax alnorum* Rare to uncommon migrant and nesting species, mid-May to mid-September. Alder and shrub swamps, edges of marshes, bogs, and ponds. Miles Wildlife Sanctuary, Mohawk SF, White Memorial Foundation.

Willow Flycatcher *Empidonax trailii* Uncommon to fairly common migrant and breeder, present in state from mid-May to mid-September. Nests in coastal and inland willow and alder thickets, wet pastures. Bluff Point CR, Durham Meadows, White Memorial Foundation.

Least Flycatcher *Empidonax minimus* Uncommon to fairly common migrant early May to early June, early August to mid-September. Uncommon to locally fairly common nesting species in northern half of state. Boston Hollow, Devil's Hopyard SP, River Road in Kent, River Road in Southbury, Station 43, White Memorial Foundation.

Eastern Phoebe *Sayornis phoebe* Fairly common migrant and nesting species, mid-March to November in open deciduous woodlands, bridges and buildings, often near water. Devil's Hopyard SP, East Rock Park, Mt. Riga, Osbornedale SP, Roaring Brook Nature Center.

Great Crested Flycatcher *Myiarchus crinitus* Fairly common migrant and nesting species, May to late September in deciduous and mixed woodlands throughout state. Boston Hollow, Bluff Point CR, Flanders Nature Center, Mohawk SF, Valley Road.

Western Kingbird *Tyrannus verticalis* Rare migrant found primarily along coast from mid-September to November. Most likely location for this species is Lighthouse Point Park.

Eastern Kingbird *Tyrannus tyrannus* Uncommon to fairly common migrant and nesting species in woodland edges, pond edges, water courses, farmlands, from late April to late September throughout state. Durham Meadows, East Rock Park, Nehantic SF, Pachaug SF.

Horned Lark *Eremophila alpestris* Uncommon to fairly common coastal migrant and winter visitor late October to April; locally uncommon breeding species in grassy fields at a few airports and other open areas along coast. Bluff Point CR, Bradley International Airport, Great Meadows Marsh, Hammonasset Beach SP, Sherwood Island SP.

Purple Martin *Progne subis* Uncommon migrant and locally uncommon nesting species from late April through September; usually seen over open water, farmland, coastal marshes near nesting boxes. Hammonasset Beach SP, Milford Point, River Road in Kent,

Tree Swallow *Tachycineta bicolor* Common migrant and nesting species, late March to late October. Can be abundant during fall migration, late August into September. Nests throughout state in tree and post cavities, nest boxes near water. Great Pond SF, Mansfield Hollow SP, River Road in Southbury, Station 43.

Northern Rough-winged Swallow *Stelgidopteryx serripennis* Fairly common migrant and nesting species throughout state from mid-April to September. Usually seen near water. Nests along waterways and ponds, in river banks, drain pipes. East Rock Park, Mansfield Hollow SP, River Road in Kent, Stevenson's Dam.

Bank Swallow *Riparia riparia* Uncommon migrant and locally common breeder found throughout state from late April to early September. Seen in open habitats, fields, waterways, open wetland edges near gravel banks. Nests in river banks, sand and gravel banks. Konold's Pond, River Road in Kent, Station 43, Stevenson's Dam.

Cliff Swallow *Hirundo pyrrhonota* Rare to locally uncommon migrant and nesting species present at scattered localities, mainly in western part of state from May to September. Open habitats along rivers, ponds;

nest mainly under bridges and on dams. American Legion and People's SF, Barkhamsted Reservoir, River Road in Southbury, Stevenson's Dam.

Barn Swallow *Hirundo rustica* Common migrant and nesting species found throughout state from mid-April into September. Seen in open habitats around farms, fields, rivers, and ponds. Nests in barns and other structures. Easy to find in appropriate habitat and season.

Blue Jay *Cyanocitta cristata* Common resident throughout state. Impressive fall migrations at Lighthouse Point Park. Nests and winters in urban, suburban, and rural habitats, open deciduous, mixed and coniferous forests. Usually easy to find throughout state.

American Crow *Corvus brachyrhynchos* Common to locally abundant resident throughout state. Form large communal roosts in winter. Farms, suburban and urban open space, small woodland stands. Large winter roosts in West Haven, Waterbury, and elsewhere. Easy to find throughout state.

Fish Crow *Corvus ossifragus* Uncommon permanent resident along coast and inland along rivers. Frequently nest in conifer groves. Connecticut College Arboretum, East Rock Park, Greenwich Point Park, Greater New Haven Harbor, Sherwood Island SP.

Common Raven *Corvus corax* Rare permanent resident, expanding range southward. Nests on ledges, cliffs, and sometimes in trees in relatively remote areas. Barkhamsted Reservoir, Boston Hollow, Nepaug Reservoir, Northwest Highlands Tour, Steep Rock Reservation.

Black-capped Chickadee *Parus atricapillus* Common widespread resident throughout state, in coniferous and deciduous woods, woodland edges, feeders, suburban open space.

Boreal Chickadee* *Parus hudsonicus* Irregular, casual migrant and winter visitor from late October to mid-April. Occasionally seen at coastal locations such as Lighthouse Point Park during migration in October and November.

Tufted Titmouse *Parus bicolor* Fairly common resident throughout state, in open woodlands, edges, residential, feeders. Bluff Point CR, Devil's Hopyard SP, Naugatuck SF, Osbornedale SP, Storrs Area Tour.

Red-breasted Nuthatch *Sitta canadensis* Uncommon, irregular migrant and winter visitor September through March; locally uncommon nesting species. Coniferous and mixed deciduous woodland. American Legion and People's SF, Barkhamsted Reservoir, Boston Hollow, Pachaug SF, White Memorial Foundation.

White-breasted Nuthatch *Sitta carolinensis* Fairly common permanent resident throughout state in deciduous, mixed woodlands, edges, feeders. Bigelow Hollow SP, Devil's Hopyard SP, East Rock Park, Osborndale SP, White Memorial Foundation.

Brown Creeper *Certhia americana* Uncommon migrant and nesting species present in small to moderate numbers throughout state from March to November, a few occur in winter. Deciduous and mixed woodlands. American Legion and Peoples SF, Mohawk SF, Natchaug SF, Nepaug Reservoir, White Memorial Foundation.

Carolina Wren *Thryothorus ludovicianus* Uncommon to fairly common permanent resident. Numbers greatly reduced after severe winters. More common along coast; residential, suburban, thicket, edge habitat, brushy woods. Audubon Center of Greenwich, Barn Island WMA, Osbornedale SP, Station 43.

House Wren *Troglodytes aedon* Fairly common throughout state from late April to mid-October; a few linger into December. Residential, gardens, urban open space, open woodlands, woodland edges. Flanders Nature Center, Nehantic SF, Osbornedale SP, Station 43.

Winter Wren *Troglodytes troglodytes* Uncommon to rare breeder, mainly northern and upland areas from late March to late September; small numbers winter. Deciduous, mixed and coniferous woodlands frequently near wetlands. Boston Hollow, Miles Wildlife Sanctuary, Mohawk SF, Mt. Riga, White Memorial Foundation.

Sedge Wren* *Cistothorus platensis* Very rare migrant, May and June, September to late October, and casual summer resident at scattered localities within state. Most records in autumn.

Marsh Wren *Cistothorus palustris* Uncommon migrant and nesting species late April into October; found primarily in coastal and tidal marshes, locally at inland marshes. Barn Island WMA, Durham Meadows, Great Island WMA, Manresa, Milford Point, Station 43, White Memorial Foundation.

Golden-crowned Kinglet *Regulus satrapa* Uncommon to fairly common migrant from late March to May, October and November, uncommon to rare in winter. Rare breeder in a few northern locations. Found in open deciduous and mixed wood, conifer plantations. Bigelow Hollow SP, Devil's Hopyard SP, White Memorial Foundation.

Ruby-crowned Kinglet *Regulus calendula* Common migrant. April to mid-May, mid-September through November. Same habitats and locations as Golden-crowned Kinglet.

Blue-gray Gnatcatcher *Polioptila caerulea* Uncommon to common migrant and nesting species late April through September. Wet, open and mixed woodlands, woodland edges, along rivers and ponds. Devil's Hopyard SP, East Rock Park, River Road in Kent, River Road in Southbury, Valley Road.

Northern Wheatear* *Oenanthe oenanthe* Casual in fall, usually seen in September and October along coastal locations. Several records from Hammonasset Beach SP.

Eastern Bluebird *Sialia sialis* Uncommon to locally common from March to October, uncommon in winter. Nests along fields, meadows, and cow pastures. Haley Farm SP, Northwest Park, Osbornedale SP, Roaring Brook NC, White Memorial Foundation.

Veery *Catharus fuscescens* Common to fairly common migrant and nesting species in deciduous and mixed woodlands throughout state, May to October. Boston Hollow, Devil's Hopyard SP, Nehantic SF, White Memorial Foundation.

Gray-cheeked Thrush *Catharus minimus* Rare migrant, mid-May to June, September and October; coniferous and mixed woodlands, woodland edges. Bluff Point CR, East Rock Park, Lighthouse Point Park, White Memorial Foundation.

Bicknell's Thrush *Catharus bicknelli* Specimen records indicate that this species is a rare migrant through the state. Identification is problematic at best.

Swainson's Thrush *Catharus ustulatus* Uncommon migrant mid-May to early June, late August to late October. Deciduous and mixed woodland, woodland edges. Bluff Point CR, East Rock Park, Flanders Nature Center, Lighthouse Point Park, River Road in Kent.

Hermit Thrush *Catharus guttatus* Uncommon from early April to November, rare but regular during winter. Coniferous and mixed woodland, frequently found near wet thickets during migration and in winter. Local breeder in scattered locales. American Legion and Peoples SF, Boston Hollow, Bluff Point CR, White Memorial Foundation.

Wood Thrush *Hylocichla mustelina* Fairly common breeder in open woodlands throughout state from May to mid-October. Bigelow Hollow SP, Devil's Hopyard SP, Nehantic SF, River Road in Kent, Valley Road.

American Robin *Turdus migratorius* Common throughout state from March into November, can be abundant during migration.

Individuals or small flocks usually found throughout winter. Suburbs, urban open space, farms, fields, thickets, gardens, edges of open woodlands. Easy to find throughout state.

Varied Thrush* *Ixoreus naevius* Very rare from December to late March, usually at feeding stations.

Gray Catbird *Dumetella carolinesis* Very common throughout state from late April to late October, rare in winter. Nests in wetlands, open woodlands, suburban yards, thickets, parks, and wet edge habitats. Pachaug SF, Cromwell Meadows, Station 43, Valley Road.

Northern Mockingbird *Mimus polyglottos* Common resident throughout the state; most common in human modified habitats; gardens, landscaped residential and commercial sites, rose thickets, woodland edges. Audubon Center of Greenwich, Cromwell Meadows, Mansfield Hollow SP, Roaring Brook Nature Center.

Brown Thrasher *Toxostoma rufum* Uncommon migrant and breeding species; population decreasing; March through October over most of state but easily overlooked when not singing. Reverting fields, woodland edges. Barn Island WMA, East Rock Park, Haley Farm SP, Mansfield Hollow SP, Northwest Park.

American Pipit *Anthus rubescens* Locally uncommon migrant from late September into November; rarer in spring, April and May. Usually found in small flocks in crop fields, coastal marshes, and shoreline. Bluff Point CR, Farmington Meadows, Griswold Point Preserve, Sherwood Island SP, Station 43, Storrs Tour.

Cedar Waxwing *Bombycilla cedrorum* Uncommon to fairly common throughout state from April through December, uncommon in winter; often occurs in medium-sized flocks in winter and during migrations. Orchards, woodland edge, river and pond edge. Connecticut College Arboretum, Cromwell Meadows WMA, Station 43, White Memorial Foundation.

Northern Shrike *Lanius excubitor* Rare and irregular winter visitor, more numerous during incursion years. Fields, meadows, farms, edges. No regular locations, but has occurred at Durham Meadows.

Loggerhead Shrike* *Lanius ludovicianus* Very rare migrant; most records from late August to October. Extirpated as a breeding species in the Northeast. Open habitats, fields, farms, woodland edges. No regular locations for this species.

European Starling *Sturnus vulgaris* Common to locally abundant and widespread throughout state. Large flocks in fall and winter. Urban, suburban, open space, farms, open woodlands.

White-eyed Vireo *Vireo griseus* Uncommon to locally fairly common nesting species and rare to uncommon migrant, mainly coastal, late April to October. Look for this species in brushy areas, coastal thickets. Barn island WMA, Birdcraft Museum, Bluff Point CR, Haley Farm SP, Hartman Park.

Solitary Vireo *Vireo solitarius* Uncommon to fairly common nesting species in coniferous woodlands in northern part of state; uncommon migrant in deciduous and mixed woodlands. Found from late April through October. Bigelow Hollow SP, Mohawk SF, Mt. Riga, White Memorial Foundation.

Yellow-throated Vireo *Vireo flavifrons* Uncommon migrant and fairly common breeder, May to September; deciduous woodlands, often near streams, lakes, or ponds. Devil's Hopyard SP, Naugatuck SF, Nehantic SF, River Road in Kent, River Road in Southbury.

Warbling Vireo *Vireo gilvus* Uncommon to locally common breeder throughout state from May into September. Trees in open areas, especially bordering bodies of water. Devil's Hopyard SP, East Rock Park, Mansfield Hollow SP, River Road in Kent, Station 43.

Philadelphia Vireo *Vireo philadelphicus* Casual migrant in May, rare from late August through September. Deciduous and mixed woodlands. Bluff Point CR, Lighthouse Point Park, River Road in Kent, Sherwood Island SP.

Red-eyed Vireo *Vireo olivaceus* Common breeder and migrant from May to October in open deciduous and mixed woodlands throughout state. Boston Hollow, East Rock Park, Roaring Brook Nature Center, Sharon Audubon Center, White Memorial Foundation.

Blue-winged Warbler *Vermivora pinus* Common migrant and fairly common nesting species throughout state; in open woodland, thickets, edge habitat from late April through September. Larson Sanctuary, Mansfield Hollow SP, Miles Wildlife Sanctuary, River Road in Kent.

Golden-winged Warbler *Vermivora chrysoptera* Rare nesting species in open, second growth adjacent to woodlands and frequently wetland edges; rare migrant in deciduous and second growth woodlands, May to early September. Population decreasing. East Rock Park, Miles Sanctuary, Mohawk SF, River Road in Kent.

Tennessee Warbler *Vermivora peregrina* Uncommon but regular migrant, May into June and August to mid-October. Usually in upper canopy of deciduous and mixed woodlands, ornamentals. Boston Hollow, Bluff Point CR, East Rock Park, Miles Wildlife Sanctuary, River Road in Kent.

Orange-crowned Warbler *Vermivora celata* Very rare migrant late April through May and again from late September through November in thickets, edges of open woodlands mainly at coastal locations. Found annually at Bluff Point CR from late September into October.

Nashville Warbler *Vermivora ruficapilla* Uncommon migrant and nesting species; old fields, pastures, woodland edges, open conifer woods from mid-April to mid-October. Bluff Point CR, East Rock Park, Mohawk SF, White Memorial Foundation.

Northern Parula *Parula americana* Uncommon to fairly common migrant in May and September to mid-October in wet deciduous woodlands, red maple swamps. Bluff Point CR, Connecticut College Arboretum, East Rock Park, River Road in Kent,

Yellow Warbler *Dendroica petechia* Common breeder and migrant throughout state, late April into September. Wetland thickets, brushy edges, shrub layer of open deciduous woodlands. Assekonk Swamp WMA, East Rock Park, Naugatuck SF, Station 43, Valley Road.

Chestnut-sided Warbler *Dendroica pensylvanica* Uncommon to fairly common breeder and migrant from May to mid-September in second growth field and edges of deciduous and mixed woodlands. Northwest Highlands Tour, Naugatuck SF, Nehantic SF, Station 43.

Magnolia Warbler *Dendroica magnolia* Uncommon to fairly common migrant from May to June, late August to mid-October; rare nesting species in open conifer and deciduous woods of the Northwest Hills. Bluff Point CR, East Rock Park, Mt. Riga, White Memorial Foundation.

Cape May Warbler *Dendroica tigrina* Rare to uncommon migrant from mid to late May, and August into October in coniferous and mixed woodlands, spruce plantings, edge habitat, parks. East Rock Park, Mohawk SF, River Road in Kent, White Memorial Foundation.

Black-throated Blue Warbler *Dendroica caerulescens* Uncommon to fairly common breeding species in northern areas of the state. Uncommon migrant in May, and August through September. Nests in open deciduous woodlands, usually with mountain laurel shrub growth. Bigelow Hollow SP, East Rock Park, Mt. Riga, Mohawk SF,

Yellow-rumped Warbler *Dendroica coronata* Common migrant from late April through May, and August through October in deciduous and mixed woodlands. Locally uncommon breeding species in conifer woodlands in northern areas of the state. Small numbers overwinter. Bigelow Hollow SP, Bluff Point CR, Great Pond SF, River Road in Kent, White Memorial Foundation.

Black-throated Green Warbler *Dendroica virens* Uncommon to fairly common migrant, late April to June, August to mid-October; locally common nesting species in conifer (mostly hemlock) woodlands. Boston Hollow, East Rock Park, Natchaug SF, Nepaug Reservoir, River Road in Kent, White Memorial Foundation.

Blackburnian Warbler *Dendroica fusca* Uncommon to fairly common migrant in May, late August to early October in coniferous and mixed woodlands throughout state. Uncommon nesting species at scattered northern locations in coniferous woodland. American Legion and Peoples SF, East Rock Park, Valley Road, White Memorial Foundation.

Yellow-throated Warbler* *Dendroica dominica* Very rare and irregular coastal migrant from mid-April to late May, accidental in fall. A single pair (?) has nested several years in Kent. Branford Supply Ponds, East Rock Park, River Road in Kent.

Pine Warbler *Dendroica pinus* Uncommon to locally fairly common migrant and breeding species from April to early November in mixed and conifer woodlands throughout state. American Legion SF, Great Pond SF, Nepaug Reservoir, Natchaug SF, White Memorial Foundation.

Prairie Warbler *Dendroica discolor* Uncommon migrant and nesting species throughout state, present from May to late September in open habitats, thickets, edges, scrubby habitats along powerlines. Flanders Nature Center, Hartman Park, Mansfield Hollow SP, Naugatuck SF,

Palm Warbler *Dendroica palmarum* Uncommon to fairly common migrant, early April to mid-May, September to late November. Understory of open deciduous woodlands, scrubby areas along pond edges, wetland thickets, coastal shrubs especially during fall. One of the earliest warbler migrants observed each spring. Bluff Point CR, East Rock Park, Station 43, White Memorial Foundation.

Bay-breasted Warbler *Dendroica castanea* Uncommon migrant mid-May to early June, August into October. Conifer plantations, open deciduous and mixed woodlands throughout state. Boston Hollow, East

Rock Park, River Road in Kent, Talcott Mountain Reservoir, White Memorial Foundation.

Blackpoll Warbler *Dendroica striata* Fairly common migrant mid-May to early June, August to mid-October, same habitats as Bay-breasted Warbler. East Rock Park, River Road in Kent, Devil's Hopyard SP, Nepaug Reservoir, Talcott Mountain Reservoir.

Cerulean Warbler *Dendroica cerulea* Rare migrant and locally uncommon breeder. May to September, in upper canopy of mature deciduous woodlands, frequently along rivers. Devil's Hopyard SP, Hartman Park, Natchaug SF, Nehantic SF, River Road in Kent.

Black-and-white Warbler *Mniotilta varia* Fairly common breeder throughout state in deciduous woodlands with mountain laurel thickets from late April through October. Boston Hollow, Devil's Den Preserve, East Rock Park, Osbornedale SP, River Road in Kent.

American Redstart *Setophaga ruticilla* Common migrant and fairly common breeder, May to mid-October; wet deciduous and mixed woodlands. East Rock Park, Hartman Park, Mt. Riga, Nehantic SF, River Road in Kent.

Prothonotary Warbler* *Protonotaria citrea* Rare migrant in April and May, accidental in fall. Open, swampy woodlands, woodland edges near water. Occurs almost annually in late April, early May at East Rock Park.

Worm-eating Warbler *Helmitheros vermivorus* Uncommon migrant and breeder found throughout most of state from May to September on dry hillsides and open deciduous woodlands. Devil's Den Preserve, East Rock Park, Nehantic SF, River Road in Kent, Valley Road.

Ovenbird *Seiurus aurocapillus* Common migrant and nesting species, May to mid-September in deciduous and mixed woodlands throughout state. Devil's Hopyard SP, Nehantic SF, Sharon Audubon Center.

Northern Waterthrush *Seiurus noveboracensis* Uncommon migrant and nesting species present from late April through September in swampy woodlands, bogs, and along slow moving wooded streams. Boston Hollow, Miles Wildlife Sanctuary, Mohawk SF, White Memorial Foundation.

Louisiana Waterthrush *Seiurus motacilla* Uncommon migrant and nesting species present from mid-April through August along wooded streams and bottomland, wooded edges of ponds and lakes throughout state. Devil's Hopyard SP, Flanders Nature Center, Miles Wildlife

Sanctuary, Osbornedale SP, Roaring Brook NC.

Kentucky Warbler *Oporornis formosus* Rare but regular migrant, mid-May to mid-June; very rare nesting species in shrub layer of deciduous woodlands, open wet woodlands. Locations include Fairchild Garden in Greenwich, East Rock Park, River Road in Kent.

Connecticut Warbler *Oporornis agilis* Rare but fairly regular fall migrant, late August to mid-October in thickets, wetland shrubs, and along woodland edges. Bluff Point CR, East Rock Park, Greenwich Point Park, Lighthouse Point Park.

Mourning Warbler *Oporornis philadelphia* Rare, regular migrant mid-May to early June and September. Brushy edges of woods, tangles, wetland thickets. Bluff Point CR, East Rock Park, Lighthouse Point Park, River Road in Kent, "W" Lot in Storrs.

Common Yellowthroat *Geothlypis trichas* Common migrant and nesting species present throughout state from late April through October in edges, thickets, especially around ponds, lakes, streams, wetlands. Audubon Center of Greenwich, Durham Meadows, Miles Wildlife Sanctuary, Station 43, numerous other locations.

Hooded Warbler *Wilsonia citrina* Rare to uncommon migrant and nesting species present from May to September in understory and along edges of deciduous woodlands. Devil's Den Preserve, Hartman Park, Naugatuck SF, Nehantic SF, Osbornedale SP.

Wilson's Warbler *Wilsonia pusilla* Uncommon to rare migrant in May, and August to late September in thickets, brushy tangles near woodland edges, and wetlands. Bluff Point CR, East Rock Park, Miles Wildlife Sanctuary, Station 43, White Memorial Foundation.

Canada Warbler *Wilsonia canadensis* Uncommon to fairly common migrant, late April into May, September into October. More common nesting species in highlands. Nest in woodlands with mountain laurel shrub layer, frequently in or near wet areas. East Rock Park, Mt. Riga Area, Mohawk SF, White Memorial Foundation.

Yellow-breasted Chat *Icteria virens* Rare to very rare migrant and former breeder, May to October. May nest at scattered localities in southeast corner of the state, no recent records. Very rare and accidental in winter. Barn Island WMA, Bluff Point CR, Haley Farm SP.

Summer Tanager* *Piranga rubra* Rare migrant late April to early June. No regular locations.

Scarlet Tanager *Piranga olivacea* Fairly common migrant and nesting species in open deciduous woodlands throughout state from May to early October. Devil's Den Preserve, Devil's Hopyard SP, Naugatuck SF, Nehantic SF, Sharon Audubon Center.

Northern Cardinal *Cardinalis cardinalis* Common resident throughout the state in suburbs, parks, thickets, woodland edges, open woodlands, gardens. Osbornedale SP, Sharon Audubon Center, numerous other locations.

Rose-breasted Grosbeak *Pheucticus ludovicianus* Fairly common migrant and breeder, late April to mid-October, in deciduous and mixed woodlands throughout state. Audubon Center of Greenwich, Boston Hollow, Mohawk SF, Naugatuck SF, Northwest Park.

Blue Grosbeak *Guiraca caerulea* Rare migrant mid-April through May, mid-September to mid-October in weedy fields, field edges, thickets, tangles mainly along the coast. In July, 1996, the first state breeding record occurred at Northwest Park. Usually found in fall, September to October, at coastal locations such as Longshore Club Park and Lighthouse Point Park.

Indigo Bunting *Passerina cyanea* Uncommon to locally common migrant and nesting species throughout the state from May into October along woodland edge, shrubby fields, powerline cuts. Flanders Nature Center, Northwest Park, Osbornedale SP, Roaring Brook NC, Station 43.

Dickcissel *Spiza americana* Rare but regular fall migrant usually seen in grassy fields along the coast, or occasionally inland from late September to mid-November, occasionally in winter. Cove Island Park, Hammonasset Beach SP, Lighthouse Point Park, Longshore Club Park.

Eastern Towhee *Pipilo erythrophthalmus* Common migrant and nesting species in open deciduous woodlands, edge habitat,thickets, throughout state from mid-April to mid-October; a few overwinter. Devil's Den Preserve, East Rock Park, White Memorial Foundation.

American Tree Sparrow *Spizella arborea* Common migrant and winter visitor late October to mid-April. Shrubby fields, edge, marshes, and sedge wetlands. Cromwell Meadows WMA, Hammonasset Beach SP, Lighthouse Point Park, White Memorial Foundation.

Chipping Sparrow *Spizella passerina* Fairly common migrant and nesting species throughout state from mid-April through October. Fields, farms, woodland edges, lawns. Nepaug Reservoir, Osbornedale SP, River Road in Southbury, Roaring Brook NC, Storrs Area.

Clay-colored Sparrow* *Spizella pallida* Casual migrant from mid-September into November, rarer in spring. Most likely found at coastal locations. Records from Hammonasset Beach SP, Lighthouse Point Park, Longshore Club Park.

Field Sparrow *Spizella pusilla* Fairly common migrant and nesting species throughout state from mid-March to November; uncommon in winter. Shrubby or weedy fields, thickets, woodland edges, hedgerows, powerline cuts. Haley Farm SP, Mansfield Hollow SP, Northwest Park, Osbornedale SP, Sunny Valley Farm.

Vesper Sparrow *Pooecetes gramineus* Rare to locally uncommon migrant and formerly a very rare nesting species present at scattered localities in state from mid-April to December. Grassy roadways and windbreaks, also cultivated fields. Hammonasset Beach SP, Lighthouse Point Park, Longshore Club Park, Sherwood Island SP, Station 43.

Lark Sparrow* *Chondestes grammacus* Casual fall migrant and early winter visitor from September into December mainly along coast.

Savannah Sparrow *Passerculus sandwichensis* Common migrant and locally common nesting species throughout state from April to November, a few linger through winter. Found in thickets, meadows, brush edges along salt and fresh water marshes. The Ipswich race winters in small numbers at coastal locations in dunes and sandy areas with sparse vegetation.Bluff Point CR, Bradley International Airport, Great Meadows Marsh, Hammonasset Beach SP, Sherwood Island SP.

Grasshopper Sparrow *Ammodramus savannarum* Rare migrant which nests at a few localities in the state from late April through October; found in dry, grassy fields and meadows. Bradley International Airport, Hammonasset Beach SP, Lighthouse Point Park, Longshore Club Park, Northwest Park.

Henslow's Sparrow* *Ammodramus henslowii* Very rare migrant in May and again from late September through October; in dry, grassy or weedy fields, coastal marsh edges. Difficult to find but has occurred at coastal locations during fall, try Hammonasset Beach SP, Lighthouse Point Park, Longshore Club Park, Milford Point.

Saltmarsh Sharp-tailed Sparrow *Ammodramus caudactus* Locally uncommon migrant and nesting species present in coastal tidal marshes from late April to November, a few overwinter. Barn Island WMA, Guilford Sluice, Great Island WMA, Great Meadows Marsh, Hammonasset Beach SP.

Nelson's Sharp-tailed Sparrow *Ammodramus nelsoni* Recent AOU taxonomic split from Sharp-tailed Sparrow. Likely to be an uncommon migrant. Same habitat and locations as Saltmarsh Sharp-tailed Sparrow.

Seaside Sparrow *Ammodramus maritimus* Rare to uncommon migrant and nesting species present in coastal tidal marshes from mid-April to mid-November. Barn Island WMA, Great Island WMA, Great Meadows Marsh, Guilford Sluice, Hammonasset Beach SP, Manresa.

Fox Sparrow *Passerella iliaca* Uncommon migrant mid-March to mid-April, mid-October through November; rare wintering species, throughout most of state in open woodlands, shrub fields, brushy edges of wetlands, farm fields, feeders. Bluff Point CR, Denison-Pequotsepos NC, East Rock Park, Hammonasset Beach SP, Longshore Club Park, White Memorial Foundation.

Song Sparrow *Melospiza melodia* Common permanent resident throughout state in edge and shrubby habitats, thickets, shrubby borders along ponds, streams, edges, powerline cuts. Common and widespread.

Lincoln's Sparrow *Melospiza lincolnii* Rare to uncommon migrant in May and October into November at scattered locations; prefers thickets, field edges, shrubby areas near wetlands. Farmington Meadows, Lighthouse Point Park, Longshore Club Park, Station 43, White Memorial Foundation.

Swamp Sparrow *Melospiza georgiana* Uncommon to fairly common migrant and nesting species in fresh water marshes, along wetland edges from late April to mid-November, rare in winter. Cromwell Meadows WMA, Durham Meadows, Lighthouse Point Park, Station 43, White Memorial Foundation.

White-throated Sparrow *Zonotrichia albicollis* Common and widespread migrant and winter visitor from mid-September into May, throughout state in fields, shrubby habitat, woodland edges, mixed woodlands. A locally uncommon nesting species in scattered northern locales. Bigelow Hollow SP, Miles Wildlife Sanctuary, Mohawk SF, Station 43, White Memorial Foundation.

White-crowned Sparrow *Zonotrichia leucophrys* Uncommon migrant in May, late September into November; shrubby habitat, thickets, hedgerows, field edges. Farmington Meadows, Hammonasset Beach SP, Longshore Club Park, Sherwood Island SP, "W" lot, Storrs.

Dark-eyed Junco *Junco hyemalis* Common migrant and winter visitor throughout state from October to May; rare to uncommon nesting species. Weedy fields, lawns, gardens, woodland edges. Bigelow Hollow SP, Hammonasset Beach SP, Lighthouse Point Park, Mohawk SF, Mt. Riga Area.

Lapland Longspur *Calcarius lapponicus* Rare but regular winter visitor late October to April mostly along coast, fields, beaches, farms. Usually found with flocks of Snow Bunting and Horned Lark. Great Meadows Marsh, Griswold Point Preserve, Hammonasset Beach SP.

Snow Bunting *Plectrophenax nivalis* Uncommon late fall migrant and rare to uncommon winter visitor, normally in small flocks November through February. Weedy fields, dry sandy fields, beaches along coast. Bluff Point CR, Great Meadows Marsh, Griswold Point Preserve, Hammonasset Beach SP, Sandy Point, Sherwood Island SP.

Bobolink *Dolichonyx oryzivorus* Fairly common migrant and nesting species in grassy fields from mid-May to mid-October. Durham Meadows, Haley Farm SP, Lighthouse Point Park, Northwest Highlands Tour, Station 43.

Red-winged Blackbird *Agelaius phoeniceus* Common to locally abundant in fresh and tidal marshes, pond and lake edges throughout state from late February to mid-November; rare in winter. Common in most wetland habitats throughout state.

Eastern Meadowlark *Sturnella magna* Uncommon and numbers decreasing, throughout state from mid-March into November; rare in winter along coastal marshes. Grassy fields, pastures, meadows, along edges of wetlands throughout state. Bradley International Airport, Durham Meadows, Horse Barn Hill in Storrs.

Yellow-headed Blackbird* *Xanthocephalus xanthocephalus* Casual visitor from the west, occasionally recorded from September to April. Fresh water and coastal marshes, farm fields.

Rusty Blackbird *Euphagus carolinus* Uncommon migrant March to late April, mid-October through November in swampy woodlands, shrubby areas near water. Cromwell Meadows WMA, Farmington Meadows, Station 43, White Memorial Foundation.

Boat-tailed Grackle* *Quiscalus major* Accidental visitor from the south found in coastal marshes. First breeding record at Great Meadows Marsh in summer, 1995.

Common Grackle *Quiscalus quiscula* Common throughout state from late February through November; abundant during peak migration days in mid-October. Fields, open woodlands. Cromwell Meadows

WMA, Durham Meadows, East Rock Park, Station 43.

Brown-headed Cowbird *Molothrus ater* Fairly common to abundant migrant, fairly common nesting species; present throughout state from late February to late November; rare to uncommon in winter. Suburbs, urban open space, farms, open woodlands, wetlands. Devil's Den Preserve, Durham Meadows, Station 43, White Memorial Foundation.

Orchard Oriole *Icterus spurius* Uncommon migrant, rare nesting species at scattered localities throughout state from May through August. Farms, woodland edges, parks, floodplains. Haley Farm SP, Manresa, Northwest Park, Osbornedale SP, River Road in Southbury and River Road in Kent.

Baltimore Oriole *Icterus galbula* Fairly common nesting species throughout state from late April to mid-October. Open deciduous woodlands, woodland edge, floodplains. Devil's Hopyard SP, Durham Meadows, Mansfield Hollow SP, Naugatuck SF, Nehantic SF.

Pine Grosbeak *Pinicola enucleator* Rare to uncommon irruptive winter visitor, late October into April. May be common during flight years. Coniferous woodlands, ornamental evergreens and plantings. No regular locations, sometimes seen on hawk watches and more northern locales in state.

Purple Finch *Carpodacus purpureus* Uncommon to common migrant mid-March to late May, late September to early December; much less common as a nesting and wintering species. Edges of open woodlands, wooded suburbs, feeders, weedy and shrubby fields. Hartman Park, Miles Wildlife Sanctuary, Mohawk SF, Nepaug Reservoir, White Memorial Foundation.

House Finch *Carpodacus mexicanus* Common to locally very common throughout state, usually in human habitats. Suburbs, urban open space and tree-lined city streets, open woodlands, orchards, farms, feeders. Very common in most suburban residential areas. Greenwich Point Park, Osbornedale SP, Pine Creek, Station 43.

Red Crossbill *Loxia curvirostra* Rare and erratic visitor from early November to April. Conifer and mixed woodlands at widely scattered localities throughout state. Difficult to predict when and where to find this species, but mainly in northern locales. Barkhamsted Reservoir, Bigelow Hollow SP, Nepaug Reservoir, Pachaug SF, White Memorial Foundation.

White-winged Crossbill *Loxia leucoptera* Rare and erratic winter visitor from early November to April. Rarer than Red Crossbill. Conifers, ornamental evergreens, occasionally feeders. Same locations as Red Crossbill.

Common Redpoll *Carduelis flammea* Erratic winter visitor, November to April. Fields, windbreaks, hedgerows, feeders. Irruptions in some winters along with crossbills, but difficult to predict when and where to find this species.

Pine Siskin *Carduelis pinus* Uncommon to fairly common but irregular and variable. Present from October to April; occasionally nests, normally following winter irruption years. Evergreen stands, woodland edges, ornamental evergreens, feeders in winter. Barkhamsted Reservoir, Bigelow Hollow SP, Miles Wildlife Sanctuary, Nepaug Reservoir, White Memorial Foundation.

American Goldfinch *Carduelis tristis* Fairly common migrant and breeder; uncommon in winter, depending on food supply. Fields, edges, hedgerows, feeders in winter. Audubon Center of Greenwich, Miles Wildlife Sanctuary, Roaring Brook Nature Center, Station 43,

Evening Grosbeak *Coccothraustes vespertinus* Irruptive, uncommon to fairly common migrant and winter visitor throughout state from October to May; very rare nesting species. Open deciduous and mixed woodlands, edge habitats. Often seen on hawk watches in October-November, irregularly at feeders in winter. Barkhamsted Reservoir, Lighthouse Point Park, White Memorial Foundation.

House Sparrow *Passer domesticus* Fairly common to abundant resident throughout the state. Urban and suburban habitats, parks, farms, fields, edge habitats.

Accidental and Casual Species

The following accidental and casual rarities have been recorded in Connecticut. In many cases this list includes species only seen once or just a few times during this century. If you are birding in Connecticut and observe one of the species listed below, marked by an asterick in the preceeding section, or a bird not described anywhere in this annotated species list, a report to the Connecticut Rare Records Committee is appropriate. Please send a detailed report on the species sighted including photographic documentation or a sketch, if possible, to: Secretary, CRRC, c/o COA, 314 Unquowa Road, Fairfield, CT 06430

Pacific Loon
Western Grebe
Northern Fulmar
Black-capped Petrel
Audubon's Shearwater
Cory's Shearwater
Greater Shearwater
Manx Shearwater
Wilson's Storm-Petrel
White-faced Storm-
 Petrel
Amer. White Pelican
Brown Pelican
Anhinga
Magnificent
 Frigatebird
White Ibis
White-faced Ibis
Wood Stork
FulvousWhistling-
 Duck
Tufted Duck
Swallow-tailed Kite
Mississippi Kite
Swainson's Hawk
Yellow Rail
Corn Crake
Purple Gallinule
Wilson's Plover
Black-necked Stilt
American Avocet
Spotted Redshank
Eskimo Curlew

Long-billed Curlew
Curlew Sandpiper
Sharp-tailed Sandpiper
Ruff
Red-necked Phalarope
Red Phalarope
Pomerine Jaeger
Parasitic Jaeger
Long-tailed Jaeger
Franklin's Gull
Mew Gull
Thayer's Gull
Ross' Gull
Sabine's Gull
Gull-billed Tern
Sandwich Tern
Arctic Tern
Bridled Tern
Sooty Tern
Dovekie
Thick-billed Murre
Razorbill
Black Guillemot
Atlantic Puffin
Band-tailed Pigeon
White-winged Dove
Northern Hawk Owl
Burrowing Owl
Great Gray Owl
Boreal Owl
Rufous Hummingbird
Black-backed
 Woodpecker

Say's Phoebe
Ash-throated
 Flycatcher
Tropical Kingbird
Gray Kingbird
Scissor-tailed
 Flycatcher
Townsend's Solitaire
Mountain Bluebird
Bohemian Waxwing
Bell's Vireo
Black-throated Gray
 Warbler
Hermit Warbler
Western Tanager
Black-headed
 Grosbeak
Painted Bunting
Green-tailed Towhee
Lark Bunting
LeConte's Sparrow
Golden-crowned
 Sparrow
Harris' Sparrow
Smith's Longspur
Chestnut-collared
 Longspur
Brewer's Blackbird
Bullock's Oriole
Hoary Redpoll

V ANNOTATED BIBLIOGRAPHY

American Ornithologist's Union. 1983. Check-list of North American Birds. 6th ed. American Ornithologist's Union, Lawrence, Kansas *Along with supplements periodically published in The Auk, contains approved scientific and common names for all North American birds.*

Askins, R. A. 1990. Birds of the Connecticut College Arboretum. Connecticut College Arboretum Bulletin No. 31. *Birds, birding, and bird research at the Connecticut College Arboretum.*

Audubon Society Videoguide. 1985. Birds of North America. 5 volumes. Nature Science Network. MasterVision, New York. *This popular video series describes all of the species likely to be found in the state.*

Bell, M. 1985. The Face of Connecticut. State Geological and Natural History Survey Bulletin No. 110. *A very readable story of the people, geology, and ecology of the Connecticut landscape.*

Bent, A. C. (Life histories of North American Birds 22 volumes). Originally published as U.S. National Museum Bulletins, reprinted by Dover Press. *Author Cleveland Bent was an indefatigable compiler of bird facts. His books contain a wealth of information about the ecology and life history of North American birds.*

Bevier, L., ed. 1994. The Atlas of Breeding Birds of Connecticut. State Geological and Natural History Survey Bulletin No. 113. *Concise, factual, and invaluable account of the status, distribution, and breeding behavior of Connecticut's nesting species.*

Billings, G. 1990. Birds of Prey in Connecticut. Rainbow Press, Torrington, Connecticut. *Basic information about hawks and owls that occur in Connecticut and the most likely places to find them.*

Brumbach, J. J. 1965. The Climate of Connecticut. State Geological and Natural History Survey Bulletin No. 99. *Description and statistics about Connecticut's weather.*

Bull, J. 1964. Birds of the New York Area. Harper & Row, New York. *Of interest to Connecticut birders because it includes information on birds from Westport to Greenwich in Fairfield County.*

Clark, W. S., and B. K. Wheeler. 1987. A Field Guide to Hawks: North America. Houghton Mifflin Co., Boston. *This field guide in the Peterson series is valuable for its illustrated comparisons of juvenile and adult plumages as well as subspecies identification.*

Connecticut Department of Environmental Protection. 1995. Connecticut's Endangered, Threatened and Special Concern Species. *The mammals, birds, reptiles, amphibians, fish, invertebrates, and plants that are currently listed by the state.*

COA Bulletin *This quarterly newsletter of the Connecticut Ornithological Association contains information on birding trips, events, and other news items for Connecticut birders.*

Connecticut Ornithological Association. Field Checklist Birds of Connecticut. 1994. Connecticut Rare Records Committee, Connecticut Ornithological Association. August, 1994.

Connecticut Warbler. *The state bird journal, published quarterly by the Connecticut Ornithological Association. Each issue contains much interesting and informative information about aspects of Connecticut birds. A good mix of scientific and popular articles.*

de la Torre, J. 1990. Owls: Their Life and Behavior. Crown Publishers, New York *Well written and well illustrated introduction to owls by a popular Connecticut birder and author. Includes all species that may occur in Connecticut.*

Dunne, P., D. Sibley, and C. Sutton. 1988. Hawks in Flight; the Flight Identification of North American Migrant Raptors. Houghton Mifflin Co., Boston. *A handy field reference with useful details and hints on identifying raptors migrating through Connecticut.*

Ehrlich, P.R., D. S. Dobkin, and D. Wheye. 1988. The Birder's Handbook: a Field Guide to the Natural History of North American Birds. Simon and Schuster, New York. *A worthy companion to your field guide. Basic information on all North American species such as where they nest, when they nest, what they eat and so forth.*

Farrand, J., Jr., ed. 1983. Audubon Society Master Guide to Birding. 3 volumes. Alfred A. Knopf, New York. *A more thorough, more detailed guide to North American birds than covered in a single volume field guide.*

Grant, P. J. 1986. Gulls: a Guide to Identification. T & A D Poyser, Calton, England. *The theme of this book is how to identify age classes as well as species. Much useful information for birders.*

Hayman, P., J. Marchant, and T. Prater. 1986. Shorebirds: an Identification Guide. Houghton Mifflin Co., Boston. *Life histories and hints on identifying the shorebird group, which includes some difficult birds to identify in the field.*

Kaufman, K. 1990. A Field Guide to Advanced Birding. Houghton Mifflin Co., Boston. *In this member of the Peterson field guide series, Ken attacks in very readable fashion how to sort out some of the problem specie such as certain herons, gulls, terns, and the Empidonax flycatchers.*

MacKenzie, L. 1961. The Birds of Guilford, Connecticut. Peabody Museum, Yale University, New Haven, Ct. *An annotated checklist of the birds observed in and around Guilford.*

Madge, S., and H. Burn. 1988. Waterfowl: an Identification Guide to the Ducks, Geese, and Swans of the World. Houghton Mifflin Co., Boston. *Identification and life history information on waterfowl.*

Manter, Jerauld A. 1975. Bird of Storrs, Connecticut, and Vicinity. *Published by the Natchaug Ornithological Society of Storrs, CT. A revised and expanded version is currently being published.*

National Geographic Society. 1987. Field Guide to the Birds of North America. National Geographic Society, Washington, D.C. *Considered by many to be one of the best field guides.*

Peterson, R. T. 1980. A Field Guide to the Birds. Houghton Mifflin Co. Boston. *The classic field guide to birds of eastern North America.*

Poole, A. Birds of North America: Life Histories for the 21st Century. *The very latest information on every North American bird species. This authoritative series is keyed toward researchers as well as birders and includes the latest information with good literature citations. Available at many libraries or by interlibrary loans.*

Proctor, N. S. 1978. 25 Birding Sites in Connecticut. Pequot Press. Guilford, CT. *The first birding guide to the best areas in the state. Still interesting and entertaining. Available in libraries.*

Proctor, N. S., and P. Lynch. 1993. Manual of Ornithology. Yale University Press, New Haven, CT. *A thorough introduction to the biology and ecology of birds.*

Sage, J.H., L. B. Bishop, and W. P. Bliss. 1913. The birds of Connecticut. State Geological and Natural History Survey, Bulletin No. 20, Hartford, CT. *Long out of print but can be obtained in many libraries in the state.*

Terres, J.K. 1980. The Audubon Encyclopedia of North American Birds. Knopf, New York. *A thorough single volume treatment, encyclopedic in scope with excellent coverage of all topics of interest to birders, many with surprising depth.*

Zeranski, J. D., and T. Baptist. 1990. Connecticut Birds. University of New England Press. Hanover, NH. *Connecticut's state bird book. Provides information on the status and distribution of Connecticut's birds.*

VI N*ATURE* O*RGANIZATIONS IN* C*ONNECTICUT*

Connecticut has dozens of environmental organizations, many of which own or manage properties in the state. Of these, the following organizations emphasize birding or offer nature preserves good for birding.

Audubon Society of
Northeastern Connecticut
P. O. Box 190
Storrs, CT 06268

Connecticut Audubon Society
2325 Burr Street
Fairfield, CT 06430

Darien Audubon Society, Inc.
P. O. Box 3313
Darien, CT 06820

Greenwich Audubon Society
P. O. Box 7487
Greenwich, CT 06836-7487

Hartford Audubon Society
P. O. Box 270207
West Hartford, CT 06127

Lillinonah Audubon Society
P. O. Box 791
Southbury, CT 06488

Litchfield Hills Audubon
Society
P. O. Box 861
Litchfield, CT 06759

Mattabeseck Audubon Society
P. O. Box 307
Middletown, CT 06457

Menunkatuck Audubon
Society
P. O. Box 214
Guilford, CT 06437

Natchaug Ornithological
Society
P. O. Box 192
Mansfield Center, CT 06250

National Audubon Society
Audubon Center in Greenwich
613 Riversville Road
Greenwich, CT 06831

The Nature Conservancy
Connecticut Chapter
55 High Street
Middletown, CT 06457

Naugatuck Valley Audubon
Society
Box 371
Derby, CT 06418

New Canaan Audubon
Society, Inc.
Box 241
New Haven, CT 06840

New Haven Bird Club
P. O. Box 9004
New Haven, CT 06532-0004

Potapaug Audubon Society
Box 591
Old Lyme, CT 06371

Quinnipiac Valley Audubon
Society
111 Mohawk Drive
Wallingford, CT 06492

Saugatuck Valley Audubon
Society, Inc.
P. O. Box 684
Westport, CT 06881

Sharon Audubon Center
R.R. 1, Box 171
Sharon, CT 06069

Western Connecticut Bird
Club
c/o John Longstreth
846 Southford Road
Southbury, CT 06488

INDEX

Vulture, Turkey 7, 50, 59, 67, 71, 75, 88, 94, 106, 116, 120, 122, 126, 135, 151, 155, 158, 169, 173, 202, 252, 258, 284, 289, 294, 316, 375, 389, 399, 410, 499, 512

Warblers 1, 2, 5, 6, 18, 42, 45, 65, 68, 86, 92, 104, 115, 130, 133, 142, 144, 148, 179, 182, 201, 226, 227, 247, 255, 266, 276, 279, 287, 289, 296, 300, 306, 318, 326, 327, 339, 340, 345, 347, 368, 389, 396, 402, 407, 424, 428, 457, 459, 460, 465, 473, 475, 482, 497

Warbler, Bay-breasted 46, 58, 71, 88, 95, 101, 110, 151, 180, 188, 213, 220, 475, 532

Warbler, Black-and-white 26, 45, 54, 58, 68, 69, 72, 80, 85, 94, 95, 101, 108, 113, 115, 135, 141, 151, 160, 164, 168, 174, 180, 188, 217, 220, 226, 236, 254, 277, 279, 284, 289, 293, 299, 318, 398, 403, 424, 454, 462, 463, 477, 489, 500, 503, 533

Warbler, Blackburnian 27, 36, 42, 46, 47, 54, 58, 65, 72, 75, 88, 90, 92, 95, 96, 101, 110, 111, 114, 115, 134, 137, 139, 180, 188, 210, 217, 220, 250, 252, 254, 257, 258, 260, 264, 403, 460, 532

Warbler, Blackpoll 46, 58, 71, 88, 101, 110, 133, 139, 151, 171, 180, 213, 217, 220, 279, 299, 403, 460, 477, 533

Warbler, Black-throated Blue 56, 58, 59, 65, 69, 75, 92, 95, 108, 133, 139, 161, 165, 180, 210, 213, 250, 252, 255, 257, 260, 280, 302, 398, 531

Warbler, Black-throated Gray 7, 51, 541

Warbler, Black-throated Green 27, 28, 36, 46, 47, 56, 58, 65, 67, 69, 72, 75, 82, 90, 92, 94, 95, 96, 101, 108, 110, 111, 113-115, 132, 134, 139, 148, 156, 170, 171, 180, 188, 210, 213, 217, 220, 250, 252, 254, 255, 257, 260, 264, 267, 271, 283, 287, 288, 289, 294, 300, 390, 398, 403, 424, 460, 532

Warbler, Blue-winged 30, 45, 48, 51, 59, 85, 87, 90, 94, 101, 103, 108, 109, 113, 116, 124, 125, 127, 133, 137, 141, 148, 150, 151, 153, 163, 173, 174, 179, 180, 188, 195, 200, 213, 217, 222, 232, 240, 264, 272, 275, 276, 279, 284, 288, 290, 293, 298, 302, 303, 313, 318, 398, 405, 410, 463, 465, 477, 482, 503, 530

Warbler, Brewster's 87, 151

Warbler, Canada 51, 56, 59, 65, 71, 72, 88, 95, 101, 108, 109, 111, 133, 135, 139, 148, 151, 161, 165, 253, 257, 260, 266, 288, 295, 369, 398, 403, 424, 460, 477, 534

Warbler, Cape May 58, 88, 92, 95, 101, 110, 133, 151, 180, 188, 213, 218, 220, 279, 403, 475, 531

Warbler, Cerulean 92, 94, 104, 108, 109, 123, 180, 255, 266, 293, 296, 299, 302, 311, 405, 533

Warbler, Chestnut-sided 48, 51, 59, 69, 85, 94, 95, 96, 101, 103, 108, 116, 125, 133, 137, 141, 150-153, 163, 180, 195, 212, 217, 222, 232, 240, 288, 290, 293, 295, 398, 405, 410, 463, 477, 482, 489, 497, 531

Warbler, Connecticut 20, 148, 168, 225, 270, 322, 323, 341, 369, 397, 401, 424, 534

Warbler, Golden-winged 2,14,87,90,94,96, 104, 108, 109, 148, 405, 475, 530

Warbler, Hermit 401, 406, 541

Warbler, Hooded 51, 135, 148, 151, 152, 153, 161, 163-166, 168, 180, 293, 296, 299, 300, 302, 341, 389,

LIST OF ILLUSTRATIONS